THE
PENTATEUCH

Old Testament Survey Series

THE
PENTATEUCH

JAMES E. SMITH

COLLEGE PRESS
PUBLISHING COMPANY

Unless otherwise noted, all Scripture references are the author's own translation.

Drawings are taken from *The Popular and Critical Bible Encyclopaedia*, (ed. Samuel Fallows; copyright 1904 by J. Mitchell Howard). Figures 2, 6, and 7 are taken from *Sacred History and Geography* by Don DeWelt (copyright 1955 Baker Book House; used by permission).

Library of Congress Catalog Card Number 88-64053
International Standard Book Number: 978-0-89900-429-7

DEDICATED TO

DR. W.W. WINTER

WHO FIRST INTRODUCED

THE AUTHOR

TO THE JOYS OF STUDYING

THE PENTATEUCH.

CONTENTS

The Book of Genesis

The Book of Exodus

The Book of Leviticus

The Book of Numbers

The Book of Deuteronomy

Charts and Diagrams

Maps

Artwork

Bibliographies

PREFACE

The term *Pentateuch* is derived from a Greek word which means "the five-volume book." The term is used to describe the first five books of the Old Testament which from ancient times have been regarded as five parts of a single work. Because these books are mainly legal in character, the Jews refer to them as the *Torah* which means "instruction" or "law."

The Pentateuch contains the foundational revelation of the Bible. These books depict God as Creator and man as fallen creature. They narrate the first stages in the Creator's scheme of redemption: the call of Abram, the Exodus from Egypt, and the covenant at Sinai.

No dearth of resources for Pentateuchal studies exists, so why another volume? For some time no adequate textbook has been available for a Bible college course in the Pentateuch. The single volume works which are in print are either too brief (e.g., Allis, *The Five Books of Moses*) or too technical (e.g., Hamilton, *Handbook to the Pentateuch*). The excellent volumes by John Davis (*Paradise to*

Prison and *Moses and the Gods of Egypt*) unfortunately cover only the first two books of the Pentateuch.

Condensing the contents of the Pentateuch into a study guide is a challenge. The amount of material to be surveyed is staggering. This section of God's Word contains 187 chapters, roughly twenty per cent of the Old Testament and fifteen percent of the entire Bible. Furthermore, the text bristles with difficulties and exegetical questions on which no consensus can be found. A constant flow of scholarly articles and monographs makes even the most avid reader despair of ever keeping abreast of current research.

Still another challenge is that of making the material interesting and relevant to the lives of students. Aside from a few stories in Genesis, most of the material is unfamiliar to those who graduate from the typical Sunday School program. The legal materials of the Pentateuch are approached with prejudice. Why brush the dust off these archaic utterances? Why would one who lives in New Testament Canaan want even briefly to traverse the terrain of this barren wilderness? Thus the challenge to one who would write a textbook on the Pentateuch is this: Make these books live! Show their relevance. Help students penetrate the peripheral in order to see the eternal principles which God communicated through the Law of Moses.

The author was first introduced to the Pentateuch in the classroom of Dr. W.W. Winter at Cincinnati Bible College. The three-volume commentary of C.F. Keil was the text. Using Keil the students were required to answer all the questions in McGarvey's *Class Notes on the Pentateuch*. This weekly exercise taught the discipline of serious biblical research. Unfortunately, the genius of this nineteenth century German scholar was lost on the freshmen in the class.

The present work is intended as a general introduction to the Pentateuch for freshmen Bible college students. In keeping with this purpose, no attempt has been made to interact with the contentions of biblical criticism. A student should first master what the Book says about itself before he undertakes to meander through the maze of what men have said about the Book. Consequently, little has been included about the theories of Wellhausen, Gunkel and others who pit verse against verse in order to overturn the Bible's own view of itself. Though the older theories have been of late modified to great extent,

14

still the majority of writers on the Pentateuch assume that these five books do not present an accurate picture of Israel's earliest history.

The present work has been written from the perspective of one who is committed to the traditional view regarding the authorship of the Pentateuch. This position has not been adopted due to any lack of exposure to the views of modern critics. The author spent five years in a graduate school of Reformed Judaism where the negative view of the Pentateuch was the presupposition of every class. These years included a course popularly called "Pentateuchalization" in which the philosophical, historical and exegetical presuppositions of the modern view were presented systematically. This course served only to underscore in the author's mind that the Documentary Theory of Pentateuchal origins is built upon a flimsy foundation.

Teaching a freshman course in Foundations of Hebrew History for seventeen years at Florida Christian College has forged some definite convictions about what is appropriate for inclusion at this level of instruction. These convictions are reflected in the content and format of this book.

Several features have been included to enhance the usefulness of this volume as a textbook. The material has been arranged in forty-five chapters of approximately equal length. Each is intended to serve as a separate lesson. For each chapter an overall aim and theme have been articulated. Forty-five charts, fourteen maps and eight drawings have been used to amplify the discussion. Fourteen bibliographies have been inserted to facilitate further research.

The author is indebted to countless scholars who previously have reflected upon the meaning of the Pentateuch. He has made free use of commentaries, surveys, and introductory and critical works. Documentation has been included where dependence has been most pronounced.

A special word of appreciation is in order to Karen McNeely, my efficient secretary, and to Linda Stark, Librarian at Florida Christian College, both of whom labored cheerfully in proofreading the manuscript. Tina VanDyke rendered yeoman service in preparing the several charts which summarize and illustrate the text.

CHAPTER ONE

The Five Books of Moses

AIM: To introduce the Pentateuch.

THEME: Ancient books for modern man!

From ancient times the first five books of the Old Testament have been considered a literary unit. These five books are known collectively as the Torah ("Law") or Pentateuch ("Five Scrolls"). The New Testament refers to these books as "the law of Moses" (Luke 24:27), "the writings of Moses" (John 5:46,47), or simply "Moses" (Mark 7:13). The divine authority of this section is indicated by Jesus when he bestowed upon it the title "the word of God" (Mark 7:13).

The importance of the Pentateuch hardly can be overstated. This section of God's Word is important historically, for here is an accurate record of the most primitive periods of the human adventure. The Pentateuch is important theologically, for here is the explanation of the predicament of the race. These books reveal the origin of sin and the necessity of redemption through shed blood. The Pentateuch is also important scientifically, for here the Creator reveals details about the formation and filling of the earth which empirical investigation could never discover. The Pentateuch is important legally, for herein is contained one of the oldest, and certainly most influential, law codes known to man. The Pentateuch is also important sociologically. These five books reveal the origins of the basic unit of society, the family.

By way of introduction to the Pentateuch, six areas are examined in this chapter: (1) scope, (2) authorship, (3) unity, (4) structure, (5) chronology, and (6) teaching of the first five books of the Old Testament.

SCOPE OF THE PENTATEUCH

The Pentateuch consists of five books divided into 187 chapters. This material constitutes a little over twenty percent of the Old Testament. One would have to read the books of Matthew, Mark, Luke, John, Acts, Romans, 1 Corinthians, 2 Corinthians, Galatians and Ephesians to read an amount equivalent in length to the Pentateuch.

The five books of the Pentateuch were clearly intended to be viewed as separate entities, as Brevard Childs has pointed out.[1] Genesis is structured around a genealogical formula ("these are the generations of") which sets that material off from the other four books. Genesis contains family history, not national history, yet the material here is integrally connected with the history of the nation of Israel which begins in the following book.

Exodus begins with a recapitulation of material from Genesis which is designed to introduce a distinct literary product (compare Ex 1:1-5 with Gn 46:8ff.). The second book concludes with the building of the Tabernacle and a summary of its role in the future wandering of God's people.

The setting of Leviticus is the same as that of Exodus, but the structure of the book is quite different. Thematically, Leviticus deals with the implementation of the cultic apparatus which is constructed in Exodus. This book employs a topical approach which often breaks the logical and chronological sequence of its continuity with Exodus. Leviticus concludes with a summary which clearly sets it apart from the book which follows.

18

The Book of Numbers focuses on the laws of the camp during the wandering period. The book begins with a precise date formula which indicates a new section of material. Numbers ends with a summary which sets it apart from the fifth book of the Pentateuch. In Leviticus God's people are stationary at Mt. Sinai, but in Numbers they are on the move from Sinai to Kadesh to the Plains of Moab.

Deuteronomy shares the same geographical setting with the concluding chapters of Numbers, yet a sharp break separates the one book from the other. The last book of the Pentateuch has a clear introduction and conclusion. The homiletical style of this book sets it apart as an independent work.

AUTHORSHIP OF THE PENTATEUCH

The authorship of the Pentateuch has been debated for decades. On the one hand, conservative scholars maintain the traditional view that these five books were authored by Moses. Modern biblical scholarship, however, refuses to recognize any significant role for Moses in the production of these books.

A. Biblical Claims.

No specific claim of authorship appears in Genesis, but the claims are abundant in the other four books. Thus in Exodus the claim is made that "Moses wrote down everything the Lord had said" (24:4); and "the Lord said to Moses, Write down these words" (34:27). About thirty-five times in Leviticus Moses is said to have received directives from the Lord. In Numbers about half the chapters begin with the claim that God communicated with Moses. Deuteronomy claims to contain the last words of Moses spoken just before his death. Without question, then, the Pentateuch makes repeated claims that its content originally was communicated to and through Moses.

The claims of the Pentateuch are echoed throughout the rest of the Old Testament. Dozens of times the Law is connected with Moses. Three examples of this claim are 1 Kings 2:3, 2 Kings 14:6 and Ezra 3:2.

Jesus also connected Moses' name with the Law. He told the cleansed leper to offer the gift which Moses commanded (Matt 8:4).

He associated the name of Moses with the divorce law (Matt 19:7-8). He quoted two specific laws regarding respect for parents and attributed them to Moses (Mark 7:10). He directed the Sadducees to consult the "book of Moses" (Mark 12:26). After his resurrection he explained how all the Scriptures "beginning with Moses" pointed to him (Luke 24:24:27). He rebuked the unbelief of his auditors by claiming "Moses wrote about me" (John 5:46).

Following the lead of their Master, the inspired apostles frequently made the connection between Moses and the Law. Peter quoted the Messianic prophecy from Deuteronomy 18 and attributed it to Moses (Acts 3:22). James, the half brother of Jesus, claimed that Moses was read in the synagogues on every Sabbath (Acts 15:21). Paul quoted passages from Exodus (Rom 9:15) and Deuteronomy (Rom 10:19) and attributed them to Moses. He spoke about the veil which covered the hearts of Jewish auditors when Moses is read (2 Cor 3:15). The writer of Hebrews affirmed that Moses proclaimed every commandment of the Law to Israel (Heb 9:19).

B. Critical Conjectures.

For almost two hundred years most biblical critics have denied that Moses wrote the Pentateuch. At first they claimed that writing had not yet been invented in the days of Moses. Archaeological investigations have now made clear that writing was common in the ancient Near East fifteen hundred years before Moses. The critics pointed to certain passages in the Pentateuch which they argued could not have been written by Moses.[2] When correctly interpreted, however, no passage in the Pentateuch rules out Moses as author with the exception of the account of his death in the last chapter of Deuteronomy. This account was most likely added by Joshua who succeeded Moses as the leader of Israel.

The critical conjecture regarding the authorship of the Pentateuch is known as the *Documentary Hypothesis*. The documentary hypothesis is the theory that the Pentateuch was a compilation of selections from several different written documents composed at different places and times over a period of several centuries. Nearly every individual critic has his own version of the theory. Most critics, however, see four distinct and contradictory strands interwoven within the five books. The Pentateuch is not Mosaic, it is a mosaic! Older critics held that these strands represented evolutionary stages in the development of Old Testament religion. More recent critics see these strands as equally ancient. Each strand evolved on its own until finally it was woven with the other three at the conclusion of Old Testament history. This revised version of the theory regarding the origin of the Pentateuch is no more compatible with the biblical claims than the older version!

The key name in the long history of the documentary hypothesis is *Julius Wellhausen* who lived in the last half of the nineteenth century. Wellhausen offered four literary arguments for his theory. (1) He pointed out that two names for God (Yahweh and Elohim) are used in Genesis. This, he speculated, indicated two authors. (2) Wellhausen pointed out what he regarded as duplicate and contradictory accounts of some events in the Pentateuch. (3) He found evidence of different and contradictory styles of writing, vocabulary, moral and religious ideas in these books. (4) When the sections and paragraphs assigned to the hypothetical strands were put together they (allegedly) formed a connected whole. Conservative scholars like E.J. Young, W.H. Green, Gleason Archer and O.T. Allis have responded to these arguments decisively.[3]

Wellhausen also turned Old Testament history upside down in an effort to show an *evolutionary* development. He then attempted to correlate this revised history with the four basic "documents" which he thought he had discovered through the literary analysis of the Pentateuch.

The Bible claims that God revealed to Moses a complex worship system about 1400 BC. This revealed religion, among other things, provided for (1) an elaborate, centralized worship center (the Tabernacle); (2) a tri-level priesthood (Levites, priests, high priest); (3) multiple sacrifices; and (4) a complex religious ritual. The critics claim, however, that all the above elements of Israelite religion *evolved* over a thousand years. They say what is described in the Pentateuch is the status of Israelite religion in the time of Ezra, a thousand years after Moses!

The issues at stake in this debate are substantial. If Moses did not write these books, then they are a forgery. At the heart of the argument is the very nature of Old Testament religion. The biblical view is that Old Testament religion is a product of *revelation*; the modern view is that it results from *evolution*. Ultimately the authority of Christ is involved in the question of the authorship of the Pentateuch, for he unquestionably subscribed to the Mosaic origin of these books.

UNITY OF THE PENTATEUCH

Pentateuchal studies have entered a dramatic new phase within the past quarter-century. Older criticism focused on hypothetical sources and internal contradictions. Recent studies have tended to view the Pentateuch holistically. Microscopic examination of textual minutiae has given way to analyzing the unifying theme of the five books as a whole. The concern today is on articulating what the Pentateuch "in its final form" is all about. A new appreciation has emerged for the literary genius of the one responsible for this work.

The Pentateuch is a distinct, unique and independent literary entity. For centuries Jews, Samaritans, Christians and even Muslims have so regarded it. Critics point to the fifth century BC as the time when the Pentateuch in its present form was created and recognized as Scripture by the masses. Conservative scholars would argue that the Pentateuch essentially in its present form is a thousand years older than what the critics imagine. Be that as it may, recognition of the thematic unity of the Pentateuch is a positive breakthrough in Pentateuchal studies.

The key to the meaning of the Pentateuch, as David Clines has pointed out,[4] is the promise made to Abraham in Genesis 12:1-3. That promise was repeated and amplified to Isaac and Jacob in the remaining chapters of Genesis. Three major ingredients of the promise are (1) *progeny*, (2) *position*, and (3) *possession*. In the first ingredient God promised to make the descendants of Abraham, Isaac and Jacob into a great nation. In the second God promised to bless the Patriarchs and enter into a covenant with them. He would be their God, and they would be his people. They would have a unique position among the peoples of the earth. The possession which was promised to the Patriarchs was the land of Canaan. These ingredients are interrelated and interdependent and are in fact facets of one promise.

Excluding the first eleven chapters of Genesis which constitute a kind of preface, the Pentateuch narrates the movement of God's people chronologically, geographically and spiritually toward the fulfillment of the Patriarchal promise. The individual books of the Pentateuch are seen by Clines to focus particularly on one of the three ingredients of that promise. Each book concludes with a thematic pointer indicating that faith in the Promise, though tested by circumstances, was still alive.

Genesis 12–50 explores the psychological, physical and spiritual tensions which resulted from snail's-pace fulfillment of the *progeny* aspect of the Promise. By the end of Genesis the covenant family has survived all manner of adversity and has safely settled in Egypt. They have not, however, become a great nation, and they are away from the Promised Land. Before his death, recorded in the last chapter of Genesis, Joseph made the sons of Israel swear that they would take his bones with them when God delivered them from Egypt (50:25). This expression of confidence in the deliverance of Israel from Egypt reminds the reader that the Patriarchal Promise is yet to be fulfilled and the story is to be continued in the following book.

Exodus and Leviticus emphasize the *position* aspect of the Promise. God entered into a covenant at Sinai. There he revealed the standards which set Israel apart from all other nations. There he also revealed the procedures for maintaining the special position with their God. Exodus concludes with the glory of the Lord taking up abode in the newly constructed portable shrine. That glorious cloud would serve to direct the travels of Israel during their journey to the Promised Land (40:36-38). Thus Exodus closes with a reminder that the Promise yet awaited fulfillment. Leviticus similarly concludes with a future orientation. The laws found in the final chapters of this book anticipate occupation of the Promised Land.

In Numbers and Deuteronomy the orientation is toward the *possession* of the land. In Numbers the march toward Canaan resumes. The book concludes with Israel camped "in the plains of Moab by the Jordan across from Jericho" (36:13). Deuteronomy is set in the same locale as Numbers. Of the five books, this last has the most decided future orientation. Deuteronomy is virtually a handbook of do's and don'ts to be observed once the entrance into Canaan has been effected.

23

As Deuteronomy closes, the Promise still has not been realized. With the death of the great lawgiver one could even say that the Promise was in jeopardy.

Thus the Pentateuch is a masterpiece of literature, carefully crafted by its author to underscore how faith in God's original Promise survived every challenge. Though full of accounts of false starts, failures, and reverses of every sort, the Pentateuch is basically optimistic. However slow and painful, progress toward the realization of God's Promise was ongoing.

STRUCTURE OF THE PENTATEUCH

The structure of the Pentateuch can be described from several perspectives. On the most obvious level, the Pentateuch consists of five separate books, each displaying its own distinct literary characteristics. On another level the Pentateuch could be described as a literary bifid. The first sixty-nine chapters of the Pentateuch (Gn 1 — Ex 19) are mainly history; the last 118 chapters are mainly legislation. On still a third level, markers exist within the text itself to indicate how the author intended to structure his work. A pattern of narrative, poetry and epilogue appears with regularity in the Pentateuch. The author appears to have shaped his work by the positioning of poetic discourses within the prose narrative.[5]

Three major predeath discourses divide the Pentateuch into its largest units. All three discourses contain blessings and curses upon sons and their descendants. In Genesis 9:25-27 (epilogue 9:28) Noah makes his predictions concerning his sons Shem and Japheth and his grandson Canaan. Genesis 49 (epilogue ch. 50) contains Jacob's predictions concerning the destiny of his sons. Finally, in Deuteronomy 33 (epilogue ch. 34) Moses just before his death announced the future of the various tribes of Israel. The strategic placement of these three similar passages in the Pentateuch suggests that the author viewed his work as covering three major epochs:

1. the Primeval age (Gn 1-9).
2. the Patriarchal age (Gn 10-50).
3. the Mosaic age (Ex 1-Dt 34).

Even within these epochs the author has signaled the movement from one period to another by means of poetic insertion. The Primeval age is divided into the Edenic (Gn 1–3) and Antediluvian (Gn 4–9) periods. Genesis 1–3 describes the creation of Adam and Eve, their habitation of the Garden and their expulsion from Paradise. This Edenic material concludes with a poetic utterance by God (Gn 3:14-19 + epilogue vv. 20-24). The Patriarchal age also has two phases, the Postdiluvian or Pre-Canaan (10:1–12:5) and Post-Canaan (12:6–50:26). The poetic call of Abram out of Haran (Gn 12:2-3 + epilogue vv. 4-5) marks the transition.

The Mosaic age is broken by poetic discourse into three subdivisions. The Egyptian or Exodus narratives conclude with the Song of Moses after the crossing of the Red Sea (Ex 15:1-18 + epilogue vv. 19-21). The wilderness narratives are marked off by the citation of some anonymous poets (Nm 21:27-30 + epilogue vv. 31-35). The final section, which might be called the Moab narratives, concludes with another Song of Moses (Dt 32:1-43 + epilogue vv. 44-52). The structure of the Pentateuch as indicated by this literary device is displayed in Chart 1.

CHRONOLOGY OF THE PENTATEUCH

A vast amount of time, the exact duration of which cannot be determined, is covered in the Pentateuch. The key to the chronology of these books is furnished by 1 Kings 6:1 which dates the construction of Solomon's Temple 480 years after the Exodus. On independent grounds the Temple project can be dated to about 967 BC. Adding the 480 years to that date places the Exodus in 1447 BC. The Exodus inaugurated a new era, and several passages mark time from that event (e.g., Ex 19:1; Nm 10:11). Using data supplied by the Pentateuch itself, and working forward and backward from that fixed point, the chronological framework of these books can be established.

The Mosaic age extended from (roughly) the birth of Moses in about 1527 BC to his death in about 1407 BC. To this span of 120 years the Bible devotes 138 chapters — all of Exodus, Leviticus, Numbers and Deuteronomy. As noted above, the life of Moses is divided by the text into three periods: the Exodus, the wilderness and the

25

Chart No. 1

STRUCTURE OF THE PENTATEUCH						
PRIMEVAL AGE		PATRIARCHAL AGE		MOSAIC AGE		
EDENIC	PRE FLOOD	PRE CANAAN	POST CANAAN	EXODUS	WILDERNESS	MOAB
Genesis 1–3	Genesis 4–9	Genesis 10:1–12:6	Genesis 12:7–50:26	Exodus 1:1–15:21	Exodus 15:22– Numbers 21	Nm 22– Dt 32

Moab periods. The chronology of the Mosaic era can be summarized as follows:

1. While the Exodus period covers eighty years (Ex 7:7), most of the biblical material is concerned only with the single year in which God afflicted Egypt with plagues and subsequently freed his people.

2. The Exodus period ended and the Wilderness period began with the crossing of the Red Sea in about 1447 BC. The key characters of the Wilderness period were Moses, Aaron and Miriam. The period of wandering following the Exodus lasted about four decades (Nm 33:38). The biblical text, however, concentrates only on the first and last years of that period.

3. The Wilderness period terminated with the crossing of the Brook Zered in the fortieth year after the Exodus (Dt 1:3; 2:13-15). The events in the plains of Moab prior to Moses' death lasted about three months (Nm 33:38; Dt 1:3).

Working backward from the Exodus in 1447 BC the following chronological notes are found in the text. The Israelites were in Egypt 430 years (Ex 12:40). This would mean that the Eisodus — the going down into Egypt — must have occurred about the year 1877 BC. Jacob was 130 at the time of the Eisodus (Gn 47:9) and therefore must have been born about the year 2007 BC. Isaac was sixty when Jacob was born (Gn 25:26) and therefore must have been born about 2067 BC. Abraham was a hundred when Isaac was born (Gn 17:17), and therefore must have been born about 2167 BC.

Abram (as Abraham was earlier known) entered Canaan when he was seventy-five (Gn 12:4) about 2092 BC. The family of Jacob left for Egypt about 215 years later in 1877 BC. With the call of Abram the Canaan phase of the Patriarchal era began. Genesis 12–45 focuses on the four main characters of this period: Abraham, Isaac, Jacob and Joseph.

The duration of the earliest periods of Pentateuchal history is not known. No clue is given in the text regarding the length of time which elapsed between creation and the expulsion from the Garden of Eden. The time covered in Genesis 4–9 — the Antediluvian period — is also uncertain. Based on the figures which are given in Genesis 5 one would have to conclude that at least 1656 years elapsed between the expulsion from the Garden and the Flood.

The time lapse between the Flood and the call of Abram in about 2092 BC also cannot be established with certainty. The chronological data in chapter 11 necessitate a span of at least 427 years. The most important event during this period was the attempt to build the Tower of Babel. Key characters of the Postdiluvian or Pre-Canaan period were Shem, Ham and Japheth (the sons of Noah) and Nimrod, who may have been the builder of the Tower of Babel.

TEACHING OF THE PENTATEUCH

The Old Testament prepared the way for the coming of Christ. Several writers have suggested the following outline of the major divisions of Old Testament literature:

Foundation for Christ	The Pentateuch (Genesis — Deuteronomy)
Preparation for Christ	The Historical Books (Joshua — Nehemiah)
Anticipation of Christ	The Devotional Books (Job — Song)
Expectation of Christ	The Prophetic Books (Isaiah — Malachi)

Chart No. 2

TEACHING OF THE PENTATEUCH		
FOUNDATION FOR CHRIST		
BOOK	THEME	LESSON
GENESIS	THE ELECTION OF ISRAEL	SALVATION ESSENTIAL
EXODUS	THE REDEMPTION OF ISRAEL	DELIVERANCE ESSENTIAL
LEVITICUS	THE SANCTIFICATION OF ISRAEL	HOLINESS ESSENTIAL
NUMBERS	THE DISCIPLINE OF ISRAEL	PERSEVERANCE ESSENTIAL
DEUTERONOMY	THE INSTRUCTION OF ISRAEL	OBEDIENCE ESSENTIAL

The teaching of the Pentateuch is foundational to the rest of biblical revelation. The theme of each book reflects God's relationship with his people Israel. The five overriding lessons taught here are truths fundamental to the scheme of redemption. These matters, which are summarized in Chart 2, will be developed at length in the pages which follow.

ENDNOTES

1. Brevard Childs, *Introduction to the Old Testament as Scripture* (Philadelphia: Fortress, 1979), pp. 129f.

2. The following alleged non-Mosaic passages are listed by H.H. Rowley: Gn 18:31 (because of the mention of kings); Gn 14:14 (because of the mention of Dan); Gn 12:6 and 13:7 ("the Canaanite was *then* in the land"); and Gn 21:32 (because of the mention of Philistines). *The Growth of the Old Testament* (New York: Harper and Row, 1963), p. 17.

3. The best defense of Mosaic authorship of the Pentateuch is Gleason L. Archer, *A Survey of Old Testament Introduction* (Chicago: Moody, 1964), pp. 96-165.

4. David Clines, *The Theme of the Pentateuch*, JSOTSupp (1984): 25-43.

5. John H. Saihamer, "The Canonical Approach to the OT: Its Effect on Understanding Prophecy," *JETS* 30 (Sept. 1987): 307-315.

BIBLIOGRAPHY: THE PENTATEUCH

Listed below are works which provide background material, commentary or devotional application respecting the Pentateuch as a whole.

Aalders, G. Ch. *A Short Introduction to the Pentateuch.* London: Tyndale, 1949.

Allis, O.T. *The Five Books of Moses.* Philadelphia: Presbyterian and Reformed, 1949.

_____. *God Spoke by Moses.* Philadelphia: Presbyterian and Reformed, 1958.

Archer, Gleason. *A Survey of Old Testament Introduction.* Chicago: Moody, 1964.

Baxter, J. Sidlow. *Explore the Book.* Grand Rapids: Zondervan, 1960.

Brooks, Keith L. *The Summarized Bible.* Grand Rapids: Baker, 1975 reprint.

Cassuto, U. *The Documentary Hypothesis.* Jerusalem: Magnes, 1961.

Clines, David J.A. *The Theme of the Pentateuch.* Sheffield, England: JSOT Press, 1984.

Eason, J. Lawrence. *The New Bible Survey.* Grand Rapids: Zondervan, 1963.

Erdman, Charles R. *The Pentateuch.* Old Tappan, NJ: Revell, 1968.

Geisler, Norman L. *A Popular Survey of the Old Testament.* Grand Rapids: Baker, 1977.

Green, W.H. *The Higher Criticism of the Pentateuch.* New York: Scribner, 1903.

Hamilton, Victor. *Handbook on the Pentateuch.* Grand Rapids: Baker, 1982.

Hendriksen, William. *Bible Survey.* Grand Rapids: Baker, 1961.

Keil, C.F. "The Pentateuch." In *Biblical Commentary on the Old Testament.* Trans. James Martin. Grand Rapids: Eerdmans, 1959 reprint. 3 vols.

LaSor, William S., David Hubbard, and Frederic Bush. *Old Testament Survey.* Grand Rapids: Eerdmans, 1982.

Livingston, G. Herbert. *The Pentateuch in its Cultural Environment.* Grand Rapids: Baker, 1974.

Mackintosh, C.H. *Notes on the Pentateuch.* Neptune, NJ: Loizeaux, 1951 reprint. 6 vols.

Meyer, F.B. *The Five Books of Moses.* London: Marshall, Morgan and Scott, 1955.

Newell, W.R. *Studies in the Pentateuch.* Grand Rapids: Kregel, 1983.

Phillips, John. *Exploring the Scriptures.* Chicago: Moody, 1965.

Thomas, W.H. Griffith. *Through the Pentateuch Chapter by Chapter.* Grand Rapids: Eerdmans, 1957.

Wolf, Herbert. *An Introduction to the Old Testament Pentateuch.* Chicago: Moody, 1991.

THE BOOK OF
GENESIS

CHAPTER TWO

Getting Acquainted with Genesis

AIM: To demonstrate the special role of Genesis in the Scriptures.

THEME: Salvation is essential!

Genesis is the watershed of revelation. The ever deepening rivers of revelation which surge through the Bible spring from this book. Genesis introduces all the questions and problems which are addressed in the rest of the Bible. The roots of redemption are planted deep in Genesis, and he who would understand God's grand plan for the ages must spend much time exploring the contents of this book. Genesis contains fifty chapters, 1,533 verses, and 32,267 words. Genesis is the seventh largest book in the Old Testament.

The title of the first book of the Bible is derived from the Latin Vulgate translation of Jerome which in turn is based on the title found in the Greek manuscripts of the book. *Genesis* means origin, birth, generation or beginning. The name is most appropriate because Genesis records the beginnings of life, history, redemption, and the fundamental institutions of society. In Jewish circles the book is sometimes designated by its first Hebrew word, *bere'shith* "in the beginning."

Genesis can be summarized in the caption "Patriarchs and Promises." The theme of Genesis is *The Election of the Nation*. In this book God selected from the midst of idolatry a family through which he would bless all families of the earth. A nation emerged from that family — a nation which would play a key role in the history of God's dealings with man. One lesson of abiding significance is underscored again and again in Genesis: *salvation is essential*. Man cannot save himself from sin and corruption. God had to act on his behalf.

COMPOSITION OF GENESIS

Genesis makes no explicit claim regarding its authorship. The book, however, has always been regarded as volume one of a fivefold collection. Internal evidence of Mosaic authorship of this collection is supported by early and persistent Jewish and Christian tradition.

Those who accept Moses as the author of this book are divided over the question of when Moses may have written this material. Some hold that he penned these chapters while he still resided in Egypt in the house of Pharaoh's daughter. The date assigned is about 1490 BC. Others think Moses devoted himself to this project when he was leading Israel through the wilderness. On this hypothesis the date of writing would be about 1425 BC.

Since Moses lived over three hundred years after the last events in Genesis a question arises as to the source of the information which he records in this book. Perhaps some of the material came to him by direct revelation. The Joseph story (chs. 37–50) reflects a strong Egyptian background. This material was most probably still circulating in oral form in Moses' day.[1] Moses may have made extensive use of written sources in composing Genesis 1–36. Some think the Hebrew expression *'elleh toledoth* ("These are the generations of") is used to mark the conclusions of ancient tablets written by the patriarchs themselves. Eight (or ten) of these "tablets" have been identified.[2] Chart 3 summarizes the result of this research.

Most scholars do not accept the "ancient tablet" theory of the origin of Genesis. The usual view is that the *toledoth* verses introduce new sections of the book. They are superscriptions employed by Moses to mark divisions in his material, not subscriptions inserted by the original writers.[3] In either case Moses was guided by the Holy Spirit in the selection of all the materials in Genesis. Believers can rest assured that Genesis is God's inerrant Word.

Chart No. 3

ANCIENT SOURCES IN GENESIS				
TABLET	OWNER/WRITER	EXTENT	COLO-PHON	CONTENT
1	(Heavens & Earth)	1:1–2:4a	2:4a	Creation
2	Adam	2:4b–5:2	5:1	Fall/Cainites
3	Noah	5:3–6:10	6:9	Sethites/Sin
4	Sons of Noah	6:11–10:1	10:1	Flood
5	Shem	10:2–11:11	11:10	Dispersion
6	Terah	11:12-32	11:27	Shem's Line
(7)	(Ishmael)*	(12:1–25:12)	(25:12)	Abraham
(8) 7	Isaac	25:13-19a	25:19a	Ishmael
(9)	(Esau)*	(ch. 36)	26:1,9	Esau
(10) 8	Jacob	25:19b–37:2a	37:2a	Isaac/Jacob
*Isaac may have been the owner/writer of a larger tablet (12:1–25:19a) into which he incorporated the record of Ishmael. The same may be true of the Esau tablet (ch. 36) which was probably incorporated into the larger Jacob tablet.				

Why was Genesis written? After the long Egyptian bondage, God's people needed to be reminded of their roots. They needed an accurate account of the promises which God had made to their fathers. Thus the immediate purpose of the author is to remind the Israelites that God had promised to deliver them from bondage (Gn 15:16; 46:4). According to MacGregor, the ultimate purpose of Genesis is to give the early history of Israel, and to define the place which Israel occupied among the other nations of the earth.[4]

PLAN OF GENESIS

Genesis is a literary bifid of unequal proportions. The first eleven chapters deal with the beginnings of the created world, and the last thirty-nine chapters focus on the beginnings of the chosen people. The spiritual plan of the book can be outlined in three words: generation, degeneration, and regeneration. Another triad conveying the same meaning is: construction, destruction, and reconstruction.[5]

The terms "generation" or "construction" describe the contents of the first two chapters of Genesis. The account systematically relates how the world which was "unformed and unfilled" took shape and was populated. The account progresses to its climax in man as a responsible and blessed being. In these chapters everything God created is good. The elements respond in perfect obedience to the commands of God and so are blessed (1:22,28; 2:3). Perfect harmony exists between the man and his mate both of whom enjoy the idyllic joy of a Garden paradise.

Genesis 3–11 depicts the process of uncreation, degeneration or destruction. Sin entered the Garden and from there spread. The chasm between man and God widened. First an individual (Adam) was affected, then a family (Cain's clan), then the society of Noah's day, and finally the nations of the earth.

This spread of sin in Genesis 3–11 is countered by increasingly severe punishments from the Lord. Yet in each case God's grace is also clearly present. Adam and Eve were expelled from the Garden, but not before God provided them with proper clothing and a promise of ultimate victory over the Serpent (Gn 3). Cain was banished from the cultivatable soil, but not before he received a divine guarantee of his safety (Gn 4). The Flood totally wiped out a violent and corrupt society, but Noah found grace in the eyes of the Lord (Gn 5–7). The nations united in defiance of God at Babel were dispersed over the face of the earth (Gn 11).

Chronologically Abram's entrance into Canaan marked a new era; thematically his response is just as significant. The consequences of the drastic and irreversible Babel judgment were mitigated somewhat by Abram's response to the Call (Gn 12:1-5). Through the descendants of this man God promised once again to bless all nations. Part of that blessing would be the unification of the nations in Christ.

The remainder of Genesis reveals God at work in reconstruction or re-creation. While the focus in the preceding section is on man's predicament, here it is on God's Promise. The process is seen at work first in the life of three individuals: Abram, Isaac and Jacob. The process continues at the family level (sons of Jacob), the society level (Joseph in Egypt), and finally the national level (Israel).

As noted in the preceding chapter, the Promise to the Patriarchs had three interrelated aspects. In the *progeny* aspect God announced that he would make of Abram, Isaac and Jacob a great nation (12:2). Some nineteen formulations of this commitment are found in Genesis 12–50. While the fulfillment of the *position* and *possession* aspects of the promise constitute minor themes in Genesis, the overriding concern of the narratives is the tension between faith in the *progeny* promise and the ever so slowly developing fulfillment of it. Other families growing from similar roots developed far more rapidly than did Israel into mighty nations (ch. 36).

Circumstances constantly challenged faith in the seed promise. Twenty-five years passed before the child of promise was born. Once born, the question of his survival (ch. 22) and marriage (ch. 24) became crucial. The accounts of the barrenness of wives and the jeopardy of mothers-to-be (chs. 12, 20, 26) are to be interpreted against this backdrop. The lives of the heirs of the promise — Ishmael, Isaac, Jacob, Joseph, Benjamin — were in danger from time to time. The Patriarchal narrative revolves around rash decisions born of frustration, dissension within the family, and painful separations. Yet at the end of Genesis the family is intact, safely settled in a fertile region of Egypt with every prospect of growth. The Promise has not yet been fully realized — they are not yet as numerous as the stars of the heavens and sand of the seashore (15:5; 22:17) — but definite progress has been made toward that destiny.[6]

Chart No. 4

STRUCTURE OF GENESIS					
The Roots of a Special People					
BEGINNINGS OF THE CREATED WORLD 1:1–12:5			**C**	BEGINNINGS OF THE CHOSEN PEOPLE 12:6–50:26	
EDENIC PERIOD	PRE FLOOD	POST FLOOD	**A**	POST CANAAN	
1:1–3:24	4:1–9:29	10:1–12:5	**L**		
FOUR PIVOTAL EVENTS			**L**	FOUR PIVOTAL PERSONS	
CREATION FALL FLOOD DISPERSION			↓ 12:1-5	ABRAHAM ISAAC JACOB JOSEPH	
MAN'S PREDICAMENT				GOD'S PROMISE	
GOD'S ULTIMATE PURPOSE					

CHRONOLOGY OF GENESIS

The Book of Genesis relates the history of the kingdom of God on earth from the time of the creation of the world to the death of Joseph in Egypt. The book begins with *creation* and ends with a *coffin*. Precisely how many years are covered in Genesis is impossible to ascertain. In the opinion of many Old Testament scholars, the earliest date in Bible history which can be computed with anything like precision is the birth of Abraham. Biblical chronology places the call of

Abram at about 2092 BC and his birth seventy-five years earlier in about 2167 BC. Most Old Testament scholars will not hazard a guess about dates prior to the birth of Abram. Notices are sufficient during the Post-Canaan or Patriarchal period to establish the chronology. The Patriarchs journeyed about in the promised land for 215 years. The Eisodus ("way into") or entering of Egypt by the family of Jacob can be dated to approximately 1877 BC. Joseph continued to hold office in Egypt for about 70 years following the Eisodus.

Five distinct periods of history can be identified in Genesis. These are displayed in Chart 5.

Chart No. 5

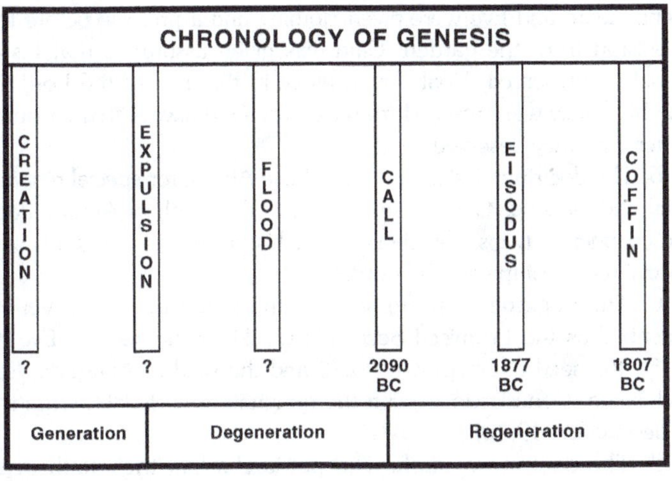

CHRONOLOGY OF GENESIS					
C R E A T I O N	E X P U L S I O N	F L O O D	C A L L	E I S O D U S	C O F F I N
?	?	?	2090 BC	1877 BC	1807 BC
Generation	Degeneration		Regeneration		

THEOLOGY OF GENESIS

Genesis is foundational in theology. Basic themes emerge here which are amplified in the rest of the Bible. Seven key doctrines characterize the book.

1. The doctrine of creation. All that exists came into being by the Word of the eternal God. Consequently, the material world is inherently good. Man is the apex of God's creative work, and therefore man has been given sovereignty over the earth.

39

2. The doctrine of sin. Sin is encouraged by a malevolent being called Serpent (Gn 3). Sin manifests itself in heinous crimes (Gn 4), in immorality and violence (Gn 6, 19), and in pride and rebellion against God (Gn 11).

3. The doctrine of judgment. God punishes sin. He pronounced sentence on Serpent, Adam and Eve after the Fall (Gn 3). Cain was banished following the murder of Abel (Gn 4). The Flood destroyed the world except for those on the ark (Gn 6–8). Those who defied God by building a tower were scattered by the confusion of tongues (Gn 11). The cities of the plain were destroyed by fire and brimstone (Gn 19).

4. The doctrine of grace. A ray of hope is evident in every judgment. Adam and Eve were given clothing and a promise before their expulsion from the garden. Cain was given assurance that his life would be preserved. Noah found grace in the eyes of the Lord. Lot and his family were rescued from Sodom. God always treated sinners better than they deserved!

5. The doctrine of election. God chose Abram for special responsibility and blessing. God chose Isaac after the death of Abram. Jacob the younger of twins was chosen over his brother to enjoy this same special relationship with the Lord.

6. The doctrine of promise. In Genesis the future Deliverer is described as the Promised Seed. He would be the seed of Eve (Gn 3:15), the seed of Shem (Gn 9:27), and the seed of Abraham, Isaac and Jacob. Genesis closes with the designation of Judah as the tribe of destiny (Gn 49:10).

7. The doctrine of faith. The patriarchs had their faith in the promise tested repeatedly. During their lifetimes they experienced but token fulfillments of each promise. Yet they continued to believe, and God counted their faith as righteousness (Gn 15:6). The supreme example of this testing is recorded in Genesis 22 where Abraham was commanded to offer his only son as a sacrifice to God on Mt. Moriah.

GEOGRAPHY OF GENESIS

The drama of Genesis unfolds on three geographical stages. The Mesopotamian river valley is the setting for the first eleven chapters.

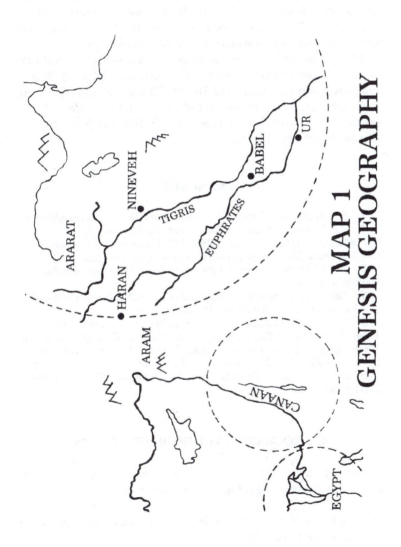

MAP 1
GENESIS GEOGRAPHY

In chapter 12 Abram is called to leave Ur of Chaldees to go to a land which God would show him. That land, as it turned out, was the land of Canaan. Chapters 12 through 38 describe the journeys of the patriarchs in Canaan and neighboring lands. The last twelve chapters of Genesis focus attention on events in the land of Egypt.

Much of the action in Genesis 12–50 centers around five great journeys: (1) Abram's journey from Ur to Canaan (11:27–12:9); (2) Abram's brief excursion into Egypt (12:10-20); (3) the journeys of Abram, Isaac and Jacob around the land of Canaan (chs. 13–28, 32–38); (4) Jacob's journey to Paddan Aram (chs. 28–31); and (5) Israel's journey into Egypt (chs. 42–46).

ENDNOTES

1. K.A. Kitchen, s.v. "Joseph," *The New Bible Dictionary*, pp. 658-659.

2. P.J. Wiseman, *Ancient Records and the Structure of Genesis*, ed. D.J. Wiseman (Nashville: Nelson, 1985); R.K. Harrison, *Introduction to the Old Testament* (Grand Rapids: Eerdmans, 1969), pp. 543-551.

3. Derek Kidner, *Genesis, an Introduction and Commentary* (London: Tyndale, 1967), pp. 23f.

4. George H. C. Macgregor, *Messages of the Old Testament* (London: Hodder and Stoughton, 1901), pp. 10-13.

5. G. Campbell Morgan, *The Analyzed Bible* (Old Tappan, NJ: Revell, 1964), p. 2; J. Sidlow Baxter, *Explore the Book* (Grand Rapids: Zondervan, 1960), pp. 27-29; W.H. Griffith Thomas, *Through the Pentateuch Chapter by Chapter* (Grand Rapids: Eerdmans, 1957), p. 28.

6. David J.A. Clines, *The Theme of the Pentateuch* (Sheffield, England: JSOT Press, 1984), pp. 45f.

BIBLIOGRAPHY: THE BOOK OF GENESIS

Listed below are works which give introductory, exegetical and devotional insight to the entire book of Genesis.

Aalders, G. Ch. *Genesis*. 2 vols. Bible Student's Commentary. Grand Rapids: Zondervan, 1981.

Barnhouse, Donald Grey. *Genesis*. Grand Rapids: Zondervan, 1970.

Candlish, R.S. *The Book of Genesis.* Grand Rapids: Kregel, 1979.

Crawford, C. *Genesis: The Book of Beginnings.* Joplin: College Press,1966–71. 4 vols.

Davis, John. *Paradise to Prison.* Grand Rapids: Baker, 1975.

Green, W.H. *The Unity of the Book of Genesis.* Grand Rapids: Baker,1979 reprint.

Kidner, Derek. *Genesis: An Introduction and Commentary.* The Tyndale Old Testament Commentaries. London: Tyndale, 1967.

Leupold, H.C. *Exposition of Genesis.* Columbus: Wartburg, 1942.

Morris, Henry. *The Genesis Record.* Grand Rapids: Baker, 1976.

Murphy, J.G. *A Critical and Exegetical Commentary on the Book of Genesis.* Reprinted by James Publications, n.d.

Phillips, John. *Exploring Genesis.* Chicago: Moody, 1980.

Roop, Eugene F. *Genesis.* Believers Church Bible Commentary. Scottdale, PA: Herald, 1987.

Sarna, Nahum. *Understanding Genesis.* McGraw-Hill, 1966.

Sauer, Erich. *The Dawn of World Redemption.* Grand Rapids: Eerdmans,1950.

Speiser, E.A. *Genesis: Introduction, Translation and Notes.* The Anchor Bible. Garden City, NY: Doubleday, 1964.

Stigers, H.G. *A Commentary on Genesis.* Grand Rapids: Zondervan, 1976.

Thomas, W.H. Griffith. *Genesis: A Devotional Commentary.* Grand Rapids: Eerdmans, 1946.

Vos, Howard. *Genesis and Archaeology.* Chicago: Moody, 1963.

Wiseman, P.J. *Ancient Records and the Structure of Genesis.* Ed. D.J. Wiseman. Nashville: Nelson, 1985.

CHAPTER THREE

God's Creative Word
Genesis 1:1-2:3

AIM: To demonstrate the personality, power and purpose of God as it is revealed in the creation account.

THEME: The Greatness of God!

Man by nature is curious about the origins of the world in which he lives. In the ancient creation myths of Mesopotamia the universe resulted from warfare among the gods. Certain parallels between these myths and the biblical narrative of Genesis 1 have been noted, but the differences far outnumber the similarities. Comparing pagan cosmogonies with biblical revelation is like comparing a pigsty to a cathedral. Any similarity is purely coincidental.

Modern secular man is in no better position than ancient man to know the truth about the origins of the universe. Though he couches his speculation in scientific jargon and bolsters his hypotheses with mathematical formulas, his efforts produce no assurance. Philosophy, not science, attempts such speculation. Since science is the systematic analysis of presently observed processes and their phenomena, any attempt to extrapolate conclusions from these observations regarding the primeval earth are clearly outside the realm of science. Scientists who pontificate about events which they allege to have occurred millions or billions of years ago do so as high priests of the religion of humanism.

To all men ancient and modern who think they know how the universe was formed the Creator asks this question: "Where were you when I laid the foundation of the world?" (Job 38:4). The question of origins is beyond the range of empirical investigation. Therefore special revelation from the Creator is needed if man is to know anything for certain about his origins.

Genesis 1 is the most amazing composition in all the literature of the world. It provides the perfect opening to God's book. The chapter is marked by simplicity. Only seventy-six different root words are used. Yet here is all that men really need to know about the facts of creation. Here is the first word and the last word regarding the beginning of all things.

Until the latter half of the nineteenth century the western world regarded Genesis 1 as an authoritative account of the beginning. The writings of Charles Darwin, Hermann Gunkel and Julius Wellhausen tended to shatter the confidence which men had in the biblical creation account. From Darwin came the attack of evolution which said in effect, "the Genesis account is not accurate." Gunkel's research in the field of comparative religions focused on other ancient creation accounts. This field of study generated the conclusion that the biblical account was not unique and therefore, not inspired. Wellhausen employed the techniques of literary criticism to argue that Genesis contains two creation accounts which are inconsistent and contradictory. Because of the influence of these three men and their disciples, "by 1900 many people had been educated to believe that the Bible's statements about creation were neither accurate, inspired, nor consistent."[1]

Four aspects of the creation narrative emphasize the greatness of God: (1) the priority of God in relation to creation, (2) the power of God as displayed in creation, (3) the process of God employed in creation, and (4) the plan of God which is evident in creation.

THE PRIORITY OF GOD

Genesis 1 begins with the grand announcement, "In the beginning *God.*" This chapter reveals the priority of God in respect to (1) time and (2) position.

A. Priority in Time.

The greatness of God is indicated in the fact that he was here when it all began. The implications of the first verse of the Bible are staggering. Here the Bible throws down the gauntlet to a number of "isms" which are antithetical to the biblical worldview. Seven items of positive revelation are contained in Genesis 1:1.

1. God exists. Thus atheism is opposed. The Hebrew word for God *('elohim)* is used over 2500 times in the Old Testament. The word conceives of God as the one who by his nature and his works rouses man's fear and reverence. *'Elohim* emphasizes the power and transcendence of God.

2. Only one God exists. The verb in verse 1 is singular necessitating the conclusion that the world was created by one God. Thus polytheism is opposed.

3. The pluralistic unity of the Godhead is suggested by the fact that the word for God *('elohim)* is plural while the verb is singular. Later revelation will make clear that the one God manifests himself as Father, Son, and Holy Spirit. Thus Unitarianism is opposed.

4. The universe had a beginning. Matter is not eternal. Thus materialism is opposed.

5. God is distinct from nature, for he created the heavens and earth. Thus pantheism is opposed.

6. Since God created the material universe, he is obviously superior to it and therefore in control of it. Thus the doctrine of fatalism is opposed.

7. In creating the material universe God, a nonmaterial being, of necessity had to interact with the material realm. Thus the doctrine of dualism is opposed.

In Genesis 1:1 the curtain of revelation rises to reveal a single actor on a cosmic stage. The spotlight in this verse and throughout

47

the chapter is on God. In the creation narrative the emphasis is not so much on *how* as on *who*. *'Elohim* is used thirty-two times in the first chapter of the Bible and with only two exceptions (1:2,27) always as the subject of a verb. Add to this total four places in the chapter where a pronoun referring to God is the subject of the action verb. Eight times the chapter emphasizes the divine satisfaction with the creation effort. Such language would be inappropriate to an impersonal force. The God who was here when it all began is intelligent, systematic, communicative, and beneficent.

B. Priority in Position.

Since God has priority in time he also has priority in position. He is God and all else is not God. He vies with no rival for sovereignty. Genesis 1 recognizes this priority in position in four ways.

1. God exercised his sovereign rights when he named various facets of his creation. He who gives a name is superior to that which is named. Often in the ancient world the conqueror of a city would give the place a new name. In Genesis 1 God named the light and darkness (1:5), the expanse (1:8), the gathering of waters and the dry land (1:10).

2. God exercised his sovereign rights when he delegated responsibility and authority. On day four God appointed the greater light to rule the day and the lesser light to rule the night (1:16). Pagan mythology deified the heavenly bodies; in Genesis they are but servants given their orders and duty by God. On day six man was given dominion over all the earth and the animals which inhabit it (1:26,28). Man then must not worship any creature, for he is superior to all save the Creator himself.

3. Since the lesser is blessed by the greater (Heb 7:7), the three blessings pronounced by God in the creation narrative are evidence of his priority of position. Thus God blessed fish and fowl on the fifth day (1:22), man on day six (1:28), and the sabbath on day seven (2:3).

4. God exercised his sovereignty by imposing restrictions on the created order. Four times God ordered various life-forms to reproduce "after their kind" (1:11,21,24,25). While there is some debate about the boundaries embraced in the word "kind" (*min*), the word certainly rules out evolution from one-cell creature to man.

48

THE POWER OF GOD

Two features of Genesis 1 underscore the power of God as displayed in creation, namely, the creation vocabulary and the fiat-fulfillment motif.

A. The Creation Vocabulary.

The key word in creation vocabulary is *bara'*, to create. This word appears at three crucial places: initial creation (1:1); the creation of conscious life (1:21), and the creation of man (1:27; 5:1-2). The word has four connotations: (1) newness—the appearance of something which did not previously exist, (2) effortlessness, (3) instantaneous action, and (4) divine activity—God is always the subject of this verb.

No small amount of discussion revolves around the issue of whether or not the term *bara'* conveys the notion of creation *ex nihilo*, i.e., creation from nothing. When the implications of the term *bara'* are placed in conjunction with the phrase "in the beginning" one can make a strong case for the doctrine of creation *ex nihilo* in Genesis 1. In the light of John 1:1-3 and Hebrews 11:3 Christians have affirmed that God spoke into being all of the material universe. In any case, if in Genesis 1:1 Moses desired to express the concept of absolute creation there was no more suitable word in the Hebrew language at his disposal.

Other verbs in Genesis 1 which point to the power of God are the following:

1. God made (*'asah*). This very common Hebrew word connotes purposeful construction. God made the expanse (1:7), heavenly bodies (1:16), land animals (1:25), and man (1:26). This verb is used to sum up the entire work of the creation week (1:31; 2:2-3).

2. God separated (*badhal*). He separated the light and darkness (1:4), and atmospheric vapors from ground waters (1:6,7).

3. God placed (*nathan*). He placed the heavenly bodies above the uninhabited world (1:17). This and the preceding word stress the organizational ability of God in creation.

B. The Fiat-Fulfillment Motif.

The power of God is emphasized by the use of the fiat-fulfillment motif. Seven commands, three of them double, appear in Genesis 1.

49

Thus God's fiat ("Let it be") is followed by the comments of the sacred historian ("And there was . . . and it was so"). The impression is conveyed that God merely spoke the universe into being. The world then is not the product of blind chance, of eons of trial and error or of struggle between God and equally powerful contrary forces. The God of Genesis 1 is in complete control from that point which can be called "the beginning" to the present.

Other Scriptures support the notion of effortless creation. "Through faith we understand that the worlds were framed *by the word of God*" (Heb 11:3). "For this they (i.e., scoffers) willingly are ignorant of, that *by the word of God* the heavens were of old, and the earth standing out of the water and in the water" (2 Pet 3:5). "*By the word of the Lord* were the heavens made . . . He spoke, and it was" (Ps 33:6,9). "Let them praise the name of the Lord, for *he commanded, and they were created*" (Ps 148:5).

THE PROCESS OF GOD

The greatness of God is indicated in the process by which he chose to bring the universe into existence. All that exists could have been brought into being in one millisecond by one command of the Almighty. God chose, however, to employ process in the work of creation. The sense of God's wisdom, majesty and power is thereby enhanced. The goodness of every aspect of the universe is thus underscored. A certain hierarchy in the created order thereby becomes evident.

A. The Beginning of the Process (Gn 1:2).

The word structure of Genesis 1:2 gives a geocentric orientation to the rest of the chapter. The condition of the earth prior to the first recorded divine fiat is described in five ways. The earth was (1) *tohu*, unformed. It did not have the physical features which would make it habitable. Thus (2) it was *bohu*, unfilled. (3) The earth was covered with water called "the deep" (*tehom*), and (4) it was enveloped in darkness. Yet (5) the Spirit of God was hovering over this primeval earth as a mother eagle might hover over her nest.

How is the condition of the earth as described in Genesis 1:2 to be explained? The Ruin-Reconstruction theory (also known as the Gap Theory) is perhaps the most widely held view among evangelicals. According to this view verse 1 describes an original perfect creation. For some reason undisclosed in Scripture, God destroyed that original creation. Verse 2 is translated, "Now the earth *became* waste and void." Advocates of the Ruin-Reconstruction Theory suggest that prehistoric men and animals were part of the original creation, not the present creation which is only a few thousand years old. Opponents of the Gap Theory often contend that it has been superimposed upon Genesis as a means of harmonizing the existence of prehistoric fossils alleged to be millions of years old on the one hand, and a biblical chronology which measures the creation of Adam in thousands and not millions of years. Advocates of the Gap Theory, however, long antedate the discovery of prehistoric fossils.[2]

Can Genesis 1:2 be translated "Now the earth *became* waste and void"? Many authorities insist that the verb *hayah* cannot be rendered *became* here.[3] The truth of the matter is that this verb more often than not expresses an action and not a state of being.[4] The Gap Theory cannot be opposed on linguistic grounds. Against the Gap Theory, however, these points can be raised: (1) No other scriptures support the concept of a universal judgment on the world before the Flood. (2) Exodus 20:11 teaches that the world and all that is in it were made in six days. (3) Genesis 1 gives the impression of describing one creation, not a re-creation of something which had previously been destroyed.

Genesis 1:2 is best viewed as a description of the earth in the first stage of a process. Perhaps the verse could be translated, "Now the earth came into being unformed and unfilled." The process of forming and filling the earth is then unfolded in the six creative days.

B. The Genesis Days.

Each of the creative days is discussed within a more or less fixed pattern which has five components: (1) The announcement—God said, (2) the fiat — let it be, (3) the report — and it was so, (4) the evaluation — it was good, and (5) the temporal framework — morning came and evening came, day number. Five major views of the nature of the creative days have found advocates.

1. The day-age theory.[5] The days in Genesis are viewed as long eons of time. In support of this theory it is argued that (1) God does not measure time as man does (2 Pet 3:8; Ps 90:4), (2) the word "day" is used in a figurative way in the creation narrative (Gn 2:4), and (3) God's "Book of Nature" reveals that long eons elapsed between the creation of the lower forms of life and man.

2. The revelatory day theory.[6] The days in Genesis were ordinary days on Mt. Sinai in which God revealed the fact of divine creation to Moses. This theory has difficulty explaining Exodus 20:11.

3. The framework theory.[7] The days in Genesis are but a literary device. The author has chosen to organize his material in a topical pattern. The succession of days reveals nothing about the actual sequence in which the present order took shape. The symmetry between the first three and the last three days is offered as evidence that they are merely a literary device.

4. The ordinary day view.[8] Advocates point out that the word "day" is defined in 1:5 as the period from sunrise to sunset. The term "day" (yom) in the singular appears some 1,150 in the Old Testament. In over ninety percent of these occurrences the word has its ordinary meaning. When a numeral is used with yom it always means an ordinary day. The phrase "evening and morning" also is thought to support this position. Finally, Exodus 20:11 is viewed as Moses' own commentary on Genesis 1.

5. The creative intervention view.[9] At strategic points in the natural development of the earth the Creator intervened. Thus the days were ordinary days, but between these creative interventions long eons of time may have elapsed.

C. The Unfolding of the Process (Gn 1:3-26).

The acts of creation are divided, not only by the six days, but also by means of the expression "God saw that it was good." That expression may be regarded as marking the successive steps or stages of the divine work. The phrase occurs seven times, but does not divide the work exactly as the days divide it. On the second day the clause does not occur at all; and on the third and sixth day it occurs twice. Combining these two indicators of divine activity the following stages in the creative process become apparent.

Day one (1:3-4) featured an act of separation resulting in the creation of light. The darkness which shrouded the earth in verse 2 was removed. God pronounced the alternation of light and darkness good.

On day two (1:6-8) God began to form the earth by means of a second act of separation. An expanse — the atmosphere — was placed in the midst of the waters thus separating the clouds above from the condensed water below.

On day three (1:9-13) the second phase of the process of ordering the waters took place. An act of separation resulted in the formation of land. The physical features of the earth were now complete and God pronounced his work good. The filling of the earth began immediately. At God's command the land produced all manner of vegetation including fruit trees. God expressed his approval for these self-perpetuating living things.

In a second triad of days Moses narrates the filling of the earth. On day four (1:14-18) the luminaries — sun, moon and stars — were placed in the expanse. Whatever the source of the light on day one, that light was now localized in these heavenly bodies. The creation of fish to fill the waters and birds to fill the heavens mark the creative work of day five (1:20-22). The appearance of beasts and man mark the climax of creation on day six (1:24-26).

D. The Conclusion of the Process (Gn 2:1-3).

Genesis 2 opens with this declaration: "Thus the heavens and the earth were completed in all their hosts." Six times during the creative week God saw what he had made that it was good. Now at the conclusion of the entire process "God saw everything he had made, and, behold, it was very good" (1:31).

On the seventh day God rested from his creative activity. This is not the rest of weariness, but simply the cessation of a particular kind of activity. Religious observance of the seventh day is not enjoined here, nor is there any evidence that men in the primeval period worshiped on the seventh day. Sabbath observance would later become a distinctive feature of the Law of Moses.

ENDNOTES

1. D.F. Payne, *Genesis One Reconsidered* (London: Tyndale, 1964), pp. 5-6.

2. Some early Jewish commentators and church fathers advocated this approach to Genesis 1. Among the more recent advocates have been Rosenmuller, Pember, Rimmer and Custance.

3. Bernard Ramm, *A Christian View of Science and the Scriptures* (London: Paternoster, 1964), p. 139. Others taking the same position are Whitcomb, Buswell, Filby and Barr.

4. Archer, *Introduction*, p. 174, n. 3. The same position is taken by Pusey, Billman, S.R. Driver and Custance.

5. Nineteenth century advocates of the day-age theory: Dana, Dawson, Godet and Zockler. More recently the theory has been advocated by Handrich (1953), Gedner (1950), and in a modified form by Davis Young (1977).

6. Advocates of the revelatory day theory are P.J. Wiseman, James Strong, Bettex (1924) and Miller (1957).

7. The view of John Davis, J.P. Lange and more recently by Filby (1963) and Ridderbos (1957).

8. The ordinary day view is advocated by Rimmer, Klotz, Zimmerman, Whitcomb and Morris.

9. The creative intervention view is advocated by Duntzweiler and Robert C. Newman (1977).

BIBLIOGRAPHY: GENESIS 1

Filby, Floyd A. *Creation Revealed*. Old Tappan, NJ: Revell, 1964.

Heidel, Alexander. *The Babylonian Genesis*. Second ed. Chicago: University Press, 1963.

Newell, Philip R. *Light out of Darkness*. Chicago: Moody, n.d.

Newman, Robert C., and Herman Eckelmann. *Genesis One and the Origin of the Earth*. Grand Rapids: Baker, 1977.

Payne, D.F. *Genesis One Reconsidered*. London: Tyndale, 1962.

Whitcomb, John. *The Early Earth*. Grand Rapids: Baker, 1972.

Young, Edward J. *Studies in Genesis One*. Philadelphia: Presbyterian and Reformed, 1964.

CHAPTER FOUR

The Crown of Creation
Genesis 2:4-25

AIM: To demonstrate the beauty and perfection of God's original creation.

THEME: God's tender concern for man.

Man is the crown of creation. The significant but brief treatment of his origin in Genesis 1 is amplified in Genesis 2. Jesus tied the two accounts together when in Matthew 19:4-5 he said: "Have you not read that he who made them at the beginning made them male and female (Gn 1:27) and said, For this cause shall a man leave father and mother and shall cleave to his wife and they twain shall be one flesh" (Gn 2:24). Thus by Jesus' own teaching example modern students are instructed to regard Genesis 1 and Genesis 2 as harmonious accounts of the same event.

New Testament usage also compels Christians to regard Adam and Eve as real people, not legendary characters or literary inventions. Jesus regarded them as the first human pair (Matt 19:4-5). Paul considered Adam to be just as historical as Moses (Rom 5:12,14). He accepted the account of Eve as reliable (1 Tim 2:13f.; 2 Cor 11:3; 1 Cor 11:8-9). Luke put Adam in the context of a list of historical personages (Luke 3:38).

That man was the crown of God's creation is indicated in four ways. The account emphasizes man's (1) uniqueness, (2) abode, (3) mate, and (4) dominion.

MAN'S UNIQUENESS
Genesis 1:26-27; 2:4-7

The amount of space allocated to the second creative act of the sixth day clearly indicates that man is at the center of the plan of God. All that was created before him was created for him. Man is unique in several ways.

A. The Uniqueness of the Planning for Man.

The uniqueness and superiority of man in the created order is underscored by the divine consultation which took place prior to his creation. "Let us make man in our image and in our likeness" (1:28). Who is this that takes counsel together? Certainly not angels. Man is never said to be created in the likeness of angels, and God is never said to take counsel with angels (cf. Isa 40:14). Is this a majestic plural such as sovereigns employ? Not likely, for this type of plural cannot be demonstrated in the court language of the Old Testament. So far in the narrative the only creative powers alluded to have been God, the Spirit of God, and the word of God. In the light of John 1:1-3 the only satisfactory explanation of the plural can be that man is the product of the contemplation of the pluralistic godhead, i.e., the Father, Son and Holy Spirit.

B. The Uniqueness of the Nature of Man.

Man is different from and superior to the animals in that he alone is made in the image (*tselem*) and likeness (*damuth*) of God. This is the only place in the Old Testament where these two terms are used in conjunction with one another. The first Hebrew term comes from a root meaning "to carve, cut off." The general significance is that man is closely patterned after his Maker. The second term is merely supplementary to or explanatory of the first term.[1] The combination of terms refers to man's intellectual, spiritual, volitional, and ethical capacity. In short the combination "image and likeness" refers to all that sets man apart from the animal kingdom. Neither term refers to man's body. God is an incorporeal Spirit (John 1:18; 1 Tim 6:16). He does not have a body analogous to that of man. Yet it is logical to assume that the body which man possesses is a worthy tabernacle for that spirit which bears the image and likeness of God.

C. The Uniqueness of Man's Sexuality.

On the fifth day God told the water creatures and birds to be fruitful and multiply (1:22). A reference to the procreative powers of these creatures is thus implied. But only in the case of man is sexuality specifically mentioned. "Male and female created he them" (1:27). The ancient pagan mind could conceive of no creative force other than sex. Sex existed before the cosmos. The gods themselves were creatures of sex. The universe was born as a result of a sexual act of gods. Not so in Genesis. The God of the Bible is sovereign over sex, for he created it.

Genesis 1 clearly indicates that both male and female are created in the image of God. The inherent equality of the sexes is thus taught. God, of course, is not a sexual being. In this respect man is not made in God's image. God most frequently is referred to by male terms in Scripture. This is appropriate because God is the initiator of life. But the fact that God is called, for example, Father should not be taken to mean that God is male. Again it must be stressed that both male and female are made in the image of God because the image of God has nothing to do with sexuality.

In the creation of the lower forms of life, multitudes were apparently created simultaneously. These creatures were told to reproduce "after their kind." God, however, only created a single pair of humankind. Thus the foundation of marriage as the cohabitation of a single male and a single female is clearly set forth. Attempts to erase the distinction between male and female are against nature and are an affront to the wisdom of the Creator.

D. The Uniqueness of Man's Creation (Gn 2:4-7).

In Genesis 2 the transcendent and all-powerful *'elohim* is identified as Yahweh, the God of redemption. The LORD God (*yahweh 'elohim*) is the Creator. This double name for God is used eleven times in Genesis 2. The name Yahweh means "he who is" or the Eternal. Yahweh is the covenant name for God in the Old Testament.

Conditions on earth just prior to the creation of the first man are spelled out in 2:4-6. The "field shrubs" and "field plants" had not yet appeared. This is not the same terminology used of the vegetation created on the third day of the previous chapter (1:11-12). Two reasons are stated for the lack of these kinds of plants: God had not sent rain on the earth, and (2) no man was present to work the ground. Prior to the first rain, the land was watered by a fountain (*'ed*) which went up from the ground. There is no indication that the rainless condition continued until the time of Noah as some have suggested. The kind of vegetation spoken of in 2:5 was the special vegetation which was put in the garden.

The crown of God's creation is called *'adam* (man), a word closely related to *'adhamah* (ground) in 1:25. Just as the land creatures came from the earth (1:24), so also did man, at least in his physical aspect. Thus Genesis 2 points to the lowly origin of man, his essential frailty and final destiny. But man was fashioned by the hand of God (2:7). The verb "formed" (*yatsar*) describes the artistic genius of a potter. Man's body is of divine origin.

The body of man was animated by the breath of God (2:7). The phrase "breath of life" (*nishmah chayyim*) is never used of animals. This breath of God in man is that which Christian theology designates as soul or spirit.

MAN'S ABODE
Genesis 2:8-17

God's tender concern for man is indicated by the way he provided a habitation for the first man. Two observations about that garden are important.

A. The Nature of the Garden.

The text does not indicate that the entire primeval earth was a paradise. The word garden (gan) signifies a place protected by a fence or wall. The garden was located "eastward" in respect to the writer and in a plain ('eden) at the confluence of four rivers (2:8,10-14). Two of the rivers can be identified — the Hiddekel (Tigris) and the Perat (Euphrates). The Pishon and Gihon are likely two of the other Mesopotamian rivers which flow into the Tigris and Euphrates. These four rivers joined to flow through the garden as one river.[2] The author seems to be describing the geography of ancient Sumer just north of the Persian Gulf in what is present-day Iraq. Ancient pagan legend remembered a paradise at the northern end of the Persian Gulf.

The garden was a scene of beauty and bounty prepared by the hand of Yahweh Elohim himself (2:8-9). This place was the perfect habitation for man in his perfection. The garden was adorned by beautiful vegetation ("every tree that is lovely to see"). The Garden trees were abundant in fruitfulness ("every tree . . . good for food"). God may have created special animals to inhabit the garden (2:19).[3] The garden was later used as the standard to measure fruitfulness and beauty (Gn 13:10; Isa 51:3; Ezek 28:13; Joel 2:3).

B. The Purpose of the Garden.

God put (sim) man in the garden (2:8), caused man to rest (nuach) in the garden (2:15). Man thus knew the conditions outside the garden before he came to experience the blessings of that place. Yet the garden was no place of idleness. God assigned man work to do. He was to cultivate ('abhad) and to keep (shamar) it (2:15). The plants, flowers and trees of Eden stood in need of cultivation from the hand of man and would speedily have degenerated without his attention.

Because the garden was an abode of innocence, it was suitable for sinless man. There man had access to the tree of life. But continued access to that tree was contingent upon man's faithfulness. Only the name of this special tree hints at its purpose. Partaking of the tree of life apparently imparted to the partaker the possibility of physical immortality.

The garden was a place of probation. A single prohibition provided man with an opportunity to function as a free moral agent, to choose for or against God. The prohibition was specific and emphatic. Of one designated tree God ordered: "You may not surely eat"

(2:17). The prohibition was light, for concerning all the other trees in the garden God had said, "You may eat freely" (2:16). The prohibition was accompanied by a warning: In the day you eat of the forbidden tree you shall surely die!

MAN'S MATE
Genesis 2:18-25

The tender concern of God for man is indicated in the mate which he provided for the first man.

A. The Need for a Mate (Gn 2:18-20).

God observed that it was not good for the man to be alone (2:18). This should not be taken to mean that God intends for every person to marry. Other Scriptures indicate that there are times when it would be better for a man or a woman to remain single. God's observation was that it was not good for Adam's personality for him to remain alone. He needed companionship. Furthermore, God's program demanded that Adam have a mate. From the beginning God looked forward to the propagation of the race, the generation of the chosen people, and the coming of the Promised Seed.

To help prepare man for the reception of his mate, God brought the garden animals before him "to see what he would name them" (2:19). This enabled man to (1) exercise the gifts of language and reason, (2) manifest his sovereignty over the inferior creatures, and (3) discover for himself his loneliness. Adam was absolutely correct in his assessment of the nature of each animal: "Whatever Adam called each living creature, that was its name." He marked each creature for what it was — inferior to himself. Adam saw clearly that for him there was no suitable helper among the animals (2:20).

The implication is that the woman about to be created would be man's helper ('ezer). The Hebrew word does not connote inferiority. She was not to be man's servant. The animals are helpers to man; but none of them is a helper corresponding to him. Animals are inferior to man; the woman is not. She renders a kind of help which animals are not suitable to offer (2:20). This word helper is elsewhere used of God himself. He is man's ultimate Helper. The word points to strength and wisdom. A woman who is truly fulfilling the role of helper to her mate is performing a God-like function to her husband.

B. The Provision of a Mate (Gn 2:21-22a).

In the Mesopotamian creation myths no special attention is given to the creation of woman. The Bible, on the other hand, indicates the significance of the first woman in several ways.

1. The time of her creation. The summary account of Genesis 1 gives the impression that man and woman were created simultaneously. Genesis 2 makes clear that an interval separated the two events. Woman was the last of God's creative works. She was the crown of the creation. She made her appearance only after everything was in the highest state of readiness for her reception: a home, provision for her maintenance, a husband who longed for her coming, who appreciated her worth.

2. The manner of her creation. God literally built (*banah*) the woman. This term is used nowhere else in the creation narrative. The verb is frequently used in the Old Testament for completing an unfinished structure. Man was incomplete without his mate.

3. The substance from which she was formed. She was formed from man's rib (*tsela'*). This indicates that woman was made of more precious material, dust doubled refined. Woman is one with man for she came from him. She had a claim upon man for protection and affection. Long ago Matthew Henry observed: "She was not made out of his head, to rule over him; nor out of his feet, to be trampled on by him; but out of his side, to be equal with him; under his arm, to be protected; and near his heart, to be beloved."[4]

C. The Union with the Mate (Gen.2:22b-25).

Woman was created to be the perfect supplement to Adam's incompleteness physically, intellectually, and socially. In man's need, and woman's power to satisfy that need, is laid the foundation for the divine institution of marriage. Three basic ingredients of marriage are present in Genesis 2: (1) the Father's consent — he brought her to Adam (2:22), (2) the woman's consent — she willingly came to her husband, and (3) the man's consent — Adam received her as his bride.

1. The intimacy of the union. The excitement of Adam upon viewing his bride is clearly indicated in the Hebrew text. Adam did not
need to be instructed by divine revelation regarding the true nature of
his bride: "She is bone of my bone, and flesh of my flesh" (2:23). He
thereby accepted her as an equal, as one to be loved and cherished.
But this is more than an affirmation of kinship with the woman. A
study of similar expressions in the Old Testament (e.g., Gn 29:14;
Judg 9:2) suggests that this is also a declaration of loyalty. Adam thus
composed the first marriage vows in which he declared his fidelity to
this mate regardless of the circumstances.

The inspired lawgiver (Moses) reflects on the observation of Adam
and sets forth three basic laws of marriage: the laws of (1) leaving, (2)
cleaving, and (3) weaving. So strong is the marriage bond that it
supersedes the ties between parents and children. He who would
marry must leave ('azabh) father and mother — physically, psychologically and economically. The Hebrew verb suggests the termination of
a loyalty. He must thereafter cleave (dabhaq) to his wife. The word
elsewhere is used to describe a covenantal commitment to God (cf. Dt
10:20). Thus by using this word the lawgiver is suggesting that marriage is a covenant between a man and woman. The lives of husband
and wife are woven together in marriage — they become one flesh.
Their union is celebrated and reaffirmed in sexual intercourse. Christ
(Matt 19:5) explained this verse as teaching the indissoluble character
of marriage.

The intimacy and innocence of the first marriage is beautifully set
forth in the words, "The man and his wife were both naked, and they
were not ashamed" (2:25).

2. The structure of the union. Fundamentally, the man and his
mate were equals. This is indicated in the following facts: (1) she was
a "helper" corresponding to him (2:18), (2) she received the creation
mandate as much as he (1:28-30), (3) Adam recognized her as "bone
of my bone" — as fundamentally like him, (4) she was the special
handiwork of God as much as he, and (5) both the man and the
woman were made in the image of God. In that first marriage, however, the man was the first among equals, i.e., he was the leader in the
relationship. He was created first and therefore had a certain priority
for that reason (cf. 1 Cor. 11:3,8,12). Adam asserted (and Eve

accepted) his leadership when he gave his bride a name (2:23): "She shall be called Woman (*'ishshah*) because she was taken from man (*'ish*). A woman who chooses to marry chooses to subordinate herself in some measure to the leadership of the man of her choice. Adam was the head; Eve was the helper.

MAN'S DOMINION
Genesis 1:28-30

God decreed that the man who bore his image and likeness should rule as his vice-regent over the earth. Plants have unconscious life, and animals have conscious life; but man alone possesses self-conscious life. He thus is superior to all other life forms created by God.

Man was to rule *(radah)* over fish, birds, cattle, creeping things, and all the earth (1:26,28). The word means tread upon, subdue, rule over. It seems to connote absolute sovereignty.

Man was to be fruitful (*parah*), multiply (*radhah*) and fill (*mala'*) the earth. God created the earth to be inhabited (Isa. 45:18).

Man was to subdue (*kabhash*) the earth. The verb means to bring under one's control or take possession of a hostile country (Nm 32:22,29), enemies or slaves (2 Chr 28:10; Jer 34:11; Neh 5:5); to assert one's superiority of power or wisdom over another. Several of the twenty-four passages where this term is used in the Old Testament suggest that the dominion should be exercised with great care. The text suggests that it is through multiplication of his race that man is to carry out his command to subdue the earth (1:28).

What are the implications of this creation mandate? Man is the crown of creation. Everything was made for him. God intended for man to develop all the potentialities of the earth. Any animal and plant forms may be freely sacrificed for the good of man. Of course this is no license to rape the earth. The authority is not absolute; it is delegated. Man is responsible to the Creator for the manner in which he interacts with his environment.

ENDNOTES

1. H.C. Leupold, *Exposition of Genesis* (Columbus: Wartburg, 1942), pp. 88f.
2. E.A. Speiser, *Genesis, The Anchor Bible* (Garden City, NJ: Doubleday, 1964), pp. 19f.
3. U. Cassuto, *From Adam to Noah* (Jerusalem: Magnes, 1961), pp. 128f. That the verb in Genesis 2:19 should be rendered as pluperfect ("had created") has been argued by Leupold, *Exposition*, p. 130.
4. Matthew Henry, *Commentary on the Whole Bible* (Old Tappan, NJ: Revell, n.d.), I, 19f.

BIBLIOGRAPHY: GENESIS 1–11

Listed below are works which focus on the entirety of Genesis 1–11. See also the general bibliography for Genesis (p. 40) and the special bibliographies on creation (p. 52) and the Flood (p. 94).

Cassuto, U. *A Commentary on the Book of Genesis.* Jerusalem: Magnes, 1961. 2 vols.

Davis, John D. *Genesis and Semitic Tradition.* Grand Rapids: Baker, 1980 reprint.

Hanson, R.S. *The Serpent Was Wiser: A New Look at Genesis 1–11.* Minneapolis: Augsburg, 1972)

Kikawada, Isaac M., and Arthur Quinn. *Before Abraham Was.* Nashville: Abingdon, 1985.

Logan, William M. *In the Beginning God.* Richmond: John Knox, 1957.

Mitchell, H.G. *The World before Abraham according to Genesis 1–11.* Boston: Houghton, Mifflin, 1901.

Nelson, Byron. *Before Abraham.* Minneapolis: Augsburg, 1948.

Pember, G.H. *Earth's Earliest Ages.* Fifteenth ed. Suffolk: Lang, n.d.

Schaeffer, Francis. *Genesis in Space and Time.* Downers Grove, IL: InterVarsity, 1972.

Thielicke, Helmut. *How the World Began: Man in the First Chapters of Genesis.* Muhlenburg, 1961.

CHAPTER FIVE

The Fall of the King
Genesis 3

AIM: To demonstrate the subtlety of Satan, the seriousness of sin, and the necessity of salvation by grace through faith.

THEME: The plight of man.

In the literary treasures of the ancient Near East no close parallel to the Fall narrative of Genesis 3 appears. This is not altogether unexpected. No fall was possible in pagan mythology because man was created evil by evil gods. He never experienced a state of innocence from which to fall. The situation, however, is quite different in the Bible. The Fall of man from an original state of purity is the silent hypothesis of the whole biblical doctrine of sin and redemption.[1] The historicity of Genesis 3 is vital to the Christian view.

Adam was the king and Eve the queen of creation. Their surrender to temptation brought sin and death into the world. In their experiences in Genesis 3 the first parents of the race illustrate seven aspects of the plight of all men.

THE TEMPTER
Genesis 3:1a

The tempter is introduced in 3:1 as *hanachash*, the serpent, or simply Serpent.[2] He is described as crafty (*'arum*), indeed more crafty than any beast of the field. Adam had named, i.e., correctly identified the nature of, every creature in the garden. In this temptation episode he is dealing with an intelligence far greater than any he had identified in the animals of his immediate environment. Scripture makes clear that Serpent is that supernatural and evil creature known elsewhere as Satan, the adversary (Rev 12:9,15; 20:2; 2 Cor 11:3; Matt 12:29; John 8:44; Acts 10:38).

How did Satan come into the world? That is a question upon which Scripture sheds little light. Biblical teaching compels Christians to assert that God is not the author of sin. Satan is a created being, for nothing is eternal save God himself. Satan, however, could not have been created evil. He must have fallen from his position as one of God's chief angels (2 Pet 2:4; Jude 6; 1 Tim 3:6). Many commentators think that Isaiah 14:3-17 and Ezekiel 28:11-19 refer to the fall of Satan. In both cases, however, the text clearly indicates that the focus is on the proud ambitions and ultimate downfall of pagan monarchs, not Satan.

Conservative commentators are not agreed as to the role of the biological reptile in Genesis 3. The traditional view is that Satan commandeered the body of a snake and in some manner spoke through that reptile. Others think that Serpent is a proper name for the devil. No biological reptile was involved. The temptation of Eve was no different from the temptation which comes to any person. These commentators regard "on your belly you shall crawl" as a figurative expression for humiliation (cf. Micah 7:17). Certainly the language used in 3:14b is not intended literally of snakes as conservative commentators acknowledge. This might signal that 3:14a should be taken in a figurative sense as well.

THE TEMPTATION
Genesis 3:1b-5

Those who battle the Tempter daily can gain valuable insight by studying the tactics employed by the Evil One in the first temptation. Satan struck fast, before practice had confirmed the first pair in obedience. He began with the woman, not because she was inherently weaker than her mate, but perhaps for two reasons: Eve had not directly heard the command of God stating the prohibition, and she had not been exposed to conditions outside the garden. On the other hand, Eve had experiential knowledge of God's goodness and mercy; she also had a clear and unambiguous word from God.

These additional points in Satan's temptation strategy should be noted: (1) he attacked when Eve was alone; (2) he selected the ground carefully, waiting until the woman was in full view of the tree; (3) he employed ambiguous and obscure language; and (4) he pretended to be seeking only the best for his victim.

Satan launched the attack by raising an insidious question about God's word: "Is it really true that God has said you must not eat from any tree in the garden?" The question makes light of the prohibition by exaggerating it. Eve's response to the question of Satan was weak. Already she was sliding into sin. She minimized the garden privileges: "We may eat from the trees in the garden" (cf. 2:16). She exaggerated the prohibition. To "do not eat" she added "nor touch it" (cf. 2:17). She watered down the warning. "In the day you eat of it you will surely die" (2:17) became simply "you will die" (3:3).

Eve's weak response encouraged Serpent to make two bold declarations. First, he denied the word of God. "No! Not true that you will surely die!" Satan's language is most emphatic in the Hebrew. Satan now had removed the first great barrier to sin: the punishment barrier.

Satan then went on to suggest that God's motives in the prohibition were not pure. "God has known all along that if you eat of the fruit your eyes will be opened and you will be like gods[3] knowing good and evil." Serpent was suggesting that experiential knowledge was a desirable, God-like quality which the Creator was jealously reserving to himself. Man is to be like God in ethical attributes, but godliness is not attempting to seize the power and prerogatives of deity. Satan had now removed the second great barrier to sin: the love of God.

THE TRANSGRESSION
Genesis 3:6

Contemplation followed temptation (3:6). Eve studied the tree. It appealed to her in three ways. Physically the tree was appealing for it was "good for food." Because it was "pleasing to the eye," the tree had aesthetic appeal. Intellectually the tree enticed Eve because she saw that it had the potential "for making one wise." Every temptation appears to have one or more of these three appeals. This is what the Apostle John referred to as "the lust of the flesh, the lust of the eyes and the pride of life" (1 John 2:15-17).

Eve surrendered to the temptation. She partook of the forbidden fruit and thus committed the first act of human rebellion against God. Eve immediately gave the fruit to her husband, and he, offering no resistance, joined his mate in transgression. Chronologically, Eve ate first; but theologically Adam is declared to be the original sinner. He was the head of the race and was responsible for its actions.

THE GUILT
Genesis 3:7-13

The consequences of partaking of the fruit were not as expected. Six indications of guilt can be seen in the narrative.

1. The eyes of their mind were opened (as Satan had promised) but they saw themselves as frail mortals, not gods. "They saw that they were naked" (3:7). Before the Fall they were innocent (2:25); now they were guilty. Why their sense of shame focused on their nakedness is not entirely clear.

2. They manifested a kind of cleverness, but not the God-like wisdom which they had sought. They sewed fig leaves together and made aprons (*chagorot*) for themselves (3:7).

3. They now knew good and evil, but not the way God does (3:22). A sick man has a knowledge of suffering which differs from the insight of the physician who treats him. So God who is omniscient knows all about evil. Man, however, knows evil by experience.

4. They lost their fellowship with God. When they heard the sound of God walking in the garden, they hid themselves. Mistrust, fear and

guilt replaced trust and free communion with God. One of the effects of Adam's sin was that he forgot that God is omnipresent and omniscient.

5. They experienced an embarrassing confrontation with God (3:9-13). The questions God asked were pedagogic, i.e., they were designed (1) to make man assess his sinful condition, and (2) lead him from shame to guilt and then to repentance. "Adam, where are you?" (v. 9). "Who told you that you were naked?" (v. 11). "Have you eaten of the tree?" (v. 11). "What have you done?" (v. 13). God interrogated Adam and Eve, not Serpent. For that Evil One there was no hope. In fact Serpent said absolutely nothing in the presence of God.

Chart No. 6

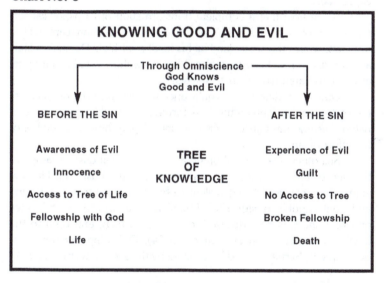

6. They indulged in self-justification. Adam blamed the woman, and (indirectly) God. "The woman *you* gave me offered me some fruit from the tree" (3:12). Sin divides the human race. Of love for the woman or anxiety for her welfare there was not the slightest trace here. For her part, Eve blamed Serpent: "He deceived me" (3:13). Both sinners freely admitted their transgression: "And I ate" (3:12f.).

THE SENTENCE
Genesis 3:14-19

God pronounced sentence both on the Tempter and those who were deceived by him.

A. The Punishment of Serpent (Gn 3:14-15).

Serpent is the first to hear the divine condemnation. For him God announced judgment with no mercy. Immediately he would be cursed above (lit., "from") both domestic and wild animals. In this context the word "from" (*min*) means, "apart from." Serpent would crawl on his belly and eat dust. Three major opinions about these words have been expressed.

1. Some hold that a complete transformation of all biological serpents took place at this time. But if a snake was the innocent vehicle of Satan, why is the snake (and all his kind) punished? Do snakes literally eat dust, or is this a metaphor? If a metaphor, could it not apply as easily to Satan himself as to snakes?

2. Others say that a new significance was given to the original status of the snake. Thus what had formerly been the mere result of nature became through this curse a kind of punishment, a symbol of the effect of sin.

3. Still others take "crawl on your belly" and "eat dust" in a figurative sense. Like the modern expression "bite the dust" the Hebrew expression "eat dust" is equivalent to being reduced to a demeaning and contemptible position (cf. Mic 7:17; Isa 65:25). This former angelic being was now debased in relation to man, and even to the lowliest creatures God ever made (3:14). Following the period of debasement, Serpent would be crushed by the seed of woman (3:15).

B. The Punishment of the Woman (Gn 3:16).

The woman was sentenced next. Her punishment had three dimensions.

1. Physically she would experience multiplied pain (*'itstsebhon*) especially as it is associated with childbirth. She who sought sweet delights in eating the fruit found not delights but pain, not joy, but sorrow.

2. Psychologically, the woman's desire *(teshuqah)* would be for her husband. She would be continually drawn toward that one who had the power to cause her great pain through impregnation. She who sought to act independently of the man would find a continual attraction for him. Some have suggested that this is a promise rather than a punishment. Even though woman would face extreme pain in childbearing, she would still desire normal conjugal relations with her husband.

3. The social aspect of the punishment was that the woman would be in subordination to her husband (cf. 1 Tim 2:14). She who sought to control her husband by leading him into temptation would now be the one controlled. Women have suffered much because sin entered the world. They have been subjected to degradation, to moral and physical slavery in many cultures. The dominion of the husband in the marriage is not harsh and unbearable where the spirit of Christ abides.

C. The Punishment of the Man (Gn 3:17-19).

The sentence on the man was equally severe. He had yielded to the love of a creature in preference to that of God; now the creation would turn against him. He had eaten forbidden fruit; now the earth would refuse him necessary food. He had disobeyed God; now the earth over which he had been given dominion would disobey him. Five aspects of his punishment are apparent.

1. Because of man the ground would be cursed (3:17). Did something happen to the ground when man sinned? Or does this mean that man would be driven from the garden into the conditions which existed outside the garden?

2. Adam would have to toil for his food (3:17). In this toil he would experience misery (*'itstsabhon).

3. The uneatable products of the earth would be multiplied thus making it difficult to cultivate the eatable herbs (3:18).

4. Continuous toil would have to be expended throughout life (3:19). The picture here seems to be of the sweat of the brow mingling with food at meal times. The words "you will eat" which appear three times in the sentence of the man are full of promise. Man's life would be difficult, but he would survive, at least for a time.

5. Ultimately the earth would reclaim Adam's body. He would return to the ground from which he was taken (3:19).

THE HOPE
Genesis 3:15,20-21

A ray of light shines through the darkness of Genesis 3. Here is a promise of salvation and here is faith in that promise.

A. The Promise of Salvation (Gn 3:15).

Genesis 3:15 has been called the Protevangelium, the first Gospel. This first Messianic prophecy comes in a most unlikely place — in the context of a curse upon Serpent. The verses assure Serpent that he would have a battle on three different levels.

1. On the personal level the woman would do battle with Serpent. She would never again be the pushover she had been in the garden. God promised to put enmity in her heart toward Serpent. This was the beginning of the successful struggle against Satan. Needless to say, God did not force this enmity upon the woman. He was responding to her sense of shame and free admission of guilt. How was this a punishment for Satan? The woman's enmity toward Satan smashed his dreams of recruiting all mankind for his rebellion against God.

2. The battle would continue between the seed of woman and the seed of Serpent. That the word "seed" here is figurative is obvious from the fact that women do not literally have seed. The seed of woman would embrace all those who share the woman's enmity toward the Devil, i.e., righteous mankind. The seed of the Devil would include all who yield to the Evil One without so much as a skirmish, i.e., wicked mankind. God was assuring Serpent that a righteous remnant of mankind would resist with God-given might the evil designs of the children of the Devil.

3. The struggle between the two seeds would reach its climax in a confrontation between Serpent himself and a single representative of the seed of woman. Serpent will strike at the heel of this champion of righteousness. He will thereby inflict great pain upon him. Ultimately, however, the representative of the seed of woman would crush Serpent's head, i.e., deal him a mortal blow. That Genesis 3:15 refers to

72

the victory of Messiah over Satan is the teaching of Galatians 4:4-5 and 3:15ff.

B. Faith in the Promise (Gn 3:20-21).

Adam took note of the hints of hope in the midst of the divine pronouncement of punishment. He demonstrated his faith in the promise of God and the future of the race when he renamed his wife Eve (chavvah), i.e., one who continues to give life (3:20). Thus was Adam expressing his faith that Eve would produce offspring as promised in 3:15. This faith implies repentance.

God expressed his acceptance of Adam's faith by clothing the sinners with skins. Those skins served to remind them of the sin they had committed. Some think this clothing foreshadowed the robe of Christ's righteousness which God provides to guilty sinners. Be that as it may, the action of God in providing garments taught Adam and Eve that (1) their sense of shame after the Fall was appropriate; (2) the beasts of the field might lawfully be used for the benefit of mankind; and (3) their bodies would need to be protected from cold and injury outside the garden.

THE EXPULSION
Genesis 3:22-24

Repentance and consequent forgiveness do not negate the temporal consequences of sin. Man had to be expelled from the garden for he had "become like one of us knowing good and evil" (3:22). God knows good and evil through omniscience. Before the fall man had experienced good and he was aware of the possibility of evil. After his transgression he knew evil by personal experience. Not knowing good and evil is living in a state of innocence. Children (Dt 1:39) and imbeciles (having only the intelligence of children) are in this state. But after confronting temptation man enters a state of accountability. That is what it means to know good and evil.

Since man was now accountable for his sin, and since he had chosen the path of disobedience, it would have been most disastrous for him to have access to that fruit which would have imparted to him imperishable physical life. Adam was sent from the garden into the world until another Adam (Christ) should come and obtain the right to partake of that tree.

God banished man from the garden (3:23). That man was reluctant to leave is indicated by the language of 3:24. God "drove" the man out. To discourage any attempt to re-enter the garden God stationed cherubim and a revolving sword-like flame at the entrance. Cherubim are a class of angels. They are usually depicted in the Bible guarding something (e.g., Ex 36:35; Ezek 1:5). Cherubim seen by Ezekiel had feet, hands, four faces and four wings (Ezek 10:21).

How long did the garden remain after the expulsion of man? Certainly for a time, or else why would God station guardians at its entrance? Did it remain until the time of the Flood? Probably, but positive proof is lacking.

ENDNOTES

1. H. Bavinck, s.v. "Fall," *The International Standard Bible Encyclopaedia*, II:1092.

2. J. Oliver Buswell, *A Systematic Theology of the Christian Religion* (Grand Rapids: Zondervan, 1962), p. 264; Walter C. Kaiser, Jr., *Toward an Old Testament Theology* (Grand Rapids: Zondervan, 1978), pp. 77f.

3. Leupold, *Exposition*, p. 150 (following the lead of the Septuagint).

CHAPTER SIX

The Two Seeds
Genesis 4:1-6:10

AIM: To demonstrate that the conflict of Genesis 3:15 began to rage at the very dawn of history.

THEME: The eternal conflict.

Over a century elapsed between the events of Genesis 3 and those of Genesis 4. Adam begat Seth at age 130 (5:3). Cain's murder of Abel must have taken place before that year because Seth took the place of Abel (4:25). In any case, in the progeny of Adam and Eve the contrast between the godly and ungodly is evident. That contrast can be traced on three levels: (1) the individual, (2) small group, and (3) societal levels.

CONTRASTING BROTHERS
Genesis 4:1-16

Cain and Abel were the initial representatives of the Serpent's seed and the woman's seed mentioned in Genesis 3:15. Several snapshots of these two brothers are contained in Genesis 4.

A. The Brothers at Birth (Gen. 4:1-2).

Genesis 4 opens with the beautiful euphemism for sexual intercourse: "Adam knew his wife." Marriage is the most intimate of human relationships. Some have concluded on the basis of the language here that there had been no sexual intercourse prior to the expulsion from the garden.

Cain was the first person ever born. His name means "acquisition, possession." He received this name *qayin* because it reminded Eve of something she had said at his birth: "I have gotten (*qaniti*) a man from Yahweh" (i.e., with the help of Yahweh). Here, as in most places where biblical names are explained, sound similarity rather than etymology is the principle employed.

Eve's comment at the birth of Cain expressed her thanksgiving at being delivered from the pains and dangers of pregnancy. Her use of the name Yahweh indicates that she regarded this birth as a token of the faithfulness of God in allowing "seed of woman" to be born. Her language suggests that Eve had repented of the garden sin. Her utterance may be regarded as a word of faith. Whether or not she expected this particular child to be the Crusher of Genesis 3:15 cannot be determined.

The text does not reveal the age difference between Cain and his younger brother. The name Abel means "vanity." Perhaps this name expresses disillusionment with the conduct of Cain. On the other hand, the name may indicate that the hard life outside the garden was beginning to take its toll psychologically.

B. The Brothers at Work (Gen. 4:2).

Cain followed in the footsteps of his father. He became a tiller of the ground. Abel became the first shepherd. No effort is being made here to exalt the pastoral pursuit at the expense of the agricultural. The difference in moral character between the two brothers is not to be traced to their respective callings. Probably their choices were determined by their talents and their tastes. The implication here is that cultivation of the soil and domestication of animals were practically coeval. Man did not have to struggle through primitive stages in order to develop some sophistication in agricultural pursuits.

C. The Brothers at Worship (Gen. 4:3-7).

Did the concept of worship through sacrifice originate in a command of God? Or did it arise spontaneously as a natural expression of devout men? Did sacrificial worship begin with Cain and Abel? Or did Adam teach his sons how to worship? What was the purpose of the offerings presented by the brothers? Were they for sin, or merely an expression of thanksgiving? Was an altar used for the offerings? Were these fire offerings? The text is not explicit on any of these questions.

Apparently the material offered was determined entirely by the occupation of the two worshipers. Cain's worship, however, was unacceptable. He brought to the Lord "some of the fruits of the ground" (4:3). His rather casual attitude toward worship revealed a lack of faith and love in his heart. "Unto Cain and his offering Yahweh did not look with favor" (4:5). The offerer is put before the offering. Cain's attitude rendered his offering unacceptable.

On the other hand, Abel's offering to God was commendable. He offered "the firstlings of the flock and the fat thereof" (4:4). He gave the best parts of his best animals. No hint is found in the text of the superiority of a bloody offering over a nonbloody offering. Rather the focus is upon the worshiper himself. Abel was "righteous" (Matt 23:35). He approached God in faith and that, according to Hebrews 11:4, made his sacrifice more excellent, literally, fuller. His sacrifice had more in it; it had faith.

How God manifested his acceptance of Abel's worship and his rejection of Cain's is not entirely clear. Here are some proposals: fire descended and consumed Abel's offering; Yahweh manifested himself to them; God spoke directly with them perhaps at the garden entrance; Abel's future efforts were blessed and Cain's were not. In any case the divine evaluation of the two worshipers was evident and Cain did not like it. He was "wroth," (lit., "it burned with Cain exceedingly"). Because of his anger against God and his resentment toward his brother, Cain's countenance fell, i.e., his attitude was clearly reflected in his facial features.

The Lord sought to warn Cain about the dangerous direction

which his life was taking because of anger. "Why are you wroth? Why is your face downcast?" The questions were designed to make Cain take pause to reflect upon the justification of his anger. A third question called attention to the basic simplicity of a right relationship with the Lord: "If you do what is right, will you not be accepted?" If Cain was determined not to do what was right, then sin, like a ferocious beast, was crouching at the door. Sin desired to overpower him; but he could and must master this beast. He must not let it dominate him (4:7). Cain made no response to this divine warning.

D. The Brothers in the Field (Gen. 4:8-10).

Cain did not heed the warning of the Lord. Anger opened the door, and sin devoured him. He was of the Evil One; therefore he slew his brother in the field. Why? "Because his deeds were evil and his brother's were righteous" (1 John 3:11-12).

The Lord brought Cain to trial immediately. "Where is Abel your brother?" This is the second time God approached sinful man with a question. Adam and Eve manifested fear following their sin. Not so Cain. He was impudent and hardened. He lied to God. To God's question about the whereabouts of Abel, Cain replied, "I know not!" He then hurled a rhetorical question at God: "Am I my brother's keeper?" (4:9). The Lord cut off all further evasion when he said, "The blood of your brother cries out to me from the ground." While the blood of the innocent man cried out to God for vengeance, the blood of Jesus "speaks better things than that of Abel" (Heb 12:24). Jesus' blood speaks of forgiveness rather than vengeance.

E. The Punishment of Cain (Gen. 4:11-15).

Now for the first time the divine curse fell on a mortal. This was not the curse of damnation. The curse contains two aspects: (1) Under God's curse, Cain must leave the ground which had swallowed up the blood of his brother (4:11). The ground which he had learned to cultivate would no longer yield its crops. (2) Cain would be forced to abandon agriculture and become a vagrant and a wanderer on the earth (4:12).

At this news Cain fell into a state of depression. "My punishment is greater than I can bear." The punishment troubled Cain, not the sin. He was concerned especially about four aspects of the punishment: (1) He would be "driven" from the face of the ground. The word used here is the same word used of Adam being driven from the garden. (2) Such an expulsion would mean that he would be "hidden from the face of God." (3) He would be "a vagrant and a wanderer." The divinely inspired dread caused Cain to become a self-made fugitive. (4) He worried about being slain by those he might encounter. How old the two brothers were when the murder took place cannot be determined. Cain's remark suggests that he may have been considerably older than is generally supposed. By the time Cain was four hundred the earth's population would have approached 100,000.

Why did God not execute Cain? Perhaps it was because the crime was not premeditated. Since no one before had ever died, Cain may not have realized that his blow would cause the death of his brother. Others have suggested that his life was spared to facilitate the hasty population of the earth. Still others have proposed that Cain's living misery would be a perpetual warning to any others who might contemplate murder.

God was more than gracious in his dealing with Cain. He proclaimed that anyone who slew Cain would suffer a sevenfold divine vengeance (4:15). This proclamation underscores the fact that vengeance belongs to God; it also serves as a warning against the crime of murder. To give Cain confidence in this promise of protection, God "appointed a sign for Cain" (4:15). What this sign may have been cannot be determined from the text.

Under the curse of God, Cain went out from the presence of the Lord. Since God is omnipresent, it is not possible to go out from his presence physically. The text must therefore refer to the spiritual direction of his life. He went forth to build a godless society east of Eden, in Nod, the land of wandering (4:16).

CONTRASTING FAMILIES
Genesis 4:17–5:32

From Cain and from Seth, the substitute for Abel, two families arose with very different values. Cain's clan was concerned with cleverness and culture. Seth's descendants were committed to spiritual values. In the development of these two families the struggle of Genesis 3:15 intensified.

A. The Seed of Serpent (Gn 4:17-24).

Genesis 3:15 predicted that enmity would exist between the seed of woman (i.e., people of faith) and the seed of Serpent. Cain "knew his wife." She had apparently accompanied him into his exile. Cain was no doubt married to one of his sisters, a circumstance which was neither morally wrong nor physically damaging in these early days of the human race. The descendants of Cain became the seed of Serpent. In the latter half of Genesis 4, Cain's clan is introduced. The highlights in the history of this family are enumerated. Ancient nations attributed the development of civilization to various gods; but the Bible underscores the fact that human culture was created by mere mortals.

1. Cain was building (Hebrew participle) the first city and named it Enoch after his son. What were Cain's motives? Was he defying the

Chart No. 7

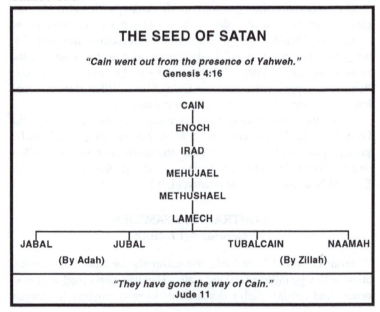

THE SEED OF SATAN

"Cain went out from the presence of Yahweh."
Genesis 4:16

CAIN
|
ENOCH
|
IRAD
|
MEHUJAEL
|
METHUSHAEL
|
LAMECH

JABAL   JUBAL   TUBALCAIN   NAAMAH
(By Adah)   (By Zillah)

"They have gone the way of Cain."
Jude 11

divine curse? Was he attempting to ensure his personal safety? In any case this was a new stage in the advance of civilization.

2. Enoch, Irad, Mehujael, and Methushael are just names on the infamous list.

3. Lamech became the first to violate the principle of monogamy. He took to himself two wives. Lamech was also the first poet. His composition was a boastful ballad celebrating vengeance (4:23-24). Whether Lamech had already slain a man or whether he is merely bragging about what he would do to any attacker is the subject of dispute among commentators.

4. The sons of Lamech became leaders in various aspects of culture. Jabal ("wanderer") became the father of those who followed the nomadic way of life. Jubal ("sound") was the father of those who were skilled with instruments of music. Tubal-Cain was the first to learn the secrets of working with metals.

B. The Seed of Woman (Gn 4:25–5:32).

Genesis 5 opens with a beautiful reminder of the great truths concerning the creation of man. Moses reminded his readers of (1) the stupendous miracle of man, namely, that he was created by 'elohim in a day; (2) the supreme importance of man, namely, he was created in the likeness of God; (3) the supreme distinction in man, namely, he was created male and female; (4) the special blessing of man; and (5) the significant name of man, namely, Adam. That God gave man this name was not narrated in the earlier account.

Genesis 5 sketches the early history of the family of faith. These patriarchs lived long lives. Their average age (excluding Enoch) was 912 years. Again with the exception of Enoch, each biography concludes with the solemn toll of a funeral bell. From Adam onward death had dominion (Rom 5:11) thus fulfilling the garden threat, "Thou shalt surely die!"

Someone has referred to the patriarchs in Genesis 5 as the "ten commitments." These men possessed faith in the promise of Genesis 3:15. They were godly men. Two — Noah and Enoch — are said to have walked with God. They bore witness against the wickedness of the world (Jude 14; 2 Pet 2:5). Seth was probably not the third child of Adam and Eve. He was born after the death of Abel. Adam's other

Chart No. 8

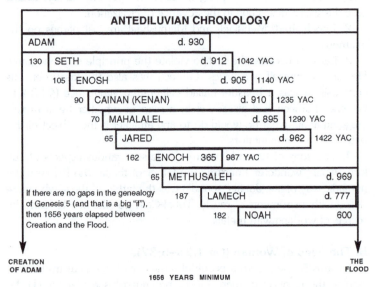

ANTEDILUVIAN CHRONOLOGY

ADAM — d. 930
130 SETH — d. 912 — 1042 YAC
105 ENOSH — d. 905 — 1140 YAC
90 CAINAN (KENAN) — d. 910 — 1235 YAC
70 MAHALALEL — d. 895 — 1290 YAC
65 JARED — d. 962 — 1422 YAC
162 ENOCH 365 — 987 YAC
65 METHUSALEH — d. 969
If there are no gaps in the genealogy of Genesis 5 (and that is a big "if"), then 1656 years elapsed between Creation and the Flood.
187 LAMECH — d. 777
182 NOAH — 600

CREATION OF ADAM   1656 YEARS MINIMUM   THE FLOOD

children probably had gone the way of Cain leaving no one to perpetuate the holy line. Eve expected Seth ("substitute") to be another Abel in respect to piety (4:25). In this expectation she was not disappointed. Seth became the first of a chosen line which would culminate in Messiah.

In the days of Enosh ("frail man") "men began to call upon the name of Yahweh" (4:26). This marked the beginning of public, organized worship of the Lord. The verse suggests that the name Yahweh was known long before Moses. The names which follow—Kenan ("possession"), Mahalalel ("praise of God") and Jared ("descendant") — are mere names on the honor roll of the faithful.

Enoch was the first man in the Bible said to have walked with God. The text suggests that his walk with God began with the birth of Methuselah his son. His commitment to God was not superficial for it endured for three hundred years. He was no hermit. He walked with God in the midst of domestic cares for he begat sons and daughters. Apparently celibacy is not a prerequisite for a committed life. After living a year of years (365 years) "he was not for God took him" (5:23). The author of Hebrews provides the inspired commentary on this statement: "By faith Enoch was taken up so that he should not see death; and he was not found because God took him up; for he obtained the witness that before his being taken up he was pleasing to God" (Heb 11:5).

Enoch's son Methuselah ("man of a dart") at 969 years was the oldest man who ever lived. His long life is covered in but three verses! Methuselah's son Lamech ("wild man") uttered a prophecy at the birth of his son Noah ("rest"). He foresaw that in some way Noah would bring comfort to the troubled race (5:29).

If one assumes that in the genealogy of Genesis 5 there are no gaps (and that is a big *if*), then 1656 years elapsed between creation and the Flood. Adam would still have been living in the days of Lamech, the father of Noah. Chart 8 illustrates how the lives of these primeval patriarchs overlapped. Most scholars, however, think that this genealogy is selective — that names are omitted.

CONTRASTING COMMUNITIES
Genesis 6:1-10

With the passing of years the seed of Serpent became ever more numerous. The seed of woman — righteous mankind — diminished to the point of being represented by one man, his three sons and their four wives. The opening verses of Genesis 6 point out the contrast between these two communities.

A. The Wicked Community (6:1-7).

The opening verses of Genesis 6 paint a dismal picture of human degradation. One manifestation of the corruption of the race was the laxness regarding marriage. The identification of the "sons of God" in 6:1 is problematic. One interpretation is that they are angels; another, that they are kings. The best interpretation is that the "sons of God" are descendants of Seth. That marriage standards among the Sethites began to erode is clear here. The "sons of God" married indiscriminately for they married the daughters of men, i.e., women from the

83

line of Cain who did not share the spiritual values of the Sethites. They married superficially for their attraction to these women was based on the sole fact that they were fair. They married polygamously, "whomsoever they chose" (NASB).

Another manifestation of the degradation of humankind is seen in the violence associated with the *nephilim* (6:4). The *nephilim* were not so much giants (KJV), as tyrants. The word comes from the Hebrew root meaning "to fall upon." The *nephilim* where those who were bullies, who fell upon others to force their will upon them. "Those were the mighty men who were of old, men of renown" (6:4). This violence is again emphasized by the narrator in 6:11. Some hold that the *nephilim* were the product of the marriages just mentioned; others think they were contemporary with, but separate from, the marriages. Still another view is that the *nephilim* were the "sons of God."

Surveying the scene on earth God declared that man was mere "flesh," i.e., he was acting on the level of the animal kingdom and not as one made in the image of God. The Judge pronounced the wickedness of man great on the earth. Every intent of the thought of man's heart was only evil continually (6:5). Man seemed incapable of even thinking a decent thought. Yahweh "repented" that he had made man. The word does not signify a change of purpose, but a change of feeling. God was "grieved in his heart" (6:6) by the corruption of man. In 6:11-12 the narrator uses the word "corrupt" both nominally and verbally to summarize the conditions which existed. This term is used of idolatry and sexual immorality. These sins were committed "before God," i.e., openly, publicly, flagrantly and presumptuously.

In 6:3,7 the great Judge pronounces sentence against his creatures. There are three aspects to the proclamation: (1) "My Spirit shall not strive with man forever" (6:3). God will not continue to let his Spirit exercise the restraining influence hitherto exerted upon sin. According to 1 Peter 3:18-20 the Spirit of Christ, through the instrumentality of the pious patriarchs, preached to the disobedient spirits of the old world. (2) "His days shall be 120 years" (6:3), i.e., there would be a grace period prior to the pouring out of judgment. (3) "I will blot out man whom I have created" (6:7). Other creatures tied to the face of the earth will suffer the same fate. The fact that angels are not subject to punishment here confirms the interpretation given to the phrase "sons of God" in 6:1.

B. The Godly Community (Gn 6:8-10).

Noah was the solitary exception to the general picture of corruption and violence on the earth. This man "found grace in the eyes of Yahweh" (6:8). Four reasons for the divine favor toward Noah are noted: (1) Noah was a righteous man (6:9). His life measured up to the standards of God. (2) Noah was perfect or blameless in his generation (6:9). The word has the idea of "well rounded, balanced." The implication is that those who live without God are warped. (3) Noah walked with God, (lit., "with God he walked to and fro"). Personal communion with God was the source of Noah's righteous-perfect life. (4) Noah became the father of three sons: Shem, Ham and Japheth (6:10). Why should these sons be named here when they have already been introduced in 5:32? Here they are named in connection with Noah's piety. Perhaps Noah had succeeded in passing on to his sons his spiritual fervor. He was their spiritual as well as their physical father.

CHAPTER SEVEN

The Great Flood
Genesis 6:11-9:17

AIM: To demonstrate that God rewards the righteous and punishes the wicked.

THEME: God's perfect salvation.

The great Flood of the Bible is one of the best attested events in antiquity. Four more or less detailed accounts of a world Flood have been discovered: the Sumerian account, Gilgamesh Epic, Atrahasis and Berossus. To these may be added the Sumerian King List which indicates that the Flood caused a total break in the political history of Mesopotamia.

Archaeologists disagree as to whether or not they have found physical evidence of Noah's Flood in the ruins of Mesopotamia. Patrick O'Connell writes convincingly of discovering a major hiatus in the occupational levels throughout the region from Jericho in the west to the Iranian highlands in the east. This hiatus, O'Connell argues,

87

was caused by the destructive waters of a massive flood about 7,000 B.C.[1]

Jesus regarded the account of the Flood as an accurate record of what happened in the ancient world. He referred to the eating and drinking of the Flood generation and to the destructive power of those waters of judgment (Matt 24:35-39). In three passages the Apostle Peter alluded to the great Flood. He referred to the patience of God during the building of the ark and to the salvation of the eight souls in that ark (1 Pet 3:20). Peter mentioned the destruction of the ancient world and the salvation of Noah, "a preacher of righteousness," and seven others (2 Pet 2:5). In a third passage he spoke more generally of the destruction of the ancient world (2 Pet 3:6-7).

As in all the Old Testament, the Christian can find in the Flood account important lessons. Three aspects of God's perfect salvation are illustrated in Noah's deliverance. The account points to (1) a perfect plan, (2) perfect protection, and (3) perfect provision.

A PERFECT PLAN
Genesis 6:11-22

The divine decision had been announced. The world was to be destroyed by a Flood. Noah, however, found grace in the eyes of the Lord. For this man and his family God had a perfect plan. That plan necessitated the construction of an ark. Four points about God's perfect plan are worthy of note.

A. Divinely Given (Gn 6:13-14).

Salvation from a worldwide catastrophe can be conceived only in the mind of God. He alone could provide for the safety of Noah and his family. Whitelaw reminds believers that "schemes of redemption may be beautiful, ingenious, attractive, hopeful; if they are not God's schemes they are worthless."[2] *'Elohim*, the great transcendent God of creation, is the one who revealed to Noah that "the end of all flesh" (i.e., the destruction of the human race) "has come before me" (lit., "to my face"). These words suggest that man's ruin had not been sought by God but had been thrust upon him as something which could no longer be ignored. God explained to Noah the reason for this judgment: "For the earth is filled with violence (*chamas*) from before them" (lit., "from their faces"). From their faces the wickedness floods upward to God's face. "Behold I am about to destroy them (*mishchitam*) with the earth." The verb translated "destroy" in 6:13 is the same verb translated "corrupted" in 6:12. Thus the Flood is fitting retribution for the conduct of mankind.

B. Minutely Detailed (Gn 6:14-16).

Noah was to build the ark according to divinely revealed specifications. (1) The ark was to be built of gopher wood (6:14). The identity of this wood is uncertain. (2) He was to build rooms in the ark (6:14). (3) The ark was to be pitched within and without to waterproof it (6:14). The term *kopher* (pitch) is known from the Assyrian language. (4) The ark was to be three hundred cubits long, fifty cubits wide and thirty cubits high (6:15). Assuming an eighteen inch cubit, the ark would have been $450 \times 75 \times 45$ feet. The gross tonnage of this vessel was 13,960. Not until modern times (1884) was a ship of this size again constructed.

Other details of the ark's construction were these: (5) A window of a cubit from the roof of the ark was to be constructed (6:16). This window appears to have been an opening for light and ventilation around the whole boat, perhaps shielded with an eave. (6) Noah was to put a single door in the side of the ark (6:16). (7) He was to construct the ark with three stories (6:16).

Reflecting upon these specifications, Whitelaw observes that the salvation of man from first to last is God's plan. God's plan admits neither of addition nor subtraction, correction nor improvement, at the hands of men.[3] Peter Jensen of Holland in 1609 proved by actual experiment that a ship constructed after the pattern of the ark, though not adapted for sailing, would in reality carry a cargo greater by one-third than any other form of like cubic content. The stability of the ark was such that it would have to be turned completely vertical before it could be tipped over.[4] The difficulty of building a vessel of such enormous magnitude may be explained by (1) the extreme simplicity of its structure, (2) the length of time allowed for its erection, (3) the physical constitution of the builders, and (4) the facilities for obtaining materials which may have existed in abundance in their vicinity.

C. Believingly Received (Gn 6:17-21).

The instructions to build the ark were accompanied by promises. For the first time God made it clear that he was about to bring a Deluge which would destroy every living thing. God promised, however, that Noah would survive the Deluge to make a new covenant with God. The plan was that he and his family would ride out the Flood on the ark which he would construct. Representatives of all the "kinds" of animals would come to him. Noah was to load them on the ark. He also was responsible to gather food for his family and for the animals (6:17-21).

Noah believed God's warning and by faith began the construction project. "By faith Noah, being warned of things not yet seen, moved with fear, prepared an ark to the saving of his house; by the which he condemned the world, and became heir of the righteousness which is by faith" (Heb 11:7). Very likely Noah was ridiculed by his contemporaries. His project was no doubt viewed as an act of folly. Perhaps he himself now and again had misgivings about the work. The building of that ark required immense labor, patient endurance and heroic self-sacrifice. Yet through all those years of his labor Noah accepted his assignment in a spirit of meek and unquestioning faith.

D. Obediently Followed (Gn 6:22).

Noah built the ark according to the divine specifications. "Thus did Noah according to all that God had commanded him" (6:22). By obedience, faith discovers its existence.

A PERFECT PROTECTION
Genesis 7:1-24

Two aspects of the perfect protection provided for Noah are instructive for believers.

A. Protection in the Ark (Gn 7:1-10).

When the ark was finished, God invited Noah and his house to enter. The reason for this gracious invitation is clearly spelled out to the Patriarch: "You have I seen righteous before me in this generation" (7:1). His righteousness was even more exceptional since it was in *that* generation.

Detailed instructions were given regarding the animals which were to be taken on board the ark. Of the clean animals he was to take literally "seven seven." This has been taken to mean (1) seven plus seven, or fourteen; (2) seven times seven, or forty-nine; (3) seven pairs; and (4) seven even seven, i.e., six pairs and a spare.

The exact basis upon which the distinction between the clean and unclean was made in this early period is not clear. Apparently the distinction was well known to Noah, and he needed no further instruction on the subject. In any case, the reason for the larger number of clean animals is clear. The extra number would provide animals for sacrifice after the Flood, some food (e.g., milk) during the Flood, and would facilitate rapid reproduction of the clean animals after the Flood.

These instructions were given to Noah seven days before the beginning of the forty days of rain. The implication is that it took Noah a week just to load the passengers on the ark. Perhaps grain and other foodstuffs had already been placed on board.

Noah's perfect obedience to the commands of God is emphasized a second time in 7:5 (cf. 6:22). His obedience was personal ("Noah went in") and influential ("his sons, his wife and his sons' wives with him"). The entrance of the animals into the ark was precise and orderly. They entered "two and two into the ark, the male and the female, as God commanded Noah" (7:8,9).

Skeptics have questioned the credibility of the account with respect to the housing of the animals. There are about a million species on earth, ninety-five per cent of which could have survived outside the ark. That leaves about 50,000 animals averaging the size of a sheep. These animals could have been contained on only one deck of the ark.[5]

B. Protection from the Flood (Gn 7:11-24).

The Genesis Flood was no ordinary happening. This act of divine judgment cannot be explained entirely by naturalistic means. The Hebrews had a special word, *mabhul*, to refer to this event. The commencement of the Deluge is dated precisely according to the year (600th), month (2nd), and day (17th) of Noah's life (7:11).

The waters of the Flood came from two sources: (1) the fountains of the great deep broke open, and (2) the windows of heaven were opened (7:12). From the beginning of the rain until the Flood reached maximum depth was a period of 150 days (7:24). Three stages in these 150 days can be distinguished: (1) For the first forty days the waters *increased* (lit., "grew great"). This enabled the ark to float (7:17). (2) The waters *prevailed* (lit., "were strong"). The ark began to move about (7:18). (3) The waters *prevailed exceedingly* (lit., "became strong exceedingly"). The mountains were now submerged to a depth of fifteen cubits (7:19-20).

Chart No. 9

THE CHRONOLOGY OF THE FLOOD												
600TH YEAR											601ST YEAR	
2	3	4	5	6	7	8	9	10	11	12	1	2
					MONTHS OF 30 DAYS							
					Ark Rested			Mts. Seen	Raven Sent		Cover Removed	Exit Orders
17th Day					17th Day			1st Day	10th Day		1st Day	27th Day
7:11					8:4			8:5	8:6		8:13	8:14

	40 Days			
	150 Days Water Prevailed		163 Days Water Receded	57 Days Waiting
	TOTAL TIME OF FLOOD: 313 DAYS			
	TOTAL TIME IN ARK: 370 DAYS			

Is the Genesis narrative describing a universal Flood? Some hold that Genesis contains an exaggerated version of a Mesopotamian river flood. Others think the narrative points to an unprecedented regional flood which covered all the inhabited world.[6] Still others argue that the Flood was geographically as well as anthropologically universal.[7] The key exegetical issue is the meaning of *'eretz*. Should it be translated *earth* or *land*.

The following statements in the text point toward the geographical universality of the Flood: (1) The whole of the animal population died (7:21). (2) The whole human population (all in whose nostrils was the breath of life) perished, save Noah and those with him on the Ark (7:22-23). (3) "All the high hills that were under the whole heaven" were covered to the extent of fifteen cubits (7:19-20). (4) The Flood prevailed 150 days. The abatement of the waters took another 220 days (8:13-14).

A PERFECT PROVISION
Genesis 8:1-9:17

In the darkness of the Deluge a ray of hope shone through: "God remembered Noah" (8:1). The emphasis in the narrative is upon the new conditions which existed after the Flood.

A. A New Earth (Gn 8:1-19).

Attention is focused first on the abatement of the waters which is attributed to three causes: (1) a special wind, (2) the stopping of the fountains of the deep, and (3) the closing of the windows of heaven (8:1-2). The narrator distinguishes eight stages in the abatement:

1. At the end of 150 days the waters had regressed enough to cause the ark to be grounded on Ararat (8:4).

2. Seventy-three days after the grounding, the tops of the mountains were visible from the ark (8:5).

3. To assure himself that the Deluge would not return, Noah waited forty days before taking action. He then opened a window of the ark and dispatched a raven (8:6-7). This window is mentioned here for the first time. The raven no doubt was selected because, as a bird of prey, it could feed upon the carrion which must have been scattered about on the ground. From the movements of this bird, however, Noah could not ascertain the condition of the ground.

4. Seven days later Noah sent forth a dove (8:8-9). The ground was apparently still too wet and muddy for the fastidious dove. The bird flew back and forth and then returned to the safety of the ark.

5. Noah anxiously waited (*yachel*) seven more days. He dispatched a dove which returned to him that evening with an olive leaf (8:10-11). Noah knew that the waters had receded to the lower elevations where olive trees commonly grow.

6. A third dove sent forth seven days later did not return to the ark (8:12). The gentle creature now found a clean, dry place to make her nest.

7. The covering of the ark was removed 163 days after the grounding of the vessel. The face of the ground was now *charabh*, i.e., dry (8:13).

8. Fifty-seven days later the earth was dry (*yabheshah*). After some 370 days on board, the eight humans and their animal cargo departed from the ark (8:14-19). The departure was divinely directed, obediently executed and orderly conducted. Noah emerged into a world cleansed from sin by judgment. God was giving the human race a second chance.

B. A New Worship (Gn 8:20-22).

Worship was Noah's first concern after exiting the ark. He built an altar, the first altar mentioned in the Bible. Noah, functioning as a priest to his family, offered on his new altar burnt offerings of every clean animal (8:20). The burnt offering was the symbol of complete consecration and gratitude.

God was pleased with the worship of Noah. The narrator anthropomorphically describes the pleasure with which God smelled the aroma of the sacrifice. God resolved that he would not again "curse the ground" because of man. Never again would there be such a massive destruction of life as occurred during the Flood. The reason for this divine resolution is clearly stated: "The imagination of man's heart is evil from his youth" (8:21). God would have to schedule worldwide catastrophes in every generation if he were to respond to human corruption as he did at that time. By demonstrating his wrath against sin in the days of Noah, God had accomplished his purpose.

The marvelous grace of God was revealed anew in the promise

which he made concerning earth's seasons: "Until all the days of earth, seed time and harvest, cold and heat, summer and winter and day and night shall not cease" (8:22). The language does suggest, however, that the present order is not eternal.

C. A New Blessing (Gn 9:1-3,7).

The divine command to be fruitful and multiply and fill the earth was at the same time a blessing. Man would fill the geographical world (9:1,7) and by so doing would exercise dominion over the animal world (9:2). He would derive his nourishment from the physical world, animal as well as vegetable (9:3). Two views regarding this verse have been expressed: (1) that meat was expressly forbidden before the Flood and now was permitted for the first time;[8] and (2) that meat was permitted before the Flood but now that implied provision is expressly renewed.[9]

D. A New Revelation (Gn 9:4-6).

The permission to eat meat must not result in a loss of respect for life. Man may shed the blood of animals, but not eat improperly drained meat (9:4). By this law God was beginning to teach man the importance of blood in the divine economy. Human blood is not to be shed. Man is made in the image of God. The person who ignores this fact and slays his neighbor forfeits his own right to live. God was here delegating to society the right to execute murderers. Implicit here is the divine authorization for human government, for if society has the ultimate authority to take a human life, then society has the right to make other laws to govern men.

E. A New Covenant (Gn 9:8-17).

God put his personal resolve regarding the future of the human race into solemn covenant form. This covenant is between God and every living thing. Never again would he destroy the world by means of a Flood (9:8-11). The rainbow was designated as the covenant sign (9:12-17). This was not necessarily the first rainbow ever seen by man. The point is that, whenever God would see the rainbow, he would be reminded of his commitment to man.

ENDNOTES

1. Patrick O'Connell, *Science of Today and the Problems of Genesis: The Deluge and the Antiquity of Man* (privately published, 1969), pp. 22-65.

2. Thomas Whitelaw, *Genesis*, The Pulpit Commentary (New York: Funk & Wagnalls, 1909), p. 112.

3. Ibid.

4. Ramm, *Christian View*, p. 157.

5. John C. Whitcomb, Jr., *The World That Perished* (Grand Rapids: Baker, 1973), pp. 23-32.

6. Regional flood advocates include: Arthur Custance, *The Flood: Local or Global* (Grand Rapids: Zondervan, 1979, pp. 13-62); Davis Young, *Creation and the Flood* (Grand Rapids: Baker, 1977), pp. 171-213; and T.G. Mitchell, s.v., "Flood," *The New Bible Dictionary*, p. 427.

7. Advocates of a universal Flood include: John C. Whitcomb, Jr., and Henry Morris, *The Genesis Flood* (Grand Rapids: Baker, 1961), pp. 1-88; Byron Nelson, *The Deluge Story in Stone* (Grand Rapids: Baker, 1968).

8. Robert Candlish, *The Book of Genesis* (Edinburgh: Adam and Clark Black, 1868), pp. 140-143.

9. Whitelaw, *Genesis*, p. 139.

BIBLIOGRAPHY: THE FLOOD

Cummings, Violet M. *Noah's Ark: Fact or Fable?* San Diego: Creation-Science Research Center, 1972.

Filby, Frederick A. *The Flood Reconsidered.* Grand Rapids: Zondervan, 1971.

Heidel, Alexander. *The Gilgamesh Epic and Old Testament Parallels.* Chicago: University Press, 1963.

Nelson, Byron C. *The Deluge Story in Stone.* Grand Rapids: Baker, 1968.

O'Connell, Patrick. *Science of Today and the Problems of Genesis.* Second ed. Privately published, 1969. 2 vols. in one.

Patten, D. W. *The Biblical Flood and the Ice Epoch.* Pacific Meridian, 1966.

Rehwinkel, A. M. *The Flood.* St. Louis: Concordia, 1951.

Whitcomb, John, and Henry Morris. *The Genesis Flood.* Philadelphia: Presbyterian and Reformed, 1961.

Whitcomb, John. *The World that Perished.* Grand Rapids: Baker, 1973.

Young, Davis A. *Creation and the Flood.* Grand Rapids: Baker, 1977.

CHAPTER EIGHT

God and the Nations
Genesis 9:18-11:9

AIM: To demonstrate the context in which God established the roots of a chosen people in this world.

THEME: God and the nations.

To compute the time which elapsed between the disembarkment of the ark and the birth of Abraham is impossible. The figures given in Genesis 11 suggest that the *minimum* would be 352 years. Probably a much greater amount of time was involved. The years between the Flood and the call of Abram are called the Postdiluvian Period. The brief account of this period in Scripture contains three important revelations concerning the nations of the world. God reveals here (1) the origin of the nations, (2) the rebellion of the nations, and (3) the distribution of the nations.

THE ORIGIN OF THE NATIONS
Genesis 9:20-29

"Now the sons of Noah who came out of the ark were Shem, Ham, and Japheth; and Ham was the father of Canaan. These three were the sons of Noah; and from these the whole earth was populated" (Gn 9:18,19). These words clearly indicate the purpose of this section. The prophecies of Noah which are narrated in 9:20-27 have to do with the the origin of the nations of the earth.

A. Background of Noah's Predictions (Gn 9:20-24).

Some time after the Flood Noah began farming and planted a vineyard (9:20). The text does not mean that Noah was the first tiller of the ground, as reflected in the translation of the RSV. Noah was not the first to plant a vineyard. Out of forty occurrences of the word "began to" only four can be rendered "was the first to." Before the Flood vineyards existed, but until this time Noah had never grown one. In recording this detail the Bible again stands squarely against ancient paganism which contended that wine-making originated with the gods. The present text underscores the proposition that growing vineyards and making wine were very human enterprises.

Here is the first mention of wine in the Bible. This does not mean that wine had never before been extracted from grapes. Noah was not the first to get drunk. Babylonian tradition knows of the abuse of the fruit of the vine in the period before the Flood, and Matthew 24:38 confirms the "drinking" in this period. Noah's drunkenness was inexcusable. He knew perfectly well what would happen if he imbibed fermented wine!

Ham saw his father's nakedness during the drunken stupor (9:22). This was no accidental glance. The Hebrew implies that he gazed with satisfaction. He then retired from the room to tell with delight what he had seen. This then is a case of gross disrespect for a parent. Perhaps more — some carnal act — was involved, but the text is silent on the matter. In any case, Moses is careful to point out that Ham was the father of Canaan. The Canaanites were notorious in the ancient world for their sexual proclivities.

The modesty and parental respect of Shem and Japheth stand in

100

stark contrast to the actions of Ham. They carried a garment upon their shoulders and backed into the room so as not to see their father's nakedness (9:23). Perhaps their actions were designed to serve as a rebuke to Ham.

When Noah awoke from his stupor, he *knew* what Ham, his younger son, had done. Did he have vague recollections about what had happened? Did the other brothers tell him? Did he know by intuition or perhaps by inspiration? The text does not indicate.

B. Noah's Predictions (Gn 9:25-29).

Before patriarchs died they uttered inspired predictions concerning their sons. Negative predictions are couched in the form of a curse; positive predictions take the form of blessings. Why Noah omits Ham from these prophetic utterances is not clear. Perhaps it was because he had already died. The patriarchal utterances of Noah may not have followed immediately upon the drunkenness incident. Noah lived 350 years after the Flood (9:28). The mention of his death immediately following the predictions, suggests that these utterances may have been made just before Noah's death. Ham may have died during those three and a half centuries between the Flood and the final days of Noah. In any case, in his prophetic pronouncement Noah spoke three times concerning Canaan, twice concerning Shem and once concerning Japheth.

1. The curse on Canaan. Canaan the son of Ham was cursed. A curse in the Bible is a negative prophecy pertaining to temporal life. Canaan was to be "a servant of servants," i.e., the lowliest of servants. The descendants of Canaan (Canaanites) would be servants first to their own brethren, i.e., other Hamites (9:25), then to the Shemites (9:26), and finally to the Japhethites (9:27). The Egyptians were Hamites, the "brethren" of Canaan. They subjugated Canaan in the fifteenth century BC. According to Genesis 10, the Assyrians and Babylonians were Hamitic peoples. They dominated Canaan from the eighth to the sixth centuries BC. When the Shemitic Israelites invaded Canaan in the fourteenth century the second part of the prediction was fulfilled. During the conquests of Alexander the Great Canaan fell under the domination of the Japhethites. The prophecies of Noah are a capsule of ancient history.[1]

The curse on Canaan had nothing to do with the origin of the black race as some have contended. Ham had three sons besides Canaan. Cush was the progenitor of the Ethiopians, Mizraim of the Egyptians, Phut of the Libyans and peoples of Africa. This curse, however, has to do only with the Canaanites, a people who manifested none of the racial characteristics of the black race. The skin texture of Israelites and Canaanites at the time of Joshua's invasion was probably very similar. The problem concerning the Canaanites was not in the color of their skin but rather in the condition of their hearts.[2]

Why the curse on Canaan? Some think it was because he was involved with his father in a carnal act against Noah. Of this there is no proof. Perhaps there is some merit to the suggestion that since the sin was committed by Ham, Noah's youngest son, the curse is placed on Canaan, the youngest son of Ham. Canaan certainly was not being punished for the sin of his father. Rather this is an announcement that the descendants of Canaan would manifest the same propensity for immorality as their progenitor Ham. The Canaanites would then be justly punished for their gross sin by being enslaved by one nation after another.

2. The blessing on Shem. Noah's utterance seems to contain two blessings for Shem. First, "Blessed be Yahweh, the God of Shem" (9:26). The language suggests that Shem had a special relationship with Yahweh, the God of covenant redemption. His descendants would preserve the knowledge of the true God and would disseminate that knowledge throughout the world. Perhaps there is also a hint here that the promised seed would spring from the loins of Shem.

The second blessing on Shem was this: "He shall dwell in the tents of Shem" (9:27). Some regard the third person pronoun as a reference to Japheth. Others have offered cogent reasons for regarding God (*'elohim*) as the subject of this sentence.[3] Taken in this way, Noah would be predicting the incarnation. God himself would come to dwell in the midst of the Shemites. The Apostle John declared that the divine Word became flesh and "dwelt," (lit., "tabernacled") among his people (John 1:14).

3. The blessing on Japheth. Japheth's blessing is stated concisely: "May God enlarge Japheth" (9:27). The Japhethites include the Indo-

European peoples as well as the brown and yellow races. In the early migrations of the human family from the cradle of civilization these peoples spread into Europe, Asia and eventually to the Americas. Noah under the inspiration of God foresaw this expansion of the Japhethites. In 539 BC Cyrus the Persian, a descendant of Japheth, conquered Babylon. The Japhethites became masters of the world. From that day to this no Semitic or Hamitic race has succeeded in breaking the world supremacy of the Japhethic peoples.

THE REBELLION OF THE NATIONS
Genesis 10:8-12; 11:1-9

The paragraph in Genesis 10 which describes the exploits of Nimrod has been linked in Jewish tradition with the tower of Babel episode recounted in Genesis 11:1-4. The linkage has some biblical support in the fact that Nimrod was the founder of the city of Babel. In any case, both paragraphs depict the rebellion of the nations against God.

A. The Conspiracy of Nimrod (Gn 10:8-12).

The text furnishes scant information concerning Nimrod. He was a descendant of Cush, a Hamite. The biblical record thus agrees with data from the ancient history of Mesopotamia which furnish evidence that the region was first ruled by a non-Shemitic people. Nimrod began to be (i.e., set out to be) a mighty one (*gibbor*) in the land (10:8). The term *tyrant* captures the intention of the original. Nimrod's very name is an encapsulation of his lifestyle. His name means, "Let us revolt." He must have been a ruthless ruler who was opposed to all existing order.

Nimrod was especially noted as "a mighty hunter before Yahweh" (10:9). One of the royal responsibilities of kings in ancient times was to keep the wild animal population thinned out so that citizens would not be threatened. The text may refer to this function. The documents, however, also speak of ancient kings *hunting* the men of a city, capturing them, and carrying them off into slavery. Perhaps Nimrod hunted men. He did this "before (*liphne*) Yahweh," i.e., in opposition to Yahweh. The Septuagint rendered, "a mighty hunter against the Lord."

Nimrod was an empire builder. He started his rise to power in Shinar, in the lower Mesopotamian river valley. He gradually extended his influence over (or possibly built) Babel, Erech, Accad and Calneh. Nimrod eventually expanded his influence into Assyria where he built Nineveh, Rehoboth, Calah and the great city of Resen (10:10-12).

B. The Construction of Babel (Gn 11:1-9).

For some time after the Flood the human family was of one language and dialect. Eventually the descendants of Shem, Ham and Japheth migrated south and east into the land of Shinar. Apparently they were a nomadic people. At some point, however, they decided to build a city, and especially a tower. Since stone was practically nonexistent in Shinar, they invented a way of making kiln-baked bricks. They used the bitumen found in the region as mortar.

The motives of the tower builders are not entirely clear. With this spectacular architectural feat they hoped to make a name (i.e., reputation) for themselves. They hoped that the tower would provide protection from another Flood or from enemies who might attempt to scatter them. So the tower pointed to man's attempt to glorify and fortify himself. The structure was a monument to lack of faith in God's promises and to disobedience to his command to spread over the earth.

Yahweh came down to see the city and the tower (11:5). This in no way implies that the Lord was unaware of the actions of his children. Rather God is here making a judicial investigation worthy of that One who is scrupulously fair in his dealings with mankind. His verdict was that the project had to cease. The people were united in their ungodly purpose, and this was only the beginning of their rebellious plans (11:6).

The judgment upon the tower builders was that their language would be confounded. The resulting confusion caused the various language groups to scatter across the face of the earth. The building project came to an abrupt halt. The place was called Babel, "confusion," to commemorate this judicial act of God (11:7-9).

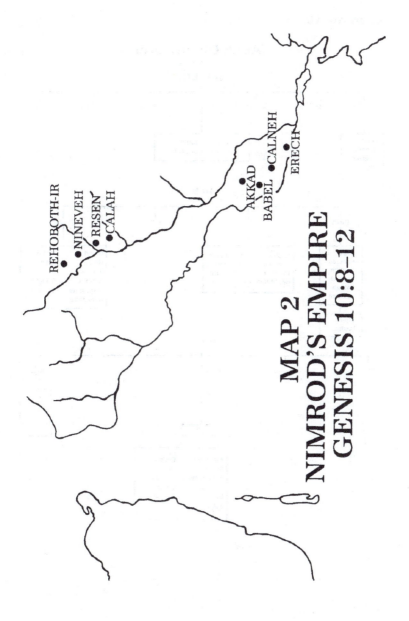

MAP 2
NIMROD'S EMPIRE
GENESIS 10:8-12

Chart No. 10

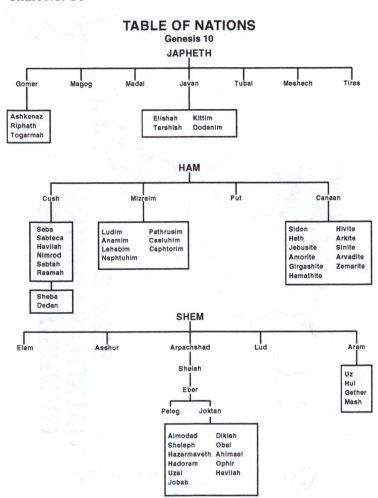

TABLE OF NATIONS
Genesis 10

JAPHETH

| Gomer | Magog | Madai | Javan | Tubal | Meshech | Tiras |

Ashkenaz
Riphath
Togarmah

Elishah   Kittim
Tarshish   Dodanim

HAM

| Cush | Mizraim | Put | Canaan |

Seba
Sabteca
Havilah
Nimrod
Sabtah
Raamah

Sheba
Dedan

Ludim   Pathrusim
Anamim   Casluhim
Lehabim   Caphtorim
Naphtuhim

Sidon   Hivite
Heth   Arkite
Jebusite   Sinite
Amorite   Arvadite
Girgashite Zemarite
Hamathite

SHEM

| Elam | Asshur | Arpachshad | Lud | Aram |

Uz
Hul
Gether
Mash

Shelah

Eber

Peleg   Joktan

Almodad   Diklah
Sheleph   Obal
Hazarmaveth Ahimael
Hadoram   Ophir
Uzal   Havilah
Jobab

THE DISTRIBUTION OF THE NATIONS
Genesis 10:1-7,13-32

The so-called Table of Nations in Genesis 10 is one of the most valuable ethnological documents from antiquity. Nothing like this Table is found in ancient literature. One of the ancient Mesopotamian myths seems to suggest that the earth was repeopled by means of magic spells after the Flood. Genesis 10, however, offers a nonmagical explanation of the rapid increase of mankind at this time. This natural proliferation was in accord with divine will.

A. The Structure of the Table.
The structure of the Table of Nations is such that the remote and less important peoples are treated first. The order of Noah's sons as they usually appear is reversed. The Table moves from general history to salvation history.

1. The Sons of Japheth (10:2-5). Japheth's descendants are listed first because he was the eldest of the three brothers, and because his descendants were of less significance in God's program. Seven sons and seven grandsons of Japheth are named. At the time of Abraham these peoples were located in Asia Minor and Europe. The oriental peoples are also Japhethic, but they are omitted because of their distance from the stage upon which the drama of redemption unfolded.

2. The Sons of Ham (10:6-20). The Hamites are treated in the second place so that the list might conclude with the Shemites. Four sons and twenty-six other descendants of Ham are named. Hamitic peoples occupied Africa, Canaan and Arabia. All the earliest civilizations of note were founded and carried to their highest technical proficiency by Hamitic people. Arthur Custance contends that almost every basic technological invention owes its origin to them![4]

3. The Sons of Shem (10:21-31). Five sons and twenty-one descendants of Shem are listed in the Table. These peoples settled in Mesopotamia and Arabia. Six generations of Shemites are mentioned. An important note is attached to Peleg in the fifth generation: "In his days the earth was divided" (10:25). Four views of this cryptic note have found supporters. The dividing of the earth may have been (1) a dispersion prior to the dispersion at the tower of Babel, (2) the map-

ping of the earth by an ancient cartographer, (3) the parting of the continents which once were one large land mass, and (4) the dispersion at Babel. The last interpretation is decidedly the best.

B. Observations Regarding the Table.

1. The rise of ethnological divisions within the human family was part of God's scheme. Ethnic diversity is a natural product of the multiplication of people; linguistic diversity and dispersion of mankind has another explanation.

2. Chapter 10 implicitly marks the rise of idolatry. Prior to this time the Bible attests universal monotheism. After the ethnic divisions of the human family appear, belief in one God seems to have been almost exclusively the possession of Abraham and his descendants.

3. Whether the Table is listing personal names or tribal names is not always clear. Even behind some of the obvious tribal names may be tribal ancestors.

4. Some names — Sheba, Ophir, Havilah — appear both in the Shemitic and Hamitic lists. Perhaps intermarriage between the two lines took place. That different peoples with the same name existed in the ancient world is also possible.

5. Chapter 11:1-9 (the Tower of Babel) is chronologically prior to the Table of Nations (cf. 10:25). Mention of Sodom and Gomorrah (10:19) may indicate a date prior to 2000 BC. The Table probably represents the state of the nations at the time of Abraham.

6. The Table classifies peoples according to ethnology. This is not, however, a treatise on ethnological theory, but a factual, historical record of the migrations of men from the land of Shinar after the Tower of Babel episode. Modern scholars classify peoples according to language groups. These language groupings do not always correspond to the ethnological divisions cited in the Table. Canaanites, for example, would be classified by modern scholars as Shemitic, while the Table traces their ancestry to Ham.

7. The Table deals with the descendants of Noah. Oriental peoples are not mentioned. Does that mean that the people of the Far East were not descendants of Noah? Some scholars so interpret. They hold that these peoples were not affected by the Flood. The Bible seems to be very clear, however, that only eight souls survived the

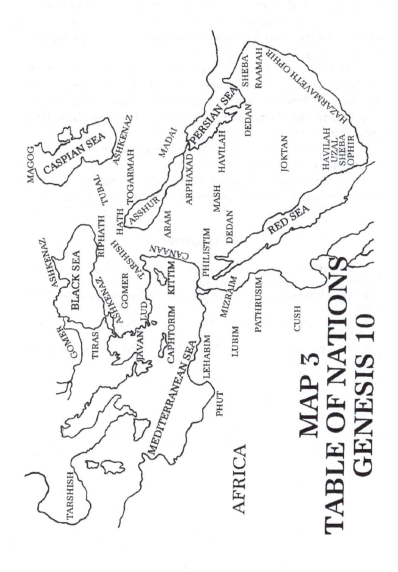

**MAP 3
TABLE OF NATIONS
GENESIS 10**

Flood. This would necessitate that the Oriental peoples were descendants from Noah. They are omitted from the Table because they are too far removed from the stage of biblical history and consequently had no dealings with the people of God.

8. The Table refers to the primary distribution of men from Shinar over certain districts. No attempt is made here to trace subsequent migrations of those peoples. The Table is one frame of a motion picture. Ancient peoples moved about, mixed, and perhaps changed languages several times over.

9. The Table says nothing about race or racial characteristics except what may be inferred from heredity.

10. Seventy names are listed in the Table of Nations. This may have influenced the selection of seventy witnesses in Luke 10:1.

ENDNOTES

1. Robert Brow, "The Curse on Ham — Capsule of Ancient History," *Christianity Today*, October 26, 1973, pp. 76-78.

2. H.L. Willmington, *Guide to the Bible* (Wheaton: Tyndale, 1981), p. 33.

3. Charles Briggs, *Messianic Prophecy* (New York: Scribners, 1891), pp. 82f. n. 1.

4. Arthur Custance, *Noah's Three Sons* (Grand Rapids: Zondervan, 1975), pp. 154-216.

CHAPTER NINE

A Journey of Faith
Genesis 11:10-13:4

AIM: To demonstrate that the journeys of Abram have their counterparts in the pilgrimage of a Christian.

THEME: The walk of faith.

Abram lived roughly two millennia before Christ. By five steps the approximate date for his birth can be computed. (1) The dates of Solomon's kingship are known. The fourth year of his reign was 967 BC. According to 1 Kings 6:1, 480 years should be added to 967 BC to establish the date of the Exodus as 1447 BC. (2) Israel was in Egypt 430 years (Ex 12:40). Add 430 years to 1447 BC to establish the date for Jacob's entrance into Egypt in 1877 BC. (3) Jacob was 130 when he stood before Pharaoh (Gn 47:9). Add 130 years to 1877 BC to establish the birth date of Jacob in 2007 BC. (4) Isaac was sixty when Jacob was born (Gn 25:26). Add sixty to 2007 BC to get the birth date of Isaac in 2067 BC. (5) Abraham was 100 when

Isaac was born (Gn 21:5). Add 100 to 2067 BC to get the birth date of Abram in 2167 BC.

With Abram God made a new initiative in the history of redemption. After setting forth the antecedents of Abram's call, the faith walk of this great man of God is narrated.

THE ROOTS OF A SPECIAL NATION
Genesis 11:10-32

According to the predictions of Noah, the Shemites were to have a special relationship to Yahweh. After summarizing the generations between Noah and Terah, the narrator focuses attention on the descendants of Terah.

Chart No. 11

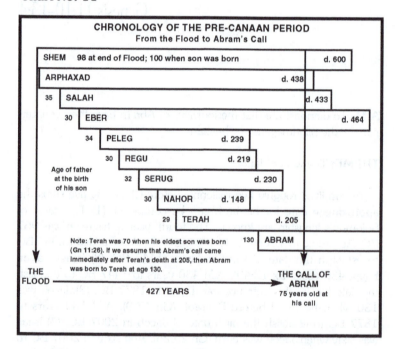

CHRONOLOGY OF THE PRE-CANAAN PERIOD
From the Flood to Abram's Call

SHEM   98 at end of Flood; 100 when son was born   d. 600
ARPHAXAD   d. 438
35   SALAH   d. 433
      30   EBER   d. 464
            34   PELEG   d. 239
                  30   REGU   d. 219
      Age of father   32   SERUG   d. 230
      at the birth
      of his son   30   NAHOR   d. 148
                                 29   TERAH   d. 205
            Note: Terah was 70 when his eldest son was born   130   ABRAM
            (Gn 11:26). If we assume that Abram's call came
            immediately after Terah's death at 205, then Abram
THE   was born to Terah at age 130.   THE CALL OF
FLOOD ──▶   ABRAM
                          427 YEARS   75 years old at
                                                               his call

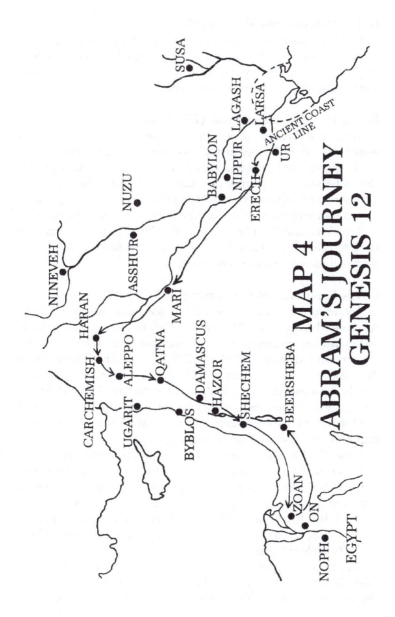

MAP 4
ABRAM'S JOURNEY
GENESIS 12

A. The Descendants of Shem (11:10-26).

Chart 11 summarizes the data concerning eight generations of Shem's descendants. At least one name, Cainan, is found in the Septuagint text which is not in the Hebrew. Luke 3:36 accepts Cainan as a legitimate link in this genealogical chain.

B. The Descendants of Terah (11:27-30).

Terah had three children: Haran, Abram and Nahor. Abram is named first in 11:26 because of his spiritual preeminence, but it would appear that Haran was Terah's firstborn. Before this family left Ur of Chaldees on its journey of destiny, Haran died. The biblical narrator thought it noteworthy that Haran died before his father. In the normal course of life, sons should bury their fathers, not vice versa.

Abram married Sarai his half-sister (Gn 20:12). Nahor married his niece Milcah (11:29). Later the Law of Moses would outlaw the marriage of those who were closely related.

C. The Emigration of the Family (Gn 11:31-32).

According to Stephen, "The God of glory appeared to our father Abraham when he was in Mesopotamia, before he lived in Haran, and said to him, Depart from your country and your relatives, and come into the land that I will show you" (Acts 7:2-3). Even though Abram had seen this theophany, Terah is credited in Genesis with organizing the expedition. Is this merely deference to the head of the family? Or did Terah's decision and Abram's instruction to leave Ur just happen to coincide? Did Terah move at the insistence of Abram or did Abram join in Terah's migration only after he received divine approval in the theophany? In any case, Terah is represented as having led his family out of Ur.

Terah "took" three members of his family: Abram, Lot his grandson, and Sarai his daughter-in-law. Terah was leading a larger group northward and he invited the three above-mentioned family members to travel with him. This is why the text says, "They went forth *with them*" (11:31). In the course of time Nahor and his wife Milcah also left Ur to settle in Haran.

The group was bound for Canaan. That was the divine intention at least. Abram did not know his ultimate destination for the apostle declares that he went forth "not knowing whither he went" (Heb

11:8). He left Ur in faith that God would providentially lead him to that place which he would receive as an inheritance. As to what precise time Abram was told that Canaan would be his final destination the text is silent.

The journey halted in Haran about six hundred miles north of Ur. The people who lived in Haran were essentially the same racially, religiously, and linguistically as those who lived in Ur. Why Terah's company should stop there cannot be determined. Perhaps Terah's health was a factor. What is clear here is that Abram, for whatever reason, stopped short of the Promised Land! His initial response to the command of God to leave Ur and family had only been half-hearted. Because of this, Abram lost precious time he could have spent walking with God in Canaan land.

Terah died in Haran at the age of 205 (11:32). Abram was seventy-five at the time (12:4). How long the group had been in Haran before the death of Terah cannot be determined.

THE JOURNEYS OF A SPECIAL PERSON
Genesis 12:1-13:4

With the call of Abram about 2092 BC a new era of Bible history began. The importance of this patriarch can be seen in the amount of space allocated to him in the sacred narrative. The entire history of the world from creation to the Flood — a time of no less than 1656 years — is recorded in six chapters. Some nineteen chapters are devoted to Abram even though his life span was but 175 years. Four phases of Abram's faith-walk are narrated in 12:1-13:4. Each sets forth a basic principle which governs the faith-walk of all believers.

A. Phase One: To Canaan (Gn 12:1-5).

In Haran God called Abram a second time (cf. Gn 15:5; Acts 7:2-4). With regard to the manner of this call only this can be said: According to Stephen, the "God of glory" appeared to Abram in Ur (Acts 7:2). This language suggests some visible manifestation. Perhaps a similar manifestation occurred in Haran.

Abram's call, which came after the death of Terah, contained the same directives which had earlier been given in Ur: Leave country and relatives and go to the land I will show you. Literally the Hebrew reads, "Go for your sake!" To follow this directive would be to his advantage. The context suggests that he was at liberty to persuade his family and friends to go with him if he was able. Even if no one went with him, however, he was to leave!

The divine directive was a challenge to Abram's faith. He was to leave all he knew for an uncertain destination. If the land had been described in glowing terms, the trial to Abram's faith would have been far less. God did not even tell him at this time that he would *give* him the land, only *show* it to him. During his lifetime Abram never gained possession of any of that land save a small plot where he buried his dead. The apostle describes his astounding faith in these words: "By *faith* Abraham, when he was called to go out into a place which he should after receive for an inheritance, obeyed, and he went out not knowing whither he went" (Heb 11:8).

A gracious Promise accompanied the call, and two dimensions of that Promise are mentioned here. First, God promised progeny to Abram. This is sometimes called the seed or the great nation promise. The descendants of Abram would be great in number and great in their importance to the plan of God. For this reason, Abram's name would be great. No man has been so widely and permanently honored as Abram. Jews, Muslims, and Christians alike honor him.

In the second dimension of the Promise God spoke of Abram's position or standing with God. Here a fourfold blessing is indicated. God would (1) bless Abram and (2) bless those who blessed him, i.e., were kindly disposed toward him. The reverse is also promised. Those who make light of Abram God would curse. (3) Abram would be a blessing to others. (4) Ultimately, all families of the earth would be blessed through Abram (12:1-3). From this time forward Abram's descendants were to perform a mediatorial function and blessing to mankind in general was to flow through them. Ultimately this promise came to its complete realization in Christ (Gal 3:8,16).

Abram obeyed the directive of the Lord, and Lot chose to travel with him. Abram took his wife Sarai, all the servants and all the possessions which he had acquired in Haran and set out for Canaan. He was now seventy-five years of age. The narrator emphasizes the fact that this time he reached his destination (12:4-5).

116

B. Phase Two: In Canaan (Gn 12:6-9).

Abram began to discover God's blessings in the Promised Land. He passed through the land surveying his inheritance in its length and breadth. At last he came to the spot which would later be called Shechem. To be more precise, he camped at the "oak of Moreh" or the teacher's oak. This was probably a well-known spot under which a religious teacher had been accustomed to sit.

At Shechem Abram discovered a wonderful revelation, a wonderful promise and a wonderful relationship. The Lord appeared to him there. The progeny aspect of the Promise was personalized. This childless man would have seed and that seed would possess the land where now he sojourned. Hence a third dimension of the Promise emerged. Abram through his descendants would one day possess the land to which his faith-walk had taken him. To commemorate this theophany, Abram built an altar and fellowshiped in worship with the God of Promise (12:6-7).

From Shechem Abram moved his tents to the hills east of what would later be called Bethel. Here again he built an altar. At Bethel Abram experienced the wonderful privilege of public witnessing because "he called upon the name of the Lord." No indication is given as to how long Abram remained in Bethel before he moved his tents into the Negev or southland (12:8-9).

In the Promised Land Abram found testing as well as blessing. First, he observed that the Canaanite was then in the land (12:6). The land which God had promised to the seed of Abram was already occupied by a proud, fierce and exceedingly corrupt people. Furthermore, soon after his arrival, a famine broke out in the land (12:10). Abram must have reflected now and again on the fertile regions of Mesopotamia which he had left in obedience to the command of God. Why would he even want this land cursed by famine and occupied by Canaanites? How could his present circumstances indicate any special standing with the Lord?

C. Phase Three: Away from Canaan (Gn 12:10-20).

Because of the severity of the famine Abram experienced a lapse of faith. He chose to abandon the Promised Land and migrate to Egypt, the granary of the ancient world. Since no divine directive is mentioned, Abram must have acted alone in this decision. For Abram Egypt was the land of doubt, sin and humiliation. Four disastrous consequences of his sojourn there are narrated:

1. Abram committed the sin of deception. Because of Sarah's beauty he feared for his life in Egypt. Abram regarded the Egyptians as far less scrupulous about murder than adultery. He requested Sarah to tell any who might inquire that she was his sister. This was standard operating procedure for Abram in his travels (Gn 20:13). Some have tried to argue that in the ancient Near East husbands adopted their wives as sisters to give them higher status. Others have excused Abram because Sarai was his half-sister (cf. Gn 20:12). In truth there is no justification for the deception. The essence of falsehood is the intention to deceive others for one's own personal advantage. Abram was willing to sacrifice the honor of his wife to protect himself. He was depressed and discouraged. Abram lacked the courage which grows out of faith.

The physical problem here of Sarai's beauty at age sixty-five must honestly be addressed. Pharaoh's officials saw that she was very "fair" and they praised her to Pharaoh. The Hebrew implies fairness of complexion, one likely to attract the attention of the darker Egyptians. Sarai died at the age of 127. At age sixty-five she was middle aged, childless, and a woman who had lived a life of ease. That the Egyptians would find her attractive would not be inherently ridiculous.

2. Abram lost his wife. She was taken into Pharaoh's house. He took Sarai to be his wife (12:19), i.e., he intended to make her one of the wives of his harem.

3. Abram brought pain and suffering on the house of Pharaoh. The Lord inflicted serious diseases on Pharaoh and his household because of Sarai (12:17). Abram was supposed to be a blessing to others, but here he brought, not blessing, but curse. Again Abram's faith in the divine Promise was being tested.

4. Abram was rebuked by a pagan king. Just how Pharaoh came to realize that his problems stemmed from the taking of a married woman cannot be determined. In any case he summoned Abram to his court and verbally chastised him with three questions. Apparently the Egyptians thought highly of the marriage connection, for as soon as he ascertained who Sarai was, he restored her to her husband.

Abram made no recorded defense of his actions (12:18-19). What a terrible humiliation when an unbeliever has higher moral standards than a believer!

In spite of his conduct Abram was blessed in Egypt. He experienced God's grace. During the time of the premarital ceremonies and purifications common in eastern lands, the Lord intervened and brought diseases upon Pharaoh's house. These diseases forced Pharaoh to restore Sarai to Abram before she had been fully received as a member of his harem.

Abram also received material enrichment from this episode. While Sarai was in the king's harem Abram received many tokens of respect from Pharaoh. He was enriched with gifts of livestock and servants. He left Egypt with greater wealth than he had when he entered that land. God seemed to bless him in spite of his sin and stupidity. Yet while he was in Egypt Abram lost time of fellowship with God in Canaan. He also lost his testimony to Pharaoh.

D. Phase Four: Back to Canaan (Gn 13:1-4).

Pharaoh gave Sarai back to Abram and ordered him to leave Egypt. An armed guard escorted Abram to the border. That Pharaoh felt it necessary to authorize such an escort was an admission that Abram and Sarai were in physical danger in Egypt. Abram left Egypt with wealth, which proved to be a cause of dissension within the family. He left Egypt with his wife. He almost had lost her there. Only by God's grace did he get her back from Pharaoh. He left with Lot, although Lot's heart still remained in Egypt. Some have suggested that the Egypt trip is an example of a more mature believer (Abram) leading a less mature believer (Lot) astray. Most likely Abram also left Egypt with Hagar, the Egyptian maid who would bring untold trouble to the family (13:1-2).

Abram retraced his steps. First he sojourned in the Negev. Then he moved station by station until he reached Bethel where he had earlier resided. There he rebuilt the altar and renewed his public witness by calling upon the name of the Lord (13:3-4).

Hebrews 11 emphasizes the faith of Abram. He believed God when he did not know *where* (v. 8), when he did not know *how* (v. 11), and when he did not know *why* (vv. 17-19).

119

BIBLIOGRAPHY: THE PATRIARCHAL AGE

Cole, C. Donald. *Abraham, God's Man of Faith.* Chicago: Moody, 1977.

Gaubert, H. "Abraham, Loved by God." In *The Bible in History.* New York: Hastings House, 1969.

_____ . "Isaac and Jacob: God's Chosen Ones." In *The Bible in History.* New York: Hastings House, 1969.

Gonzales, Angel. *Abraham, Father of Believers.* Trans. Robert Olsen. New York: Herder, 1967.

Hill, Dorothy B. *Abraham: His Heritage and Ours.* Boston: Beacon, 1957.

Holt, John M. *The Patriarchs of Israel.* Nashville: Vanderbilt University, 1964.

Hunt, I. *The World of the Patriarchs.* Englewood Cliffs, NJ: Prentice-Hall, 1967.

Mazar, Benjamin, ed. "Patriarchs." In *The World History of the Jewish People.* New Brunswick, NJ: Rutgers University, 1970.

Parrot, Andre. *Abraham and His Times.* Trans. James Farley. Philadelphia: Fortress, 1968.

Pfeiffer, Charles F. *The Patriarchal Age.* Grand Rapids: Baker, 1961.

Van Seters, John. *Abraham in History and Tradition.* New Haven, CT: Yale University, 1975.

CHAPTER TEN

Consolation amidst Crisis
Genesis 13:5-15:21

AIM: To demonstrate that God's Word brings encouragement to those who courageously deal with crisis.

THEME: Growth through crisis.

Abram — later to be called Abraham — plays a key role in the teachings of the three great monotheistic faiths. His life unfolded in four phases circumscribed by five events. Besides his birth and death, his call, and the births of Ishmael and Isaac were the key events in Abram's life. Chart 12 outlines what is known about the life of this great patriarch.

Abram returned to Canaan, not because the famine was over, but because he was no longer welcome in Egypt (12:30). Chapter thirteen suggests that he had learned his lesson from his tragic trip to Egypt. After his return to Canaan, Abram faced two crises, both of which involved his nephew Lot. The promises made to this fledging believer in Haran were tested again and again, but with each crisis came consolation from God.

CONTENTION WITHIN THE FAMILY
Genesis 13:5-13

Believers are not exempt from family problems. "There was strife between the herdsmen of Abram's cattle and the herdsmen of Lot's cattle" (13:7a). Here the narrator reveals the reason, result and resolution of the strife.

Chart No. 12

LIFE OF ABRAHAM									
B I R T H	PHASE ONE 75 YRS.	2 N D	PHASE TWO 11 YRS. 75-86	I S H M A E L	PHASE THREE 14 YRS. 86-100	I S A A C	PHASE FOUR 75 YRS. 100-175	D E A T H
	Marriage to Saraï	C	Lot (ch. 13)		Gap of 13 Yrs. / 99th Year		Moriah (ch. 22)	
	Initial Call	A	Melchizedek (ch. 14)				Macpelah (ch. 23)	
	Move to Haran	L L	Furnace (ch. 15)				Rebekah (ch. 24)	
			Hagar (ch. 16)					
	11:27-32		Chs. 12–16		Chs. 17–20		Chs. 21–25	
2165 BC		2092 BC		2081 BC		2067 BC		1992 BC
	ABRAM					**ABRAHAM**		

A. The Reason for Contention (Gn 13:5-7a).

What was the problem? On the surface it would appear that the problem was Lot's wealth. Lot possessed flocks and herds and tents. The sparse pasture area and water supply in southern Canaan simply was not sufficient for the combined livestock of both Abram and Lot.

Lot's *wealth*, however, was only the superficial reason for the family dispute. The real reason for the problem was Lot's *walk*. It was fleshly, unbelieving and carnal. Lot was greedy. His ambition knew no bounds.

B. The Result of Contention (Gn 13:7b).

The contention between the two groups of herdsmen was a powerful testing for Abram. Did not God promise him that he would be a blessing to others? Yet twice, within a matter of months, Abram has been at the center of controversy with those among whom he lives. Surely the family problem must have been a source of discouragement to this man of God. Yet he did not give up his faith in God's Promise.

The dispute between the herdsmen also resulted in a poor testimony before the heathen. "The Canaanite and the Perizzite were also living in the land at that time" (13:7b). These two groups were closely related. The former dwelled in fortified cities while the latter were hamlet dwellers. The critics seize upon this statement as proof that Genesis could not have been written by Moses. The book must have been written at a time long after the Canaanites ceased to be in the land. They lived in the land *then*, but not at the time the book was being written. This forced and unnecessary interpretation completely misses the spiritual significance of the verse.

Moses made the statement about the Canaanites and Perizzites for two reasons. First, he was explaining that Abram and Lot had to share the pasture and water with others who lived there. Then too he was suggesting that unbelievers were looking on as the dispute between the herdsmen intensified. Unbelievers always rejoice when believers quarrel.

C. The Resolution of Contention (Gn 13:8-13).

Abram took the initiative in settling the difficulty with Lot. He could have insisted upon his "rights," but instead he suggested that the two part company. Better a geographical separation than an escalation of bitterness. He also graciously offered to let Lot choose the area where he wished to live. Here perhaps is a model for settling disputes among brethren.

Lot chose for himself the best part of the land, the Jordan valley. Before the Lord destroyed the cities of the plain, this region was lush and fertile. To Lot it looked like the proverbial garden of Eden, like the rich Nile delta in Egypt. Lot's choice reveals much about his character. His choice reveals: (1) his pride, for the younger should submit to the elder (1 Pet 5:5-6); (2) his worldliness, for what mattered to him was that the region was "like the land of Egypt;" (3) his selfishness, for he took the best for himself; (4) his unbelief, for he walked by sight and not by faith, "he lifted up his eyes;" (5) his recklessness, for he pitched his tents near Sodom in spite of the notorious reputation of the place.

So the brethren separated. The dispute was resolved because of the gracious spirit of Abram. Within a few months, however, Lot's choice would involve both men in dangerous circumstances.

CONSOLATION FOR ABRAM
Genesis 13:14-18

Family problems often destroy faith. In the present case, however, the Lord used the strife within the family to challenge Abram's faith. Here there is a repetition of the promises and a call for reaffirmation of faith.

A. Promises Repeated (Gn 13:14-16).

The Lord appeared to Abram for the fourth time at Bethel. Abram needed encouragement at this time, and the Lord did not fail him. Although he had been walking by faith, the Lord told him to lift up his eyes and look toward the four directions of the compass. God thus undergirded the faith of this man by showing him exactly what his inheritance would be.

Two aspects of God's Promise to the patriarch were amplified. Two significant enlargements of the possession aspect were made.

The ambiguous "this land" of 12:7 became "all the land which you see" from the region of Bethel. The adverb "forever" underscored the permanence of the gift (13:14-15). To the progeny aspect of the Genesis 12 Promise a magnificent metaphor was added. God would make Abram's descendants "as the dust of the earth."

B. Faith Reaffirmed (Gn 13:17-18).

Following the repetition of the promises, God challenged Abram to reaffirm his faith. He was to walk through the length and breadth of the land. In this symbolic way Abram would be demonstrating that he believed and claimed God's promises. Intellectually claiming God's promises is quite different from claiming those promises for oneself.

Abram moved his tents to live near the great trees of Mamre at Hebron (13:18). Mamre appears to have been a famous man in that region. Here Abram built his third altar to the Lord. True faith always manifests itself in obedience and worship.

CONFLICT IN THE REGION
Genesis 14:1-24

Genesis 14 records the most unusual incident in the life of Abram. This chapter is unique in four ways: (1) Abram appeared in a new role, as the head of a sizable desert clan and as an astute military chieftain. (2) Abram was given the title "the Hebrew" (14:13). (3) The chapter contains an unusual number of proper names both of persons and places. (4) Five times the chapter contains explanatory notes about the geographical proper names. The author wished to make this ancient account understandable to his audience.

Lot was involved indirectly in creating a second crisis for Abram. In Genesis 14 Abram became embroiled, because of Lot, in international conflict in the area. This is no Jewish fantasy designed to glorify Abram. The account bears all the earmarks of sober history. Thematically the chapter serves to illustrate again the principle "those who bless you I will bless, and those who curse you I will curse" (Gn 12:3). In 12:15 Sarah was "taken" by Pharaoh and this resulted in plagues on the takers. Here Lot was taken (14:12) by foreigners with equally devastating results. The narrative unfolds in four stages.

A. Reason for the Conflict (Gn 14:1-7).

The kings of the five cities of the area where Lot had settled served Chedorlaomer, king of Elam. After twelve years, the kings formed an alliance and rebelled against their overlord. This probably means that they withheld the annual tribute. To date scholars have not been able to identify these relatively minor city kings, but their names have a genuine Palestinian flavor. The name of the king of Bela (Zoar) is not given. If the chapter is pure fiction as some critics maintain, there would have been no reason for not concocting a name for this king too. The following chart summarizes what is known of the other four kings.

CITY	KING	MEANING OF NAME
Sodom	Bera	"Conqueror"
Gomorrah	Birsha	"Large Man"
Admah	Shinab	"Sin (the moon god) is Father"
Zeboiim	Shemeber	"His Name is Mighty"

Not much can be said with regard to the identity of the four invading kings. The leader of the group was Chedorlaomer, king of Elam. Other Elamite names of this construction have surfaced, but this particular king has not been identified in the documents. No exact identification of Amraphel, king of Shinar, can be made at this time either. Tidal seems to have been a Hittite royal title. The name Arioch was a Babylonian name (cf. Dan 2:14). Arioch ruled Ellasar (Larsa) which was located near the city of Ur in the lower Euphrates river valley.

The invasion route of the four kings from the east and their crushing success in battle along the way are briefly narrated. The Rephaim, Zuzim and Emim, the earliest known inhabitants of the area of Transjordan, were the first victims of the expedition. Sweeping southward into the hill country of Seir, the four kings crushed the Horites. On the march westward toward En Mishpat (Kadesh) the Amalekites were defeated. Bypassing momentarily Sodom, the powerful army overran the Amorites at Hazazon Tamar. This set the stage for the crucial confrontation with the five allies at the southern end of the Dead Sea.

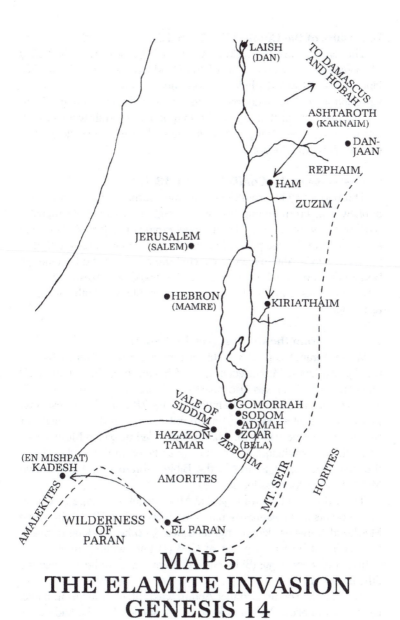

MAP 5
THE ELAMITE INVASION
GENESIS 14

B. Results of the Conflict (Gn 14:8-12).

The five kings of the plain drew up their battle lines in the Valley of Siddim at the southern tip of the Dead Sea. Apparently the five kings were not able to hold out long against the superior forces of Chedorlaomer. The defenders fled for safety to the hills. Many fell into the bitumen pits in that region. Sodom and Gomorrah were sacked. Since Lot was then living in Sodom, he and all his possessions were carried off by Chedorlaomer.

C. Response to the Conflict (Gn 14:13-15).

Through a fugitive from Sodom Abram learned of the plight of his nephew Lot. From among his own servants he was able to mobilize 318 men who were joined by an undetermined number of Canaanite allies. This small army pursued Chedorlaomer as far as Dan. In a daring night attack Abram's army effected the rescue of the hostages of Sodom. This man, who was told that he would be a blessing to others, found himself involved in armed conflict. Abram's faith was being tested again.

D. Return from the Conflict (Gn 14:16-24).

When Abram returned from his victory over Chedorlaomer he was met by two kings. Melchizedek, king of Salem, brought to him bread and wine. This king was also priest of 'el 'elyon ("God most High"), another ancient name for Yahweh (cf. Ps 78:35). The priest/king pronounced a blessing over Abram and praised God Most High for the victory that he had won. Abram responded by giving Melchizedek "a tenth of everything," i.e., of the spoils taken in the battle. This is the first instance of tithing in the Bible. Abram may have known Melchizedek before this incident.

The writer of Hebrews regarded Melchizedek as a type of Christ. These points of similarity are noted in Hebrews 7:4-10: (1) the name Melchizedek means "king of righteousness"; (2) he was king of Salem ("peace"); (3) he was a priest of God (4) but "without mother and father," i.e., genealogy; (5) he blessed Abram; and (6) he received the tithe from him.

The king of Sodom also met Abram when he returned from battle. He offered to allow Abram to keep all the spoils which he had recaptured from the kings. Abram, however, had taken an oath not to accept any gift from the Sodomite. He had once eagerly accepted monetary reward from Pharaoh. His attitude was now different. This believer did not ever want it to be said that he had gained his wealth because of the generosity of an unbeliever. Abram would accept only expenses — the food which his servants had eaten. Abram's Canaanite allies Aner, Eshcol and Mamre were not bound by the oath and consequently did receive their share of the spoils.

CONSOLATION FOR ABRAM
Genesis 15:1-21

Again in Genesis 15 the principle of consolation following crisis is evident. Here the actual institution and confirmation of the covenant are described. All aspects of the Call Promise are repeated and amplified. God does most of the speaking here. In fact only two questions (15:2,8) are attributed to Abram. Genesis 15 narrates the fifth appearance of God to the patriarch. The chapter unfolds in six movements.

A. God's Affirmation (Gn 15:1).
After the battle with the kings, the Lord came to Abram in a vision. In attacking superior forces Abram had acted impulsively. Perhaps posttrauma trepidation had set in. In any case, Abram was encouraged not to be afraid. Two incentives for courage were offered. God affirmed that he was Abram's "shield," and his exceeding great reward. Thus for the believer, God is both protector and provider.

B. Abram's Supplication (Gn 15:2-3).
In response to God's gracious affirmation, Abram burst forth in a prayer of complaint. For ten years now his faith in the Promise had been tested. The tension was unbearable. In his prayer Abram suggested that he wanted an heir, not a reward. As matters stood, his servant, and perhaps adopted son, Eliezer of Damascus would inherit all his wealth. Abram in effect was asking for an explanation from God.

C. God's Confirmation (Gn 15:4-5,7).

Responding to Abram's discouragement, God confirmed two of the promises made to his servant a decade earlier. Abram would indeed have a son, not an adopted son, but a son of his own loins. Using the night sky as a pledge, God even promised that the seed of Abram would become as numerous as the starry host. In confirming the land promise, God reminded Abram of his name. He was Yahweh, God of redemption. He had brought Abram out of Ur in order to give him possession of the land in which he now was a sojourner.

D. Abram's Justification (Gn 15:6).

Abram's senses told him that he would never father a child. Yet he believed God! Here is the first use in the Bible of the important verb *believe*. God revealed to Moses that he credited that faith to Abram as righteousness. To be righteous is to measure up to the demands of God. No man is righteous, no not one. God's plan, however, accepts obedient faith as equivalent to righteousness (Rom 4:2f.; Jas 2:20-24).

E. God's Demonstration (Gn 15:8-12,17).

Abram believed God's promises, but his faith was in dire need of encouragement. The God who takes note of even mustard seed faith graciously condescended to bind himself by means of an oath — to even place himself under a potential curse — to fulfill his promises. Abram knew full well the legal implications of the action he was required to perform.

Abram was told to bring three animals — a heifer, a goat, and a ram — as well as two birds — a dove and a pigeon. The animals were to be cut in two, and a path formed between the carcasses. To walk that path was to pronounce a self-malediction as if to say, May this terrible fate befall me if I fail to keep the promise I have given (cf. Jer 34:18f.). All day long Abram waited for what he knew would be the most dramatic manifestation of God's presence that he had yet experienced. He drove away the birds of prey whose presence would detract from the sacredness of that spot.

As the sun was setting Abram fell into a deep sleep (*tardemah*). Terror fell upon him, and deep darkness, symbolizing the ominous character of the revelation about to be presented. After the sun had set, the blessed theophany took place. A smoking fire pot with a blazing torch appeared and passed between the animal carcasses. A fire pot was a portable clay oven a couple of feet high. It resembled an inverted bowl with a hole in the upper side for draft. The explanation of this theophany is clearly stated in verse 18: "On that day Yahweh made a covenant with Abram."

F. God's Declaration (Gn 15:13-16,18-21).

The divine declaration which accompanied the theophany explained to Abram when the land promise would be fulfilled. The land of Canaan would belong to his descendants after five conditions had been met: (1) his descendants would spend four hundred years in a strange land where they would become slaves, (2) the land which enslaved them would be judged, (3) his descendants would come out of that land with great substance, (4) Abram would die in peace at an old age, and (5) the sin of the Amorites would have reached its full measure. Thus in the fourth generation (counting a generation as a hundred years) Abram's descendants would return to Canaan.

Genesis 15 concludes with specific boundaries for the Promised Land. Abram's descendants would occupy the land which stretched between the river of Egypt (not the Nile, but the Wadi Alrish) to the river Euphrates. At that time that region was occupied by ten different peoples. Someday, according to the oath of God, that land would belong to Abram's descendants.

CHAPTER ELEVEN

Divine and Human Wisdom
Genesis 16-17

AIM: To demonstrate the contrast between man's wisdom and God's wisdom.

THEME: Faith is living without scheming!

Abram had been living in the land of Canaan for ten years. He was now eighty-five and still he had no heir. The promise of God seemed to have failed. Perhaps God expected him to take matters in his own hands. After all, God helps him who helps himself. This kind of worldly logic led Abram into a scheme of which God could hardly approve. In Genesis 16 and 17 the stark contrast between two kinds of wisdom becomes evident.

THE WORLDLY SCHEME
Genesis 16:1-6

When God's promises do not seem to materialize, believers sometimes resort to their own devices. The opening verses of Genesis 16 give the sad details of a desperate scheme by Sarai and Abram to help God keep his word.

A. The Proposal by Sarai (Gn 16:1-3).

Barrenness was viewed as an intolerable curse by women in Old Testament times. Sarai must have blamed herself for the continued disappointment of her husband in not having an heir. At her age little hope of conception in the ordinary way existed. She may have regarded it as her responsibility to offer her handmaid to Abram. The practice of offering a servant to be a surrogate mother for a barren woman can be documented in the law codes of that period. By this worldly scheme Sarai hoped to *build* a family through her servant. She thus viewed the family as a structure in which the children were building blocks.

Sarai's own feelings as a wife gave way to her concern about her husband's glory and happiness. Her motives may have been pure. Faith, however, is living without scheming. Sarai's faith must have been at low ebb the day she made this proposal to Abram. In a word, she made an evil proposal in the vain expectation that some good might come. She recognized God's providence in her childlessness (16:2), then pled this fact as grounds for contriving this worldly scheme. In effect she blamed God for her desperate plan.

Sarai's servant girl was named Hagar. Most likely she had been acquired during the Egyptian sojourn some ten years before (Gn 12:20). In the intervening years she may have come to share the faith of Abram and Sarai in the one true God. Hagar may even have been desirous of playing this role in helping God fulfill his Promise to her master.

Sarai's scheme was another test for Abram, and this test he flunked. The text indicates no protest on his part, no resistance to his wife's suggestion. He surely was fully persuaded that his wife's plan was in harmony with the will of God. After all, God had never said that *Sarai* would have a child. So Abram made a deliberate choice, a reckless and inexcusable choice. He chose the path of worldly wisdom. In the previous chapter Abram listened to the voice of God and exercised faith. Here he hearkened to the voice of his wife, and fell into sin.

In this scheme, Hagar became Abram's concubine *(pilgash)*, i.e., a wife of secondary rank. Sarai presented the bride to her husband! To implement her plan cost Sarai deeply. Abram would have no part of a casual affair. His relationship to Hagar would have legal standing under the laws of that period. Nevertheless, what is legal is not always what is righteous! God never intended that a man have more than one wife. However noble Abram's motives may have been, and the approval of Sarai notwithstanding, the marriage to Hagar constituted a failure of faith and a sin on the part of the patriarch.

B. The Consequences to the Family (Gn 16:4-6).

The ill-advised measure taken by Sarai and Abram created a chain of negative consequences. Sarai experienced humiliation. When Hagar saw that she was pregnant, she began to despise her mistress. Sarai was apparently under much duress due to the haughty conduct of Hagar. The harmony between Abram and Sarai was shattered. She blamed him for her plight. Hagar was his wife. He was responsible for exercising family discipline. Because of her priority in marriage, Sarai had legal rights. A second wife could not treat her in this manner. Sarai shows no inclination to acknowledge her own role in the ill-fated scheme. Assuming that her husband would not take action, Sarai recklessly appealed to God for justice (16:3). Such hasty and passionate appeals to heaven reveal an impious spirit. God's name must be invoked with reverence.

Intimidated by the verbal abuse of his wife, Abram relinquished his responsibility to discipline his concubine. He placed Hagar under the jurisdiction of Sarai again. Abram may have been responding to his wife kindly. On the other hand, his response may indicate weakness. In any case, Sarai retaliated against the arrogance of the Egyptian by treating her harshly. The situation became so unbearable for Hagar that she fled from her mistress. She set out toward Shur on the border of Egypt. She would return to her native land.

Thus, worldly scheming resulted in humiliation for Sarai herself, misery to Abram and oppression to Hagar.

GOD'S PLANS FOR HAGAR
Genesis 16:7-16

Hagar tried to escape an unpleasant situation by fleeing. She was unaware that she had an important part to play in God's plan, and that plan called for her to remain for a time at least in the camp of Abram.

A. Hagar's Encounter (Gn 16:7-12).

Hagar could flee from her mistress, but happily not from God. By the spring on the way to Shur she had a most wonderful experience. Hagar encountered the angel of the Lord. This is the first recorded appearance of this personage in the Old Testament. Hagar referred to him as Yahweh (16:13). He addressed her in a style befitting only the Most High (16:10). He promised to perform only what God alone can do, and he foretold only what God alone could know. This, then, was no ordinary angel. The angel of the Lord was a theophany (manifestation of God). That he would choose to appear to Hagar perhaps indicates that the handmaid was of a godly disposition. Four words summarize the encounter with the Angel.

1. *Arrestment (16:7-8).* The angel had the purpose of stopping Hagar in her tracks. This he did in several ways. (1) He addressed Hagar by her name. (2) He called her Sarai's handmaid rather than Abram's wife. The Lord would thus lead her back to the humility of former times. (3) He asked her questions designed to arouse in her a sense of her plight. She was leaving a favored home for a very uncertain future.

Hagar made no effort to conceal the reason for her flight, but she could not answer the question about her destination. From the perspective of a few miles' journey into the wilderness, Hagar's mistreatment by Sarai must have seemed inconsequential.

2. *Commandment (16:9).* Hagar was given two direct commands by the heavenly messenger. She was to return to Sarai and submit to her authority. The implication is that Hagar had done wrong in despising her mistress, and endangering the fruit of her womb by this reckless trek. Returning to Abram's house would be in Hagar's best interest. Submission to Sarai would be a manifestation of repentance.

3. Encouragement (16:10-11). Promise follows quickly on the heels of command. (1) Hagar would have numerous offspring. (2) The child she was carrying would be born. (3) The child would be a son. (4) The child would wear a name which would commemorate God's intervention on her behalf in the present instance, and which would pledge a special measure of grace to help her deal with her hostile mistress. The name Ishmael means "God hears." God often sweetens onerous commands with precious promises, glimpses of future glory, and grace to deal with present frustrations.

4. Enlightenment (16:12). Hagar received a snapshot of the future of her child. What mother has not cradled a newborn son in her arms and wondered what manner of man he would become? Through the revelation by the angel of the Lord, Hagar knew! Her son would be a wild ass of man, i.e., he would roam over desert lands. He would be a powerful man, more than holding his own against all who might oppose him. He would dwell as a free man in the midst of his brethren, a reference to Abram's future descendants by Sarah. This characterization was to fit not only her son Ishmael but also his descendants.

B. Hagar's Response (Gen 16:13-16).

Hagar responded in faith to the command and promise of the angel. To demonstrate her faith she did three things. (1) She expressed her gratitude for the appearance of the Lord in a special name for God. *'el roi,* she called him, the God who sees. Here commenced a custom of memorializing each appearance of God with a new name for him. She rejoiced that God had seen her in the barren wilderness; she marveled that she had been permitted to see him as well. (2) Hagar marked the spot of the visitation. She called the well Beer-lahai-roi, the well of the one who lives and sees. Parenthetically, the sacred historian notes that this well was situated between Kadesh and Bered. The exact location of Bered is unknown, but the reference to Kadesh indicates that Hagar had not traveled far before the angel confronted her. (3) Hagar returned to the camp of Abram. A male child was born as the angel predicted. At the suggestion of Hagar Abram named the boy Ishmael. In this act the patriarch was acknowledging the child as his own (16:13-15).

Genesis 16 ends with an important chronological note. Abram was eighty-six when Hagar bore Ishmael. He had now been in Canaan for eleven years.

GOD'S PLANS FOR ABRAM
Genesis 17:1-27

A thirteen year gap exists between Genesis 16 and 17. Those years of divine silence may have been intended as chastisement to Abram for his participation in Sarai's scheme. Abram was ninety-nine when the Lord appeared to him once again. Like chapter 15, Genesis 17 focuses on the institution and confirmation of the covenant. The chapter is full of promise. God is the speaker, Abram offering but one exclamatory comment (17:18).

A. The Covenant Confirmed (Gn 17:1-8).

In this appearance the Lord identified himself as El Shaddai. The derivation and meaning of *shaddai* are uncertain, but "the Almighty" seems to be the best translation. This name of God characterized the patriarchal period. It emphasized the power of God in working out his plan in the lives of his people (17:1). No obstacle whatever could stand in the way of the complete fulfillment of the word of promise.

Before God renewed his commitment to Abram, he asked for a renewed commitment on the part of his servant. The sequence here suggests that the covenant with Abram was conditional. Two imperatives identified his responsibilities. (1) He must walk before the Lord, i.e., live a circumspect life that would meet with divine approval. (2) He must be blameless, i.e., be upright and sincere (17:2).

Commandment was followed by promise. God would make (lit., "give"), i.e., fix, appoint or confirm, a covenant with Abram. The reference is to the covenant which God had made with Abram some twenty-four years earlier. Though Abram had at this time only one son, the essence of God's covenant with him was that he would have many descendants. This was now the fifth divine declaration that his progeny would be numerous. Abram responded to the appearance of the Lord and the tremendous implications of his words with humble reverence. He fell on his face before his God (17:2-3).

138

Five new elements appear in this amplification of the covenant details. (1) Abram was to be the father, not of one nation through Ishmael, but of many nations. To commemorate this aspect of the promise, Abram was to change his name to Abraham (17:4-5). The change was greater in sense than in sound. Abram ("exalted father") became Abraham ("father of a multitude"). The new name universalized Abraham's experience for he is to be the father of many nations. (2) Not only nations, but kings would come from the loins of Abraham (17:6). Later prophecies identify one of those kings as the anointed one par excellence, the Messiah.

(3) God's special covenant relationship with Abraham would continue throughout the generations of his descendants. The covenant was an "everlasting covenant" (*berit 'olam*), lit., a covenant enduring to the far distant future. (4) The essence of the covenant was summed up in the promise to be the God of Abraham and his descendants after him. Besides gifts of grace which he pours out, God gives himself freely to his people (17:7). (5) Though Abraham had been for almost a quarter of a century a "stranger" in the land, God would give to him and his descendants all the land of Canaan. The land would be for them "an everlasting possession" (*'achuzzat 'olam*), i.e., one which would extend into the distant future (17:8). The Hebrew word *'olam* does not always convey what the English word "everlasting" connotes.

B. The Commandment Given (Gn 17:9-14).

Abraham and his descendants must "keep the covenant" (17:9). The outward sign of the covenant was the circumcision of every male child. Abraham, even though he was ninety-nine, must set the example and circumcise himself. The rite of circumcision *particularized* Abraham's experience with God. The importance of circumcision is indicated by the amount of space devoted to it in this chapter. Nine verses set forth the commandment, and five verses describe the obedience to it.

Circumcision was to be performed on the eighth day. The law applied to both native Israelites and slaves who might come among the people of the Lord. A male who refused to submit to circumcision was to be "cut off from his people." Does that expression refer to execution, eternal death, excommunication or premature death? Is it a punishment executed by man or by God? These are questions upon which no scholarly consensus exists.

Other nations practiced circumcision; but for Israel this was the badge of citizenship. This was no hygienic act; it was a religious rite. Circumcision had at least four purposes. The rite (1) symbolized the putting away of the filth of the flesh, (2) distinguished the seed of Abraham from Gentiles, (3) perpetuated the memory of the covenant, and (4) reminded them of the duty of cultivating moral purity (cf. Dt 10:16).

That the identifying mark of the Hebrew male should be on his sex organ is most appropriate. Far from being disreputable, this was the most sacred part of his whole body. Thus if this, the most private of body parts, was dedicated to God, so must be his whole person. With this organ man became, in a special sense, a co-worker with God in producing godly offspring. In circumcision the sexual act was dedicated to God's glory. When the wife became one flesh with her husband she too became sexually dedicated to the glory of God.

C. The Conception Announced (Gn 17:15-22).

For the first time God specifically announced that Sarai was yet to become a mother. To symbolize her change of fortune Abraham was to change her name to Sarah (17:15). Both names mean "heroine;" but Sarah was a newer form of the feminine ending and it was employed here to give renewed emphasis to the meaning of her name.

Even though Sarah would bear only one son, yet she would become the mother of nations. This promise embraced her spiritual posterity (Rom 4:11), Gentiles of every nationality who have faith in Christ. Among the descendants of Sarah would be kings (17:16).

Abraham fell on his face and laughed. Did he laugh for joy or was there a tinge of disbelief here? Incredible though it seemed, a man of one hundred, and a woman of ninety were about to become parents. In this period of Bible history procreation at these ages was indeed a miracle. Abraham's joy was mitigated a bit, however, by his concern about Ishmael. If Sarah was to have a child, what would become of Ishmael? How would he fit into God's plan? In a beautiful fatherly prayer for his boy, Abraham presented his petition that Ishmael might live forever before the Lord (17:18).

Before answering his petition regarding Ishmael, God focused the attention of Abraham on the child yet to be born. This son of Sarah was named by God. The name Isaac means "laugh" and it commemorated Abraham's joyous response to the news of his birth. God's everlasting covenant would be established through Isaac and his descendants after him.

What about Ishmael? God heard the prayer of his servant. He promised to bless Ishmael with fruitfulness, and cause him to multiply exceedingly. Twelve princes would come from his loins and his descendants would become a great nation. The covenant, however, would be with Isaac. Then came the greatest news of all. The miraculous birth would take place the very next year (17:20-21).

D. Abraham's Faith Response (Gn 17:22-27).

The verbal revelation to Abraham ended when "God went up from him" (17:22). This expression indicates that the "appearance" of God involved something that was externally visible, i.e., a theophany.

Abraham believed the Lord and acted that very day to carry out his instructions. He circumcised himself, his thirteen-year-old son Ishmael, and all the males born in his house as servants or acquired through purchase. Faith responds with immediacy and precision to the direct commands of the Lord.

CHAPTER TWELVE

Judgment on Sodom
Genesis 18-19

AIM: To demonstrate the terrible consequences of sin.

THEME: Divine visitations.

The events recorded in Genesis 18–19 took place in Abraham's ninety-ninth year, about 2068 BC. These chapters record two divine visitations. In Genesis 18 God visited Abraham as one friend might visit another (Jas 2:23). In Genesis 19 he visited Sodom as a wrath-filled enemy to destroy the place because of its sin.

GOD'S VISIT TO MAMRE
Genesis 18:1-33

While Abraham was encamped near a grove at Mamre, God made yet another appearance to the patriarch (18:1). His purpose here was twofold: to repeat the promise of a son, and to make known to Abraham the proposed destruction of Sodom. Four words capture the essence of Genesis 18.

A. Visitation (Gn 18:1-8).

The heat of the day is the period of rest in the Near East. For guests to arrive at that time of day was unusual. Abraham was sitting in the shade of his tent door enjoying what air might be stirring when he lifted up his eyes and saw three men standing nearby. At least to all outward appearances they were only men. Two of the strangers were created angels (19:1). The third was the same divine personage who appeared to Hagar at Beer-lahai-roi, namely, the angel of the Lord. The first verse of the chapter alerts the reader to this identification, and the subsequent narrative confirms it.

In the exaggerated hospitality so characteristic of the region, Abraham ran to meet his guests and bowed himself to the ground before them. This action was a gesture of respect for distinguished visitors. It had no religious connotations, for the patriarch at first was not aware of the true character of his guests. Abraham addressed the leader of the three with great respect ("my lord") and referred to himself deferentially ("your servant"). He promptly extended an invitation to his guests to tarry with him and refresh themselves. This invitation was humbly offered ("if I have now found favor in your sight") and modestly described ("a little water . . . a morsel of bread"). Such language is designed to relieve the guests of any anxiety which they might have about being burdensome to their host. Washing the hot and dusty feet of travelers was the first act of hospitality performed for guests in the Patriarchal period. The three visitors promptly accepted the gracious offer (18:2-5).

Abraham knew nothing about these visitors. He was ignorant of their station, their nationality, their destination or mission. They had arrived unannounced and at the most inopportune time of day. Yet Abraham rolled out the proverbial red carpet for them. He ran to them, eager to extend a welcome. His courtesy was instinctive. Little wonder, then, that the apostle used this incident to encourage Christians to give themselves to hospitality (Heb 13:2).

Abraham and Sarah busied themselves in preparing a sumptuous meal for their three guests. Sarah prepared three *seahs* (about 22 liters) of fine flour as cakes. Abraham selected a tender calf for preparation by a servant. Meat was considered a luxury served only on special occasions. Curds (a thick milk by-product) and milk were also

144

served. Abraham stood by to wait upon his guests as they ate. The amount prepared by the hosts would far exceed what three men could eat. The leftovers would be given to the servants (18:6-8).

B. Proclamation (Gn 18:9-15).

Following the meal, the guests inquired concerning Sarah's whereabouts. The question must have surprised Abraham, for in that culture a gentleman never inquired about the wife of another gentleman. Even more surprising was the fact that these strangers knew the name of Abraham's wife, and her new name at that! The question was asked to arouse Sarah's interest in the conversation. Her faith needed to be raised (18:10).

Assured that Sarah was listening, the leader of the three made an emphatic announcement which clearly revealed his identity to Abraham. He announced that (1) Sarah would have a son, and (2) this son would be born one year hence (18:10). In the miracle of the birth of Isaac, God actually did return to the camp of Abraham one year later.

Sarah received the announcement with skepticism. The patriarch and his wife were old and their capacity for procreation and conception was extinct. Sarah laughed within herself. She was too old (lit., something that is worn out by age) to enjoy any sexual pleasure with her mate (18:11-12). Sarah's respectful reference to her husband as "my lord" in this passage is commended by the Apostle Peter (1 Pet 3:6). Even in her moment of spiritual weakness the Lord found something praiseworthy in her!

By two questions addressed to Abraham the visitor solemnly confirmed the astonishing proclamation just made. The first question called attention to the skepticism of Sarah. The second directed attention to the unlimited power of God. "Is anything too hard for the Lord?" Later in Bible history that same question would be asked again by the Lord to a doubting prophet (Jer 32:27). As unbelievable as this proclamation seemed to Sarah, the heavenly visitor would return to her and she would bear a son!

The omniscience of the guest in knowing Sarah's true opinion of the promise clearly identified him as a heavenly messenger. Sarah was afraid. She quickly lied to cover up her lack of faith. The visitor, however, would not accept her denial. "You *did* laugh!"

145

C. Communication (Gn 18:16-22).

The guests arose and "looked toward Sodom," i.e., they began to walk in that direction. Following oriental custom, Abraham accompanied them as they departed on their journey. One of the three guests at this point in the narrative plainly is identified as Yahweh. Speaking to his two companions, Yahweh indicated three reasons why he should share with Abraham what he was about to do. (1) Abraham would become a great nation. He would be in a position to transmit to this nation the warning concerning God's wrath against immorality. (2) All nations of the earth would be blessed in Abraham, i.e., his influence would spread beyond the bounds of his own biological descendants. (3) God had *known* Abraham, i.e., chosen him for a special mission.

As God's chosen vessel, Abraham was to be a spiritual teacher inculcating in his children (1) the way of the Lord, (2) righteousness and (3) justice. Here is a specific stipulation that a righteous life among Abraham's descendants was to be a condition for the fulfillment of the covenant promises which God had made to the patriarch (18:17-19).

Addressing Abraham, Yahweh announced his plan. He was about to make a judicial investigation of Sodom and Gomorrah. That is the meaning of the expression "I will go down and see." God already knew what he would find there. The wickedness of the place virtually cried out for God's wrath (cf. Gn 4:10). God, however, frequently condescended to social conventions so as to leave his absolute justice beyond question. Thus prior to pouring out his wrath on the cities of the plain, the supreme Judge dispatched his two representatives to investigate the situation (18:20-22).

D. Intercession (Gn 18:23-33).

Yahweh's remarks regarding Sodom jarred Abraham. He knew that an outpouring of divine wrath was inevitable. Thoughts of his nephew living in the midst of that doomed city spurred Abraham to one of the most dramatic intercessory prayers recorded in the Bible.

Five observations regarding this prayer are in order: (1) The prayer grew out of holy boldness, for Abraham *drew near* to the Lord. (2) The prayer is undergirded with the conviction that the Judge of all

146

the earth would certainly do what was right (18:25). (3) The prayer is based on the premise that God would not slay the righteous with the wicked (18:23,25). (4) The prayer demonstrates fervent importunity. Six times Abraham posed a hypothetical situation to God. Starting with fifty righteous persons, he systematically reduced the number to ten. If there be this number of righteous people in the city would God destroy those righteous souls along with the wicked in the city? (5) The prayer is a model of reverent humility, and the more so as the prayer moves through its successive stages. At one point Abraham referred to himself as "dust and ashes" (18:27). The patriarch began the last stage of his prayer by begging, "Let not the Lord be angry and I will speak but once more" (18:32).

Abraham's intercession was successful. He got all for which he asked. As a matter of fact, Abraham quit asking before God stopped giving. If Lot had won his own family plus only two neighbors God would have spared Sodom. So why did not Abraham go below ten in his importunity? Perhaps because to do so would have degraded the noble intercession to a narrow plea for his relatives. On the other hand, perhaps Abraham himself could not believe that there could be less than ten righteous souls in Sodom.

GOD'S VISIT TO SODOM
Genesis 19:1-38

The content of Genesis 19 centers around three topics: (1) what the angels found in Sodom, (2) what the angels did in Sodom, and (3) what Lot lost in Sodom.

A. What the Angels Found in Sodom (Gn 19:1-8).

The two angels who had visited with Abraham in the previous chapter came to Sodom in the evening. What did they find there?

1. They found Lot sitting in the gate of Sodom (19:1). The "gate" was a complex of buildings where city business was transacted. That Lot was sitting there suggests that he had attained some social standing in the city.

2. They found Lot to be a very humble and gracious host (19:2-3). Lot apparently recognized these visitors as good men. The two at first

refused Lot's hospitality. They intended to follow the custom of many travelers to wrap up in their mantles and sleep in the open square just inside the gate. Lot, however, knew full well what fate would befall those men if they lodged in the open spaces. So Lot insisted that they go to his house. There he provided his guests a sumptuous feast.

3. They experienced first hand the perverse wickedness of Sodom (19:4-7). All the men of the city, old and young, were involved. They surrounded Lot's house and demanded that he deliver over to them his guests so that they might *know* them, i.e., homosexually rape them. Lot tried to reason with the mob. He called these perverts *brethren*. He referred to their proposed act as *doing wickedly*.

4. They found a righteous man with a warped sense of value (19:8). Lot offered his two virgin daughters to appease the lust of the men of Sodom. Why did he do such a horrible thing? His actions are difficult to understand, much less justify. Several factors, however, should be recognized.

The situation was desperate and dangerous. Lot did not have time to think through his action. His action must be seen as the product of sheer desperation. Furthermore, the hospitality code in that time compelled the host to do all within his power to protect the safety of those who entered his home. Another possibility is that Lot may have been attempting to use "shock therapy" on the attackers. That he was willing to sacrifice his virgin daughters to prevent their attack would dramatically demonstrate his revulsion toward homosexuality.

Two other factors should be considered. If the two girls were those who had "married" Sodomite men, perhaps he thought they would be safe. They would not dare harm girls engaged to their fellow citizens. In Bible days a betrothed woman was considered "married" and her "husband" was regarded as a son-in-law by her family. Of course Lot may have had two married daughters as well as two virgin daughters. Since only two daughters are mentioned specifically in the narrative, the former interpretation is preferable. Finally, Lot was resorting to the principle of the lesser of evils. He regarded a heterosexual rape, as bad as that is, to be less evil than an unnatural sex act.

Having said what can be said in defense of Lot, his conduct in this situation is reprehensible. One cannot avoid sin with sin! Nonetheless, this lapse must be put in the context of Lot's generally righteous life.

He was oppressed by the filthy conduct of the Sodomites day by day (2 Pet 2:8).

B. What the Angels Did in Sodom (Gn 19:9-29).

In their brief visit to Sin City the two angels were quite busy. Five actions are attributed to them. First, they rescued Lot from the men of Sodom (19:9-11). The Sodomites resented Lot as a newcomer; they resented his righteousness which condemned their lawless acts. They threatened Lot and pressed against him as they pushed toward the door. The angels reached out and pulled Lot inside and slammed the door. They smote the attackers with *blindness,* i.e., mental confusion, so that they could not even find the door (cf. 2 Kgs 6:18). The Sodomites finally became weary and retired from the house.

Second, the angels warned Lot of impending judgment (19:12-14). They urged Lot to take all of his relatives out of the city, for they had a commission to destroy the place. The wickedness of the city cried out before the face of the Lord for judgment. Lot believed the message; but he could not convince his sons-in-law. They thought Lot was jesting!

Third, the angels led Lot's family out of Sodom (19:15-16). This was necessary because Lot did not heed the urgent appeals of the angels early in the morning to hasten out of the city. He lingered. Because the Lord had determined to be merciful to Lot, the angels grabbed the hands of all four souls and brought them out of Sodom.

Fourth, the angels gave Lot directions regarding a place of safety (19:17-24). He was to escape to the mountains. In his flight, he was not to look back toward the city. Lot apparently thought that he would not be able to make it to the mountains before the judgment fell. He pled with the angels to allow him to take refuge in the nearby town of Bela. Surely God could spare this small town! The patience of the angels with Lot seems unbounded. The small town would be spared. Again, however, the angels urge haste. Nothing could be done to Sodom until Lot was safe. From this incident the town of Bela received the name Zoar, "small."

Finally, the angels destroyed the cities of the plain (19:24-29). The destruction was supernatural. "Yahweh rained fire and brimstone on Sodom and Gomorrah." Actually four towns in the plain south of the

149

Dead Sea were destroyed at this time (Dt 29:23). The area became a barren waste where nothing grew. Topographical changes resulting from the overthrow of these cities brought the waters of the Dead Sea down over that region which once was very fertile.

The destruction of the cities was a miracle, but God used physical elements near at hand to effect it. The plain contained deposits of asphalt (Gn 14:10). This substance could have easily developed enormous pressures of flammable gasses beneath the crust of the earth. An earthquake probably triggered an explosion which propelled heavenward huge quantities of sulfur, which also abounds in the region. The mass of gas and sulfur could have been ignited by lightning thus creating the rain of fire and brimstone (sulfur). Such, at least, is the explanation of Aalders.[1]

The Apostle Peter saw in the Sodom narrative both warning and encouragement. The ashes of that place were an eternal warning to those who lived ungodly lives. The rescue of Lot, on the other hand, was an illustration to the godly of how the Lord can deliver his own out of temptation (2 Pet 2:4-9).

C. What Lot Lost in Sodom (Gn 19:30-38).

Though Lot was a righteous man, he paid dearly for his choice to live in Sodom. First, he lost his wealth. All that he had worked so hard to accumulate over the years went up in smoke. He learned too late how transitory earthly riches are.

Lot also lost his wife. She must have been behind the others as they fled the city. Perhaps she was not making a determined effort to leave. Her heart was still in Sodom! In disobedience to the instructions of the angels, she longingly looked back to the city. Overcome by the sulfur fumes, she collapsed and died. Before her body had time to decay she became salt-encrusted — a pillar of salt (19:26). The text does not necessitate the view that she instantaneously was converted into a salt pillar. In any case, Jesus directed his disciples to remember Lot's wife (Luke 17:32). Christians who are tempted to look back to the world from which they were delivered should remember her opportunity, her stupidity, and her destruction.

Lot lost his children. On the basis of 19:12, some think Lot had sons who died in Sodom. His two sons-in-law, those who were betrothed to his daughters, laughed his warning to scorn. They died in the overthrow of the city. Some think Lot had at least two married daughters as well as his two virgin daughters. If so, they too perished in Sodom. Certainly he lost his two single daughters for they committed a loathsome sin not long after leaving Sodom.

Fearing that Zoar too would be destroyed, Lot and his two daughters chose to live in a cave in the mountains. The daughters feared that in that isolated area they would be deprived of male companionship and thus die childless. The girls contrived a plan to get their father drunk, lie with him, and raise up seed by him. They convinced themselves that the terrible deed which they conceived also would be in the best interests of their father. The plan worked. Lot was so intoxicated that he did not know when the girls lay down and when they arose. Both became pregnant. Lot sinned by allowing his daughters to get him drunk. How utterly guilt-stricken he must have been to discover his daughters were with child. The girls had been removed from Sodom, but apparently Sodom had not been removed from the girls — or their father.

A footnote to this sordid narrative relates that the sons born to this incestuous union were Moab and Ben-Ammi, ancestors of the Moabites and Ammonites who figure so prominently in later biblical history.

ENDNOTES

1. G. Ch. Aalders, *Genesis,* Bible Student's Commentary (Grand Rapids: Zondervan, 1981), II:19.

CHAPTER THIRTEEN

Testing and Triumph
Genesis 20:1-22:19

AIM: To demonstrate that the testing of the believer does not end when God's promise is received.

THEME: Times of testing and triumph.

Twenty-five years had passed since Abraham heard the call of God in Haran for the second time. His faith in the divine promises had been tested again and again. The testing continued and even reached its climax during the next twenty years. Yet in each instance Abraham's faith triumphed. Genesis 20–22 contains five pictures of a believer in times of testing and triumph.

ACTING IN A DISGRACEFUL WAY
Genesis 20:1-18

Genesis 20 presents many problems to the interpreter. Abraham's actions here are inexplicable in view of the divine announcement that the child of promise would be born within the year. Furthermore, at age ninety, pregnant, and "worn out," to use her own words, Sarah was still physically attractive to a pagan king it seems. For these reasons some have proposed that this chapter is not in chronological order.[1] Without question chronological dislocation can be demonstrated in the patriarchal narratives. Here, however, there does not appear to be sufficient grounds for transposing this episode to an earlier phase of Abraham's life. In five thought movements the narrative unfolds.

A. Indiscretion by Abraham (Gn 20:1-2).

Abraham renewed his journeys, this time traveling into the Negev. He camped between Kadesh on the southern edge of the Negev and Shur on the border of Egypt. The territory was known as Gerar. Some authorities place Gerar much further north near Gaza, but this interpretation would necessitate two moves by Abraham in a very short period of time. Abraham had remained some twenty years at Mamre, and no hint is given as to why he now moved. Aalders speculates that it was because of an influx of Hittites into the area of Hebron (cf. Gn 23).[2]

In Gerar Abraham repeated an old sin. He identified Sarah as his sister (cf. Gn 12:13). Whitelaw observes that "a sin once committed is not difficult to repeat, especially if its legitimate consequences, as in the case of Abraham and Sarah, have been mercifully averted. One is apt to fancy that a like immunity will attend its repetition."[3] The lie was unjustified and it was worthless. "Abimelech sent and took Sarah." As it turned out, the lie was also unnecessary for Abimelech was a man with high moral standards, higher in fact than Abraham himself. In the previous chapter Lot offered his daughters to the men of Sodom. In the present chapter under far less dangerous circumstances Abraham in effect offered his wife to a pagan king. God would have the reader know that his choice of Abraham had nothing to do with merit!

The problem of Abimelech's desire for a pregnant, ninety-year-old woman must be honestly faced. Some have suggested that Sarah had been rejuvenated in order to have children. Others have suggested that the marriage had nothing to do with physical attraction. Abimelech, so they say, was seeking a marriage alliance with the clan of Abraham.

B. Intervention by God (Gn 20:3-7).

God dealt with Abraham here better than he deserved. Divine grace intervened and rescued both Abimelech and Abraham from a potentially disastrous situation. Five aspects of grace can be seen in these verses.

1. Revealing grace. God came to Abimelech in a dream warning him that he had taken another man's wife into his harem. Abimelech pled innocent of any intention to commit adultery.

2. Restraining grace. God had prevented Abimelech from having a sexual relationship with Sarah and thus sinning against God. That the act of adultery had not actually been consummated was certainly not due to Abraham's actions!

3. Protecting grace. The purity of the promised seed was protected by the restraint placed on Abimelech.

4. Directing grace. Abimelech was told to restore Abraham's wife immediately. Abimelech still could be forgiven of the sin he innocently committed through the intercessory prayer of the prophet Abraham. If he disobeyed this divine directive, he and all his family would die.

5. Chastening grace. The Lord had brought the curse of infertility on the house of Abimelech because he had taken Sarah. Taking another's spouse is so serious a sin that it must be punished even if done in ignorance.

The Bible does not whitewash its characters. In no way is Abraham exonerated for what he did. Not one word of defense is offered on his behalf. God's intervention must be seen, not as his approval of what was done, but as his determination to fulfill the covenant promise in spite of the moral lapses of his servant.

C. Confrontation with Abraham (Gn 20:8-13).

Abimelech was eager to comply with the directive of God. Early the next morning he assembled his servants and briefed them concerning what had happened. They were afraid when they heard that their master had committed this offense against God.

Abimelech next called Abraham to the assembly and interrogated him. His probing questions were designed to rebuke Abraham publicly. Abimelech was being most charitable in his words when he said: "You have done deeds to me that ought not to be done!" In the mind of the king there had to be some logical explanation, some grand scheme behind such a dastardly deception.

Abraham gave three explanations of his conduct: (1) He thought his life was in danger in Gerar because of Sarah. Pagan kings took the women they wanted even if it meant killing a husband. Where the fear of God is absent there is no respect for the rights of others. Abraham never dreamed that these pagans would be God-fearing men. (2) Sarah was in fact his half sister. The two shared a common father. Therefore Abraham told a half-truth. (3) Claiming a brother-sister relationship was a strategy going back to the days when God called the patriarch from Ur of Chaldees. The scheme was Abraham's. (At least give Abraham credit. He did not try to blame the whole idea on his wife!) Apparently the sibling relationship was more universally respected than the marital relationship in this period.

D. Vindication of Sarah (Gn 20:14-16).

Abimelech restored Sarah to Abraham as the Lord directed. He then made three other gestures to demonstrate his contrition over the incident: (1) He gave Abraham a gift of sheep, oxen, male and female servants. (2) He invited Abraham to dwell in the land of Gerar anywhere he pleased. (3) He gave an additional gift of a thousand pieces of silver to Sarah's *brother*. Abimelech spoke sarcastically. This was to be Sarah's vindication. People would be reluctant to ridicule Sarah when they observed how richly she had been blessed.

E. Intercession by Abraham (Gn 20:17-18).

In Genesis 20 Abraham appears again in the role of an intercessor (cf. Gn 18). In spite of his sin, Abraham still had his standing with God. He was a prophet (20:7). God was better to Abraham than he deserved, for he was made the medium of bestowing blessing on Abimelech. God answered the prayer of Abraham and healed the infertility of the king's house. How ironic that Abraham's prayers opened the wombs of Philistine women, but for twenty-five years his own wife had not been able to conceive.

REJOICING IN A GIFT FROM GOD
Genesis 21:1-8

While in Gerar the Lord *visited* Sarah, i.e., intervened in her life. She conceived and bore a son at the appointed time. The promise which had been made one year earlier (17:15-21; 18:10-14) was now fulfilled.

In obedience to the command of 17:19 Abraham named the child Isaac ("laughter"). The name recalled Abraham's joyous laugh (17:17) and Sarah's mocking laugh (18:12) at the announcement of his birth. The name also commemorated Sarah's joy at the birth of the child, and the joy of all who would hear the report of his birth. On the eighth day the child was circumcised according to the previous commandment of the Lord. Isaac was now officially a child of the covenant.

Eastern women nurse a child until about age three. The weaning of the child was an occasion of great celebration. So Abraham made a feast on the day Isaac was weaned. The joy of the occasion quickly faded, however, when a family problem became evident.

STRUGGLING WITH FAMILY PROBLEMS
Genesis 21:9-21

The problem was Ishmael. He was continually mocking (*mestacheq*) Isaac. This word is never used of harmless playing. Perhaps Ishmael made fun of the promises that God had made in respect to Isaac. Paul used the word *persecuted* (*dioko*) to describe what was taking place (Gal 4:29). The Hebrew also indicates repetitive action. Ishmael was seventeen years old at the time of Isaac's weaning.

When Sarah observed the actions of Ishmael, she demanded that her husband drive out the handmaid and her son. More than motherly prejudice is involved here. Sarah recognized better than her husband the difference between the child of promise and the child of the flesh. The inheritance must be Isaac's exclusively. Both the teenager who scoffed at God's promises, and his mother, must be removed from the camp (21:9-10).

157

Sarah's demand may seem harsh, but the Apostle Paul put his stamp of approval upon it (Gal 4:30). Because he loved Ishmael so much, Abraham was grieved with the demand of his wife. What Sarah asked was not only personally painful, it was illegal under the law codes of that day. A special revelation was required to convince Abraham that he should go beyond the law and drive out Hagar. The patriarch was to listen to his wife. This direction was accompanied by a word of promise concerning the two sons. In Isaac Abraham's seed was to be called; yet because he was Abraham's seed, God would also make a great nation of Ishmael (21:11-13).

The divine directive was implemented with great tenderness the next morning. Abraham gently placed provisions upon the shoulder of Hagar. He delivered into her care the seventeen-year-old Ishmael and sent the two of them away (21:14).

Apparently bewildered by what had happened, Hagar wandered about in the wilderness of Beersheba north of the region of Gerar. She did not head toward her native Egypt as she had done when she fled from Sarah. When the water was exhausted, both mother and son were faint unto death. She being the stronger of the two, helped her son to the most comfortable spot she could find under a shrub. She walked a distance from him so she would not be forced to watch his dying gasp. Unable to do anything more for herself or for her son, she wept tears of desperation (21:15-16).

God was nearer than Hagar realized. He heard the voice of the lad. The angel of God who earlier had appeared to Hagar (16:7) directed her to return to the lad, take him by the hand, and help him to his feet. The angel then renewed the promise he had made to her seventeen years earlier, namely, God would make of Ishmael a great nation. Hagar's eyes were then opened to see a well of water. Wells in the wilderness usually were covered over to prevent evaporation. She filled her water skin and gave the boy a drink (21:17-19).

God exercised providential care over Ishmael. He grew to maturity in the wilderness where he became a skilled archer. The Wilderness of Paran where he settled lay between the Gulf of Aqaba and the Gulf of Suez to the south of Kadesh. Eventually his mother took for Ishmael an Egyptian wife (21:20-21).

ENJOYING ABUNDANT BLESSING
Genesis 21:22-33

Abimelech the ruler of Gerar observed the blessing enjoyed by Abraham. He rightly concluded that God was with the patriarch in all that he did. Abimelech wanted a covenant with Abraham which would guarantee friendship between the two peoples forever. Up to this time Abraham had been a nomadic visitor in the region of Gerar. Now Abimelech recognized him as a ruler of equal station (21:22-23).

Abraham was willing to make such a covenant, but first an obstacle needed to be removed. Abimelech's servants had seized a well of water from Abraham. Abimelech pled ignorance, and Abraham seemed satisfied. Apparently Abimelech immediately returned the well to Abraham (21:24-26).

Abraham provided sheep and oxen to be slain to *cut* the covenant in the manner illustrated in Genesis 15. Since the ratification ceremony took place on his territory, Abraham was obligated to provide the necessary animals. He also gave to the king a special gift of seven ewe lambs. These lambs apparently were given so as to guarantee Abraham's sole right to the well which had been in dispute. As a result of this new arrangement with Abimelech, Abraham was able to sojourn many days in the land of the Philistines (21:27-30).

Abraham named that spot Beersheba ("well of the oath or seven"). The earlier use of this place name (Gn 21:14) was by way of anticipation of this narrative. At this point, for the first time, the region of Gerar is identified as *the land of the Philistines*. While the main force of Philistines would not invade the region until about 1200 BC, a sizable enclave of this people seems to have settled in the southern coastal plain at a very early age (Gn 26; Ex 13:17).

Abraham planted a tamarisk tree at Beersheba as a memorial to the covenant with Abimelech. There he also "called upon the name of Yahweh," i.e., he engaged in public worship. A new name, *'el 'olam*, the everlasting God, characterized this worship. Thus did Abraham seek the Lord's blessing on the new relationship with Abimelech (21:31-34).

The covenant with Abimelech paved the way for Abraham to return to the land of the Philistines. Since Beersheba was located in the northern part of Abimelech's domain, this would not have been a long move. There Abraham dwelt many days.

FACING THE SUPREME TEST
Genesis 22:1-19

Genesis 22 portrays the climax of faith in the life of Abraham. The chapter can be treated under the themes of trial and triumph.

A. Abraham's Trial (Gn 22:1-10).

A number of years are passed over in silence in the Abraham narrative. According to Josephus, Isaac was twenty-five when God tested Abraham with respect to his son. Another Jewish tradition says Isaac was thirty-seven.

Satan tempts men to bring out the worst in them; God tests them to help bring out the best. The most severe tests come from the Lord; yet the greatest blessings accompany them. In Genesis 18–19 Abraham tried to get God to reconsider. He asked questions and demanded answers. Here in Genesis 22 the patriarch quietly followed divine directions.

Abraham was told to take his beloved Isaac to the land of Moriah and offer him as a burnt offering. Exact location of the land of Moriah is not known. Most likely this Moriah was not the Mt. Moriah which was one of the mountains of Jerusalem. A three-day journey from the region of Beersheba would put Abraham somewhere in the region of Hebron (22:1-2).

Abraham responded without hesitation to the unexplained and unexpected command of his God. Early in the morning he hastily split some wood. Scarcity of wood in Canaan made this preparation necessary. He then set out with two servants and his son for Moriah. The length of the journey would guarantee that Abraham was not making any spur of the moment decision (22:3).

On the third day the mountain was in sight. The servants were left behind as Abraham announced for the first time the purpose of his trip. He and Isaac would go to Moriah to worship. Then, said he, *we will return to you*. Abraham was expressing his confidence that somehow Isaac would survive this experience (22:4-5). The writer of

Hebrews asserts that Abraham believed that God could raise Isaac from the dead (Heb 11:19).

The wood was laid on Isaac's back. This is an indication that Isaac was no longer a small child. Abraham carried the container of hot coals and the knife. When Isaac inquired about the sacrificial lamb, Abraham responded: "God will provide for himself the lamb." The Hebrew literally reads, "God sees before him the lamb for the sacrifice." At the designated spot Abraham built an altar. He arranged the wood. He bound Isaac and laid him on the wood. He raised his knife to slay his son. So determined was Abraham to carry out the divine directive, that Isaac was as good as dead (22:6-10).

B. Abraham's Triumph (Gn 22:11-19).

At that moment the angel of the Lord spoke from heaven to announce that the test was over. "Now I know that you fear God, seeing you have not withheld your only son from me." God did not desire the death of Isaac, but the heart of his father. "Now I know" is anthropomorphic language which is intended to underscore Abraham's triumph in his test (22:11-12).

Abraham then noticed a ram caught in a nearby thicket which he hastened to offer as a joyous burnt offering before the Lord. As he did so, he gave a commemorative name to the spot: *yahweh yir'eh* ("Yahweh will provide"). Abraham realized that in the ram God was providing a substitute for his son. This incident was foundational for the Mosaic and later Christian teaching of substitutionary atonement. A proverb arose which commemorated the Moriah test. Some disagreement exists as to how the proverb should be translated. Some render it, "On the mountain of the Lord it will be provided." Aalders argues for an active rendering, "On the mount the Lord provides." In either case the meaning is captured by Aalders:[4] When God's people reach the summit of their faith, the Lord will always provide (22:13-14).

The episode on the mount concluded with a repetition of the covenant promises. Some new elements were included in this statement of the Promise. God here swore by himself that he would bless Abraham. God swears oaths by himself because there is no one above him upon whom he can call to witness the oath. God promised to multiply Abraham's descendants, not only as the stars of the heaven, but

161

MAP 6
JOURNEYS OF ABRAHAM
GENESIS 20-22

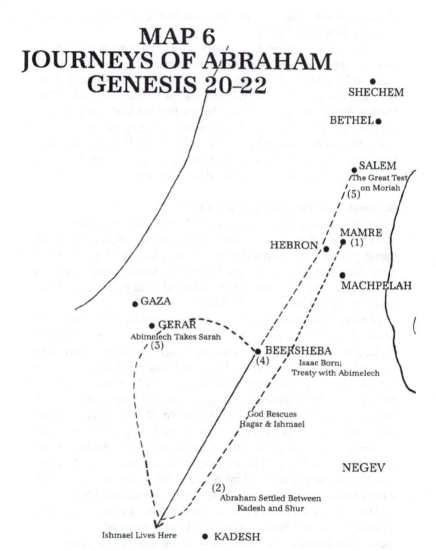

SHECHEM

BETHEL

SALEM
The Great Test on Moriah
(5)

MAMRE
(1)

HEBRON

MACHPELAH

GAZA

GERAR
Abimelech Takes Sarah
(3)

BEERSHEBA
(4)
Isaac Born;
Treaty with Abimelech

God Rescues
Hagar & Ishmael

NEGEV

(2)
Abraham Settled Between
Kadesh and Shur

Ishmael Lives Here   KADESH

WILDERNESS OF PARAN

also as the sand of the seashore. His posterity would possess "the gate of their enemies," i.e., be victorious over their enemies. This is probably a reference to the conquest of the Promised Land (Gn 15:7). Because Abraham obeyed God, all nations of the earth would be blessed through him. The dramatic test on Moriah concluded, Abraham returned to his home in Beersheba (22:15-19).

Ultimately Genesis 22 reveals more about God than Abraham. The climax comes in verse 14 with the giving of the name *yahweh yir'eh*. This name draws attention to God, not Abraham. The emphasis in not on Abraham's *performance* but on God's *provision*.

ENDNOTES

1. The Roman Catholic Heinisch and the Dutch Protestant Ridderbos are cited by Aalders, *Genesis*, II:25-27.

2. Ibid., II:27,28.

3. Whitelaw, "Genesis," p. 263.

4. Aalders, *Genesis*, II:50.

CHAPTER FOURTEEN

Patriarchal Milestones
Genesis 22:20-25:26

AIM: To demonstrate how faith functions in the varied circumstances of life.

THEME: The hills and valleys of life.

After the incident on Moriah, Abraham received welcome news of his relatives who lived in Aram Naharaim (NIV) or Mesopotamia (NASB), the region of the conjunction of the Euphrates and Habor rivers. Nahor, Abraham's brother, had traveled as far as Haran when the family left Ur of Chaldees. Like his brother, Nahor had a wife (Milcah) and a concubine (Reumah). Like Jacob he had twelve sons, eight by his wife and four by his concubine. Abraham was most glad to hear that Nahor's son Bethuel had a daughter named Rebekah. No doubt from the moment that news arrived, Abraham began to think in terms of trying to secure a wife for Isaac from among those relatives (22:20-24).

Almost twenty years of Abraham's life are passed over in silence following the Moriah experience. Abraham was 137 when Sarah died, and 140 when he sought a wife for Isaac. Isaac was forty when he married, and sixty when his twin sons were born. The deaths of Abraham and Ishmael are not recorded in chronological order (25:7-18). Abraham died at age 175 when the twins Jacob and Esau were fifteen. Ishmael's death occurred forty-eight years later when Isaac was 123 and his twin sons sixty-three.

The life of the believer has its hills and valleys, its joys and its sorrows. Through both kinds of experiences the patriarchs walked by faith. In 23:1–25:26 three important funerals, two marriages and a special birth are narrated.

BURYING A FAITHFUL WIFE
Genesis 23:1-20

Though Sarah had her moments of weakness, the Scriptures regard her as a model wife (1 Pet 3:1-6). She was 127 when she died. Abraham was living at Kiriath-arba (Hebron) when his wife died. Thus it would appear that he had moved northward again after his lengthy sojourn in the land of the Philistines. The narrator emphasizes especially the fact that she died *in the land of Canaan.*

Abraham mourned the loss of his wife, but he sorrowed not as others who have no hope (1 Thess 4:13). Apparently much earlier he had purchased a plot near Shechem (Acts 7:16); but he had either lost possession of that spot, or he considered the distance too far to travel to bury his wife. Early interment was imperative in that climate. Burial often took place on the day of death.

Abraham entered into negotiations with the sons of Heth to purchase a suitable burial spot for Sarah. Earlier the Amorites had occupied this region (20:1). Apparently the Hittites had now filtered into the area.

Abraham approached the sons of Heth with all due courtesy. He acknowledged that he was only a foreigner and a sojourner in that region and consequently had no ownership rights. Acquiring a burial plot was a favor and not a right. The sons of Heth, however, regarded Abraham as a "mighty prince," richly blessed by God. They would not withhold from him even the choicest of the burial places (23:4-6).

Abraham now arose in acknowledgment of the graciousness of his Hittite neighbors. He made it clear that he wished to buy a plot rather than accept the offer to use a Hittite burial ground. Abraham was interested in the cave called Machpelah which was situated on the end of Ephron's field. Selling that cave would not break up Ephron's holdings. The patriarch was willing to pay the full price of that cave to Ephron. Following eastern protocol, Abraham requested the group to approach Ephron on his behalf (23:7-9).

Ephron spoke at this point. He did not wish to sell just the cave; he wanted Abraham to take both the cave and the field of which it was a part. Three times Ephron used the word *give*. Westerners are likely to think that Ephron intended literally to give the real estate to Abraham. In Oriental business transactions, however, *give* simply means *sell* (23:10-11).

Hittite law codes may explain why Ephron was insisting on the sale of the entire field. If Abraham owned the whole field he would have to assume the Hittite tax (called *ilku*) obligations.

Ephron set the price of the land at four hundred shekels of silver. Judging by the real estate contracts recovered from Mesopotamia, this was an exorbitant price. Ephron probably expected Abraham to haggle in typical Oriental fashion. Abraham, however, did not quibble over the price. No amount was too great for a proper burial place for his beloved wife. He weighed out publicly the shekels in the currency of the merchants which would have been accepted by all peoples of the region. The property including the cave, the field and the trees on the property were deeded to Abraham. Hittite deeds frequently contained allusions to the trees on the property (23:14-18).

In the cave of the field of Machpelah near Mamre Abraham buried Sarah (23:19-20). Though he had spent much of his life outside the Promised Land, he was finally able to bury his wife in Canaan. This the text twice emphasizes (23:2,19). Even in his hour of grief, however, his faith was being tested. Sixty years earlier he had received the promise that the land of Canaan would be his. Yet he did not own a plot of ground suitable to bury a loved one. Abraham was forced to purchase from a pagan, land that in reality already belonged to him. What is more, he had to obligate himself to pay taxes to a foreign monarch. This perhaps explains the detailed description of the negotiations with Ephron.

SELECTING A COMMITTED MATE
Genesis 24:1-67

The longest chapter in Genesis focuses on a most important matter, the selection of a proper wife. The material here can be summarized in four words: concern, commitment, choice and comfort.

A. Abraham's Concern (Gn 24:1-9).

Three years after the death of Sarah Abraham became especially concerned about securing a wife for his son Isaac. Though he had been blessed in all things, yet this burden weighed heavy on his heart. So Abraham summoned his oldest servant, probably Eliezer, and asked him to put his hand under the patriarch's thigh. This apparently was the common practice in a most solemn oath (cf. Gn 47:29). Eliezer was to swear by the God of heaven and the God of earth.

The oath had a twofold thrust. On the negative side, the servant was never to take a wife for Isaac from among the Canaanites. Abraham knew full well the gross idolatry and immoral worship which characterized Canaanite religious life. On the positive side, he was to go to the kindred of Abraham to secure the wife. Worship of the true God among these kinsmen, while not entirely pure, was far superior to Canaanite religion (24:1-4).

Before swearing the oath, the servant wisely inquired as to the implications. If no woman could be found who would accompany him back to Canaan, should he then take Isaac back with him to Paddan Aram? Abraham's answer was an emphatic "No." God had given Canaan to his descendants. For his son to forsake the land even for a wife would be inappropriate. If the woman would not return to Canaan, then the servant was released from his oath (24:5-6). The implication here is that it is better to remain single than to marry the wrong woman (or man).

All talk of what might happen if the marital prospect refused to return with the servant was academic. Abraham believed that God would send his angel before the servant. That fact would crown his mission with success. Here then is the logic of faith. God had made promises, and he would keep those promises. Isaac belonged to God, for Abraham had laid him on the altar long before. Therefore, God

168

would supply the need now as surely as he supplied the ram on Moriah (24:7-8).

Having explored the stipulations of the proposed oath, and having heard Abraham's optimistic forecast about the mission, the servant put his hand under Abraham's thigh and swore the oath (24:9).

B. The Servant's Commitment (Gn 24:10-49).

The servant lost no time in departing on his mission. Ten camels were loaded with supplies and gifts for the bride-to-be. These animals would also serve to carry the new bride and her retinue back to the land of Canaan. The servant's destination was the city of Nahor (Haran), a city of Aram Naharaim, Aram of the two rivers. This region is also known as Mesopotamia (24:10).

The servant arrived at the city well in the evening when the women normally would go out to draw water. There he made his camels kneel. The servant bowed his head and prayed for success. He would ask the maidens for a drink. If a maiden also offered to water the camels, he would know that the Lord had led him to the right woman (24:11-14).

Before he was finished with his prayer, Rebekah came to the well to draw water. This virgin was very beautiful. As she ascended the steps from the well, Abraham's servant approached her asking for a drink of water. The girl cheerfully complied. When he had finished drinking, she offered to water his camels also. This would be no easy task. Camels are notorious for the amounts of water they consume after a long desert journey. The servant remained silent during this period, wondering in his mind whether or not this was the girl who had been chosen by the Lord (24:15-21).

When the camels were through drinking, the servant gave to the maiden a valuable nose ring and two bracelets. He then inquired about her family, and asked if lodging might be available at her house. Rebekah was not hesitant to extend to the stranger an invitation to lodge at her home. The servant bowed his head and thanked the Lord for leading him so quickly to the family of Abraham (24:22-27).

Rebekah ran to tell her family what had transpired at the well. When her brother Laban saw the valuable jewelry which the maiden had received, he was anxious to meet the stranger. He ran to the well where

Abraham's servant was waiting for an invitation from the head of the house (24:28-30). Laban the brother rather than Bethuel the father appears to have been acting as family head. Why this was so is not clear.

Laban formally extended an invitation to the servant. He invoked the name of Yahweh when he addressed the stranger. This was further confirmation that the servant had come to the right place. At the house, the camels were first unloaded and tended. The feet of the travelers were washed, and food was placed before them. Abraham's servant would not eat, however, until he had related the purpose of his visit (24:31-33).

The servant began by emphasizing the wealth of Abraham and the fact that Isaac was to inherit all this wealth. He then related the circumstances which brought him to Haran, how he had prayed at the well, and how Rebekah had fulfilled precisely the requirements which had been stipulated in his prayer. The servant then called upon his hosts to give some indication of how they were responding to this request so that he might determine his next move (24:34-49).

C. Rebekah's Choice (Gn 24:50-61).

Laban and Bethuel were impressed by the sequence of events which the servant narrated. They were convinced that God himself had selected Rebekah for Isaac's wife. They felt that they had no right to interfere in any way. They gave approval for the servant to take Rebekah with him back to Canaan (24:50-51).

The servant was overjoyed with this immediate and devout response. He thanked the Lord for what had happened, and he gave rich gifts to Rebekah and to her mother and brother. Then the servant and those with him ate and went to bed (24:52-54).

In the morning the servant bade leave of his hosts to return to Canaan. The mother and brother thought this departure to be too hasty. They wanted to give Rebekah a proper send-off. Ten days would be required for them to prepare her for such a journey. The servant, however, persisted in his request for an immediate departure. Finally the mother and brother decided to let Rebekah herself decide. She was willing to leave immediately (24:54-58).

Having secured her assent, the father, mother and brother pronounced a blessing upon Rebekah. They expressed the hope that she

170

would have a multitude of descendants and that those descendants would be powerful enough to possess the gate of their enemies. Rebekah's old faithful nurse who had tended her since infancy was sent on the journey along with several maids. So the small camel caravan departed (24:59-61).

D. Isaac's Comfort (Gn 24:62-67).

In contemplation of his forthcoming marriage, Isaac had visited the sacred site of Beer-lahai-roi where the angel of the Lord had once appeared. He appears to have separated himself from the camp of Abraham for he was living in the Negev at this time. Isaac went out to the field one evening "to meditate" *(lasuach)*, a word used only here in the Old Testament. He lifted up his eyes and saw the caravan approaching. How his heart must have pounded with excitement as he contemplated meeting for the first time his bride.

Rebekah noticed a man coming across the field to meet the camels. When she learned that this was Isaac, she got down from her camel, and covered her face with a veil. She was demonstrating modesty and respect for her future husband. When the servant rehearsed the details of his journey, Isaac knew that Rebekah was his divinely chosen mate.

Isaac honored his bride by assigning her to the tent of his beloved mother. After arrangements could be made, Isaac married Rebekah. Even though there had been no lengthy courtship considered so essential in Western culture, Isaac loved Rebekah. She supplied that womanly charm and companionship which brought Isaac comfort in the loneliness he experienced after the death of his mother Sarah.

TAKING A SECOND WIFE
Genesis 25:1-6

Abraham was 137 when Sarah died (23:1), yet following her death he married Keturah. Since Moses does not always arrange the material in Genesis in chronological order, some have suggested that the marriage to Keturah took place long before Sarah was dead. They think that it would be impossible for one who at age one hundred was thought to be too old to have a son, to father six sons after age 137.

Perhaps, however, the rejuvenation which enabled Abraham to father Isaac was not transitory.

The list of Keturah's sons and peoples descended from them is given in 25:2-4 for two reasons. First, several of these peoples are mentioned frequently in later biblical history. Then too, this list demonstrates the fulfillment of the promise that Abraham would become the father of many nations.

Isaac was Abraham's heir. He inherited all his father's wealth. Before he died, however, Abraham bestowed generous gifts upon the sons of his *concubines*. The plural certainly includes Keturah and Hagar, and possibly other unnamed concubines. These sons of Abraham occupied the desert to the east of Canaan.

Chart No. 13

ABRAHAM'S SONS AND GRANDSONS		
BY HAGAR	**BY SARAH**	**BY KETURAH**
Ishmael I Nebaioth Kedar Abdeel Mibsam Mishma Dumah Masaa Hadad Tema Jetur Naphish Kademah	Isaac I Jacob Esau	Zimran Jokshan— Medan Midian— Ishbak Shuah Ephah Epher Hanoch Abida Eldaah Sheba Dedan
Gn 25:13-51	The Covenant Line	Gn 25:2-4
"You shall be the father of many nations" (Gn 17:4).		

TWO OTHER FUNERALS
Genesis 25:7-18

Abraham lived to be 175 years old. He is described as "an old man and satisfied with life." At his death he was "gathered to his people," i.e., he rejoined his loved ones who had gone on before. Isaac and Ishmael, reunited after almost seventy years, buried their beloved father in the cave of Machpelah where Sarah had been interred thirty-eight years earlier.

After the death of Abraham, God blessed Isaac. He was still residing near Beer-lahai-roi at this time. Isaac was seventy-five when his father died, and 123 when his brother Ishmael died. Therefore, forty-eight years of Isaac's life are passed over in silence in Genesis 25.

Like his father, Ishmael was "gathered to his people." The narrator mentions three points in which the prophecies regarding Ishmael found fulfillment: (1) Twelve tribal rulers came from Ishmael (cf. 17:20). (2) His descendants lived in the desert area from Havilah (location unknown) to Shur near the border of Egypt (cf. 16:12). (3) The Ishmaelites lived in hostility toward all their brethren (cf. 16:12).

THE BIRTH OF TWINS
Genesis 25:19-26

Isaac was forty when he married and sixty when his twin sons were born. For twenty years his faith, like that of his father before him, was tested by the barrenness of his wife. Rebekah here is said to have been from Paddan Aram. In 24:10 that area was called Aram Naharaim. Probably Paddan Aram was a district within the larger kingdom of Aram Naharaim (25:19-20).

Isaac knew that covenant promises demanded that he and Rebekah have children. He therefore went to his knees on behalf of his barren wife. God answered that prayer and Rebekah became pregnant (25:21).

Rebekah experienced a difficult pregnancy. Twins jostled within her. This was a foretaste of future difficulties between the brothers. Rebekah regarded her pain as an ominous sign. She went to inquire of the Lord, probably at the home of some prophet. Her petition was, according to Leupold, "For what am I destined?" Others would have her utter a cry of despair, "Wherefore do I live?"

Through the prophetic intermediary the Lord gave Rebekah a fourfold response: (1) Rebekah would bear twins who would be ancestors of two great nations. (2) Two separate and distinct people would

173

emerge from these twins. (3) One of these peoples would exceed the other in strength. (4) The older son would serve the younger. The Hebrew here is ambiguous and could just as well be rendered, "The small shall serve the great." This might account for the differences in the way Rebekah and Isaac regarded the two boys.

Even in birth a sharp distinction between the twins was noted. The whole body of the firstborn was covered with hair, giving him a reddish brown color. The technical name for this condition is hypertrichosis. The firstborn was named Esau, a name which some scholars relate to the term "hairy." The second son came out with his hand grasping his brother's heel. He appeared to be trying to restrain his brother. This child was named Jacob, which some have interpreted to mean "heel grabber" (25:24-26). The spotlight falls on Jacob in ten of the next eleven chapters. Only in Genesis 26 is he absent from the narrative.

CHAPTER FIFTEEN

Trouble in the Family
Genesis 25:27-28:22

AIM: To demonstrate how sinful man stands in need of the trans-forming power of God.

THEME: Coping with trouble.

In Genesis 25–36 the focus shifts from Abraham to his grandson Jacob with a few side glimpses of Isaac. The lengthy Jacob cycle is framed by the genealogies of two individuals who are not a part of the chosen line — Ishmael (25:12-18) and Esau (36:1-43). Hamilton sees a basic theme in this cycle: (1) the need for transformation (25:19–28:9), (2) preparation for transformation (28:10–32:21), (3) transformation (32:22-32), and (4) the results of the transformation (33:1–36:40).[1]

Some seventy-seven years are covered in this chapter, from Isaac's sixtieth to his 137th year. Isaac's life lies intertwined with the biographies of his father and his sons. Not much is known about this somewhat colorless patriarch. From what little is recorded about Isaac, this much is clear: in every stage of his life he had to deal with unhappiness.

TROUBLESOME RIVALRY
Genesis 25:27-34

The twins were very different personalities. Esau became a skilled hunter and outdoorsman. Jacob was a quiet lad who stayed around the tents with the women. Isaac especially loved Esau, while Jacob was mother's darling. No doubt much dissension resulted from the obvious favoritism of these parents.

The twins were very different spiritually as well as physically. Esau was immoral and godless (Heb 12:16), while Jacob possessed some spiritual perception. Jacob coveted the birthright which belonged to Esau. The birthright involved (1) headship of the family, (2) family priesthood, (3) a double portion of wealth, and (4) designation as covenant channel.

While Jacob properly valued the birthright, he was unscrupulous in the way he secured it for himself. Esau came in from the field very hungry and requested that Jacob give him some of the stew he was preparing. Jacob demanded first that his brother sell him the birthright. Regarding his immediate need as more important than the privileges which might be his in the future, Esau swore an oath and sold his birthright for a mess of pottage. Isaac may have lost the wealth he had inherited from his father. If so, the birthright would have been materially worthless. Esau despised it for this reason.

Because he craved the reddish color stew, Esau received the nickname Edom which sounds very much like the Hebrew word for "red." His descendants settled the land of Edom and were known as Edomites.

TROUBLESOME TRAVELS
Genesis 26:1-35

Genesis 26 records the only incidents in which Isaac is the chief character. The action can be outlined geographically.

A. Isaac in Gerar (Gn 26:1-16).

A severe famine forced Isaac to move from his long-time home at Beer-lahai-roi. He made his way southward. His intended destination

176

was Egypt, but the Lord warned him not to leave the area. This was the first recorded revelation to Isaac. The land promise, the seed promise and the blessing promise were reiterated. These promises belonged to Isaac because of the faithful obedience of Abraham. So Isaac remained in the Philistine territory of Gerar (26:1-6). The Abimelech who ruled this region no doubt was a son or grandson of the Abimelech with whom Abraham made a covenant many years earlier (cf. 21:22-31).

In Gerar Isaac repeated the sin of his father. When the men of that place asked him about his wife, he told them that Rebekah was his sister. This sin grew out of fear that he would be killed on account of his beautiful wife. Abimelech discovered the ruse when he spied Isaac caressing Rebekah. Isaac was summoned and roundly rebuked by the king. Abimelech was horrified to think that one of the men might have taken sexual liberties with a married woman thus bringing great guilt upon his city. Orders were issued protecting Isaac and Rebekah from any molestation (26:7-11).

In spite of his sin, God blessed Isaac in Gerar. The patriarch ventured into agriculture with spectacular results. That year he reaped a hundredfold, and that in an area not noted for its fertility. Isaac became wealthy. He had so many flocks, herds and servants that the Philistines envied him. They even tried to make things difficult for this stranger by plugging up his wells. Finally the king urged Isaac to move out of his land (26:12-15).

B. Isaac in the Valley (Gn 26:17-22).

Isaac moved from Gerar, but not far. He settled in a nearby valley. There he reopened the wells dug a century earlier by his father, and gave them the same names his father had given them. Ownership of a new well he dug was disputed by the local herdsmen. This well Isaac named Esek ("dispute"), and moved on to dig another well. Again a dispute arose. Isaac named the well Sitnah ("opposition") and moved on to dig a third well. No dispute arose over this well probably because Isaac had moved beyond the region which the herdsmen could claim as their territory. Isaac named it Rehoboth ("room"). He interpreted the absence of contention here as a good sign that now he could flourish in the valley of Gerar (26:17-22).

C. Isaac in Beersheba (Gn 26:23-35).

Eventually Isaac moved back into the land of Canaan and settled at Beersheba. That very night the Lord appeared to him for the second time. The Promise was renewed that for the sake of Abraham, God would wondrously increase the descendants of Isaac. To commemorate this theophany, Isaac built an altar there and "called upon the name of the Lord," i.e., instituted public worship.

Abimelech had second thoughts about sending Isaac out of his land. He and two chief officers came to Beersheba to negotiate a treaty with Isaac similar to the earlier treaty with Abraham (21:22-31). The king did not wish to be on bad terms with one so obviously blessed of God. Isaac indicated his interest in discussing a formal treaty with these neighbors by ordering a feast to be prepared. Early in the morning the two men swore an oath to one another, and Abimelech departed in peace. When men get in the right relationship with the Lord, their relationship with their neighbors often improves (26:26-31).

On the very day Isaac entered the covenant with Abimelech, his servants reported finding water in the well they were digging. Isaac called the well Shibah ("oath" or "seven") thus reemphasizing the name given to that spot long before by Abraham (21:31). Beersheba ("well of the oath") remains the name of that spot even to this day (26:32-33).

When Isaac was one hundred, Esau, who was then forty, married two Hittite women. This is further confirmation of the lack of spiritual values in Esau. These pagan daughters-in-law made life miserable for Isaac and Rebekah (26:34-35).

TROUBLESOME TRICKERY
Genesis 27:1-40

Jacob's exploitation of his brother was bad enough; but in Genesis 27 Jacob stoops even lower by deliberately deceiving his senile and physically incapacitated father. In the preceding chapter Isaac was the deceiver; now he is the one deceived. Genesis 27 has four focal points: a declining father, a doubting mother, a deceitful son, and a despairing brother.

178

A. A Declining Father (Gn 27:1-4).

Isaac was 137 when he fell ill and thought he was going to die. (As it turned out he lived to be 180). Jacob and Esau were seventy-seven at this time. The old, blind father called his beloved son Esau and asked him to kill some wild game and prepare a meal of it. He was anxious to pronounce the patriarchal blessing, a blend of benediction and prediction, upon his beloved son. The festive meal would express the great dignity of the occasion. Had he willfully forgotten the prediction that the older would serve the younger (25:23)? Or did he regard those words as sufficiently ambiguous to allow for his discretion in the matter? In any case, the patriarchal blessing was a very solemn and holy act, performed "in the presence of the Lord" (27:7).

B. A Doubting Mother (Gn 27:5-17).

Rebekah had been told that Jacob would receive God's blessing; yet she schemed and plotted to make sure he got it. Her plan was to prepare a meal of goat meat which might resemble the wild game Isaac craved. Two kids would make possible a larger platter of meat such as might come from venison. Rebekah never entertained the thought of going to God in prayer as she had done many years earlier during her troublesome pregnancy (25:22). She was confident that through this strategy Isaac would be deceived into pronouncing the blessing upon Jacob (27:5-10).

Jacob was not so confident. He had no reservations about the deception itself; but he was desperately afraid of being caught in a lie. A mere touch by the old man would expose the hoax because Esau was a hairy man and Jacob had smooth skin. Isaac might pronounce a curse rather than a blessing if he suspected trickery. Rebekah persisted, however, by indicating that she would accept any curse which might result from the ruse (27:11-13).

Jacob must have known that God had chosen him as the recipient of the promise, yet he listened to his mother. He brought the goats to her, and she prepared the meat. She dressed Jacob in Esau's clothing, and covered his exposed smooth skin with the goat skins. Rebekah had lost all confidence in the promise of God or else because of that promise she thought she was justified in helping things along (27:14-17).

179

C. A Deceitful Son (Gn 27:18-29).

Jacob told three lies to his aged father. He said, (1) I am Esau, (2) I have done as you told me, and (3) eat some of my venison. Isaac was amazed that it was possible for his son to kill and prepare the game so quickly. Jacob explained this, however, as due to the special blessing of Yahweh. This is one of the most blatant abuses of God's name in Scripture (27:18-20).

Jacob was not able to disguise his voice, and Isaac was suspicious. He asked for his son to come near so he could verify by the sense of touch the identity of this one who came seeking his blessing. The goat skins attached to Jacob's arms were not quite convincing. The voice sounded too much like that of Jacob! So Isaac inquired one last time, "Are you Esau?" Again Jacob lied! (27:21-24).

Isaac ordered the meal to be served before the blessing was granted. After the meal the patriarch asked his son to kiss him. This would be the final test. If this son smelled of the wild, he undoubtedly was Esau. Thanks to his mother's foresight, Jacob passed the test and so his father blessed him (27:25-27).

The blessing is in poetic verse. It begins with an allusion to the wonderful smell of outdoors. Then Isaac petitioned God to grant Esau the dew of heaven so essential to agricultural success in that arid climate. This dew would insure that Esau would have the richness of the earth, i.e., grain and new wine (27:27-28).

The blessing takes on political overtones in verse 29. (1) Nations and peoples would bow to Jacob. (2) He would be lord over his brothers. (3) Those who cursed him would be cursed, and those who blessed him would be blessed. With the exception of a few brief periods in the parallel history of the two peoples, the Israelites were able to completely dominate the Edomites.

The blessing is couched in the language of petition, but patriarchal blessings were in reality predictions. Is Isaac attempting to annul God's original verdict about the relationship of the twins? Had Rebekah never informed him of the word of God concerning the boys? Or was the language so ambiguous as to allow Isaac to bestow this blessing on the son he thought was Esau?

D. A Despairing Brother (Gn 27:30-40).

Esau returned just as Isaac finished blessing Jacob. He prepared the venison and took it to his father with the request that Isaac pronounce the blessing upon him. Isaac trembled when he realized that God had overruled his attempt to give Esau the blessing. By the law of that day, a deathbed testament could not be revoked (27:30-33).

When Esau heard his father's words, he burst out in a loud cry. The New Testament states that he sought the blessing with tears (Heb 12:17). With bitterness he recalled the earlier incident when Jacob had taken from him the birthright. He continued to ask his father for at least one blessing.

Under inspiration of the Holy Spirit Isaac began to utter poetic predictions regarding Esau. He and his descendants would (1) dwell in the barren wastes away from the dew of heaven, (2) live by the sword, and (3) serve Jacob. The only note of consolation in this prediction is that there would be times when the descendants of Esau would throw off the yoke of Jacob (27:38-40). Perhaps for the first time Isaac saw clearly that Esau did not measure up to the ideals of the patriarchs.

TROUBLESOME ANIMOSITY
Genesis 27:41–28:9

Despair was replaced by malice in the heart of Esau. He planned to murder his brother as soon as Isaac died. While Esau did not share the faith of his father, he nonetheless loved and respected him. He did not wish to do anything which might hasten Isaac's death (27:41).

Esau did not keep his intentions to himself. Somehow Rebekah heard of his murderous plan. She summoned Jacob at once and strongly urged him to take refuge with her brother in Haran until Esau's anger subsided. Rebekah obviously anticipated a short separation. She would send for him the moment she was convinced that he was no longer in danger from his brother. Rebekah worried that if Esau killed Jacob, he would forfeit his own life under the principle of blood revenge. Then she would lose both of her sons in one day (27:42-45).

Rebekah did not mention Esau's plot to Isaac. He probably would not have believed her anyway. She chose rather to raise another matter

181

of concern, namely, where would Jacob get a wife? She knew full well
that Isaac loathed the Hittite women Esau had married. If Jacob married
a Hittite woman, life would be absolutely unbearable. Rebekah wanted
Isaac to send Jacob away, for then Esau would not interfere (27:46).

Isaac summoned Jacob and commanded him not to marry a
Canaanite. He was to depart immediately for Paddan Aram and take a
wife from among the relatives of his mother. Isaac had another blessing for Jacob, and this one he pronounced "in faith" (Heb 11:20). He
said nothing of the deceit used to secure the first blessing, doubtless
because he himself was not entirely without fault in that incident.

The second blessing is similar in some respects to the first. El
Shaddai (God Almighty) would make Jacob a community of peoples.
The ultimate fulfillment of this prediction awaited the Messianic age
when Gentiles became part of the new Israel of God. Jacob would
inherit all the blessings of Abraham, including the land in which he
presently resided as an alien. With these prophetic words of blessing,
Isaac sent Jacob on his way (28:1-5).

For the most part, Esau appears in these narratives as a spiritual
dimwit. When he heard of the marriage commands his father had
issued to Jacob, he realized how displeasing his Hittite wives were to
his parents. Esau took a third wife, this time from among the Ishmaelites. The text does not indicate whether or not she was a believer. Esau probably did not care about that. He aimed to please his
father by marrying someone who was connected, albeit loosely, with
the covenant family (28:6-9).

Isaac's long life was filled with unhappiness. His faith, like that of
his father, was tested again and again. A barren wife and the disappointment with his older son tested the progeny promise. A famine in
the land and the conflict over water with the herdsmen of Gerar tested the land and blessing promises.

A COMFORTING REVELATION
Genesis 28:10-22

One episode en route to Paddan Aram was of singular importance
in the life of Jacob. In a place which he would later call Bethel, Jacob
(1) saw a vision, (2) heard a voice, and (3) made a vow.

182

A. A Vision (Gn 28:10-12).

Jacob had traveled for some three days when he settled down for the night near Luz. The sun had set, and already the gates of the city had been closed for the night. Jacob made himself as comfortable as possible using a stone for his pillow. That night he had a dream. He saw a ladder or stairway reaching from earth to heaven. Angels were ascending and descending that ladder, and standing at the top of it was Yahweh himself. This was the first of seven recorded revelations to Jacob.

The purpose of the dream was to strengthen Jacob's faith. The significance of it was as follows: the angels ascending and descending represent the petitions of Jacob being carried heavenward, and the answers of God being carried earthward. Between heaven and earth there was uninterrupted communication mediated by angels.

B. A Voice (Gn 28:13-15).

A voice spoke to Jacob in the dream. The speaker identified himself as the God of Abraham and Isaac. What had been promised to Jacob before his birth (25:23) and had been bestowed on him in two blessings pronounced by his father (27:27-29; 28:3-4) now was confirmed by God himself. He would have numerous descendants, though at the time he was seventy-seven and unmarried. God would give him Canaan, though at the moment he was a fugitive fleeing the land. Through Jacob all nations of the earth would be blessed, though within the past few weeks he had been anything but a blessing to his father and brother. God was challenging Jacob to believe the incredible!

To these covenant promises, God added a personal promise appropriate to Jacob's immediate situation. He would (1) be with Jacob, (2) watch over him, (3) bring him back to Canaan, and (4) never forsake him until he had fulfilled his promises to him.

C. A Vow (Gn 28:16-22).

Jacob's initial reaction to the dream was that of fear. The infinitely holy Yahweh had appeared to him, a sinful mortal. Jacob regarded the spot as "the house of God," i.e., a place where he had been brought into the very presence of God. He also called the spot "the gate of heaven," i.e., a place where he could meet God again (28:16-17).

183

MAP 7
JOURNEYS OF ISAAC
GENESIS 25-28

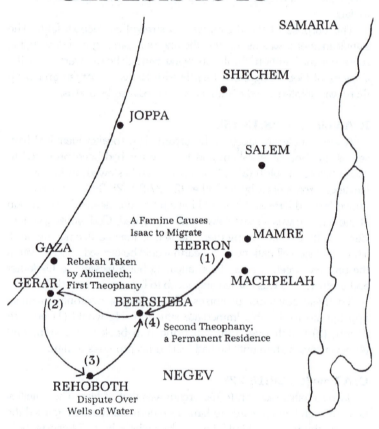

Early the next morning Jacob took his pillow and made a pillar out of it. He poured oil upon that stone. The text gives no hint that the stone was meant to be an object of worship, and the pouring of the oil an act of worship. This was Jacob's way of dedicating himself and that spot to the Lord. The stone was but a memorial. Jacob gave the spot the name "Bethel," the house of God (28:18-19). Eventually that name came to be applied to the nearby city of Luz.

Jacob made a vow at Bethel. This is the first recorded vow in the Bible. The vow is usually understood as Jacob's effort to bargain with God: If God will do certain things for me, then he will be my God and I will give him the tenth. Another view is that Jacob is expressing amazement for all God had done for him: If after all I have done, God (1) will be with me, (2) keep me on this journey, (3) give me food, (4) cause me to return, and (5) will be my God, then this stone shall be his house, and I will give him a tenth of all he gives me (28:20-22). Tithing was a practice attributed first to Abraham (14:20).

ENDNOTES

1. Victor Hamilton, *Handbook on the Pentateuch* (Grand Rapids: Baker, 1982), p. 119.

CHAPTER SIXTEEN

Jacob the Exile
Genesis 29-31

AIM: To demonstrate how God prepares a sinner for a transforming experience.

THEME: The discipline of a sinner.

The age of Isaac when he blessed his sons is not stated. His age, however, can be computed from the chronological data given here and there in the text. Isaac was 137 at that time, and the twins were seventy-seven. Jacob was absent from Canaan for twenty years. For him those were years of discipline. God was preparing Jacob for spiritual leadership in the chosen family. Part of that discipline was in forcing Jacob to see himself as he really was, a worldly, deceitful schemer. Laban, his employer, was a mirror image of Jacob with respect to character, and for twenty years the patriarch had to look at that disgusting image.

WORKING FOR LABAN
Genesis 29:1-30

From the spiritual mountaintop of Bethel Jacob descended into the practical everyday life at Haran. He spent twenty years with his kinsman Laban. During these years he reaped the sad consequences of his sins. At the same time he was disciplined for future service.

A. Jacob's Introduction to Laban (Gn 29:1-14).

Continuing his journey, Jacob came eventually into "the land of the eastern peoples," the Syrian desert east of Damascus. As he approached Haran, he saw a well with three flocks of sheep nearby. This was probably not the same well at Haran mentioned in 24:11. The shepherds apparently had an agreement to wait each day until all the flocks were gathered before they removed the large stone which covered the mouth of the well. There Jacob interrogated the shepherds about his uncle Laban. As chance would have it, Laban's daughter Rachel was approaching the well that very moment with her father's flock (29:1-6).

Jacob urged the shepherds to water their flocks and return to pasture. He obviously wanted some time alone with Rachel at the well. The shepherds were bound by their agreement to wait until all the flocks had gathered. Meanwhile Rachel arrived with her sheep. Jacob, not bound by any local agreement, removed the large stone from the well and watered his uncle's sheep. That he could single-handedly remove that large stone may suggest that Jacob was above average in physical strength.

After he watered the flock Jacob identified himself and gave Rachel the kiss of kinsmen. He wept for joy over his good fortune of having met his cousin for the first time. Rachel ran to tell her father the good news (29:9-12).

When Laban heard that his nephew had arrived, he hurried out to welcome him. Laban embraced Jacob, kissed him and escorted him to his home. Here Jacob rehearsed the events which brought him to Haran. After hearing Jacob report "all these things," Laban was convinced that this stranger was his "flesh and bone," i.e., his blood relative (29:13-14).

B. Jacob's Marriage Contract with Laban (Gn 29:15-30).

After Jacob had been his guest for a month, Laban suggested that a more formal working arrangement be negotiated. He asked Jacob to name his wages. Jacob had already fallen in love with Rachel, the younger of Laban's two daughters. The older daughter Leah is described as having "weak eyes," i.e., unattractive eyes. This was considered a major defect for a young lady in the East. Rachel, on the other hand, is described as lovely in form and beautiful. Since he had no wealth to offer as the *mohar* customarily given to the father of the bride, Jacob offered to work seven years for Rachel. Laban thought this proposal was excellent. Better that Rachel should marry in the family than be given to some unbeliever (29:15-19).

The seven years of servitude seemed only a few days to Jacob because of the love that he had for Rachel. When the time was up, Jacob reminded Laban of their agreement. Laban ordered that a marriage feast be prepared. Jacob was to receive his bride on the first night of the week-long celebration. Laban, however, conceived a scheme by which he could keep the service of Jacob for another seven years. He substituted Leah for Rachel. Because of the thick veils worn by the bride, and the poor light in the tent, Jacob did not discover the deception until morning. Laban's plot could not have been carried out without the willing cooperation of Leah (29:20-24).

Whitelaw points out the irony in this matter:

> Though indefensible on the part of Laban, the substitution of Leah for Rachel was a deserved punishment of Jacob. Having wronged Esau his brother, he is in turn wronged by 'a brother' — Laban. Having substituted the younger (himself) for the older (Esau), he is recompensed by having the older put into the place of the younger. As Isaac knew not when he blessed Jacob, so Jacob knows not when he marries Leah. As Jacob acted at the instigation of his mother, Leah yields to the suggestion of her father.[1]

Laban explained his action as being necessitated by the custom of the area, namely, always to give the older daughter in marriage first. At the completion of the week-long marriage celebration he would give to him Rachel also, but only if Jacob would agree to work another seven years. After he had consummated the marriage sexually, Jacob could not morally and legally return Leah to her father (29:26-27).

Laban kept his word and gave the younger daughter to his nephew. The marriage was an unhappy experience for Leah, for Jacob loved Rachel more than her sister. Considering the circumstances of his marriages, this is not surprising. Though he had been deceived, Jacob honored his word and worked another seven years for Laban (29:28-30).

BUILDING A FAMILY
Genesis 29:31–30:24

God took pity on Leah because she was not loved. He opened her womb, while Rachel remained barren. Leah named her firstborn Reuben, which in Hebrew sounds very much like "he has seen my misery." She anticipated, albeit wrongly, that presenting her husband with a male heir would make him love her.

A comment is necessary regarding the names given by Leah and Rachel to their sons. What is true of the name Reuben is true also of the other names given in this chapter. Sound similarity rather than strict etymology determined the name selection. The comments which follow regarding the meanings of the names must be interpreted in the light of this general principle.

Leah regarded the birth of her second son as a divine response to her misery of being unloved. She named this son Simeon, "one who hears." When her third son was born, again Leah thought that Jacob would be attached to her. She named this son Levi, "attached." By the time her fourth son was born, Leah apparently had faced reality. Producing offspring would not change Jacob's attitude toward her. So this time Leah simply praised the Lord for the successful delivery. She named this son Judah, "praise." Then she ceased bearing (29:33-35). Two of the most important Old Testament institutions have their origins in an unwanted marriage. From Judah came the institution of kingship, and from Levi the priesthood.

Rachel was jealous of her sister. Irrationally, she blamed her infertility on Jacob: "Give me children or I will die!" Jacob became angry with his wife. Conception was God's business. How could she blame him for her barrenness? (30:1-2).

Rachel resorted to the scheme which Sarah had employed to cope with her barrenness. She offered Jacob her handmaid Bilhah. She could

190

bear children "for me," literally, "on my knees." Apparently Rachel wanted to participate in the process of the birth of the children to her slave girl. Rachel hoped that through Bilhah she could "build a family." This is the same expression used earlier by Sarah (cf. Gn 16:2).

Jacob acquiesced, and the plan succeeded. In rapid succession two sons were born to Bilhah. Rachel assumed the role of mother and gave them appropriate names. The first was named Dan, "he has vindicated," because she viewed this birth as divine vindication of her scheme. Bilhah's second son was named Naphtali, "my struggle." Rachel thought that through her scheme she had won in her personal struggle with Leah (30:3-8).

Leah was determined to stay ahead of her younger sister in producing children for her husband. She imitated her sister and gave her handmaid Zilpah to Jacob. In rapid succession Zilpah bore two sons: Gad, "good fortune" and Asher, "happy" (30:9-13).

The terrible dissension in Jacob's family is illustrated in the episode of the mandrakes. During wheat harvest (May/June) little Reuben innocently brought to his mother a present from the fields, a bouquet of mandrake plants. The yellow berries of mandrakes, sometimes called Love Apples, were believed to be an aphrodisiac and an aid to fertility. Rachel asked her sister to give her some of the mandrakes, but Leah was in no mood to share with her rival. Rachel had to surrender her conjugal rights that night to secure the mandrakes (30:14-15). That these sisters would barter for the sexual favors of their husband is not a very uplifting revelation. God would have all self-righteous Israelites to realize the context of jealousy and superstitution out of which the twelve tribes emerged.

Leah met Jacob when he returned from the fields. She announced to him that she had secured conjugal rights that night by the sale of her mandrakes. Not wishing to contribute further to the jealousy of the women, Jacob spent that night with Leah (30:16).

As if to rebuke the use of magic potions, God opened Leah's womb and continued to seal Rachel's. Leah bore two more sons to Jacob: Issachar, "reward," and Zebulun, "honor." Having produced six sons for her husband, Leah fully expected that Jacob would treat her with proper honor. Some time later Leah gave birth to Dinah, the most prominent of Jacob's daughters (30:17-21).

When magic failed, Rachel cried out to God for children. Finally, God remembered Rachel and she bore her first son. She praised God for removing her disgrace. A childless woman was viewed with disdain in those lands. Rachel named her son Joseph, "may he add." His name was a prayer that she might bear yet another son (30:22-24).

ACCUMULATING WEALTH
Genesis 30:25-43

After he had completed his fourteen years of obligatory service to Laban, Jacob requested leave to return to his homeland. Laban had been blessed during the years of Jacob's service, and through *divination* (some would translate *deduction*) he had learned that the blessing had come through his son-in-law. Laban urged Jacob to stay as an employee, and suggested that he could set his own wages. Jacob realized how valuable he was to Laban, but he refused to take credit to himself. He attributed Laban's blessing to the Lord. While he had spent his time building up the livestock of Laban, however, Jacob still had nothing for his own household, and that concerned him (30:25-30).

Jacob did not ask fixed wages. He suggested that the speckled, spotted or dark colored sheep and goats be culled from Laban's livestock and given to him. Sheep in that region were usually white, and goats were usually solid dark color. Realizing this, Laban quickly agreed to the terms of his son-in-law thinking that Jacob had made a terrible mistake.

Still Laban did not trust Jacob. He therefore culled from the flock the marked animals, and removed them three days' journey from his own livestock. Laban did not want to take any chances that they would mingle with his stock and contaminate them (30:31-36).

Jacob knew of a plan by which he could get solid-colored animals to produce spotted or striped offspring. He did three things. First, he removed bark from branches in such a way as to produce a striped effect. These branches were then placed in the water troughs when the flocks were in mating season. Seeing the striped branches triggered some presently unknown mechanism which caused the animals to produce striped or spotted young. Aalders claims that this is a well-known technique among stock breeders and has been used with varying results.[2] Others regard this as pure superstitution on Jacob's part.[3]

Second, Jacob separated spotted lambs from their mothers as soon as possible. The solid-colored animals mixed and soon mated with the spotted ones which increased the likelihood that more spotted ones would be born. Third, Jacob used the above techniques only with the strong and robust animals, thus insuring that he would have quality as well as quantity in his flocks.

Thus did Jacob build his wealth. He came to possess large flocks and many servants as well as other livestock. He observed the terms of his agreement with Laban to the letter; but his methods were morally questionable. Jacob the schemer was up to his old tricks again.

LEAVING HARAN
Genesis 31:1-21

After working twenty years in Paddan Aram Jacob was ready to return to Canaan. He was now ninety-seven. He had eleven sons, at least one daughter, two wives, two concubines, and large flocks and herds.

Several factors rekindled Jacob's desire to leave Paddan Aram. Laban's sons were complaining to their father that Jacob had gained his wealth at his expense. Under the nagging influence of his sons, Laban's attitude toward Jacob was changing. Tensions were mounting. At that time God appeared to Jacob in a dream. God showed Jacob that his great wealth was not produced by his own cleverness, but by divine favor. God reminded Jacob of Bethel and directed him to return to Canaan (31:1-3, 10-13).

Jacob's first hurdle was to convince his wives that he should leave Haran. He called them to the field where he could converse with them privately. Jacob described his dissatisfaction with the way he was being treated by his employer. Laban had changed his wages ten times. He told his wives about his dream (31:4-13).

Jacob received a sympathetic response from his wives. Their father treated them as if they were foreigners. Laban had squandered the wealth which, by the sweat of his brow, Jacob had paid for these wives. Most of what their father owned was already theirs.

193

They encouraged their husband to do whatever God commanded (31:14-16).

Laban had gone a distance to shear sheep when Jacob left Haran. Rachel took advantage of her father's absence to steal his teraphim, i.e., household gods. Possession of these small statues legally guaranteed an inheritance.[4] Jacob put his wives and children on camels, while he drove the flock in front. Uppermost in his mind was the impending reunion with his beloved father. Crossing over the Euphrates River, the small company made its way hastily toward the hill country of Gilead (31:17-21).

ENTERING A COVENANT
Genesis 31:22-55

On the third day Laban learned that Jacob had fled. After a chase of seven days, he caught up with his son-in-law in the hill country of Gilead. His intentions obviously were hostile. God appeared to Laban in a dream warning him not to try to prevent Jacob from continuing his journey by any means good or bad (31:22-24).

Laban launched into a pompous harangue against Jacob. He accused him of kidnapping his daughters, of depriving him of saying a proper farewell to his loved ones, and of stealing his teraphim (31:25-30).

Jacob was firm in his response to Laban. In ancient law a son-in-law surrendered all if he left the house of his father-in-law. Jacob had been afraid that Laban would take his wives from him. He invited Laban to search his camp for the teraphim. Anyone found with them would be executed. Jacob did not know that Rachel had stolen the gods (31:31-32).

Laban searched the camp. Rachel was able to conceal the teraphim in her camel's saddle. She sat on them and excused herself from rising on the grounds that she was in her period (31:33-35).

When Laban returned sheepishly from his empty search, Jacob gained confidence in speaking up to his father-in-law. He declared his innocence of any wrongdoing. Laban could not produce a single item that had been taken wrongfully. He had labored hard and suffered much in Laban's employment. Yet Laban had attempted to keep him poor by changing his wages ten times. Only because of the intervention of the God of Abraham, the Fear of Isaac, had Jacob been able to come through his experience in Haran with any possessions.

Laban maintained his haughty attitude. He regarded everything in Jacob's camp as his own, yet he would not press his ownership claims. His hands were tied by divine warning. He therefore proposed that he and Jacob enter into a covenant. A stone was erected as a pillar with other stones heaped up about it. This monument would mark the spot of the covenant. Laban gave the place an Aramaic name, Jegar Sahadutha ("witness heap"), while Jacob gave it a Hebrew name, Galeed, which meant the same thing.

The spot was also called Mizpah ("watchtower"). Laban invoked the Lord as a witness. Jacob was not to take additional wives nor attempt to return to Haran. Laban pledged that he would not go beyond that monument to harm Jacob. The God of Abraham, Nahor and their father would enforce this covenant by watching both parties to it. Laban did not trust Jacob, and vice versa (31:48-50).

Jacob agreed to the terms stipulated by Laban. He offered a sacrifice to seal the covenant, and prepared a meal to which all were invited. Early in the morning Laban bid his daughters and grandchildren farewell, and departed for Haran (31:51-55).

ENDNOTES

1. Whitelaw, "Genesis," p. 361.
2. Aalders, *Genesis*, II:124.
3. John Davis, *Paradise to Prison* (Grand Rapids: Baker, 1975), p. 249.
4. Cyrus Gordon, "Biblical Customs and the Nuzu Tablets," *The Biblical Archaeologist Reader,* ed. David N. Freedman and Edward F. Campbell (Garden City, NY: Doubleday, 1964), II:25f.

CHAPTER SEVENTEEN

Back to Bethel
Genesis 32-36

AIM: To demonstrate the necessity of a pilgrimage back to Bethel.

THEME: Submission the key to spiritual power.

At age ninety-seven Jacob left Haran to return to the land of Canaan. Genesis 31–36 covers about eleven years. During these years Jacob experienced a marvelous transformation which began at the river Jabbok and reached its climax in a return to Bethel (35:1-15). Jacob's return to the land of promise occurred in three stages. In each of these stages he faced grave difficulties.

DIFFICULT ENCOUNTERS
Genesis 32:1–33:17

Jacob had three difficult encounters as he continued his journey back to Canaan. He met (1) the angels of God, (2) the Lord himself, and (3) his brother Esau.

A. Encounter with Angels (Gn 32:1-23).

At the edge of the Promised Land Jacob was met by the angels of God. This encounter was intended to remind Jacob of God's care, and of Bethel. Jacob called the spot Mahanaim, "two camps," by which he referred to his own camp and the camp of the angels (32:1-2).

Encouraged by this encounter with the angels, Jacob sent a conciliatory message to his estranged brother. Esau was then living south of the Dead Sea in the land of Seir. Jacob hoped to find favor in Esau's sight by (1) his humble demeanor ("your servant") and (2) the fact that he was now a man of wealth. His messengers returned, however, with the news that Esau was coming to meet him with four hundred men. Jacob was terrified (32:3-6).

Expecting the worst, Jacob set about making preparations for the confrontation with his brother. He did four things: (1) He organized his people and livestock in two groups, thinking that if Esau attacked the one, the other could perhaps escape. (2) He prayed, thanking God for the great blessing he had already bestowed, reminding God of the promises he had given, and asking God to save him from his brother. (3) He organized a peace offering of sizable proportions. As Esau approached the camp of Jacob he would encounter one servant after another with gifts of sheep, goats, camels and other livestock. Jacob hoped that the cumulative effect of these peace offerings would cause Esau to receive him in peace. (4) That night Jacob helped his family ford the Jabbok. This stream was about thirty feet wide and hip deep. He felt that this night crossing was less dangerous than a possible attack by Esau during a daylight crossing (32:7-23).

B. Encounter with the Lord (Gn 32:24-32).

Jacob remained alone on the north bank of the river. He probably wanted privately to pour out his heart to the Lord. There in the darkness he experienced a theophany, an appearance of God in humanlike form. The *man* who met him there was none other than the angel of the Lord who appeared earlier to Hagar and to Abraham. Jacob might have thought at first that the stranger was Esau or one of his agents. Reconstructing what preliminaries might have taken place is difficult. That Jacob and the stranger became locked in a mighty struggle is clear. This contest went through three phases.

1. Through most of the night the two fought on equal terms. Without recourse to supernatural powers, the angel could not prevail over Jacob. Some hold that the contest was entirely spiritual. The angel was attempting to get Jacob to surrender his all to the Lord, attempting to humble him.

2. The angel then employed his supernatural strength. He touched Jacob on the socket of his hip and wrenched it out of joint. Though in great pain, still Jacob refused to give up the struggle. Now, however, he realized that this was no mere mortal with whom he struggled. Whether Jacob's affliction was permanent or only temporary is not indicated.

3. Toward daybreak the angel begged Jacob to let him go. For Jacob to see the face of this angel would be dangerous (cf. Ex 33:20). Jacob, however, would not release the opponent until he received a blessing. He may have feared that he had offended the angel by his stubborn resistance. He certainly realized now that the angel could, and probably should have crushed him. This was the first indication that a transformation was taking place in the soul of Jacob. He had outwitted and defeated Esau, Isaac and Laban. Now he had met his match. He was the victim.

Jacob turned to fervent prayer and tears (Hosea 12:4). The purpose of the angel had now been accomplished. Jacob was now begging for *spiritual* strength with which to face the dangers of the next day. Here was the second indication of transformation: an all-consuming hunger for God. Above all else Jacob wanted the blessing of God.

The angel asked Jacob to repeat his name. When Jacob did so, he was admitting his scheming, sinful nature. "Jacob" was *what* he was as well as *who* he was. This confession of unworthiness is the third indication of transformation.

The encounter with the angel of the Lord had four positive results for Jacob: (1) The angel gave Jacob ("the deceiver") a new name, Israel, "he who struggles with God." The name pointed to a new, spiritual character in Jacob. (2) He received a new blessing. When Jacob inquired about the name of his adversary, the angel refused an answer. His identity was obvious. He then blessed Jacob and brought the encounter to a close. (3) Jacob had a new testimony. He named the spot of this heavenly encounter Peniel, "face of God." He knew that he had come face to face with God on that long, lonely night. (4) He lived to see a new day. Jacob had seen God, but his life had been spared. That sunrise was very special to him. It signaled the beginning of his walk with the Lord.

Jacob received a physical reminder of his own weakness. He *limped* away from Peniel to face his brother. The narrator closes this strange account with the note that the Israelites would not eat the tendon attached to the socket of the hip. This custom commemorated the lameness which Jacob experienced as a result of his confrontation with the angel of the Lord.

C. Encounter with Esau (Gn 33:1-16).

Spotting Esau and his four hundred men coming in the distance, Jacob prepared his family. The concubines and their children were put in front, then Leah and her sons, and finally Rachel and Joseph. He planned to introduce his family to Esau in the order of their importance. Jacob himself was out in front of all his family. Here is a new courage which is further evidence of the transformation. As he approached his brother, he bowed seven times to the ground, a custom attested in the literature of the ancient world. Here is a new humility which points again to the change in Jacob (33:1-3).

Esau would have none of this exaggerated homage. He ran to Jacob, embraced and kissed him. The two brothers wept. Esau was surprised to see Jacob's family, and was anxious to meet them. One by one the concubines and wives with their children came and bowed down before Esau (33:4-7).

When the introductions were over, Esau asked about the several droves of livestock which he had met as he approached Jacob's camp. Jacob explained that these were gifts which he wished to give to his brother. The transformed Jacob possessed a new generosity. Esau would have none of that either. He had accumulated his own material wealth. He needed nothing which his brother was offering. Jacob insisted, however, because this amicable reunion deserved such celebration. Seeing Esau's face was like seeing the face of God! Finally Esau agreed to accept the gift (33:8-11).

Esau then offered to accompany Jacob on the remainder of his journey. Jacob, however, rejected this offer on the grounds that he had to move his children and livestock very slowly. Jacob urged Esau to go on ahead. He would join his brother in Seir later. Esau then offered to leave some of his men to assist in the journey. Jacob again declined, citing the favor of his brother as more than enough compensation for the generous gifts. So Esau departed to return to Seir. The text does not record Jacob's visit to Seir (33:12-20).

DIFFICULT EXPERIENCES
Genesis 33:17–35:29

Five places are associated with Jacob's return to Canaan. His experiences at these places can only be described as very difficult.

A. A Temporary Experience (Gn 33:17).

For a while — perhaps as much as nine years — Jacob stopped short of Canaan. Near the Jabbok he built for himself a place and constructed booths for his cattle. This spot he appropriately named Succoth, "shelters."

B. A Tragic Experience (Gn 33:18–34:31).

Eventually Jacob crossed the Jordan into Canaan and camped near Shechem. Jacob obviously intended to reside there for awhile because he purchased his camping ground for four hundred *kesitahs.* The value of this unit of money is unknown. He also set up an altar there and named it *'el 'elohe yisra'el,* "mighty is the God of Israel" (33:18-20).

At this point Dinah, Jacob's teenaged daughter, rebelled against her parents. She went out to visit the pagan women of the land. Unattached females in that day were considered fair game. Shechem, son of the Hivite ruler of the city, raped Dinah. Shechem fell desperately in love with his victim and "comforted her" with a marriage proposal. He then asked his father to make the marriage arrangements (34:1-4).

Jacob did nothing about the rape of Dinah until his sons came from the field. Somehow they learned of what had happened and hurried home. The sons were sad and angry at the disgraceful thing which had been done. Hamor, however, proposed that the family of

201

Jacob should intermarry with the local Hivites. This, he urged, would open up trading opportunities (34:5-10).

Shechem also spoke on his own behalf. He agreed to pay any bridal price which Jacob and his sons might name. The sons, however, acted deceitfully, protesting that they could not give their sister to an uncircumcised man. Only if all the men of Shechem submitted to circumcision could intermarriage between the two clans take place (34:11-17).

In a public meeting at the city gate Hamor and Shechem were able to convince the Hivite men to submit to circumcision. Intermingling with Jacob's clan would prove to their advantage, they argued. They could share Jacob's wealth (34:18-24).

Three days later while all the men of Shechem were in intense pain, Simeon and Levi attacked the city and killed every male. They took Dinah from Shechem's house. The other sons looted the city and confiscated everything of value including the women and children (34:25-29).

Jacob did nothing in the way of punishing Simeon and Levi other than deliver a mild rebuke. His real concern was not the sins of his sons, but the possibility that the Canaanites would unite against him. The sons defended their crimes by arguing that Shechem had treated their sister as a common whore (34:30-31).

C. A Transforming Experience (Gn 35:1-15).

God intervened at this point to direct Jacob to move his family to Bethel. He was to build an altar to the God who had appeared to him there so many years before. Jacob knew that he needed to make spiritual preparations before going back to that sacred spot. He urged his family to remove all foreign gods, purify themselves and symbolize the same by changing apparel. The family complied. Jacob buried all the pagan paraphernalia of his family under the oak at Shechem. God kept his word to bring Jacob safely back to Bethel, for his terror fell upon the Canaanites and they were afraid to attack Jacob (35:2-5).

At Bethel Jacob built an altar which he called 'el beth'el, "God of Bethel." The joy of returning safely to Bethel was marred, however, by the death of Deborah, Rebekah's nurse. She was buried under the oak there (35:6-8). Deborah may have come to live with Jacob's clan after the death of Rebekah.

Chart No. 14

LIFE OF JACOB *"THE SUPPLANTER AND SAINT"*			
IN **BEERSHEBA** Gn 25:19–28:9	IN **PADDAN ARAM** Gn 28:10–31:55	IN **CANAAN** Gn 32:1–45:28	IN **GOSHEN** Gn 46:1–49:33
With His Parents	With His In-laws	With His Sons	With His Grandsons
Birth to 77 (77 Yrs.)	Age 77-97 (20 Yrs.)	Age 97-130 (33 Yrs.)	Age 130-147 (17 Yrs.)
Antagonist: Esau	Antagonist: Laban	Antagonists: Sons	No Antagonism
Gains: Birthright & Blessing	Gains: Wives & Wealth	Loses: Wives & Children	Regains: Family
ACQUIRING BLESSING	**ACCUMULATING WEALTH**	**SUFFERING ADVERSITY**	**EXPERIENCING TRANQUILITY**

God appeared again to Jacob at Bethel. The purpose of this revelation was to confirm the promises made in the first Bethel appearance. *Renewal* is the key word in analyzing this revelation and the aftermath of it.

At Bethel God renewed Jacob's spiritual name, Israel. Earlier when he had received this name at Peniel, Jacob had been alone; now his family was with him. God renewed the Promise that a great company of nations and kings would come from Jacob. The Land Promise was renewed. Jacob renewed the stone monument there, pouring out upon it a libation (probably of wine) and oil as he had done years before. The patriarch also renewed the name of that place. He publicly named the spot Bethel, "the house of God" (35:10-15).

MAP 8
JOURNEYS OF JACOB
GENESIS 28-38

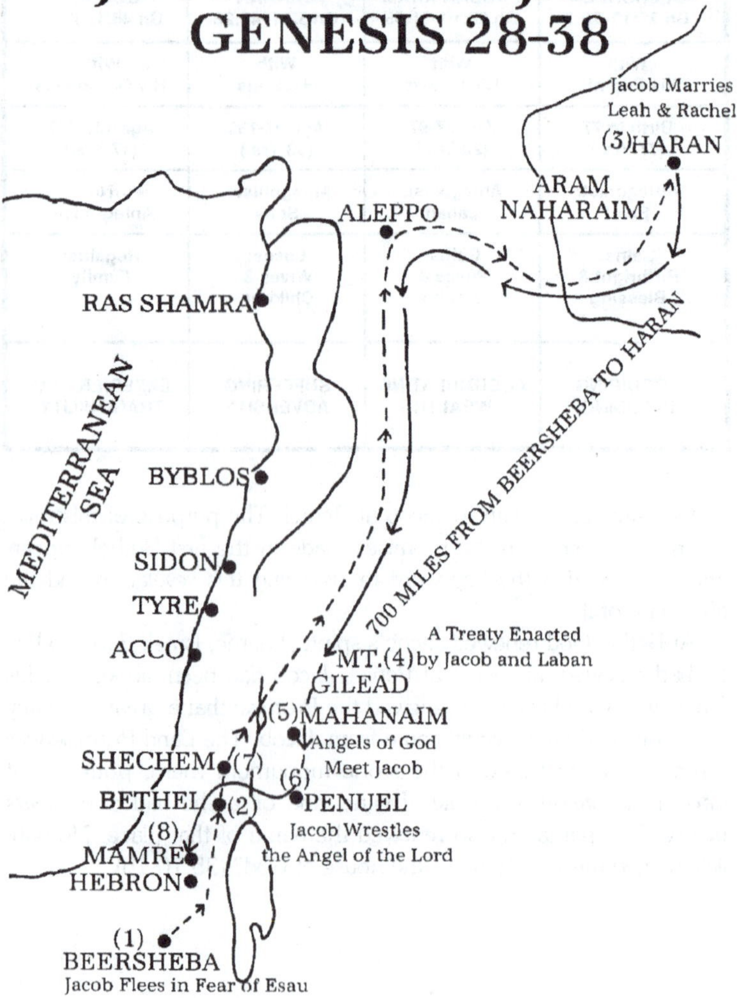

Jacob Marries
Leah & Rachel

(3)HARAN

ARAM
NAHARAIM

ALEPPO

RAS SHAMRA

700 MILES FROM BEERSHEBA TO HARAN

MEDITERRANEAN
SEA

BYBLOS

SIDON

TYRE

ACCO

A Treaty Enacted
MT.(4) by Jacob and Laban
GILEAD

(5)MAHANAIM
Angels of God
Meet Jacob

SHECHEM (7)
(6)
BETHEL (2) PENUEL
(8)   Jacob Wrestles
MAMRE   the Angel of the Lord
HEBRON

(1)
BEERSHEBA
Jacob Flees in Fear of Esau

D. Trying Experiences (Gn 35:16-22).

Jacob's clan moved from Bethel after a stay of unstated duration. Rachel was pregnant with her second child. Near Ephrath (later Bethlehem) Rachel experienced hard labor. With her dying gasp she named the male child Ben-oni, "son of my trouble." Because of his love for that child, Jacob renamed him Benjamin, "son of my right hand."

Jacob lost his beloved wife at Ephrath. Shortly thereafter he lost his son Reuben at Edar. While he was living in that region, Reuben went in and slept with his stepmother Bilhah. Israel, i.e, Jacob, heard of the incident, but exercised no immediate discipline in the matter. According to the Chronicler, however, "When he defiled his father's marriage bed, his rights as firstborn were given to the sons of Joseph; so he could not be listed in the genealogical record in accordance with his birthright" (1 Chr 5:1). The life of Reuben can be summed up in four greats: (1) great expectation (29:32), (2) great privileges (49:3), (3) great sin (35:22), and (4) great loss (1 Chr 5:1).

E. A Touching Experience (Gn 35:27-28).

Jacob eventually was reunited with his father who was then living at Mamre near Hebron. According to the chronological notices in the book, the two would have spent at least twelve years together. Isaac was 180 when he was gathered to his people. Jacob and Esau were 120 at the time. The two brothers joined in burying their father.

NOTE ON CHAPTER 36

Genesis 36 goes into great detail about the descendants of Esau through his three wives. Why such detail about one who was not part of the covenant line? The key seems to be in verse 31. Kings were promised to Jacob's line (35:11). At the time Moses wrote Genesis the descendants of Esau already had achieved this state of national development while Israel had not. The comparatively slow political development of Israel was a challenge to their national faith through the centuries. Also God had made promises to Esau (27:39), and this chapter confirms that God keeps his word!

CHAPTER EIGHTEEN

From the Pit to the Palace
Genesis 37:1-45:24

AIM: To demonstrate how God overrules the sinful designs of men.

THEME: God's providence.

Joseph was born when Jacob was ninety-one. Joseph was seventeen when he was sold into slavery in Egypt. Since Jacob was 120 when Isaac died, the selling of Joseph into Egypt took place before the death of Isaac. Therefore, the note about the death of Isaac in 35:27ff. is not in chronological order. Approximately twenty-two years are covered in this chapter, from Joseph's seventeenth to his thirty-ninth year.

Leupold has observed that divine providence shines forth here more brilliantly than anywhere else in sacred history.[1] In the life of Joseph this providence is seen at work in four situations.

A FAVORED SON
Genesis 37:1-36

Joseph was Jacob's favorite son because he was the son of his old age and the son of his beloved wife. Two main points are brought out respecting Joseph's home life: he was the object of his brothers' (1) envy, and (2) enmity.

A. The Object of His Brothers' Envy (Gn 37:1-11).

Even believers have family problems. The stupid actions of both Jacob and Joseph triggered the dangerous emotions of envy and jealousy in the other sons. Three reasons for the envy of the brothers are indicated. First, Jacob made for Joseph a special coat which was a constant reminder that he was the chosen one. The brothers so hated Joseph that they would not even talk to him. Joseph's tattling on his brothers also stirred bitterness toward him (37:1-4).

Joseph related two dreams to his brothers that made them hate him all the more. The first was set in the field. Joseph's sheaf of grain stood upright, while the sheaves of the brothers round about bowed down. In a second dream the sun, moon and eleven stars bowed down to Joseph. The brothers were infuriated over the implications of these dreams. Even Jacob questioned the second dream. Would his mother and father bow before him? Neither dream is represented in the text as being a revelation from God (37:5-11).

B. The Victim of His Brothers' Enmity (Gn 37:12-36).

Jacob dispatched Joseph to see about the well-being of his brothers. They were grazing the flocks near Shechem several miles north of Hebron. Not finding his brothers in the city, Joseph began to search the pasture lands. A man who found him there directed him further north to the area of Dothan (37:12-17).

As Joseph approached, the brothers recognized him and plotted to kill him. They would be rid of that dreamer once and for all. Reuben argued that they should not shed blood, just throw Joseph into a cistern and leave him. Reuben hoped to be able to go back and release Joseph at a later time (37:18-22).

Joseph was stripped of his special coat and thrown into an empty

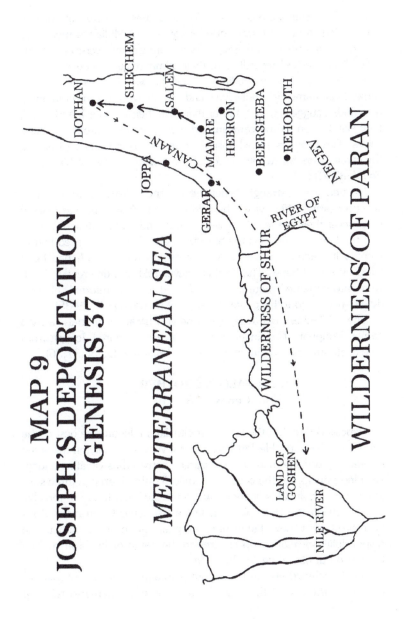

MAP 9
JOSEPH'S DEPORTATION
GENESIS 37

cistern. The brothers, oblivious to Joseph's cries for help, sat down to eat. During the meal they spotted a caravan of Midianite merchants making their way toward Egypt. Such caravaneers were apparently called "Ishmaelites" regardless of their ethnic origins. Judges 8:22-24 expressly identifies the Midianites and Ishmaelites as one and the same. Dual names for individuals and groups were common in antiquity. Judah suggested that, rather than slay their own flesh and blood, they sell Joseph to the caravan and thus gain some profit for themselves. The brothers pulled Joseph from the cistern and sold him to the caravaneers for twenty pieces of silver. Joseph was on his way to Egypt (37:23-28).

Reuben was distraught when he returned to the cistern to find Joseph missing. What would he tell his father? A scheme was devised to conceal their crime. They slew a goat and dipped Joseph's robe into the blood. They took the bloody robe to Jacob and asked him to identify it. Jacob jumped to the conclusion that Joseph had been killed by a wild beast. The brothers never told him differently. Jacob went into sustained mourning and refused to be comforted. He was determined to go to his grave in a state of mourning (37:29-35).

The Midianites sold Joseph to one of Pharaoh's officials, a man named Potiphar. The finger of providence had spared Joseph from sure death and placed him in a strategic position in Egypt (37:36).

A FALLEN BROTHER
Genesis 38:1-30

Genesis 38 depicts the lack of spirituality in Judah, the best of the rest of Jacob's sons. He *left* his brothers. Was the family on the verge of breaking up? He married a Canaanite woman thus violating a long-standing principle in the covenant family. To that marriage three sons were born. Er, Judah's firstborn, was so wicked that the Lord took his life. Following the principle of Levirate marriage, Onan married his dead brother's widow. He wanted the gratification of sex without the responsibility of rearing up children in the name of his brother. The Lord also put him to death (38:1-10).

Judah withheld his third son from marriage to the widow using as an excuse the age of the boy. Tamar devised a scheme to raise up seed for her dead husband. She removed her widow's garb, put a veil on her face, and stationed herself on the road to Timnah where her father-in-law was going to shear sheep. According to ancient law, the Levirate responsibility could pass to the father-in-law if there were no brothers to fulfill it. Tamar was scheming to attain her legal right (38:11-14).

Judah thought Tamar was a prostitute and went in to her. He promised her a goat for her services. She demanded his seal and staff as pledge that he would fulfill his obligation. Judah later sent his friend the Adullamite with the goat. Meanwhile Tamar had returned to her widow's garb and to her father's house. No one in the area knew anything about a "cult prostitute" in the area (38:15-23).

When Judah heard that Tamar was pregnant, he ordered her to be burned to death. Tamar had sinned against the man to whom she was pledged—Judah's third son—and the penalty for that infidelity was death. When he saw the staff and seal, however, he declared Tamar more righteous than himself. He never slept with with Tamar again. In the course of time Tamar gave birth to twin sons (38:24-30). She is one of three women listed in the lineage of Jesus (Matt 1:3).

What purpose does Genesis 38 serve? It underscores the contrast between the immorality of Joseph's brothers, and the high standards of Joseph himself as recorded in the following chapter. Still more important, the chapter points out the imperative of getting the covenant family out of Canaan. The family was becoming submerged in Canaanite culture. A stay in Egypt was part of God's providential plan to maintain the purity of his people. Egyptians despised shepherds, and Jacob's family would be left relatively free from the corrupting influence of idolatry.

A FAITHFUL STEWARD
Genesis 39:1-20

Against the black backdrop of Judah's sin, the uplifting story of Joseph continues in Genesis 39. Joseph's life is a series of exaltations and humiliations. In Egypt his master observed that everything the Hebrew did was blessed with success. Step by step Joseph rose to prominence, from (1) Potiphar's personal attendant to (2) chief of household servants to (3) manager of the entire estate. Everything was entrusted to his care. The Lord showered blessing upon Potiphar's house. The Egyptian came to trust Joseph implicitly (39:1-6).

Joseph faced severe temptation in the house of Potiphar. His master's wife had her eyes on the handsome youth. She constantly urged him to become sexually involved with her. Joseph firmly rejected her advances with two sound reasons: (1) he could not betray the trust of his master, and (2) he could not sin against God. He certainly had the right perspective on sexual sin (39:7-10).

Joseph was the victim of misrepresentation at the hands of the scorned woman. She embraced him one day when they were alone in the house and urged him to lie with her. Joseph fled from her presence leaving his coat in her clutches. The infuriated woman then screamed, showed the coat to the other men of the house and accused Joseph of attempted rape. Potiphar was convinced by his wife's story. He ordered Joseph thrown into the royal prison (39:11-20).

A FORGOTTEN SERVANT
Genesis 39:21–40:23

In the prison house Joseph was forgotten by his master, but not by his God. The Lord was with him and blessed him. Once again Joseph began a rise to leadership. The warden so completely trusted him that he made Joseph chief administrator of the prison (39:21-23).

Two of Pharaoh's personal staff officers were in prison at the same time. In one night the two of them had dreams. Joseph could tell by the look on their faces the next morning that they were perplexed about something. He encouraged them to relate their dreams because dream interpretations belong to God (40:1-8).

The cupbearer related a dream in which he had seen three grape branches. He saw himself taking the grapes from that vine and squeezing them into Pharaoh's cup. Joseph interpreted this to mean that within three days the cupbearer would be restored to his position. In return for this interpretation Joseph asked that the cupbearer tell Pharaoh about the injustice which had been done him, first by being forcibly carried off from the land of the Hebrews, and then by being framed for rape (40:9-15).

Encouraged by the favorable interpretation rendered for the cupbearer, the chief baker related his dream. Three baskets of baked goods were on his head, and birds were eating these goods from the top basket. Joseph indicated that within three days the baker would be hanged and the birds would eat his flesh (40:16-19).

On the third day, at a birthday banquet, Pharaoh lifted up the heads of his two officers. The cupbearer was restored to his position, the baker was hanged. In spite of the obvious implications of Joseph's uncanny ability to interpret dreams, the cupbearer did not remember him (40:20-23).

The exact chronology of Joseph's stay in prison cannot be determined. He may have been in prison for ten years prior to meeting Pharaoh's officers. Two years elapsed before the cupbearer remembered Joseph.

A FAMOUS SOVEREIGN
Genesis 41:1–45:24

In Genesis 41–45 the forgotten servant becomes a famous sovereign. These five chapters contain four units which can be labeled (1) unexpected promotion, (2) stressful visitation, (3) skillful investigation, and (4) joyous reconciliation.

A. Unexpected Promotion (Gn 41:1-57).

Pharaoh experienced two revelatory dreams which greatly troubled him. In the first, seven fat cows emerged from the Nile to graze among the reeds. Seven thin cows followed them, and ate the fat cows. In the second dream seven heads of healthy grain were swallowed up by seven blighted heads. None of the Egyptian wise men was able to interpret these dreams (41:1-8).

Pharaoh's consternation over his dreams jogged the memory of his cupbearer. He told Pharaoh about the Hebrew who had interpreted accurately the two dreams in the prison. The king immediately sent for Joseph and he was quickly brought from the dungeon. Joseph shaved, changed his clothes and stood before Pharaoh. He disclaimed

213

any personal ability to interpret dreams, but Joseph assured Pharaoh that God would give him the answer he sought (41:9-16).

Pharaoh graphically described his two dreams to Joseph, and the Hebrew did not hesitate a moment to declare that both dreams had the same meaning. Egypt would experience seven years of great abundance followed by seven years of dreadful famine. The double dream underscored the certainty of the prediction (41:17-32).

Without waiting to be asked, Joseph proceeded to give to Pharaoh a strategy for dealing with this foreboding future. Pharaoh should establish a commission under a wise leader to gather into storehouses twenty per cent of the crops during the seven years of abundance. These stores would preserve the land during the famine years. Pharaoh liked the plan, and came to regard Joseph as the best possible administrator of the taxation program (41:33-40).

So Joseph was elevated to the position of prime minister, second only to Pharaoh himself. The symbols of his office were Pharaoh's signet ring, a gold chain, fine robes and a personal chariot. Runners prepared the way before him wherever he went. Pharaoh gave him an Egyptian name (Zaphenath-paneah) and gave him a wife (Asenath) who came from one of the most prominent families in the land. Joseph was thirty when he received these honors (41:41-46).

During the seven years of abundance Joseph heaped up stores of grain in cities scattered throughout Egypt, so much grain in fact that he stopped keeping records of the amount. Two sons were born to him during those years. He named them Manasseh ("forget") and Ephraim ("double fruitful"). The abundance he now enjoyed had made him forget the bitter past (41:46-52).

When the seven years of famine arrived, Pharaoh continued to trust Joseph's leadership. Joseph opened the storehouses and sold grain, not only to the Egyptians, but to buyers from distant lands (41:53-57). Here is a fulfillment of the promise, "Those who bless you, I will bless" (12:3). When Joseph was elevated by the Egyptians, he became the means of saving Egypt from disaster.

B. Stressful Visitation (Gn 42:1-28).

Jacob dispatched ten of his sons to go down to Egypt to purchase grain. Benjamin stayed at home. Joseph immediately recognized his brothers in the audience, but they did not not recognize him. Joseph's aim was twofold: (1) to elicit information about his father and brother, and (2) to ascertain whether or not his brothers had changed during the past twenty years. He did this by (1) charging them with espionage, (2) challenging their credibility, (3) putting them in jail for three days, (4) demanding that the younger brother to whom they referred be brought to Egypt, and (5) insisting that one brother be left in Egypt as surety that the others would return with Benjamin (42:1-20).

Joseph was deeply moved as the brothers discussed among themselves their past sins against Joseph. Since he had spoken to them only through an interpreter, they assumed that he could not understand them. Joseph ordered his servants to return each brother's silver in his sack of grain. The brothers were no little perplexed when they discovered their silver. Jacob was greatly distressed when he heard of all that had transpired. He had lost Joseph, and now Simeon, and he was not about to allow Benjamin to go to Egypt with his brothers. Reuben pled with his father to entrust Benjamin to his care. If he did not bring Benjamin home, Jacob could put to death Reuben's two sons. Reuben meant well, but his gesture was not very reassuring (42:21-38).

C. Skillful Investigation (Gn 43:1-44:34).

Jacob finally realized that another trip to Egypt was necessary. Judah reminded him of what the Egyptian ruler had said. They must take Benjamin with them. Judah offered to be a surety for his younger brother and bear the blame forever if anything happened to him. Reassured, Jacob authorized the trip. He ordered his sons to take double the money from the previous trip as well as some products from Canaan which were not affected by the famine. Jacob wished his sons Godspeed and sent them on their way in sorrow (43:1-14).

When Joseph saw Benjamin with his brothers, he ordered a noon feast prepared, and the men taken to his house. The brothers assumed the worst, that something dreadful was about to happen because of the silver which had been returned to their sacks on the first visit. They approached Joseph's steward to explain about the silver and offer to repay it. The steward assured them that he had indeed received their silver, and that they could regard the silver found in their sacks as a blessing from God. At this point Simeon was permitted to rejoin his brothers. The men then washed and made preparations for their noon luncheon with the prime minister (43:15-25).

When Joseph arrived, the brothers presented him with their gifts and bowed before him. Joseph again sought to elicit information from them about his father. When he was introduced to Benjamin, he had to make a hasty exit from the room to weep for joy. Then he returned to the chamber where he sat at a table apart from his brothers because Hebrews were detestable to the Egyptians. The brothers were astonished to observe that the seating arrangement was in order of their ages. When the portions were served from Joseph's table, Benjamin received five times as much as anyone else (43:26-34).

Joseph had to perform one last test before he could reveal himself to his brothers. Again each man's silver was to be returned in his sack, but in Benjamin's sack the steward was to put the prime minister's silver cup. When the brothers left the city, Joseph sent his steward after them to accuse them of having stolen the silver cup. He who was guilty was to become a slave in Egypt. From firstborn to youngest, the steward made his search, knowing full well that he would find the cup in the sack of Benjamin where he had hidden it. In utter disbelief the brothers reloaded their donkeys and returned to the city (44:1-13).

Judah spoke for the brothers before Joseph. He and the others were fully prepared to become slaves just as they had pledged earlier to the steward (44:9). Joseph, however, insisted that only the guilty brother would be retained as a slave. Judah then made an eloquent appeal in which he offered to become a slave in place of Benjamin. Judah expressed touching concern over the emotional state of his father if Benjamin should not return. That the hearts of his brothers had changed was now obvious to Joseph (44:14-34).

D. Joyous Reconciliation (Gn 45:1-24).

Joseph could no longer contain himself. He ordered all servants out of the room. Then he revealed himself to his brothers. The joyous weeping was so loud that the Egyptians heard it and reported it to Pharaoh (45:1-2).

216

Chart No. 15

JOSEPH IN EGYPT Genesis 39–55				
SERVANT 39:1-19	PRISON 39:20–40:23	PLENTY 41:1-52	FAMINE 41:53–47:26	SOJOURN 47:27–50:26
Potiphar's House	Meets the Butler and the Baker	Two Children Born	Brothers, Benjamin Arrive ┌── 17 Yrs ──┐ Jacob Arrives 1877	Goshen Jacob Dies 1860
Age 17-19 (2+ Yrs.)	Age 19-30 (11 Yrs.)	Age 30-37 (7 Yrs.)	Age 37-44 (7 Yrs.)	Age 44-110 (70 Yrs.)
1901–1898 BC	1898–1887 BC	1887–1880 BC	1880–1873 BC	1873–1807 BC
Steward	Dream Interpreter	PRIME MINISTER		

Joseph was full of forgiveness. He interpreted his sale to Egypt as due to divine providence. Through Joseph's position in Egypt, God would preserve a remnant of his people through the famine. He urged his brothers to return to Canaan and convince their father that he should move to Egypt where Joseph could provide for him during the balance of the five years of famine (45:3-15).

Pharaoh was pleased with the news that Joseph's brothers were in Egypt. He too invited the family to dwell in his land. Joseph provided ten carts to assist in making the move. He gave new clothing to each of the brothers, with extra money and clothing for Benjamin. He sent twenty donkeys loaded with the best things of Egypt as a gift for his father. His parting words to his brothers were that they should not quarrel along the way home, i.e., they should not be accusing one another of past sins (45:16-24).

ENDNOTES

1. H.C. Leupold, *Exposition of Genesis* (Columbus: Wartburg, 1942), p. 949.

CHAPTER NINETEEN

The Last Days of Jacob
Genesis 45:25-50:26

AIM: To demonstrate the importance of perseverance.

THEME: Faithful unto death!

The last chapters of Genesis focus on Jacob, with a few glimpses of Joseph. Jacob was 130 when he entered Egypt in 1877 BC. He lived there with his sons for seventeen years before his death. His faithfulness to the Lord is evident in the last five events of his life.

JACOB'S LAST JOURNEY
Genesis 45:25–47:12

Jacob was initially incredulous and stunned at the news that Joseph was alive and that he was a mighty ruler in the land of Egypt. Not until he saw the carts which Joseph had sent did he believe the story. Once he was convinced, however, he did not hesitate to make plans to go to Egypt to see his beloved son (45:25-28).

According to 37:14 Jacob's last residence had been at Hebron, and it is from that place that his journey to Egypt began. At Beersheba on the southern border of Canaan, the family paused so that Jacob could offer sacrifices. He may have used the very altar which his father had erected in that place many years earlier (26:25).

Chart No. 16

DESCENDANTS OF JACOB		
c. 1877 BC		
Descendants of Leah (32*)		
1. REUBEN	13. LEVI	23. ISSACHAR
2. Hanoch	14. Gershon	24. Tola
3. Pallu	15. Kohath	25. Puah
4. Hezron	16. Merari	26. Jashub
5. Carmi		27. Shimron
	17. JUDAH	
6. SIMEON	Er	28. ZEBULUN
7. Jemuel	Onan	29. Sered
8. Jamin	18. Shelah	30. Elon
9. Ohad	19. Zerah	31. Jahleel
10. Jakin	20. Perez	
11. Zohar	21. Hezron	( ) DINAH
12. Shaul	22. Hamul	

Descendants of Zilpah (16)		*Descendants of Bilhah (7)*	
32. GAD	40. ASHER	48. DAN	50. NAPHTALI
33. Zephon	41. Imnah	49. Hushim	51. Jahziel
34. Haggi	42. Ishvah		52. Guni
35. Shuni	43. Ishvi		53. Jezer
36. Ezbon	44. Serah		54. Shillem
37. Eri	45. Beriah		
38. Arodi	46. Heber		
39. Areli	47. Malkiel		

Descendants of Rachel (14)		
	55. BENJAMIN	
( ) JOSEPH	56. Bela	61. Rosh
( ) Manasseh	57. Beker	62. Muppim
( ) Ephraim	58. Ashbel	63. Huppim
	59. Naaman	64. Ard
	60. Ehi	65. Gera

Genesis 46:9-25
NIV

*Genesis 46:15b gives the total of Jacob's "sons and daughters"
by Leah as 33, probably using a different tallying system.

In a vision of the night God appeared to Jacob for the last time. The Lord calmed his fears about the future of the covenant family by making some wonderful promises to him. God promised to (1) make a great nation of him there, (2) go down to Egypt with him, (3) bring him back to Canaan, and (4) cause Joseph to close his father's eyes in death (46:1-4).

The entire family of Jacob migrated to Egypt (46:5-7). The text contains a catalog of the names of the heads of families who would later lead prominent clans within the family. These points stand out in the list found in 46:8-27: (1) Four sons of Reuben are named, whereas 42:37 suggests he had but two. Two sons must have been born to him in Egypt. (2) Ten sons of Benjamin are listed. All of them probably were born in Egypt. (3) Of many daughters and granddaughters, only two are listed, Dinah and Serah, a daughter of Asher. (4) Adding Joseph, his two sons, and Dinah, the most prominent daughter of Jacob, yields the total figure of seventy who migrated to Egypt.

Judah preceded the clan to Egypt to confirm the arrangements for settlement in the land of Goshen. When the family arrived a few days later, Joseph went out in his chariot to meet them. Over two decades had elapsed since the father and son had seen each other. After a tearful reunion Jacob expressed his satisfaction with life. He was ready to die now that he had seen for himself that his son was still alive (46:28-30).

Joseph thought it wise to secure Pharaoh's approval of the plans for the settlement of his family. He would explain to the king that his family were shepherds by trade and that they had brought their flocks and herds with them. He coached his family to identify their occupation as shepherds. This was no deception on their part, for shepherding was the *primary* occupation of these men. Since shepherds were detestable to the Egyptians, Pharaoh would authorize Jacob's clan to settle in the more or less isolated area of Goshen. Joseph had the covenant idea. He wanted his family to be insulated as much as possible from the evil influences of Egyptian culture (46:31-33).

Joseph went to his sovereign and reported the arrival of his family. He selected five of his brothers to stand before Pharaoh. As anticipated, Pharaoh interrogated the brothers about their occupation, and they responded as coached by Joseph earlier. They then requested

221

that they be allowed to settle in the pasture lands of Goshen. Pharaoh directed Joseph to settle his family in the best part of the land. Any of his brothers with special ability were to be given royal appointment over Pharaoh's livestock (47:1-6).

At this point Joseph brought his father in before Pharaoh. The aged patriarch blessed the king. When asked as to his age, Jacob responded "The years of my pilgrimage are a hundred and thirty." He evaluated those years as "few and difficult" and not equal in length to the years of the pilgrimage of his father Isaac who died at 180, or his grandfather Abraham who died at 175. Jacob here reflects the covenant idea. Life is a pilgrimage en route to a city whose maker and builder is God! After pronouncing a second blessing, Jacob departed from the presence of Pharaoh (47:7-10).

Following the directions of Pharaoh, Joseph settled his family in the best part of Goshen, a region called Rameses. Provisions of food were awarded to each head of household according to the number of children (47:11-12).

JOSEPH'S ADMINISTRATION
Genesis 47:13-27

The narrator digresses briefly to further emphasize the genius of Joseph's farm policy in Egypt. Five stages in this policy are evident.

1. Before the famine the government confiscated twenty per cent of all grain and stored it in store cities throughout the land (41:47-49). The result was that grain was available during the years of famine.

2. In the first stage of the famine the people were able to buy grain from the government (41:56-57). The result was that the people had food, but their money supply was soon exhausted.

3. Joseph then accepted flocks and herds in exchange for grain. Within a year Joseph had purchased all the livestock in Egypt (47:13-17).

4. The following year the people offered to sell themselves and their land to Pharaoh in exchange for food. Pharaoh thereby came to claim title to all land except that of the priests. All the people of the land were now considered slaves (47:18-22).

5. As the land began to produce again, Joseph gave seed to the

farmers with the stipulation that one fifth of the crop would always belong to Pharaoh. The people received this ruling with gratitude. "You have saved our lives," they exclaimed. They were quite willing to place themselves under bondage to Pharaoh. The twenty per cent tax on crops was still the law of the land in the days of Moses (47:23-26).

The purpose of this lengthy description of Joseph's administrative policy is twofold. These verses (1) justify the necessity of the Israelite migration to Egypt by depicting the severity of the famine, and (2) point out the contrast between the enslavement of the people of Egypt and the comparative prosperity of the Israelites. While the Egyptians were losing their lands, the Israelites acquired property through the land grant of Pharaoh. There in the land of Goshen the children of Israel began to increase rapidly in number (47:27).

JACOB'S LAST REQUEST
Genesis 47:28-31

At age 147 and approaching death Jacob became concerned about his place of burial. Seventeen years in Egypt had not dulled his love for the Promised Land. He summoned Joseph and asked him to assume the posture for a solemn oath, i.e., with his hand under the thigh of his father. Jacob requested that Joseph swear to bury him where his fathers were buried in the land of Canaan. Joseph complied with his father's request. Then the old man bowed in worship and thanksgiving as he leaned on the top of his staff (or the top of his bed) for support.

JACOB'S LAST BLESSING
Genesis 48:1-22

When he heard that Jacob had fallen ill, Joseph took his two sons with him to his father's side. The old man rallied his strength and sat up on the bed. Jacob then did nine things.

1. He rehearsed to Joseph the story of the wonderful theophany which he had experienced at Bethel. Jacob referred to the second Bethel appearance narrated in 35:9-13. He reminded Joseph of the

divine promise to multiply the number of his descendants, and to give to them the land of Canaan as an everlasting possession (48:3-4).

2. He adopted Joseph's two sons as his own. They would have equal standing with Reuben and the others. In the future inheritance of the land all other sons of Joseph would be reckoned as belonging to either Ephraim or Manasseh.

3. He reminded Joseph of the circumstances of the death of his mother Rachel (cf. 35:16-20). She was buried there in the land of Canaan. That would be an added incentive for Joseph's sons someday to return there (48:7).

4. He took his two grandsons upon his knees, embraced them and kissed them (48:8-10).

5. He expressed his amazement at the grace of God. He thought he would never see Joseph again. Now the Lord had permitted him to see Joseph's children as well (48:11).

6. He prepared for the blessing of the boys by crossing his hands, putting his right hand on the head of Ephraim and his left on the head of Manasseh the firstborn of Joseph (48:12-14).

7. He blessed Joseph in the person of the two boys. The deity here is identified as "the God before whom my fathers walked," "my Shepherd," and "the Angel who has delivered me from all harm." Jacob called upon this God to bless the boys. He prayed that they would wear the family name proudly and increase greatly (48:15-16).

8. He uttered a prophecy regarding the relationship between the two boys. Joseph was upset with his father for placing his right hand on the head of Ephraim. He moved the hand to the head of his first-born Manasseh. The patriarch, however, refused. Ephraim would take precedence over Manasseh. The older boy would become a great people, but his younger brother would become "a group of nations." He predicted that in the future one would invoke the names of Ephraim and Manasseh when pronouncing a blessing on others (48:17-20).

9. He willed to Joseph, i.e., his descendants, that part of the land of Canaan which he had taken from the Amorites with sword and bow. This is the only reference to any war waged by Jacob. The reference is probably to the piece of land Jacob purchased from the sons of Hamor (33:19). The Amorites must have reclaimed this land and Jacob was forced to counterattack and take it back (48:21-22).

JACOB'S LAST MESSAGE
Genesis 49:1-28

Before he died, Jacob uttered patriarchal prophecies regarding the future of all of his sons. The expression "last days" (49:1) is regarded by some as always embracing in some sense the Messianic age.[1] Others think the expression simply means something like, "in the distant future."[2] In any case, the eleven paragraphs which follow outline Jacob's predictions regarding his sons. The sons are not all mentioned in the order of their birth and no satisfactory explanation for this unusual order has been suggested.

1. Reuben, Judah and Joseph are directly addressed by Jacob. Reuben was the firstborn who once excelled over his brothers in honor and power. Reuben, however, was like unstable water, easily aroused. He defiled his father's bed when he lay with Bilhah, Jacob's concubine (35:22). Therefore, Reuben would lose his preeminence among the sons (49:3-4).

2. Jacob disassociates himself from the violence which characterized the brothers Simeon and Levi. Jacob cursed their anger and predicted that they would be scattered throughout Israel (49:5-7).

3. The first positive word concerned Judah. In effect Judah is given the rights of the firstborn. He whose name means "praise" would be the object of the praise of his brothers. They would bow before him, an obvious prediction that Judah would be the royal tribe. Judah would put his feet on the neck of enemies, i.e., he would be successful in combat against them. He would become like a lion which no one had courage to arouse (49:8-9).

Judah would continue to bear the scepter, i.e., exercise leadership over the other tribes, until Shiloh came. While several interpretations of this term have been proposed, those commentators who see in this Shiloh ("rest bringer") a reference to the Messiah are probably correct. The prophecy does not directly assert, but does strongly suggest, that Messiah would come from the tribe of Judah.[3]

The obedience of nations would be rendered to this Shiloh. The age of Shiloh would be an age of great prosperity. Vines would be so plentiful that donkeys would be tethered to vines, and garments washed in wine. An abundance of wine and milk would produce a healthy color in the citizens of his kingdom (49:10-12).

4. Zebulun would live by the seashore toward Sidon. This tribe would be a haven for ships (49:13). The tribe of Zebulun was not actually given an inheritance on the coast. Apparently the meaning of the prediction is that this tribe would have direct access to the sea and would enjoy the abundance of sea commerce.

5. Issachar is likened to a strong donkey loaded down with saddle-bags. Some see in the saddlebags a reference to two great elevations which marked the boundaries of this tribe. Issachar would be comfortable in his pleasant land. He would rather be a slave and have peace than resist oppression and have liberty (49:14-15).

6. Dan would provide justice for his people. For horse riding strangers who might pass through his territory, however, he would be like a dangerous snake in the grass. Jacob's inspired expectation was that God would sustain this tribe during these times of trial (49:16-18). Samson's victories over the Philistines may be in view here.

7. Gad would be attacked by a band of raiders, but he would be able to drive them away (49:19).

8. Asher would have a fruitful land producing rich foods fit for a king (49:20).

9. Naphtali is likened to a doe that bears beautiful fawns (49:21). The exact import of this figure is obscure.

10. Joseph is likened to a fruitful vine. Jacob then alluded to Joseph's personal struggles in the past. The hostility against Joseph is likened to an archery attack. With the help of the Lord, Joseph did not weaken under this attack. The several titles for the deity in this paragraph are remarkable. He is the Mighty One of Jacob, the Shepherd, the Rock of Israel, the Almighty.

Looking to the future, Jacob emphasized the blessings which Joseph would experience: (1) the "blessings of the heavens above," i.e., the dew, rain and sunshine necessary for abundant harvest; (2) the "blessings of the deep that lies below," i.e., streams and subsurface waters; (3) "blessings of the breast and womb," i.e., rapid multiplication of children and livestock. All of these are described as (4) "the blessings of your father" which are said to be greater in magnitude than the ancient mountains (49:22-26).

11. Benjamin is likened to a ravenous wolf which plunders by night and devours the prey by morning light. The Benjamites are depicted as wild and vigorous warriors throughout Old Testament history (49:27).

To all of his sons Jacob repeated the instructions regarding his burial which he had earlier given to Joseph privately. He wished to be laid to rest in the cave in the field of Machpelah where Abraham, Sarah, Isaac, Rebekah, and Leah were already buried. Jacob then drew his feet up into his bed, breathed his last, and was gathered to his people (50:29-33).

JACOB'S LAST RITES
Genesis 50:1-21

Joseph was particularly distraught by his father's death. He threw himself over his father's body, wept, and kissed him. Regaining his composure, Joseph assumed responsibility for the final arrangements for his father. He ordered the physicians to embalm Jacob. That process took a full forty days. A seventy-day official period of mourning was observed by the Egyptians as well as the Israelites (50:1-3).

After the period of mourning, Joseph requested permission from Pharaoh's court to fulfill his oath to go up to Canaan to bury his father. Why Joseph did not directly approach Pharaoh is not clear. In any case the permission was granted. A large company of dignitaries and family members began to make its way northward with chariots and horsemen providing security (50:4-9).

The burial procession, perhaps for political reasons, did not travel the usual route to Canaan. It traveled around the Dead Sea and up the east side of the Jordan. The group paused for seven days at Atad, a threshingfloor near the Jordan. There Joseph observed another week of mourning for his father. Apparently this was the custom of that area. The local Canaanites were much impressed with this display of grief and gave the spot the name Abel Mizraim, "mourning of the Egyptians" (50:10-11).

Finally the mission was completed. Jacob was laid to rest by his sons in the cave in the field of Machpelah near Mamre. The Egyptian dignitaries left this final rite to the family alone. After the burial the entire group returned to Egypt (50:12-14).

Joseph's brothers completely misjudged the forgiveness which their brother had offered to them seventeen years earlier. They thought Joseph had refrained from punishing them out of consideration for their father. Now the brothers feared Joseph's wrath. They sent word to him that Jacob had left instructions that he should forgive them of their transgressions against him forty years earlier. The brothers added to this plea from Jacob their own petition for forgiveness. Joseph was moved to tears by this appeal (50:15-17).

When the brothers heard of Joseph's response, they came and threw themselves before him as his slaves. Again Joseph calmed their fears. He was not going to assume the role of God to judge his brothers. God had overruled their evil intent in selling him to Egypt and had brought good out of it. This was God's plan for saving the lives of the covenant people! So Joseph reassured his brothers with these kind words, promising to continue to provide for them and their children (50:18-21).

JOSEPH'S DEATH
Genesis 50:22-26

Genesis closes with the account of Joseph's death. He lived to see the third generation of his children i.e., his grandchildren. When he died at age 110 he had held office in Egypt for some eighty years.

Joseph had the covenant idea. In prophetic spirit he predicted that someday God would take up his brothers (i.e., their families) out of Egypt to the Promised Land. This would not be a natural tribal migration, but would be the result of divine intervention. Joseph insisted that when this day of deliverance came, his family should carry his bones with them to the Promised Land (50:24-25). Having secured this commitment from his family, Joseph died. They embalmed him and placed him in a coffin in Egypt (50:26).

ENDNOTES

1. To Leupold the "end of days" were "the future culminating in the messianic age"; to E.J. Young "the time when messianic salvation will be accomplished."

2. The position of Aalders, Kidner and von Rad.

3. For a discussion of the various interpretations of Shiloh see James E. Smith, *What the Bible Says about the Promised Messiah* (Joplin: College Press, 1984), pp. 55-58.

Chart No. 17

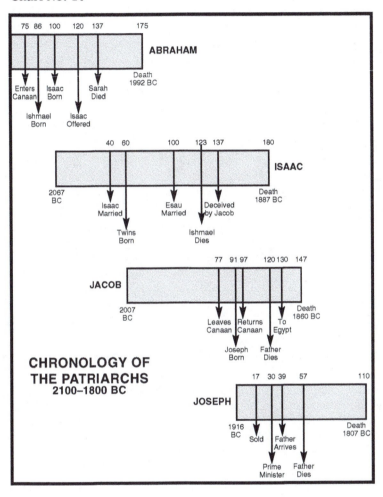

Chronology of the Patriarchs

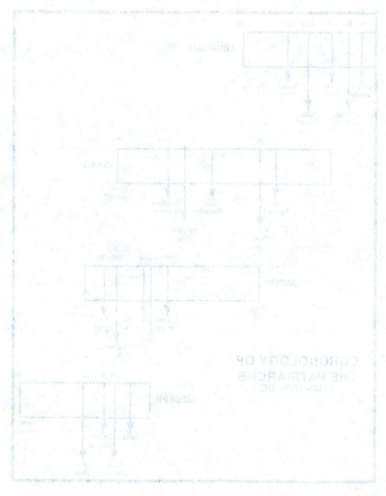

THE BOOK OF
EXODUS

CHAPTER TWENTY

Getting Acquainted with Exodus

AIM: To demonstrate that the Book of Exodus contains important truths vital to the Christian life.

THEME: Deliverance is essential!

The Book of Exodus has been an inspiration to believers through the centuries. Hebrew poets and prophets quoted frequently from it and applied its lessons of deliverance, faith, and hope in their generations. Likewise, Exodus was a source of frequent quotation by the Apostles in the New Testament. Jews and Christians alike have found in this book a rich mine of inspiration.

Exodus has fewer chapters (forty), and verses (1,213) than Genesis but is actually a bit larger than the first book by word count (32,692). Exodus is the sixth largest book of the Old Testament. The name comes ultimately from the Greek and means "the way out." The ancient Jews used the first significant word of the Hebrew text, *she-moth* ("names") to designate this book.

Exodus claims to be the product of Moses' writing under inspiration of the Holy Spirit (Ex 24:4). The historical details in the book support this claim. Exodus contains details about the stay in Egypt and the journey to Mt. Sinai which could have been recorded only by an eye witness. The author, for example, takes special note of the number of palm trees and springs at Elim (Ex 15:27). Moses probably penned these words during the stay in the wilderness about 1444 BC.

The background of Exodus can be briefly summarized as follows: About 1877 BC the family of Jacob descended into Egypt. Because of Joseph's position in that land the Israelites were treated cordially. A Pharaoh arose, however, who did not know Joseph. The Israelites were gradually persecuted and then enslaved. Toward the end of the 430 year stay in Egypt, God raised up a deliverer for his people.

The immediate purpose of Exodus is to narrate the history of the Israelite nation from the birth of Moses, through the Exodus, to the erection of the Tabernacle. The ultimate purpose of the book is to reveal through law, ritual and symbol the character of God.

FOCAL POINTS IN EXODUS

The Book of Exodus can be summarized in the caption "Plagues and Precepts." The first half of the book concentrates on the plagues which resulted in the release of God's people. The latter half of the book contains the precepts by which God governed his people. The theme of Exodus is *the redemption of the nation.* Exodus contains the account of how God redeemed his people from Egyptian bondage. The abiding lesson in Exodus is that *deliverance is essential.* Man in the bondage of sin needs the intervention of God to set him free. Just as the blood of the Passover lamb applied to the door protected an Israelite family from death, so the blood of the perfect Lamb of God shed on Calvary protects the believer from the second death. Thus in Exodus the Christian sees a picture of Christ, the Perfect Lamb.

Five literary keys open up the meaning of Exodus. The key passage in the book is 19:4-6a: "You have seen what I did unto the Egyptians, and how I bore you on eagles' wings, and brought you unto myself. Now therefore, if you will obey my voice indeed, and keep my covenant, then you shall be a peculiar treasure unto me above all people: for all the earth is mine. And you shall be unto me a kingdom of priests, and a holy nation." Others have nominated 3:8 as the key verse: "So I have come down to rescue them from the hand of the Egyptians and to bring them up out of that land into a good and spacious land, a land flowing with milk and honey." Still others see 12:51 as epitomizing the contents of the book: "And on that very day the Lord brought the Israelites out of Egypt according to their hosts."

The key word in Exodus is *deliver* which occurs in various forms some nine times. The key expression is "As the Lord commanded Moses." The key thought is *redemption*. God redeemed his people from the bondage of Egypt. While Genesis focuses on several human actors, Exodus highlights only one, Moses. He is the key character in this book.

A number of literary forms appear in this book: historical narrative, song (ch. 15), genealogies, lists, and prayers. A large portion of Exodus is couched in legal language. A threefold classification of laws is found in Exodus: (1) *commands* which pertain to moral life (chs. 19–20), (2) *judgments* relating to social life (chs. 21–23), and (3) *ordinances* concerning religious life (chs. 24–40).

STRUCTURE OF EXODUS

The structure of Exodus differs from that of Genesis. No genealogical formulae are present here to mark divisions of the book. In the middle chapters an itinerary is in evidence,[1] but it does not provide any overarching framework for the entire work. A chronological principle was followed in arranging the material of Exodus.

Exodus begins with an introduction (1:1-17) which serves to forge a link with the preceding book. The book then recounts in order the following episodes: the birth of Moses, the exile and return of Moses to Egypt, the deliverance of Israel, the journey to Sinai, the covenant at Sinai, and the construction of the Tabernacle.

The Ten Commandments (Ex 20:1-17) occupy a strategic position in Exodus. The prologue of this unit summarizes the previous eighteen chapters. The Decalogue was delivered to those who had been rescued from slavery in Egypt. The Ten Commandments themselves serve as "an interpretative guide to all succeeding legal material."[2] The Decalogue, then, binds law to historical experience. Israel's law was not the result of centuries of juridical evolution. The Mosaic code grew out of episodes in which God revealed himself and his will. Israel did not discover God's will through meditation or reason. God's will had to be revealed.

Since no formal literary markers are present in the book, no uniformity of opinion has been expressed regarding the major divisions of Exodus. One threefold outline of Exodus which has been suggested is this: (1) Israel's call out of Egypt (chs. 1–19), (2) Israel's consecration at Sinai (chs. 20–24), and (3) Israel's construction of the Tabernacle (chs. 25–40). Another suggestion is this: (1) the Exodus from Egypt (chs. 1–15), (2) the wilderness journey (15:22–18:27), and (3) the Sinai covenant (chs. 19–40).

The book follows a format which is observable in documents from the ancient Near East, namely, triumph of deity followed by construction of a sanctuary. In the plagues God proved his superiority over the gods of Egypt, including the deified king. Then in fifteen chapters the details concerning the Tabernacle are chronicled. Chart 18 reveals the various sub-divisions of Exodus.

Chart No. 18

STRUCTURE OF EXODUS *"The Formation of the Nation"*		
CONFRONTATION IN EGYPT	CONSECRATION AT SINAI	CONSTRUCTION OF TABERNACLE
Persecution chs. 1–6	Commandments	Designed chs. 25–31
Plagues chs. 7–12	Judgments	Delayed chs. 32–34
Pilgrimage chs. 13–19	Ordinances	Dedicated chs. 35–40
EXODUS 1–19	EXODUS 20–24	EXODUS 25–40
GOD'S POWER	GOD'S PRECEPTS	GOD'S PRESENCE

236

THEOLOGY OF EXODUS

The theological themes of Exodus yield precious ore to the perceptive student. Three major emphases are especially worthy of note.

A. The Self-Revelation Theme.

One of the great themes of Exodus is that of the self-revelation of God. He made himself known in the mighty acts which he wrought against Egypt and on behalf of Israel. When confronted with the demand that he release Israel, Pharaoh responded, "I do not know Yahweh." The events which followed were designed to teach Pharaoh, his people and even Israel who Yahweh was, the eternally existing One, the only deity.

1. When the Egyptians witnessed the release of Israel from bondage, and when they saw their own army destroyed at the Red Sea they would come to know by experience that "I am Yahweh" (7:5; 14:1-4,18). At the end of the tenth plague the Egyptians urged the Israelites to hurry their departure. They were afraid they would all die if the Israelites stayed much longer. They showered upon their former slaves gifts of gold and silver to encourage their hasty departure (12:33-36).

2. At various times during the plagues Pharaoh would came to know the uniqueness of Yahweh (8:10; 9:14), the sovereignty of Yahweh (9:29), and Yahweh's choice of Israel (11:7). In short he learned that "I am Yahweh" (7:17). At one point Pharaoh acknowledged that he was wrong and Yahweh was right. He called for Moses to pray to Yahweh for him (9:27). As he issued the order for the Israelites to be released, Pharaoh requested that Moses bless him (12:32).

3. The plagues against Egypt were signs designed to help the Israelites know that "I am Yahweh" (10:2). When they saw the great power which Yahweh displayed against the Egyptians, the people feared Yahweh and put their trust in Yahweh and in Moses his servant (14:31).

Two other individuals, Moses and Jethro, came to know Yahweh through the mighty deeds of the Exodus. Moses praised Yahweh and acknowledged his supremacy in chapter 15. When Jethro heard of all that Yahweh had done to Egypt and for Israel he confessed, "Now I know that Yahweh is greater than all other gods" (18:11).

B. The Grace of God Theme.

According to Exodus the foundation of the covenant between God and Israel was mercy and forgiveness. The election of Israel was not conditioned on obedience to the Law (20:2), but derived solely from the kindness of God (19:4). So also the continuing relationship between God and Israel was grounded in God's grace, not Israel's faithfulness. This is particularly clear in chapters 32–34. Here can be traced the interwoven themes of judgment on disobedience, intercession for forgiveness and prayer for God's continued presence. From the outset Israel's covenant relationship with God stood under the shadow of disobedience. When Israel offered worship to a calf of gold the nation was repudiating the covenant which had been sealed only days before. Though the nation deserved destruction for this act of treason, God responded to the prophetic intercession of Moses and spared Israel. The God of Exodus was inclined to be positive toward his people. He looked for reasons to forgive. Exodus instructed Israel that true repentance and genuine intercession can avert divine wrath even when their conduct had been the most offensive.

C. The Perpetual Sinai Theme.

Thirteen chapters of Exodus describe the preparation for (chs. 25–31) and the actual building of (chs. 35–40) the Tabernacle. This constitutes about thirty-seven per cent of the book. Why is so much attention focused on this portable religious shrine? The answer comes in the final chapter of Exodus. The purpose of the Tabernacle was to perpetuate the Sinai experience.

In Exodus 24:16f. the "glory of Yahweh" settled atop Sinai in the form of a devouring fire. The same imagery is used of the Tabernacle in 40:34. Moses had been able to ascend the mountain. He could not, however, enter the glory of Yahweh which filled the Tabernacle (40:35). The sons of Aaron, however, could approach God's altar after they had gone through certain rituals (40:31). Just as Moses served as the mediator between Israel and God at Sinai, so the Aaronic priesthood would serve in that capacity perpetually.

238

CHRONOLOGY OF EXODUS

Exodus opens with a brief notation regarding the Eisodus, the descent of the family of Jacob into Egypt about 1877 BC. For some time after the death of Joseph (c. 1807 BC) the children of Israel prospered (1:7). This period of prosperity lasted perhaps 150 years. About 1730 BC a new Pharaoh arose who knew not Joseph (1:8) and an era of hostility toward Israelites began. This period of persecution lasted perhaps 280 years.

Moses was born about 1527 BC in the midst of the persecution of Israel. At age forty he was forced to flee Egypt (c. 1487 BC). At age eighty he returned to demand the release of Israel from bondage. A year of plagues (Ex 7-12) brought the Egyptians to their knees and forced Pharaoh to give the Israelites their freedom about the year 1447 BC.

For Israel to travel to Sinai required a month and a half (chs. 13-18). Moses was in the mount for eighty days receiving instruction from the Lord (chs. 19-34). Chapters 35-40 narrate the construction of the Tabernacle which took a bit more than seven months. The Tabernacle was erected about 1446 BC.

For Israel the Exodus marked the beginning of a new era. Four chronological notes appear in the book. The first three of these notes allude to that historic year of deliverance. The first Passover was conducted on the fourteenth day of the first month (Ex 12:2,6,18). Israel entered the desert of Sin on the fifteenth day of the second month (Ex 16:1). They entered the desert of Sinai on the first day of the third month (Ex 19:1). The Tabernacle was erected on the first day of the first month of the second year (Ex 40:2,17).

Correlating the chronological data with the chapter divisions yields the following breakdown: Chapter 1 covers 350 years, from the Eisodus to the birth of Moses; chapters 2-6 cover eighty years, from the birth of Moses to the plagues. The plagues (chs. 7-12) occupied about a year. Chapters 13-18 cover forty-five days, from the Exodus to Mt. Sinai. In chapters 19-34 Moses was in the mount for eighty days. About seven months were required for Israel to construct the Tabernacle (chs. 35-40). The chronological setting of Exodus is displayed in Chart 19.

Chart No. 19

CHRONOLOGY OF EXODUS			
1877–1446 BC			

1850 1800 1750 1700 1650 1600 1550 1500 1450 1400			
1877			
PROSPERITY (1:7) 150 Yrs.	PERSECUTION (1:8–6:30) 280 Yrs.		
	EXODUS 1–6		EXODUS 1447 BC
	FOCUS ON TWO YEARS 1447–1446 BC		
PLAGUES ON EGYPT	PATH TO SINAI	PRECEPTS FROM THE MOUNT	PALACE FOR THE KING
Ex 7:12	Ex 13–18	Ex 19–34	Ex 35–40
1 Year	45 Days	80 Days	7 Months

Correlating biblical chronology with Egyptian chronology yields the following picture. Moses was born during the reign of Thutmose I, a mighty conqueror. His daughter Hatshepsut may have been the one who rescued Moses from the river and adopted him as her son. After the brief and inconsequential reign of Thutmose II, Hatshepsut became the Pharaoh. She was married to her brother, Thutmose III, who hated her. He most likely hated Moses as well. Eventually Thutmose III was able to wrest the reins of government from his sister/wife. During his reign Moses fled to the wilderness of Sinai. When Moses returned to lead Israel out of Egypt, Amenhotep II was ruling Egypt. He was the Pharaoh of the plagues and the Exodus.

The so-called early date theory of the Exodus harmonizes quite well with other chronological data in the Old Testament. In the light of 1 Kings 6:1 and Judges 11:26, the period of the Judges must be about 345 years long. Another theory, more popular in biblical studies places the Exodus in the reign of Pharaoh Rameses about 1275 BC. This theory is forced to compress the period of the Judges into about 176 years.[3] Chart 20 contrasts these two theories of the date of the Exodus.

Chart No. 20

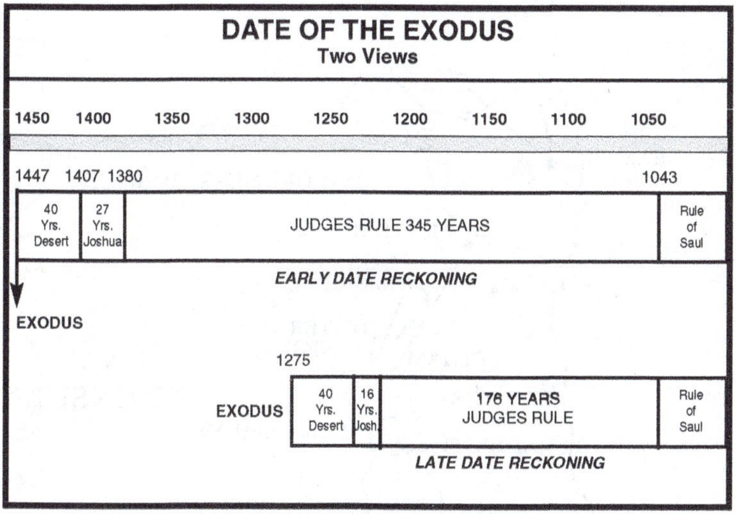

DATE OF THE EXODUS
Two Views

1450	1400	1350	1300	1250	1200	1150	1100	1050

1447 1407 1380   1043

40 Yrs. Desert	27 Yrs. Joshua	JUDGES RULE 345 YEARS		Rule of Saul

EARLY DATE RECKONING

↓
EXODUS

1275

EXODUS	40 Yrs. Desert	16 Yrs. Josh.	176 YEARS JUDGES RULE	Rule of Saul

LATE DATE RECKONING

GEOGRAPHY OF EXODUS

Geographically, Exodus has three divisions: (1) Israel in Egypt & Moses in Sinai (chs. 1–12), (2) Israel en route to Sinai (chs. 13–18), and (3) Israel at Sinai (chs. 19–40).

The most crucial geographical issue in Exodus is that of the route of the Israelites as they left Egypt. Five locations in their march are mentioned: Rameses, Succoth, Etham, Pi-hahiroth and the crossing point of the Red Sea. None of these spots has been identified with certainty. A survey of maps in Bible atlases reveals a number of different views of where Israel crossed the Red Sea, or Sea of Reeds as it was known in ancient times. The key verse in determining the general direction of the route is 13:17 which explicitly says that God directed Israel southward from Rameses. He did not permit them to take the shorter northern route through the land of the Philistines. J.W. McGarvey visited the region before the construction of the Suez canal. He scouted both sides of the Red Sea with Bible in hand and concluded that only one spot met all the biblical requirements for the place of crossing. McGarvey's conclusions are reflected in map 10.[4]

241

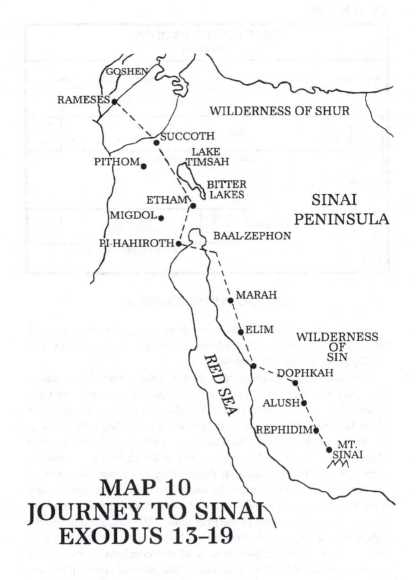

MAP 10
JOURNEY TO SINAI
EXODUS 13-19

TYPOLOGY OF EXODUS

Exodus is full of Christ. The book contains no direct prophecies, but it is full of previews or pictures called *types*. *Typology* is the study of these foreglimpses of Christ and the Christian age. Persons, places, objects and even events can be typical of New Testament realities. A type is more than just an analogy between something in the Old Testament and something in the New. A type was created by God with the intention of foreshadowing the coming age. Without revelation the certain identification of types is impossible. In other words, only those persons, places, objects or events of the Old Testament which are identified as types in the New Testament can strictly speaking be classified as such. Some of the more outstanding types in Exodus are the following:

1. Aaron, or at least the office of high priest which he occupied. The writer of Hebrews repeatedly refers to the ministry of Aaron and the more glorious ministry of the Christian high priest Jesus Christ.

2. Paul saw the crossing of the Red Sea as a type of baptism in 1 Corinthians 10:2.

3. The Passover lamb clearly depicted the Lamb of God. Paul declared that Christ is the Christian's Passover (1 Cor 5:7).

4. The wilderness manna was typical of the bread from heaven which Jesus declared himself to be (John 6:48-51).

5. The rock from which water sprang forth pointed forward to the water of life supplied by Christ (1 Cor 10:4).

The grand type in Exodus is the Tabernacle which Israel constructed at Sinai. While some have carried the typology of the Tabernacle to extremes, the New Testament does make clear that certain aspects of this structure were typical. These are:

1. The bronze altar. Hebrews declares that Christ is the Christian's altar (Heb 13:10).

2. The bronze laver is used in Titus 3:5 to portray baptism.

3. The incense altar points to the prayers of the saints of God (Rev 8:3-4).

4. The golden lampstand points to Christ the light of the world, and to the Christians who reflect that light.

5. The table of showbread seems to be a type of Christ, the bread

of life, and of the Lord's table which commemorates the body and blood of the Lord (1 Cor 10:21).

6. The holy of holies was a picture of heaven into which the Christian's high priest, Jesus, has entered upon his ministry (Heb 9:24; 10:34).

ENDNOTES

1. The itinerary is in evidence in the following places: 12:37a; 13:20; 14:1; 15:22a; 17:1a; 19:2. This itinerary reappears in the Book of Numbers.

2. Brevard S. Childs, *Introduction to the Old Testament as Scripture* (Philadelphia: Fortress, 1979), p. 174.

3. Advocates of the early date include: John Davis, *Moses and the Gods of Egypt* (Grand Rapids: Baker, 1971); G.L. Archer, *A Survey of Old Testament Introduction* (Chicago: Moody, 1964). John Bimson dates the Exodus as early as 1470 BC in *Redating the Exodus and Conquest* (Sheffield: Almond, 1981). Advocates of the thirteenth century date include: K.A. Kitchen, *Ancient Orient and Old Testament* (Chicago: InterVarsity, 1966); R.K. Harrison, *Introduction to the Old Testament* (Grand Rapids: Eerdmans, 1969); and Jack Finegan, *Light from the Ancient Past* (Princeton: University Press, 1959).

4. J.W. McGarvey, *Lands of the Bible* (Cincinnati: Standard, 1880), pp. 438-447.

BIBLIOGRAPHY: THE BOOK OF EXODUS

Cassuto, U. *Exodus: A Complete Commentary.* Trans. Israel Abrahams. Jerusalem: Magnes, 1968.

Childs, B.S. *Exodus, A Commentary.* Old Testament Library. Philadelphia: Westminster, 1974.

Davis, John J. *Moses and the Gods of Egypt.* Grand Rapids: Baker, 1971.

Fields, Wilbur. *Exploring Exodus.* Bible Study Textbook Series. Joplin: College Press, 1976.

Finegan, Jack. *Let My People Go: A Journey through Exodus.* New York: Harper and Row, 1963.

Gispen, W.H. *Exodus.* Bible Student's Commentary. Grand Rapids: Zondervan, 1982.

Goldman, Solomon. *From Slavery to Freedom.* Harper, 1958.

Gore, Norman. *Tzeenah u-reenah: A Jewish Commentary on the Book of Exodus.* Vantage, 1965.

Gutzke, Manform G. *Plain Talk on Exodus.* Grand Rapids: Zondervan, 1974.

Meyer, F.B. *Exodus.* London: Marshall, Morgan and Scott, 1952.

Murphy, James. *A Critical and Exegetical Commentary on the Book of Exodus.* Minneapolis: Klock and Klock, 1979 reprint.

Pink, Arthur W. *Gleanings in Exodus.* Chicago: Moody, 1967.

Youngblood, Ronald. "Exodus." In *Everyman's Bible Commentary.* Chicago: Moody, 1983.

CHAPTER TWENTY-ONE

The Bondage of God's People
Exodus 1-4

AIM: To demonstrate that God is aware of the suffering of his people.

THEME: Preparing for deliverance.

The focus in the first eighteen chapters of Exodus is on the deliverance of Israel from Egyptian bondage. In these chapters the Exodus is projected through Moses (chs. 1–4), obstructed by Pharaoh (chs. 5–11), and effected by the Lord (chs. 12–18).[1] The first four chapters speak of the situation which necessitated the Exodus, as well as the anticipation of that event. Three pictures of God in these chapters drive home the point that God was aware of the suffering of his people and was working behind the scenes to prepare for their deliverance.

THE CRY OF A PEOPLE
Exodus 1:1-22

Exodus 1 demonstrates the necessity for the deliverance by portraying Israel's (1) expansion in Egypt and (2) her oppression by Egypt.

A. Israel's Expansion in Egypt (Ex 1:1-12).

Exodus 1 is a sequel to Genesis. The chapter is carefully connected with what precedes by means of a threefold recapitulation in verses 1-6: (1) the names of Jacob's children (cf. Gn 35:22-26), (2) the number of Jacob's descendants who went down into Egypt (cf. Gn 46:27), and (3) the death of Joseph (cf. Gn 50:26). According to verse 6 Joseph's brothers also died in Egypt. For some time after Joseph's death the Israelites multiplied phenomenally in accordance with God's promise to Abraham (1:7).

A new dynasty — the Eighteenth — arose in Egypt. This dynasty inaugurated a new policy toward the Israelites. Having just driven the foreign Hyksos from their land, these kings were especially sensitive to the possibility that some other foreign adversary might attempt to push into Egypt. They feared that the Semitic Israelites might aid any invader from the north (1:8-10).

The persecution intensified through four phases. Exodus 1 vividly portrays the struggle between one king who would destroy God's people through various programs, and the heavenly King who was determined to preserve them. In spite of every Egyptian effort to thwart them, the Israelites continued to increase. The miraculous growth of Israel was God's countermeasure in support of his people.

Taskmasters were appointed to supervise forced labor. The Israelites were required to build the store cities of Pithom and Rameses. In spite of the rigorous labor the Israelites continued to multiply (1:11-12).

B. Israel's Oppression by Egypt (Ex 1:13-22).

In the second phase of the persecution the forced labor intensified. The Egyptians worked the Israelites ruthlessly. Not only were they engaged in hard labor in bricks and mortar, but also in the fields.

248

Josephus indicates that they were forced to dig canals, and Deuteronomy 11:10 alludes to work on irrigation projects (1:13-14).

In the third phase of the persecution the Egyptians resorted to population control. Two chief Hebrew midwives, Shiphrah and Puah, were ordered by Pharaoh to kill all male infants at the birth stools. The birth stools were nothing more than two stones over which the women would crouch at the time of birth. These two godly women could not bring themselves to commit infanticide. When Pharaoh called them to account, they excused themselves by pointing to the vigor of the Hebrew women in childbirth. The children would already be born before the midwives could arrive. Perhaps there was some truth in what the midwives said, but it was not the whole truth. God blessed these two courageous midwives with families of their own. Meanwhile, the Israelites continued to increase in Egypt (1:15-21).

In the fourth phase of the persecution Pharaoh gave the order to throw Israelite male infants into the river. The Israelites themselves were subject to this order, and no doubt they were under a death sentence if they did not carry it out (1:22).

THE CULTIVATION OF A PERSON
Exodus 2:1-25

As the persecution against Israel intensified, so also did God's countermeasures. The Exodus is anticipated by the preparation of a leader through whom God would effect the deliverance of his people. Two stages in the preparation of that leader are indicated in Exodus 2.

A. Moses' Preparation in Egypt (Ex 2:1-15a).

The Egyptian phase of Moses's preparation involved (1) his birth, (2) his education, and (3) his failure.

1. The birth of Moses (2:1-4). Moses was born about 1525 BC to Amram and Jochebed of the tribe of Levi (Ex 6:20).[2] Aaron his brother was three years older (7:7), and Miriam older still. The faith of his parents is lauded in the New Testament. Seeing that their new son was a "proper child" (Heb 11:23) and "exceedingly fair" (Acts 7:20), they were not afraid of the king's command. The beauty of the child was taken as a sign that God had something special in store for him.

By faith they hid the child for three months. By faith they committed him to the Nile River in a waterproof ark made of the sticky papyrus found along the Nile. His mother took two precautions: (1) she placed the ark among the reeds near the bank where it could not be swept along with the current, and (2) she stationed Miriam nearby to guard against any unexpected danger.

2. *The education of Moses (2:5-10)*. God used the tears of the infant to touch the heart of Pharaoh's daughter as she came down to the sacred Nile to take her ritual bath. The princess recognized the baby as a Hebrew not because of his circumcision (Egyptians also circumcised), but because he was an abandoned male. Miriam who was hiding nearby then stepped forward and offered to secure a Hebrew nurse for the infant. Miriam brought Jochebed to the princess who contracted with her to nurse the baby. That his mother would be paid by an Egyptian princess to nurse her own son is ironic and even humorous.

The baby Moses stayed in the home of his real mother until he was weaned. If the word "weaned" is used here in its literal sense, she had her son for two or three years. If the word here is interpreted figuratively, Moses may have stayed with his parents until he was age twelve. In any case, Moses was the adopted son of Pharaoh's daughter. During his stay in the palace Moses became learned in all the wisdom of the Egyptians. He is described as mighty in words and in deeds (Acts 7:22).

3. *The failure of Moses (2:11-15a)*. When Moses was come to years, i.e., when he reached maturity, he made the first in a series of faith decisions. He refused to be called the son of Pharaoh's daughter. He chose to suffer affliction with the people of God rather than to enjoy the pleasures of sin for a season. Those people who cherished the Messianic hope suffered reproach. To Moses, however, that reproach was more valuable than all the treasures of Egypt. He knew that ultimately God would reward his faith (Heb 11:24-26).

At age forty Moses left the luxury of the palace to visit his countrymen. Seeing an Egyptian beating a fellow Hebrew, Moses was roused to anger. Checking to see that no one was watching, he slew the Egyptian and hid his body in the sand. Moses here was acting at the wrong time, for the wrong motive, and he employed the wrong method. Moses' rash act was punished by his exile in the land of Midian for forty years.

Moses *thought* that his own people would recognize that God was using him to rescue them, but they did not (Acts 7:25). The very next day he tried to assert his leadership among his people by intervening on behalf of a Hebrew being victimized by a fellow Hebrew. The aggressor responded to Moses' efforts with two rhetorical questions: "Who made you a ruler and judge over us? Do you intend to slay me as you slew the Egyptian?" This Hebrew man saw in Moses only a meddler. Moses now realized that his violent deed was known to his own countrymen and surely must eventually be revealed to Pharaoh. He was afraid, not so much of Pharaoh (Heb 11:27), but of the opinion of his fellow Hebrews. When Pharaoh heard what Moses had done, he sought to kill him.

B. Moses' Preparation in Midian (Ex 2:15b-22).

Moses' flight to Midian can be viewed as an act of faith (Heb 11:27) in that he made no effort to defend himself or reconcile himself to Pharaoh. The next forty years he lived in Midian. Through those difficult years Moses endured "as seeing him who is invisible" (Heb 11:27). Four developments in Moses' life during this period are clear.

1. Even after his leadership setback in Egypt, Moses was still willing to champion the cause of the weak. The seven unmarried daughters of Reuel, following the custom of that region, were shepherdesses. They had come to water their father's flock at a well, but some shepherds drove them away. This injustice aroused Moses' anger. He rescued the daughters and even watered their flock for them (2:15b-17).

2. Moses lodged in a godly home. Reuel ("friend of God"), was a "priest of Midian." Reuel is called Jethro in 3:1, a name which appears to be a title meaning "highness." He seems to have been a worshiper of Yahweh. This is not surprising since the Midianites were descendants of Abraham by Keturah. When Reuel heard of the kindness performed by Moses at the well, he rebuked his daughters for their lack of hospitality and sent them to seek out the "Egyptian." Reuel was so impressed with Moses that he invited him to live with him and manage his flocks. Moses agreed, and for the next forty years he lodged in the camp of Reuel (2:18-21a).

3. Moses eventually married Zipporah, one of the daughters of Reuel. By her he fathered Gershom ("sojourner there"). The name of the child reflected Moses' discouragement at being an exile from the land of his birth and from his people (2:21b-23).

4. Moses tended the flock of Reuel and learned the discipline of the desert for forty years (3:1a).

THE CALL OF A PROPHET
Exodus 2:23–4:31

The Pharaoh who sought Moses' life died, but the government policy of oppressing the Hebrews did not change. At this point the people of God turned with one accord to the Lord. They groaned and cried out to God for help. Four verbs stress the divine response: God *heard* their groaning; he *remembered* the covenant with the patriarchs; he *looked* on the Israelites; and he was *concerned* about them (2:23-25). The divine concern was translated into concrete action when God called a prophet to be their deliverer. The commissioning of Moses unfolded in three stages.

A. God Appeared to Moses at the Bush (Ex 3:1-10).

In the course of his duties of tending Jethro's flock, Moses came into the region of Horeb, the mountain of God. This mount may have been sacred already to the worshipers of the Lord. On the other hand, the text may call the place the "mountain of God" proleptically, i.e., in anticipation of what would shortly transpire there. Horeb actually refers to a range of mountains. The particular peak where God appeared was known as Sinai. At that mount the heavenly silence of four centuries was broken (cf. Gn 46:2-4).

The angel of Yahweh appeared to Moses in flames of fire from within a bush. This is not a visionary or inner experience.[3] What happened there cannot be explained on any naturalistic basis.[4] This was a genuine theophany, a manifestation of God. Moses observed that, while the bush was on fire, it was not consumed. He moved closer to investigate, and when he did, he heard the voice of God speak six words:

1. A word of address. God called Moses' name two times. Thus did God arrest the attention of the shepherd and at the same time indicate a personal acquaintance with him.

2. A word of warning. Moses must come no closer. He was standing on holy ground in the presence of God. He must show respect for the spot by removing his sandals. Sandals pick up dirt during a journey, and man must be clean when he approaches God!

3. A word of identity. The deity identified himself as the God of your father (singular), and the God of Abraham, Isaac and Jacob. Hearing this, Moses quickly covered his face, for he knew that it meant death to look upon God.

4. A word of compassion. Four precious indications of divine grace were given: "I have seen . . . I have heard their cry . . . I know . . . I am come down." God always is concerned about the welfare of his people.

5. A word of promise. God promised to bring his people out of Egypt and bring them into a land flowing with milk and honey.

6. A word of challenge. Moses was informed that he was being sent to lead the Israelites out of Egypt.

B. God Answered Moses' Objections (Ex 3:11–4:17).

Moses did not exactly jump at the chance to assume the leadership of a nation of slaves. That was an awesome task, and he shrank from it. Moses raised five objections to his appointment.

1. He pled lack of standing (3:11-12). "Who am I that I should go to Pharaoh?" The forty years in the wilderness obviously had humbled Moses. He felt woefully inadequate. God responded to this first objection with a twofold promise. First, the Lord promised to be with Moses. The believer's source of power is not who he is, but who is with him! Second, God promised Moses success. He would bring the people out of Egypt to worship their God on Mt. Sinai.

2. He cited ignorance (3:13-22). If he were asked, he would not be able to tell the Israelites the name of the God who was sending him. God answered this objection by telling Moses his name: *I am*. The statement "I am who I am" can be rendered a number of different ways in English. The statement basically emphasizes the timelessness of God. He is the self-existing one, the Eternal, the one without beginning or end. The God of Israel's ancestors was to be identified by the name Yahweh (He who is) throughout the generations.

After answering Moses' protest of ignorance regarding the divine name, God outlined the entire campaign against Egypt.

First, Moses was to go to the elders of Israel and tell them that God had appeared to him. He was to communicate to them God's concern for their plight, and his promise to bring them out of Egypt to a wonderful land. The land promise which had been given to the patriarchs was now renewed through Moses. Thus, as with any true prophet, the message of Moses was in agreement with earlier revelation. God assured Moses that the elders would believe him.

Second, the elders and Moses were then to go to Pharaoh to announce the appearance of God. They were to request permission to make a three-day journey into the wilderness to offer sacrifices to him. Pharaoh would not listen.

Third, God would smite Egypt with wonders, i.e., miraculous judgments.

Fourth, before they left Egypt, the Israelites would plunder Egypt. This also conforms to the promise made to Abraham (cf. Gn 15:14). Softened by blows from God, the Egyptians generously would bestow upon their former captives articles of gold and silver as well as clothing. The God of Israel would triumph so thoroughly over Egypt that women and children would carry away the spoils.

3. He complained that he lacked credentials (4:1-9). Moses feared that the people would not believe his claims regarding this encounter. The promise of a *future* sign in 3:12 did not quiet Moses' fears. God responded by granting to him three signs as proofs of his power. First, he was told to cast down his rod. Moses did as he was told, and the rod became a serpent. He was told to take up the serpent, and it became a rod. Second, he was told to thrust his hand inside his cloak, and it became leprous. He was told to put his hand back into his cloak, and it was whole again. Third, if his detractors would not believe the first two signs, he was to pour the water of the Nile on the ground where it would become blood.

4. He called attention to his lack of ability (4:10-12). Moses described himself as "slow of speech and tongue." He did not regard himself as an orator. God responded that he was in ultimate control of man's communication faculties. He promised to help Moses speak and to teach him what to say. During this encounter Moses addressed God twice (4:10,13), but in neither case did he use the name which God had revealed to him!

5. He pled with God to send someone else (4:13-17). This unwill-
ingness to serve angered the Lord. Aaron his brother was on his way
to the wilderness. He would serve as Moses' mouth. Moses, however,
would be "as God" to Aaron, i.e., he would be the ultimate human
leader of the nation. With his staff he would be able to perform miraculous signs, and that staff would be his symbol of authority.

C. God Assured Moses in the Way (Ex 4:18-31).

Five factors reinforced Moses' reluctant decision to accept the
divine challenge.

1. Moses received no protest from his father-in-law when he
requested leave to return to Egypt. Moses, however, did not reveal to
Jethro his full purpose (4:18).

2. As he set out for Egypt with his wife and sons (plural), he
received a further revelation from the Lord (4:19-23). Moses was to
perform his wonders, not just before Israel, but before Pharaoh as
well. God would harden Pharaoh's heart. He would not release Israel,
God's firstborn son, and so the Lord would slay the firstborn of the
king. Thus at the very outset Moses knew the final outcome of his
confrontation with Pharaoh.

3. Moses received divine discipline in the way (4:24-26). The designated leader of God's people had neglected to circumcise his
youngest son. God disciplined Moses through deathly sickness to
remind him of his obligations. A leader must first set things right in his
own household. This narrative contains a warning for every Israelite.
Even the great prophet Moses could not get by with failing to circumcise his son.

The reason for her husband's jeopardy was immediately perceived
by Zipporah. To save the life of her husband, she took a flint knife
and grudgingly circumcised her son. Just as shrewd action by Rachel
saved Jacob from Laban's wrath, so alert action by Zipporah saved
Moses from God's wrath. Her disgust at the rite of circumcision, however, is clear. She seems to have returned to her father's house after
this incident.

4. Moses met Aaron in the wilderness (4:27-28). This joyous reunion
fulfilled the earlier promise of God (cf. 4:15). His brother believed all that
Moses told him about what had transpired on the mount.

5. The elders of Israel gave Moses and Aaron a favorable reception just as God had promised (cf. 3:18). Aaron related to them all that God had spoken to Moses. He (Moses? or Aaron?) performed signs for them and they believed. The signs, no doubt, were those which were described in 4:3-9. Hearing of the compassion which God had for them, the people bowed down and worshiped (4:29-31).

ENDNOTES

1. J. Sidlow Baxter, *Explore the Book* (Grand Rapids: Zondervan, 1950), I:74.

2. Kitchen, *Ancient Orient,* pp. 54-55.

3. Roy L. Honeycutt, Jr., "Exodus," in *Broadman Bible Commentary,* ed. Clifton J. Allen (Nashville: Broadman, 1969), p. 328.

4. Werner Keller reports two types of naturalistic explanations: (1) the explosion of a gas plant native to the region; and (2) an optical illusion created by angles of sunlight reflecting off crimson berries or leaves. *The Bible as History* (New York: Morrow, 1956), p. 131.

BIBLIOGRAPHY: THE MOSAIC PERIOD

Beegle, Dewey M. *Moses, the Servant of Yahweh.* Grand Rapids: Eerdmans, 1972.

Gaubert, H. "Moses and Joshua." In *The Bible as History.* New York: Hastings House, 1969.

Rowley, H.H. *From Joshua to Joseph.* Oxford, 1950.

Taylor, W.M. *Moses the Lawgiver.* Grand Rapids: Baker, 1961 reprint.

von Rad, G. *Moses.* World Christian Books. London: Lutterworth, n.d.

CHAPTER TWENTY-TWO

Confrontation with Pharaoh
Exodus 5-8

AIM: To demonstrate the fairness of God's demands upon Pharaoh.

THEME: The King of Pharaohs.

In the fullness of time God intervened in a mighty way on behalf of his people. During the 430 years in Egypt, Israel had learned to trust God. The people had developed socially and numerically. The nation Israel was forged in the furnace of Egyptian suffering. At the same time, circumstances were ripe for God to bring judgment upon his enemies. The iniquity of the Amorites was now about full (cf. Gn 15:16), and the pretentious idolatry of Egypt cried to heaven for judgment.

In Exodus 5-15 two great leaders engage in a battle of the wills. Representing the people of God was Moses, a man raised in the Egyptian royal court and disciplined by the desert. His adversary was the Pharaoh of Egypt, an autocratic despot with delusions of deity.

INITIAL CONFRONTATION
Exodus 5:1-21

Bolstered by the expressions of confidence voiced by the people of Israel and by the promises of ultimate victory given in the wilderness, Moses and Aaron boldly marched to Pharaoh's palace to deliver God's demand (5:1,3). Pharaoh rejected out of hand any idea of releasing the Israelite slaves and issued orders which he believed would break up this incipient rebellion (7:2,4-9). His strategy seemed to work, as the Israelites turned against Moses and Aaron (5:10-21); and Moses, the designated deliverer, was overcome by debilitating discouragement (5:22-7:9).

A. God's Demand (Ex 5:1,3).

Seven times in Exodus 5–10 God demanded of Pharaoh, "Let my people go!" (5:1; 7:16; 8:1,20; 9:1,13; 10:3). The original demand was quite modest. Moses requested to lead the Israelites into the wilderness a journey of three days where they might offer sacrifices to Yahweh. Disaster might befall the Israelites if they failed to heed Yahweh's call to worship, Moses argued (5:1,3). This demand, modest though it was, set the stage for a confrontation which had repercussions for Pharaoh, Moses and Israel. Not without significance is the fact that in the first confrontation with Pharaoh no miraculous sign was requested by the Egyptian nor offered by Moses.

B. Pharaoh's Response (Ex 5:2,4-9).

Pharaoh responded to the divine demand with four utterances:

1. He asked an arrogant question: "Who is Yahweh that I should obey his voice?" He had never heard of a God by this name (5:2).

2. He categorically rejected the demand of Yahweh. Since he did not know Yahweh, he did not intend to release Israel (5:2).

3. He attacked Moses and Aaron, accusing them of taking his workers away from their labors. Since they were now a numerous people (an admission of the failure of past government policy), they were a threat to the crown (5:4,5).

4. He issued a new directive to his taskmasters and foremen (lit., scribes or tally men). No more were they to supply straw to the

Israelites. Yet the daily quota of bricks was not to be diminished. As Pharaoh saw it, the Israelites were simply lazy, and they were using the proposed religious pilgrimage as an excuse for suspending the work. They were being misled by Moses (5:6-9).

Pharaoh intended to drive a wedge between his Israelite slaves and their would-be deliverer. That he was able to do. The Israelites, embittered by their new burdens, turned their wrath against Moses.

C. The Foremen's Anger (Ex 5:10-21).

The taskmasters delivered the edict of Pharaoh to the Israelite workmen. The people fanned out over the whole land in search of stubble to use for straw. That the slaves would fail to meet their brick quotas was inevitable. Israelite foremen were beaten by the taskmasters (5:10-14).

The situation must have been desperate for the foremen dared to complain to Pharaoh about their treatment. How was it possible for them to meet their quotas when the Egyptians would give them no straw? Pharaoh offered them no sympathy. He accused them of being lazy and attributed their demands for a religious pilgrimage to that laziness (5:15-18).

The foremen now realized that the failure of the taskmasters to provide straw was not an administrative snafu, but state policy. The foremen found Moses and Aaron waiting for them, and they bitterly attacked the brothers. They called upon Yahweh to judge the two for having made the Israelites odious to Pharaoh and his servants. Far from delivering them from oppression, Moses and Aaron had given the Egyptians an excuse to kill Israelites (5:19-21).

INITIAL DISCOURAGEMENT
Exodus 5:22–7:9

Caught off guard by this sudden reversal of popular support, Moses plunged into discouragement (5:22–7:9). He went to the Lord (*'adonay,* master, boss) with a prayer of complaint. No deliverance had been effected by presenting God's word to Pharaoh. On the contrary, the plight of the people was worse than before. Moses wondered why he had been sent to Pharaoh at all if only to bring trouble (5:22-23).

A. A Reminder (Ex 6:1-5).

The word of God is a powerful antidote for discouragement. God responded to Moses' discouragement by reminding him of four things:

1. His promise. Because of God's mighty hand (twice mentioned) Pharaoh would not merely allow Israel to leave Egypt, he would drive them out (6:1).

2. His name. In patriarchal times God had revealed himself as *El Shaddai*, God Almighty, the God whose power worked in the lives of faithful men. Now he was revealing himself as Yahweh, the eternal, self-existing, self-consistent God. This name he had not made known, i.e., explained, clarified, in the days of the patriarchs (6:2-3).

3. His covenant. God's covenant with the patriarchs was that he would give them the land of Canaan where they lived as aliens (6:4).

4. His compassion. God had taken note of the groaning of his people, and he remembered his covenant (6:5).

B. An Assignment (Ex 6:6-12).

Discouragement festers in inaction. God directed Moses to get back to work. He was to speak again to the Israelites and tell them three things:

1. The eternal God would be true to his promises. He intended to redeem Israel with an outstretched arm and mighty acts of judgment (6:6).

2. By delivering Israel from bondage God would thereby be choosing them as his own. Israel would then know by experience that they were a most favored nation (6:7).

3. He would honor the oath which he had given to the patriarchs. He would give them a land of their own (6:8).

Moses obeyed the Lord and delivered the message. The discouragement of the Israelites, however, was so great that they would not listen to the words which he spoke (6:9).

God then gave Moses another assignment. He was to return to Pharaoh to demand the release of God's people. Moses objected. If the Israelites would not listen, what hope was there of any positive response from Pharaoh. Moses again brought up the matter of his speaking ability. He was a man of "uncircumcised," i.e., faltering, lips (6:10-12).

C. A Battle Plan (Ex 6:13–7:9).

In response to Moses' renewed discouragement, God did four things:

1. He repeated the charge to Moses and Aaron. They were to bring the Israelites out of Egypt, and this could only be done by confronting Pharaoh (6:13).

2. He renewed Aaron's appointment. Moses would receive divine revelation; Aaron, like a faithful prophet, would make that revelation public. Moses would be as God to Pharaoh, albeit a God to whom Pharaoh would not listen (7:1-2).

3. He revealed to Moses in more detail the fivefold course of events: first, miraculous signs and wonders would be performed in Egypt. Second, God would harden Pharaoh's heart. Third, God would perform mighty acts of judgment against Egypt. Fourth, the deliverance of the Israelites would be effected. Finally, the Egyptians would recognize that Yahweh was God (7:3-5).

4. He authorized his servants to use the first miracle in the presence of Pharaoh (7:8-9).

Two parenthetical notes amplify this section of Exodus. The ancestry of Moses and Aaron is given in 6:14-27. They were Levites of the clan of Kohath. Amram their father had married his aunt Jochebed. That type of marriage would later be forbidden in the Law of Moses (Lv 18:12; 20:19). Aaron's family is mentioned for the first time here. His wife Elisheba was of the tribe of Judah. By her Aaron had four sons who played a prominent role in later events. The other parenthetical note reveals the ages of Moses (80) and Aaron (83) when they appeared before Pharaoh (7:7).

SECOND CONFRONTATION
Exodus 7:10-13

In the second confrontation with Pharaoh the Egyptian king demanded miraculous credentials from the Israelite brothers. Aaron threw the rod on the ground and it became a large snake *(tannin)*. This is not the ordinary word for "serpent" used in 4:3. The basic meaning of the Hebrew root is something large, powerful or mighty. Some writers think a crocodile is intended.

In any case, Pharaoh summoned his wise men (counselors), sorcerers, and magicians. They did the same thing with their secret arts. How were they able to duplicate the miracle? Was this an optical illusion?[1] A Satanic miracle?[2] Sleight of hand magic?[3] Kitchen has suggested that the magicians made use of the techniques of snake charming. By pressing certain muscles in the back of the neck an asp can be made to appear rigid.[4] Be that as it may, the serpent which came from Aaron's staff swallowed up the other serpents. In spite of this Pharaoh hardened his heart.

RIVER PLAGUES
Exodus 7:14–8:14

To bring Pharaoh to his knees before his Creator, God launched an elaborate, gradually intensifying, program of disciplinary disasters against Egypt. The first two plagues were connected with the waters of Egypt, especially the Nile. This river, which was sacred to the Egyptians, was attacked by God with two plagues, the plagues of blood and frogs. These were nuisance plagues which, while loathsome and annoying, neither resulted in material loss nor in severe human affliction. Both were announced in advance by Moses. Both were imitated by the magicians. The first made no impact at all on Pharaoh; the second forced him to ask Moses to intercede for him.

A. Plague of Blood (Ex 7:14-25).

For a third time Moses confronted Pharaoh, this time at the Nile River where, no doubt, the king had gone to perform some religious ablution. Moses repeated his earlier claim to be an emissary of the the Lord, God of the Hebrews (cf. 5:1). As God's ambassador he employed the traditional messenger formula ("Thus says Yahweh") which was employed by high ranking diplomats when bearing messages from a superior king to his subordinates. To credential his claim to be the spokesman of deity, Moses announced what he was about to do with his rod. "In this," he said, "you (singular) shall know that I am Yahweh" (7:14-19). He would smite the waters of Egypt with his rod, and they would turn to blood.

Moses made good on his threat. The waters of the Nile with all of its streams and canals turned to blood. The water smelled so foul that the Egyptians could not drink it. Even water standing in vessels was contaminated. Eventually the Egyptians were forced to dig wells (or perhaps filter pits) to secure drinking water. Nonetheless, Pharaoh hardened his heart because his magicians could imitate the miracle with their magic arts. This plague lasted at least seven days (7:20-25).

B. Plague of Frogs (Ex 8:1-7).

Again Moses confronted Pharaoh with the demand for freedom and a threat. He would make the land swarm with frogs. When Aaron stretched forth his staff over the waters, that is exactly what happened. Again the magicians were able to imitate the miracle. This plague was more serious than the first in that the very homes of the Egyptians were invaded. Frog plagues were common in Egypt. The miracle here lies in the timing and abnormal multiplication of these creatures.

During the plague of frogs Pharaoh summoned Moses and Aaron for the first time. He would allow the Israelites to go offer their sacrifices if the frogs were removed. Moses challenged Pharaoh to name the time for the removal. He then announced that the frogs would be removed, according to the word of Pharaoh, the next day. The two leaders cried unto the Lord, and the frogs died out on the land. The rotting carcasses were piled up throughout Egypt. The land reeked of them. When Pharaoh saw that his land had relief, however, he hardened his heart just as the Lord had predicted (8:8-15).

NUISANCE PLAGUES
Exodus 8:15-32

In the second pair of plagues God used tiny blood-sucking insects to make life miserable for the Egyptians. The first of these plagues was unannounced, as if to punish Pharaoh for revoking his commitment to release the Israelites. The second —the plague of flies — was announced. At the conclusion of this pair of plagues the haughty Egyptian king explored the possibility of compromise with his adversary Moses.

A. Plague of Lice (Ex 8:16-19).

The Hebrew word *kinnim* has been translated lice, fleas, gnats and even mosquitoes. Obviously some blood-sucking insect is involved. This plague was unannounced. Aaron struck the ground with the rod and the *kinnim* appeared from the dust. The magicians tried to imitate the miracle but could not. Were the *kinnim* too small for magical manipulation? Did God restrain the demonic power of the magicians? Perhaps they simply gave up in discouragement. The magicians quit the contest with the announcement that this was the result of the finger of God. Nonetheless, Pharaoh hardened his heart.

B. Plague of Flies (Ex 8:20-32).

The first round of plagues ended as it had begun, with the freedom demand accompanied by a threat. The next day swarms of flies would attack the Egyptians, but not Goshen where the Israelites lived. That is exactly what happened. Jewish tradition makes this the plague of vermin, but probably the blood-sucking dog fly is intended. No mention is made of the use of the rod in producing this plague.

Pharaoh was now ready for compromise. He was willing to allow the Israelites to sacrifice to God as long as they did it in the land of Egypt. Moses countered by saying that the Israelite sacrifices would antagonize the Egyptians to the point of murderous attack. Sheep were an abomination to the Egyptians (Gn 46:34), and bulls and heifers were sacred to the Egyptians.

Pharaoh offered a second compromise. The Israelites could go into the desert to offer their sacrifices, if they did not go far. Moses interpreted this as equivalent to the three-day journey which he had been demanding, so he agreed to pray for the cessation of the fourth plague. In answer to Moses' prayer the flies totally disappeared. Pharaoh again hardened his heart.

ENDNOTES

1. F.C. Cook, ed., *The Holy Bible with Explanatory and Critical Commentary* (New York: Scribners, n.d.), I:276.

2. Merrill F. Unger, *Biblical Demonology* (Wheaton: Scripture Press, 1965), p. 112.

3. George Rawlinson, "Exodus," in *Ellicott's Commentary on the Whole Bible*, ed. Charles John Ellicott (Grand Rapids: Zondervan, n.d.), p. 121.

4. K.A. Kitchen, s.v. "Magic and Sorcery," *The New Bible Dictionary*, p. 769.

CHAPTER TWENTY-THREE

Conflict with Egypt
Exodus 9-10

AIM: To demonstrate the progressive severity of God's judgment upon his enemies.

THEME: The power of Israel's God!

The river plagues and nuisance plagues were followed in turn by six additional plagues. These may be viewed in three pairs: the disease plagues, the destruction plagues and the darkness plagues. Though Pharaoh continued to renege on promises to free the Israelites, some movement on his part is observable throughout the contest. During the plague of frogs he had asked Moses to pray to Yahweh to have the plague removed. After the plague of flies the Egyptian offered two compromises to Moses. Yet more compromise followed during the last six plagues.

DISEASE PLAGUES
Exodus 9:1-12

As the contest escalated, God sent upon Egypt the plagues of murrain and boils. From the first of these the livestock throughout Egypt died. The second affliction fell upon man as well as beast. From both plagues the land of Goshen was exempt.

A. Plague of Murrain (Ex 9:1-7).

The fifth plague again began with the freedom demand and a threat. If Pharaoh refused to heed, a terrible disease would afflict the cattle of Egypt the next day. Again the area of Goshen would be exempt. So it was. Egyptian livestock by the thousands died. Pharaoh sent servants to investigate conditions in Goshen and found them just as Moses had predicted. Yet Pharaoh still would not release the Israelites. No mention is made of Aaron in this plague.

B. Plague of Boils (Ex 9:8-12).

As in the case of the third plague, no direct prediction is recorded prior to the plague of boils. God directed Moses to take handfuls of soot from a furnace and toss them into the air in Pharaoh's presence. That Moses said nothing threatening while performing this action is difficult to imagine. In any case, festering boils broke out on men and animals throughout the land. This plague may have lasted for weeks. The bodies of the magicians were so disfigured that they could no longer appear before Moses. The people suffered more under this plague than any of those which preceded. At this point, for the first time, the text states that *God* hardened Pharaoh's heart.

DESTRUCTION PLAGUES
Exodus 9:13–10:29

In the seventh and eighth plagues God destroyed the crops of Egypt by means of hail and locusts. Moses was the executor in these two plagues.

A. Plague of Hail (Ex 9:13-35).

For the seventh time Moses confronted Pharaoh with the demand of Yahweh. Thus far Yahweh had restrained himself. In his prior refusals to release the Israelites, Pharaoh was creating the occasion through which God could show his power. The name of the Lord would be proclaimed throughout all the earth because of what would happen in Egypt. The next blow against the land would be a hailstorm, the worst that had ever befallen Egypt. Pharaoh was advised to order all his livestock to be brought in from the field lest they be killed. Some of Pharaoh's officials heeded this warning.

When Moses stretched his hand toward the sky, the hail fell. Lightning streaking to the ground, and thunder made the storm that much worse. The barley and flax crop which had ripened in the field was devastated; the trees were stripped. Animals and their keepers in the open fields were slain. The only place where the killer storm did not strike was in Goshen.

Pharaoh summoned Moses and Aaron. This time, when he had been emphatically warned beforehand, he admitted being in the wrong. He promised to release the Israelites if the plague were removed. Moses agreed to pray, but he expressed doubt that Pharaoh really feared Yahweh.

Moses was right. As soon as the storm subsided Pharaoh sinned again. He and his officials hardened their hearts and refused to order the release of the Israelites. Thus the Lord's original prediction regarding the hardening of Pharaoh's heart continued to be fulfilled.

B. Plague of Locusts (Ex 10:1-20).

Pharaoh had so hardened his heart that God determined to abandon him to the consequences of his hardness. Thus the text states that God hardened Pharaoh's heart. Against this hardened sinner God would perform wonders which would be rehearsed for generations to come. In the plagues the Israelites would come to know that their God was Yahweh, the Eternal One.

Again the alternative to obedience was made clear to Pharaoh. On the next day locusts would sweep across Egypt destroying the vegetation, especially the wheat and spelt, which had survived the hail. Egypt had experienced devastation by locusts before, but this plague would be far worse. With this Moses turned and left the presence of Pharaoh.

With Moses absent the officials finally cracked. They urged Pharaoh to allow the Israelites to depart to worship their God. Egypt had already been ruined by the first seven plagues. Moved by the appeals of his advisors, Pharaoh had the two Israelite brothers brought again into his chamber. He attempted to negotiate. Pharaoh was willing to allow the men to go worship, but they must leave women and children in Egypt as hostages. When Moses refused to agree to this proposal, he and Aaron were driven from the presence of Pharaoh.

When Moses stretched out his rod over Egypt, an east wind began to blow across the land. By morning the ground was black with the insects. Every green thing was devoured, even the fruit of the trees. Again Pharaoh summoned Moses. He confessed his sin, begged forgiveness, and asked the prophet to pray that the plague be stayed. When the prophet prayed, the Lord reversed the winds and drove all the locusts into the Red Sea. Still God hardened Pharaoh's heart, i.e., he *permitted* his heart to remain hard by doing nothing to soften it.

PLAGUE OF DARKNESS
Exodus 10:21-29

No specific prediction accompanied the ninth plague. Moses' gesture toward the sky brought a darkness which could be felt in the land. Surely this gesture was performed in the presence of Pharaoh and accompanied by a threatening announcement. This plague seems designed to herald the tenth and final plague which occurred in the darkness of the night and involved the darkness of death.

What seems to be described here is what is called the *khamsin*, a sand storm of such proportions that the light of the sun was blotted out completely. For three days the Egyptians dared not leave the safety of their dwellings. Yet in the land of Goshen there was light!

Pharaoh summoned Moses and suggested another compromise. The women and children could go with the men, but the livestock must be left behind as surety. Moses responded that the animals would be needed to provide sacrifices in the worship. At this point Moses did not know how many sacrificial animals would be needed, nor what varieties the Lord would require.

Pharaoh was now exasperated! Moses would not compromise. He ordered the prophet out of his presence, and threatened to kill Moses if he ever laid eyes on him. Moses agreed never to see the king again (10:27-29).

OBSERVATIONS ABOUT THE PLAGUES

The terminology "ten plagues" is not found in Scripture. Only six plagues are mentioned in Psalm 78:42-51 and eight in Psalm 105:28-36. Having now surveyed the plague narratives, it is appropriate to make some general observations about (1) the nature, (2) purpose, and (3) chronology of the plagues as well as (4) the hardening of Pharaoh's heart.

A. Nature of the Plagues.

A rich terminology is used in reference to the ten plagues. These terms are:

1. Wonders (*mopheth*). Used four times in Exodus and eleven other places. Basic idea: something that draws attention; a miracle.

2. Wonders (*pala'*). Used once in Exodus and once elsewhere. Basic idea: something extraordinary or wonderful.

3. Signs (*'oth*). Used six times in Exodus and thirteen times elsewhere. Basic idea: that which points to the power of God.

4. Plagues (*maggephah*). Used once in Exodus and once elsewhere. Basic idea: blows or smitings.

5. Stroke (*nega'*). Used once. Basic idea: a touch or smiting.

6. Blow (*negeph*). Used once. Closely related in meaning to the word for "plagues."

The terminology thus suggests that the plagues were miracles designed to point to the almighty power of God; and they were acts of judgment against Egypt.

A Bible believer cannot possibly accept the conclusion of Rylaarsdam that the accounts just surveyed were "fantastic stories" which are to be regarded as "symbolic rather than historical."[1] More common among the critics is the view that the plagues were intensified natural disasters. These disasters were triggered by a volcanic eruption at the head of the Nile,[2] or in the Mediterranean.[3] According to the latter theory, the eruption would result in reddish water, whirlwinds, volcanic hail, darkness, and eventually a tidal wave at the Red Sea which would drown Pharaoh's host! Of those who have taken the intensified natural disaster view, Greta Hort has worked out the most comprehensive theory.[4] According to Hort the sequence of events went something like this:

1. The blood red river was caused by the red silting of Nile when it was in flood stage. Minute organisms sucked up the oxygen, thus accounting for the fish kill.

2. The frogs were driven on to land by the decaying fish in the river.

3. *Kinnim* are identified as mosquitoes which laid eggs in pools left by receding waters of Nile in late October or November.

4. The flies hatched in the decaying fish and frogs. Breezes kept Goshen in the north free of these flies.

5. The murrain was caused by the anthrax bacteria contracted by the frogs from the dead fish. Cattle in the field fed on grass contaminated by the waste of these frogs, thus contacting the disease.

6. The boils were skin anthrax carried by the flies of the fourth plague.

7. Cool, moist air of the Mediterranean meeting the hot air of Upper Egypt created this violent hail storm. In Goshen the temperature was too cool to form hail.

8. Hot wind drove the locusts over Egypt from their usual path over the Red Sea. A sea breeze cleared the land.

9. A reversal of normal wind patterns brought a sand storm from the desert which blotted out the sun and created a darkness which could be felt. Goshen was protected by the hills and mild winds.

Hort thus demonstrates what would appear to be an interconnection between the plagues. There are data in the account, however, which she ignores. These data point to the view that the plagues were separate miracles.

1. *Intensification* marks those plagues which represent a "natural" phenomenon like frogs, flies, murrain, hail, locusts and darkness. Disasters of these proportions had never before been experienced in Egypt.

2. The *immediacy* of the plagues points to divine miracle. Plague conditions developed immediately after a word or gesture.

3. The plagues were carefully *controlled*. This was not Mother

Nature on the rampage. God's servant could call forth a plague or make one cease at will.

4. The element of *prediction* makes these plagues miracles. They came and ceased exactly as Moses predicted. In one case Pharaoh was allowed to name the time of the removal of a plague (8:9).

5. Beginning with the fourth plague a *discrimination* between Israel and Egypt in the administration of the plagues is evident. Explanations of this fact on naturalistic grounds are strained.

6. The plagues reveal a certain *progressiveness*. An escalation of suffering and personal loss by the Egyptians is indicated. A progression in the demonstration of the power of God (9:14), the fear of the Egyptians, and the hardening of Pharaoh is also clear.

7. The *reaction of the Egyptians* indicates that the plagues were more than natural disasters. At the end of the third plague the magicians commented, "This is the finger of God!" When the eighth plague was threatened, the closest advisors of Pharaoh pled with him to release the Israelites because Egypt was ruined.

8. The *source* of some plagues points to miracle. Water turning to blood, dust into lice, and ashes into boils are not "natural" phenomena.

B. Purpose of the Plagues.

The plagues had momentous ramifications in five different areas.

1. The plagues were designed to discredit the gods of Egypt. Before the tenth plague God asserted, "I will bring judgment on all the gods of Egypt" (Ex 12:12; cf. Nm 33:4). This is especially evident in the first, second, fifth and ninth plagues. In the first plague the sacred Nile was affected. By the end of the second plague the Egyptians detested Ptha, the frog-headed god and Heka, a frog goddess. Apis the sacred bull could not spare his kind from the ravishing effects of the murrain. Ra the sun god could not penetrate the darkness in which Yahweh wrapped Egypt in the ninth plague.

2. The plagues also served to discredit the religious leaders of Egypt. The counsel of Pharaoh's wisest men, the sorcery and magic of his personal ministers could not prevent or remove the plagues. In the third plague the magicians retreated from the contest; in the sixth plague they were rendered unclean by the festering boils and thus disqualified from officiating in their priestly role.

3. The plagues revealed the impotence of Pharaoh as a ruler and god. His total lack of integrity, his stubbornness, arrogance, and mortality are clearly shown in the narrative. He was forced during the contest to offer four compromises to Moses, and in the end he was compelled to release the Israelites.

4. With respect to the Israelites, the plagues were designed to free them from bondage and convince them of the sole divinity of Yahweh. They were a visual lesson of God's awesome power.

5. The plagues were also God's judgment on the land of Egypt for the years of mistreatment of his people.

6. The plagues were designed gradually to magnify the power of God. In the first two plagues the power of God was imitated by the magicians. They, however, were unable to remove the plagues. In plagues three through six the restrained power of God was manifested. God's unbridled power was manifested in plagues seven through ten (9:14).

The above six purposes can be summed up in the word *know*. The contest began when Pharaoh declared that he did not *know* Yahweh. This word thereafter becomes a key word in the narrative. Through the plagues all parties would come to *know* Yahweh — Israel (6:7; 10:2; 11:17); the Egyptians (7:5; 14:4,18); and Pharaoh (7:17; 8:10,22; 9:14,29). To *know* Yahweh means to recognize him because of personal experience and then submit to his authority.

C. Chronology of the Plagues.

The duration of the plagues is indicated only with respect to the first and ninth plagues. Exodus 7:25 seems to suggest, but does not necessarily demand, that the Nile remained blood-like for seven days. In the ninth plague darkness enveloped the land for three days (10:22). How long the other plagues lasted is not stated. Each may have lasted days, weeks or even months.

In attempting to reconstruct the chronology of the plagues it is necessary to begin in reverse order. The Passover celebration on the night of deliverance falls in the spring of the year, in late March or early April (13:4; 23:15). The plague of the locusts probably took place in early March when this insect migrates. The plague of hail must have taken place in late January or early February when barley and flax are ripe (9:31). No clue is found in the text with regard to the passage of time during the first six plagues. Beegle would place the first plague in August and the plague of *kinnim* in October or November.[5] If his reconstruction is correct, the plagues lasted for approximately nine months. Most writers conclude that the plagues lasted a year or less.

Chart No. 21

THE PLAGUES AGAINST EGYPT				
RIVER PLAGUES	NUISANCE PLAGUES	DISEASE PLAGUES	DESTRUCTION PLAGUES	DARKNESS PLAGUES
1. BLOOD	3. LICE	5. MURRAIN	7. HAIL	9. DARKNESS
2. FROGS	4. FLIES	6. BOILS	8. LOCUST	10. DEATH
Aug.	Nov.	Jan.	Mar.	Apr.
All Egypt Affected	GOSHEN EXEMPT			
Aaron Performs Symbolic Acts	Predicted without Action	Moses Performs the Symbolic Act		Pre-dicted

D. Hardening of Pharaoh's Heart.

Twenty times in Exodus 4–14 statements are made regarding the hardening of Pharaoh's heart. Three different verbs are used to describe the act of hardening:

1. *Kabed*, to be heavy, is used six times. This word is used of the failure of an organ due to age or disease. Hence, when Pharaoh's heart was "heavy" it was no longer receptive to outside positive influences.

2. *Chazaq*, to be strong, hard or "bullheaded," is used twelve times.

3. *Qashah*, to be hard, difficult, severe, is used one time.

Ten times God is the subject of the verb. Four times Pharaoh hardens his own heart. Six times Pharaoh's heart is hardened. Before the plagues commenced, God predicted twice that he would harden Pharaoh's heart (4:21; 7:3). No notice, however, is given to the active role of God in the hardening until after the sixth plague (9:12). At least seven times before the sixth plague the text indicates either that Pharaoh hardened his heart or that his heart was hardened. The hardening, then, would appear to be an example of the permissive will of God. God permitted Pharaoh to continue in his self-imposed hardness and withdrew from him whatever inducements there might have been to listen to the demands of Moses. Paul argued that God raised up Pharaoh (i.e., allowed him to come to power) so that in dealing with him the magnitude of divine power might be manifested (Rom 9:17).

ENDNOTES

1. J. Coert Rylaarsdam, "Exodus," in *The Interpreter's Bible*, ed. George Buttrick (New York: Abingdon, 1952), I:839.

2. W.J. Phythian-Adams, "The Volcanic Phenomena of the Exodus," *Journal of the Palestinian Oriental Society*, XII (1932).

3. Reported by John Lear, "The Volcano that Shaped the Western World," *The Saturday Review*, Nov. 5, 1966.

4. Greta Hort has pointed out that the first nine plagues form a logical and connected sequence beginning with the abnormally high Nile inundation in August and ending about March. Cited by K.A. Kitchen, s.v. "Plagues of Egypt," *The New Bible Dictionary*, p. 1001.

5. Beegle, *Moses*, p. 102.

CHAPTER TWENTY-FOUR

Death and Deliverance
Exodus 11:1-15:21

AIM: To demonstrate the typological significance of the events surrounding the Exodus.

THEME: Free at last!

At the end of the ninth plague, three things transpired. First, God hardened Pharaoh's heart (10:27). The king was not willing to let the Israelites go free. Second, Pharaoh banished Moses from his presence (10:28). Moses would die if he saw Pharaoh's face again. Third, Moses spoke prophetic words. He predicted that he would not indeed see the face of Pharaoh again. Before he left the presence of the king for the last time, however, Moses described in detail to him the devastation of the tenth and final plague (11:4-8).

PLAGUE OF DELIVERANCE
Exodus 11:1-10;12:29-36

In regard to the tenth plague, the text indicates how the plague was (1) revealed, (2) announced, and (3) implemented.

A. The Revelation (Ex 11:1-3).

Even before Moses had left Midian, he was told that the campaign to free Israel would necessitate the death of the firstborn in the land of Egypt (4:23). Apparently a more detailed explanation of that plague had been given to Moses sometime during the last triad of plagues. Exodus 11:1-3 is parenthetical. Prior to his last appearance before Pharaoh, God had indicated to Moses that there would be one last plague. After that plague the Israelites would be free! In fact, Pharaoh would drive them out of his land!

God had promised Abraham that his descendants would come out of Egypt with great possessions (Gn 15:14). God had told Moses at the bush how the promise of great possessions would be fulfilled. That provision of the deliverance was now about to be implemented. The Israelites were to ask their neighbors for valuable objects of gold and silver. As if to justify this incredible directive, the narrator points out that by this time the attitude of the Egyptians toward the Israelites was quite different from that of the government. Moses was highly regarded throughout the land, even by the officials, and the Egyptians were favorably disposed toward the Israelites (11:1-3).

B. The Proclamation (Ex 11:4-10).

Before he left the presence of Pharaoh for the last time, Moses described in graphic detail what was about to befall the land of Egypt. Yahweh declared that he himself would pass through the land. Every firstborn in the land would die, including the firstborn of animals and even the heir to the throne. A wail would go up such as Egypt had never before experienced. Among the Israelites, however, not so much as a bark of a dog would be heard. Pharaoh would see clearly that this was no ordinary pestilence, for God would be showing that the Israelites were a special people. Pharaoh's officials would come to Moses, bowing in respect, and requesting that he and all his followers

278

leave Egypt. All of this would happen "about midnight," but on what night Moses did not say (11:4-8).

Before the execution of the last terrible plague the narrator reminds his readers of the prediction which God had made at the outset of the struggle. Pharaoh would refuse to comply with the demand to release the people. This refusal would necessitate the performance of mighty wonders in the land. With each new wonder, Pharaoh became more stubborn in his determination to resist the demands of Moses. In this sense God hardened Pharaoh's heart. By sending the plagues in gradually increasing intensity, God provided the occasion in which Pharaoh hardened his heart to his own destruction (11:9-10).

C. The Execution (Ex 12:29-36).

The plague of the firstborn struck in the middle of that very night. Every home experienced loss as Yahweh struck down the firstborn males of Egypt. Even the firstborn of the livestock were affected. No naturalistic explanation for this plague can successfully be maintained. A believer certainly cannot countenance the view that a pestilence struck Egyptian children, and later tradition remembered this as affecting only the firstborn.[1] No more acceptable is the view that the term "firstborn" is used in a loose sense and means only "the choice young men."[2] What is recorded here is true miracle, for no disease attacks only the firstborn of men and beasts. Certainly the Egyptians were not looking for naturalistic explanations of their calamity. They were too preoccupied with expressing their grief. A loud wailing could be heard throughout the land of Egypt (12:29-30).

Breaking his own word that he would never again see Moses, Pharaoh summoned the Israelite brothers during the night. He offered no further compromises. Pharaoh totally capitulated. The Israelites were to go to worship their God with their flocks and herds as they had requested. Before they left, however, Pharaoh requested that they pronounce a blessing on him. Hearing of this edict from Pharaoh, the Egyptians urged the Israelites to leave hastily. They feared for their own lives if the slaves remained much longer in the land (12:31-33).

Taking advantage of the mourning of the Egyptians, the Israelites "plundered" their captors before leaving. No physical violence was employed. They simply followed Moses' instructions and asked the

Egyptians for articles of silver and gold. Through the events of recent months, the Lord had made it clear to the Egyptians that the Israelites were a special people. Consequently the Egyptians were favorably disposed toward the Israelites, and gave them whatever they wanted (12:34-36).

PASSOVER OF DELIVERANCE
Exodus 12:1-28

Before the execution of the tenth plague, the Lord made clear that the month of deliverance, the seventh month on the civil calendar, was henceforth to be considered the first month of the year. This month was called Abib, but after the captivity the name Nisan was adopted. Abib corresponds to late March or early April on the present calendar. The night of deliverance was to be observed by a special celebration called "Yahweh's Passover." The Passover centered around (1) the slaying and (2) eating of a lamb, and (3) a festival of unleavened bread.

A. Slaying the Lamb (Ex 12:1-7).

Pertaining to the selecting of the Passover lamb, the following regulations applied:

1. Each household was to have its own lamb. Smaller households, however, could join together for the observance.

2. The animal could come from either the sheep or goats. A lamb, however, was most common.

3. The lamb was selected on the tenth day of the first month.

4. The animal selected had to be a one-year-old male without spot or blemish.

5. The lamb was to be kept apart for four days. Some see in this an allusion to the four generations which the Israelites remained in Egypt.

"Between the evenings" on the fourteenth day of Abib the lamb was to be slain. The first "evening" was immediately after noon; the second, after sunset. "Between the evenings" refers to mid-afternoon.

The blood of the lamb was to be smeared on the top and sides of the doorframes of the house where the Passover meal was to be

280

eaten. The blood was applied with a bunch of hyssop. The destroyer (an angel? pestilence?) would not enter the house where the blood had been applied. No one, however, was to leave his home that night (12:22f.).

B. Eating the Lamb (Ex 12:8-14).

The regulations regarding the eating of the Passover lamb are as follows:

1. The lamb was to be roasted whole over an open fire, thus giving it the appearance of a sacrificial animal.

2. It was to be eaten with bitter herbs, to remind them of the bitterness of their bondage.

3. It was to be eaten with unleavened bread, a reminder of the haste with which they left Egypt.

4. It was to be eaten at one sitting. Passover relates only to one night. This regulation also prevented spoilage and the treating of the meat as common.

5. It was to be eaten in haste. They were to be dressed for abrupt departure. Their sandals should be on their feet, their staff in their hand and their robe tucked into their belt, which was customary when a person had to engage in strenuous activity. This rule seems to apply only to the original Passover, not later observances (12:8-11).

The Passover was to be eaten annually as a joyful memorial feast (12:14). Through "the Passover sacrifice" future generations could be taught concerning the Exodus (12:24-27).

C. Unleavened Bread (Ex 12:15-28).

Closely associated with the Passover was the Feast of Unleavened Bread. The regulations governing the future observance of this feast were as follows:

1. The feast was to last seven days. No leavened bread was to be eaten during this time.

2. Leaven was to be removed from the house on the first day of the feast.

3. The first and seventh days are designated as days of *miqra' qodesh*, "sacred assembly" (NIV) or "holy assembly" (NASB). No work was permitted on these days except food preparation.

4. The celebration began on the fourteenth day of the first month, the same day when the Passover lamb was slain.

5. Anyone who ate leavened bread during the seven days was to be cut off from the congregation of Israel.

Twice the narrative emphasizes how the Israelites carried out precisely the Passover instructions which they had received from Moses (12:28,50).

PATH OF DELIVERANCE
Exodus 12:37–14:31

Station by station the journey to freedom proceeded: Rameses, Succoth, Etham, Pi Hahiroth. Once the Israelites crossed the Red Sea, they were free at last!

A. At Rameses (Ex 12:37-42).

The point of departure was one of the cities which the Israelites had built. Seven facts regarding the beginning of the march are narrated:

1. About six hundred thousand men participated.[3] Counting women and children, the group must have numbered about two million.

2. A large number of non-Israelites joined in the Exodus. They may have been motivated by the devastated condition of Egypt and the promise of a new land.

3. The march must have been slow, for large flocks and herds were taken along.

4. Because of their hasty departure the only food they had were cakes baked from the unleavened dough which they carried with them.

5. They departed on the 430th anniversary of Jacob's entrance into Egypt.[4]

6. The march was organized in military fashion, for the text speaks of "Yahweh's divisions."

7. Yahweh was leading his people that night and this was cause for celebration (12:37-42).

B. At Succoth (Ex 12:43–13:16).

At Succoth God taught his people. Four sets of instructions were given. First, additional instructions regarding Passover observance were set forth. Passover was only for the circumcised. Gentiles who accepted circumcision, i.e., were converted, could also participate. Passover was a home celebration. No part of the lamb was to be eaten outside the house. No bone of the Passover lamb was to be broken. The prophetic symbolism of this restriction is brought out in John 19:36 (12:43-51). These additional instructions were necessary because of the many non-Israelites who had joined in the Exodus.

Second, Moses gave instructions regarding the perpetual observance of the Feast of Unleavened Bread. Israelites were not to forget this feast when they came into Canaan. Unleavened Bread must be observed annually in order to (1) provide an opportunity to teach children; and (2) serve as a reminder constantly to speak of the law of God (13:3-10).

Third, Moses set forth instructions regarding the firstborn. Since God had spared the firstborn of Israelite men and animals, he had a claim upon their lives. The firstborn henceforth belonged to God (13:1-2). Firstborn sons could be redeemed. Firstborn of unclean animals (represented by the donkey) had to be redeemed with a lamb or destroyed. The law of the firstborn was also designed to provoke inquiry from children (13:11-16).

Finally, instructions were given regarding travel. God directed his people south toward the Red Sea rather than northward on the *Via Maris* through the land of the Philistines. The Israelites went up in martial array. Moses saw to it that the bones of Joseph went with them (3:17-19).

C. At Etham (Ex 13:20-22).

Etham was on the edge the desert. Here for the first time mention is made of the visible leading of the Lord in the pillar of cloud by day and the pillar of fire by night. This pillar was the proof of God's presence, and an expression of his love and care for Israel. The view that this cloud emanated from a volcanic Mt. Sinai must be rejected.[5] Mt. Sinai was not volcanic. Worse still is the suggestion that the cloud resulted from a fire brazier carried by a guide on a long pole![6]

D. At Pi Hahiroth (Ex 14:1-20).

From Succoth God told his people to "turn back" from their direct course to Sinai and encamp near Pi Hahiroth. The purpose of this unexpected directional change was to lure Pharaoh into thinking that they were lost and confused, hemmed in by the desert. By this move, God would harden Pharaoh's heart, i.e., create the occasion by which he would determine to make the effort to enslave the Israelites again. God's purpose here, as during the ten plagues, was to perform a wonder so spectacular that the Egyptians would come to "know" him as supreme deity (14:1-4).

Just as God predicted, when Pharaoh received word of the whereabouts of his former slaves, he and his officials reevaluated their options. They decided that they could not afford to lose this labor force. An army, led by six hundred of the best chariots and Pharaoh himself, set out to capture the runaway slaves. Normally such chariots were manned by a driver and an archer. In this case, each chariot had a third man, "an officer." The king probably led the army out of his capital a short distance, and then returned to his palace. The text indicates that *the Egyptians,* not Pharaoh, overtook the Israelites as they camped by the sea (14:5-9).

The Israelites went out of Egypt "with a high hand," i.e., under the protection of a high hand (14:8). Nevertheless, when they saw the enemy approaching in the distance, they panicked. To the east was the sea, to the south and west were mountains, and Pharaoh was pressing in from the north. First they cried to the Lord. Then they turned on Moses with a series of "I told you so" questions. In their despair they evaluated their servitude to Egypt as better than a slaughter by Pharaoh's army in the desert. Moses urged the people to be calm and stand their ground. He promised them that they would (1) see the deliverance of Yahweh, (2) never see the Egyptians again, and (3) observe how Yahweh fights for his people (14:10-14).

Moses privately cried out to God in desperation, and God gently rebuked him for it. He was told to raise his staff over the waters so that a path for God's people would be provided through the sea. Seeing the Israelites making their way through the waters would provide an occasion for the Egyptians to "harden their hearts," i.e., suppress their fear of drowning and plunge forward in pursuit of the escaping

Israelites. God would "gain glory" over Pharaoh's army there. The Egyptians would come to realize that even the greatest fighting force of that age was no match for the God of Israel (14:15-18).

The Israelites had protection as they prepared to cross the sea. The angel of God who had been leading the host, and the pillar of cloud, moved to the rear of the encampment and stood between the Egyptians and the Israelites. The cloud brought darkness to the Egyptians that night, while on the other side of the cloud light shone throughout the night (14:19-20). Beegle offers the rationalistic explanation: the flaming brazier moved to the rear of the camp to prevent a sneak attack during the night![7]

When Moses stretched out his staff over the sea, the waters parted. The text makes only three statements about this stupendous miracle: (1) that the Lord used a strong east wind to drive the waters back all the night, (2) that the path through the sea was dry land, and (3) that a wall of water was upon the left- and right-hand side of that path. This last detail eliminates the explanation that they crossed during a prolonged low tide.[8] The width of the path is not indicated. Obviously the Israelites did not cross the sea in single file, or even two abreast, for that would have taken more than one night (14:21-22).

In the morning watch, i.e., early in the morning, the Egyptians attempted to pursue the Israelites through the sea. From the fiery cloud the Lord looked down upon this scene.[9] He threw the Egyptian army into confusion, perhaps by means of a thunderstorm (cf. Ps 77:18-19). Their chariot wheels began to swerve or jam up, as some ancient versions have it. The Egyptian commander realized he was fighting against Yahweh, and ordered his men to retreat (14:23-25).

At daybreak, when the Israelites could witness the miracle, God ordered Moses to stretch out his hand over the sea. When he did so, the waters rushed back together. Not one member of Pharaoh's army which followed Israel into the sea survived. The dead Egyptians washing up on the shore reinforced faith in the power of God to save among the Israelites. The people feared Yahweh, and put their trust in him and his servant Moses (14:26-31).

PRAISE FOR DELIVERANCE
Exodus 15:1-21

The decisive defeat of Pharaoh turned the *sighing* of 2:23 into *singing*. The song of Moses is a litany of praise to the Lord. He is mentioned some forty-five times in eighteen verses. Eleven times his personal name Yahweh is used, once in the shortened form Yah (v. 2). Once he is called *'adonay*, ("master"), and twice *'el*, ("mighty One"). The song has three major divisions.

In the first five verses the singers refer to themselves in the first person, and God in the third person. Here is a personal confession of faith. Yahweh is praised as a warrior who defeated his enemy.

In verses 4-12 the song amplifies what happened at the sea. God is addressed in second person in these verses and to the end of the song. The destruction of Pharaoh's host is attributed to God's right hand, i.e., power, and to his burning anger. The murderous intentions of the Egyptians and consequent danger to Israel are clearly indicated. The hymn celebrates God's incomparable nature ("majestic in holiness") as well as his mighty acts (15:11).

In verses 13-18 the song dwells upon the implications of the Red Sea victory for the future. Because of his unfailing love, Yahweh would lead his redeemed people to the place of his dwelling. Other nations of the area would hear of what had transpired, and would tremble. God would bring his people to the Promised Land where he would plant them and reign over them forever.

Miriam for the first time was inspired by the Lord to exercise leadership. For this reason she is called a prophetess. She took a tambourine in hand and began to sing back to the men the opening lines of their song. The other women "went out after her" in a dancing chorus. Miriam was more than ninety at this time (15:19-21). Micah 6:14 names Miriam along with Moses and Aaron as one of the leaders in the Exodus.

ENDNOTES

1. Beegle attributes the plague to "some infection related to the anthrax of the previous plagues." That the plague involved only the firstborn and that it hit every house, according to Beegle, "is due to the selectivity of tradition." *Moses*, p. 134.

2. Immanuel Velikovsky, *Ages in Chaos* (Garden City, NJ: Doubleday, 1952), I:32-34.

3. Serious questions about the credibility of this figure have been raised. The questions have been addressed effectively by John Davis, *Biblical Numerology* (Grand Rapids: Baker, 1968), pp. 58-86.

4. The Septuagint translation of Exodus 12:14 reads: "who dwelt in the land of Egypt and in the land of Canaan" rather than simply "in Egypt." This rendering would suggest that the 215 years of the Patriarchal Period were included in the 430 years. This would cut in half the duration of the Egyptian sojourn.

5. Hugo Gressman argued for this interpretation. Cited by Rylaarsdam, "Exodus," I:931.

6. Beegle, *Moses*, p. 149.

7. Ibid., p. 159.

8. Rawlinson ("Exodus," p. 239) holds that the path through the sea was the result of the combination of a strong natural wind and the ebb tide.

9. The expression "pillar of cloud" is used eight times, "pillar of fire" five times. These phrases are combined in Ex 14:24.

BIBLIOGRAPHY: THE EXODUS

Listed below are special works dealing with the date and route of the Exodus. See also the general bibliography on the Book of Exodus (p. 240) and the Mosaic Period (p. 252).

Bimson, J.J. *Redating the Exodus and Conquest.* JSOTSupp 5. Sheffield, England, 1978.

DeWit, C. *The Date and Route of the Exodus.* London: Tyndale, 1960.

Griffiths, J.S. *The Exodus in the Light of Archaeology.* 1923.

Hebert, Gabriel. *When Israel Came Out of Egypt.* Richmond: John Knox, 1961.

Hoskins, Franklin E. *From the Nile to Nebo.* Philadelphia, 1912.

Jack, J.W. *The Date of the Exodus.* Edinburgh: Clark, 1925.

Pfeiffer, C. *Egypt and the Exodus.* Grand Rapids: Baker, 1964.

CHAPTER TWENTY-FIVE

Problems in Their Pilgrimage
Exodus 15:22–18:27

AIM: To demonstrate that God is sufficient for every problem which may arise in the pilgrim walk.

THEME: More than conquerors!

Israel's path to the Promised Land was not covered with rose petals. After crossing the Red Sea the Israelites went into the wilderness of Shur, part of what today is called the Sinai. *Shur* means wall, and here probably refers to a defensive wall on the eastern frontier of Egypt. The region today is largely a desolate wilderness, but some evidence exists that it was a bit more hospitable in ancient times. Some vegetation must have grown there or else Moses would not have led his flock to that area. Nevertheless, the Sinai was never an easy place to maintain an existence. Even before they reached Mt. Sinai, the redeemed of the Lord faced five serious problems.

PROBLEM OF WATER
Exodus 15:22-27

Moses now was the acknowledged leader. After he led the Israelites into the Desert of Shur, the group traveled for three days without finding water. A promising oasis proved to be a disappointment. The water there was bitter, but no more than the people who had expected to drink it. That spot was named Marah, which means "bitter" (15:22-23).

The grumbling people turned their anger against Moses. They expected him to know all the water holes in the Sinai. Moses in turn cried out to the Lord. God directed his attention to a piece of wood which he was to throw into the brackish water. The solution to the problem was near at hand. It often is.

Why the piece of wood? Some think that this was a particular kind of wood that could make brackish water drinkable.[1] Documentation of the claim that modern Arabs make use of such a method of water purification is lacking. Casting this object into the water was probably intended to be a symbolic action designed to convey to the grumbling crowds that something had been done about the water. The sweetening must have been temporary, for the water in that region is today brackish (15:24-25).[2]

God not only gave his people sweet water at Marah, he also gave them something much sweeter, namely, a promise. Obedience to the voice of God would guarantee to them good health. None of the diseases with which God had smitten Egypt would come upon Israel. Yahweh is a healer, and he would rather heal than inflict disease as he did in Egypt (15:26).

As the Israelites pressed on in their pilgrimage they found an abundance of water at Elim. This oasis was in a large plain said to be about a two-hour camel ride south of Marah. It contained twelve springs and seventy palm trees. This detail is added by the eyewitness narrator to suggest that the journey to that spot, however difficult, was well worth it (15:27). Too many believers encamp permanently at Marah, and never press on in their pilgrimage to taste the refreshment which is waiting at Elim!

PROBLEM OF FOOD
Exodus 16:1-36

The contents of Exodus 16 can be divided into four paragraphs revolving around hunger and the provision of food.

A. Pain of Hunger (Ex 16:1-3).

From Elim the Israelite host began to move eastward toward the Desert of Sin, named after the moon god Sin. They had now been marching for one month. What little food they had brought from Egypt was now exhausted and the group was too large to live off the land. For the third time within the month the congregation began to grumble against Moses and Aaron. Their hunger caused them to idealize their sojourn in Egypt. They remembered having all the food they wanted. Now it appeared that they would starve to death, not in a glorious Promised Land, but in "this desert."

B. Prediction of Food (Ex 16:4-12).

The Lord first communicated to Moses his solution to the hunger problem. He would rain down bread from heaven. The language clearly eliminates naturalistic explanations. The Lord gave precise instructions regarding the heaven-sent bread. The people were to gather day by day only enough bread for that day. On the sixth day they were to gather and prepare twice as much food. With these instructions God would test the obedience of his people (16:4-5).

Moses and Aaron conveyed the announcement of God to *all* the people, for all had apparently been involved in the complaint. They pointed out that the grumbling had not been against them, but against God. The grumblers would realize anew that the Lord had brought them out of Egypt when they (1) saw the glory of the Lord and (2) experienced the provision of meat and bread on the next day. The Lord would make these provisions, not because it was his good pleasure to do so, but because he had heard the grumbling against him. Yahweh was accepting the challenge which had been hurled at Moses and Aaron (16:6-8). The "glory of Yahweh" here is the splendor and majesty that became visible in the pillar of cloud and fire.

Moses then directed Aaron to summon the people to an assembly "before the Lord," i.e., a worship assembly. As Aaron addressed the assembly, the people observed the glory of the Lord appearing in the cloud toward the desert. The cloud still concealed so much of that glory that the people could observe it without risking death. Once again the Lord directed Moses to make a public prediction of the coming meat and bread (16:9-12).

C. Provision of Food (Ex 16:13-18).

That evening the quail came and covered the camp. These were not flying fish or locusts as some have conjectured, but feathered fowl as Psalm 78:27 makes clear. Twice during the wilderness wandering God provided these fowl in abundance for his people (cf. Nm 11:31). Large flocks of quail migrate north from Africa and Arabia in the spring, and back south in the fall. The miracle here is in bringing these birds from their normal migratory route to the camp of Israel. Quail fly only a few feet above the ground which makes them relatively easy to catch.

In the morning the Israelites awoke to find a layer of dew about the camp. When the dew dried, they noticed thin flakes like frost on the ground. The people were asking one another that morning about this strange substance. Moses told them it was "the bread of the Lord" (16:13-15).

Moses directed the people to gather as much of the bread of the Lord as they needed. He suggested an omer (about two quarts) for each person living in a tent. Gathering the manna by hand the people had to estimate how much they had accumulated. Some had more, some less than the suggested amount; but a miracle occurred when they measured their gatherings by the omer standard. Each person had exactly what he needed (16:16-18).

Two theories have been advanced to try to explain the manna rationalistically. The so-called "tamarisk manna" is the secretion of two kinds of insects on tamarisk trees. The drops range from the size of a needle head to that of a pea. The sun causes this substance to drop from trees. During the night it hardens. The "worms" were really ants which carried off the grains in the morning when the ground temperature reached seventy degrees about 8:30 AM. The secretion droppings are gathered by natives of the region during June and July. Josephus must have been alluding to this substance when he affirmed that in his day (first Christian century) the manna still fell on the Sinai peninsula.[3]

The second theory advanced by the rationalists traces the manna to a certain lichen which grows on rocks in the region. Pea-sized globules, blown by the wind, could have been scattered about the camp of Israel. Older writers describe how the natives gathered and ate these sweet-tasting nuggets. The use of this substance has not been attested in the last century and a half.[4]

Many explicit statements within the account must be ignored in order to embrace either of these theories about the manna. The quantity of manna needed constantly through forty years and the fact that no manna appeared on the seventh day are but two of the problems which confront the rationalist as he attempts to rid the account of the miraculous element.

One should not conclude that the Israelites had *nothing* to eat except manna during the wandering period. Some foods would have been provided by the desert. They had with them flocks which produced meat and milk. Deuteronomy 2:6 records an attempt to buy food from the Edomites. No doubt other tribes of the region were similarly approached.

D. Precepts for the Food (Ex 16:19-30).

Two major restrictions were placed on the use of the bread of the Lord. First, it was not to be kept overnight. The people were to trust the Lord to provide their daily bread. Some ignored this command, and by morning the bread of the Lord stunk and was full of maggots. Moses became angry at the deliberate disobedience of the people to this first precept (16:19-20).

On the sixth day the people began to gather twice the amount of the bread of the Lord as they had gathered on the preceding days. When this was reported to Moses, he revealed a second divine command, namely, that the seventh day was to be a day of rest. All food preparation was to be done on the sixth day. Moses endorsed the extra accumulation of the bread of the Lord on the sixth day. This was necessary because none of the substance appeared on the

293

ground on the seventh day. That which was preserved from the sixth to the seventh day did not spoil (16:21-26).[5]

Some of the people tested the second precept. They went out to gather the bread of the Lord on the seventh day and found none. The Lord gave new instructions to Moses regarding the observance of the seventh or Sabbath day. God had given the seventh day to Israel as a day of rest. That explained the extra amount of the bread of the Lord which he permitted them to gather on the sixth day. People were not to venture out of their tents on the Sabbath (16:27-30).

E. Preservation of Manna (Ex 16:31-36).

The bread of the Lord was given the name "manna" ("What is it?"). The color and taste of the substance are described by the narrator. Manna was white like a coriander seed, and had a honey-like taste. The coriander plant found in Egypt and Palestine bears seed-like fruit. The dried leaves are used for seasoning and oil is produced from the seeds.

At a later point in the wilderness wandering God directed Moses to preserve some of the manna for posterity. Aaron collected an omer of manna in a pot and placed it "before Yahweh," "before the Testimony." This can only be a reference to the tables of the Law which later were placed in the ark of the covenant in the Tabernacle. Future generations would be able to see that which God had provided for his people in the desert. At the direction of Moses, Aaron implemented the command to preserve a memorial jar of manna (16:31-34).

The narrator closes the account by noting that the Israelites ate manna for forty years, until they reached the border of the Promised Land. He adds the detail that an omer was one tenth of an ephah. This explanation suggests that the omer was an uncommon unit of measure (16:35-36).

PROBLEM OF THIRST
Exodus 17:1-7

The Israelites eventually came to Rephidim in their journey. Here they found no water. For the fourth time the people complained. This time they went beyond grumbling; they *quarreled* with Moses. Murmuring is an attitude that God is insufficient in difficulties. At Marah they had asked Moses, What shall we drink? At Rephidim, after the three food miracles they had already witnessed along the way, they demanded that Moses produce water.

Moses considered himself powerless. Quarreling with *him* would do them no good. He warned them that they were putting God to the test with their demand. Hebrews 3:7-13 refers to this incident and concludes that murmuring leads to hardness of heart and loss of standing with God.

Moses' warning had a temporary calming effect upon the people, but soon they were grumbling again. They continued to accuse Moses of leading them out into the wilderness to their death. The crowd was on the verge of stoning him, and this drove the prophet to his knees (17:1-4).

The Lord directed Moses to leave the camp and take some of the elders with him to serve as reliable witnesses. The people it seems had forfeited their right to witness any miracle which God might perform. Moses was to take his staff and strike a rock beside which the Lord himself would be standing (17:5-6a).

Moses did as the Lord instructed, and when he struck the rock water gushed forth. Some have suggested that he struck a thin layer of limestone rock that covered a vein of water. The problem with this view is that the rocks in that area are granite, not limestone. In 1 Corinthians 10:4 this rock is compared to Christ.

Moses gave two names to that spot: (1) Meribah ("quarreling") and (2) Massah ("testing"). Whenever God's people began to demand a miracle to prove that God is in their midst, they are repeating the sin of Israel at Massah (17:6b-7).

PROBLEM OF WAR
Exodus 17:8-15

While the Israelites were encamped at Rephidim they were attacked by the Amalekites. These people were descendants of Esau (Gn 36:12,16). The Amalekites pounced upon the stragglers who were weary and worn out from the journey (Dt 25:17-19).

Joshua, mentioned here for the first of twenty-seven times in the Pentateuch, was delegated to organize a fighting force to deal with the threat. Moses promised to undergird his efforts with intercession on a nearby hill. He would hold in hand his staff, symbol of the power of God at work among his people. Moses' reliance on the staff, however, did not exclude the action of Joshua (17:8-9).

As long as the Israelite fighters could see the upraised staff of Moses on the hill they prevailed in battle. When the staff was lowered because of fatigue, however, the course of the battle changed. Noting this, a stone was rolled into position for Moses to sit upon. Aaron and Hur stationed themselves on either side of him and propped up his hands until the sun set. (Jewish tradition identifies Hur as the husband of Miriam.) Joshua was thus enabled to overcome the Amalekite army (17:10-13).

Battles as well as blessings mark the course of a believer's pilgrimage. Sometimes the Lord fights for his people (as at the Red Sea), and sometimes through his people. In any case believers can be confident that he who is in their midst is greater than any enemy which may be encountered in the way.

Moses was told to write "this," namely, (1) the victory over Amalek, and (2) the prediction of Amalek's destruction. Five times in the Pentateuch Moses was told specifically to write something. He was also to impress orally upon Joshua God's utter hostility toward Amalek. That Joshua was destined for even greater leadership is clear in this incident. The divine sentence against Amalek was national extinction. God would blot out the memory of Amalek from under heaven (17:14).

To commemorate the victory over Amalek, Moses erected an altar and called it *Yahweh Nissi* ("my banner"). All of Israel needed to realize that they fought under the banner of their God. The hand raised toward heaven, the throne room of God, was a symbolic gesture of intercession. Moses proclaimed a perpetual hostility of Yahweh toward the Amalekites. Those who attack the people of the Lord incur the wrath of God (17:15).

PROBLEM OF LEADERSHIP
Exodus 18:1-27

Exodus 18 narrates how Jethro, Moses father-in-law, visited the Israelites while they were in the vicinity of Mt. Sinai.

A. Jethro's Arrival (Ex 18:1-8).

The reports of what God had done for the Israelites had reached the ears of Jethro. Sometime after the circumcision episode en route to Egypt (4:24-26), Moses "had sent" Zipporah and his two sons back to Jethro. Moses' first son Gershom was introduced in 2:22; he named his second son Eliezer ("my God is helper") because God had saved him from the sword of Pharaoh (18:1-4).

Jethro sent word to Moses that he was coming to meet him with Zipporah and *her* two sons. Was this intended to be a mild rebuke to his son-in-law? In any case, Moses went out to meet Jethro and greeted him respectfully and warmly. Inside his tent Moses rehearsed at length all that Yahweh had done to the Egyptians for Israel's sake. He then traced the journey from bondage indicating how Yahweh had delivered his people from all the hardships along the way (18:5-8).

B. Jethro's Confession (Ex 18:9-12).

Jethro was delighted to hear about all the good things which Yahweh had done for his people. He burst forth into praise to Yahweh. This is not Jethro's conversion, as some commentators imagine, but his elation that his own God had been so gracious. First, Jethro praised the Lord for rescuing Israel from the hand of the Egyptians and Pharaoh. Based on this dramatic experience of divine power, Jethro expressed renewed confidence that Yahweh was greater than all other gods. The word "know" does not necessarily mean "come to the realization," but rather "know by personal experience" (18:9-11).

Jethro then offered a burnt offering and other sacrifices to God. Aaron and the elders of the nation were invited to eat a sacrificial meal with Jethro "in the presence of God." From Jethro Aaron may have learned the priestly craft (18:12).

C. Jethro's Counsel (Ex 18:13-27).

The next day Jethro observed Moses exercising his judging function. People stood in line all day long to have Moses expound the will of God in settling their disputes. Jethro was dumbfounded that Moses would attempt to shoulder this burden by himself (18:13-16).

Jethro had some sound advice for his son-in-law. Moses of course should remain the representative of the people before God. He must teach them God's decrees and laws and show them the duties which they should perform. Moses, however, should appoint subordinate judges over groups of tens, fifties, hundreds and thousands. Difficult cases would still be brought to Moses. The appointees should possess three qualifications: they should (1) fear God, (2) be trustworthy men, and (3) hate dishonest gain. Jethro concluded that there would be two positive benefits from this arrangement. First, the people would be better satisfied; and second, Moses would be able to stand the strain of his office (18:17-23).

Moses accepted the wise counsel of Jethro, but the plan was not implemented immediately. According to Deuteronomy 1:9-15 judges were selected after the law was given on Sinai a few weeks later (18:24-26).

Jethro elected to return to his own country, but apparently Zipporah and the children stayed with Moses. Moses sent his father-in-law on his journey by traveling a short distance with him (18:27).

ENDNOTES

1. Rawlinson ("Exodus," *Pulpit Commentary* [New York: Funk & Wagnells, 1907], II:29) thinks it probable that a tree or shrub in the vicinity had natural purifying power. The miracle would consist of pointing out the tree to Moses.

2. McGarvey (*Lands*, p. 446) notes that "the bitterness of the water varies at different seasons, and some travelers have found it palatable."

3. F.S. Bodenheimer, "The Manna of Sinai," *The Biblical Archaeologist Reader*, ed. G. Earnest Wright and David N. Freedman (Garden City, NJ: Doubleday, 1961), pp. 76-80.

4. Ohle refers to "manna moss" which grows on rocks and produces pea-sized globules which are light enough to be blown about by the wind. The "manna rain" of seeds from this plant has never been observed in the Sinai. Cited by W.H. Gispen, *Exodus*, Bible Student's Commentary (Grand Rapids: Zondervan, 1982), p. 157.

5. The Sabbath concept is introduced seven times in Exodus, three times* at the conclusion of main sections: 16:23-29; 20:8-11; 23:10-12; 24:16*; 31:12-17*; 34:21; 35:1-3*.

CHAPTER TWENTY-SIX

The Law of God
Exodus 19:1-24:11

AIM: To demonstrate the wisdom of the law of God.

THEME: The majesty of God's law.

A nation must have a constitution and law to govern it. The only law ever revealed from heaven was received by Israel at Mt. Sinai. The Rabbis counted 613 specific injunctions in this law, 248 positive commands and 365 prohibitions.

The Scriptures indicate at least six reasons for the revelation of this law. The Law (1) revealed God's glory and holiness (Dt 5:22-28), (2) manifested the sinfulness of man (Rom 7:7,13; 1 Tim 1:9ff.), (3) marked Israel as God's chosen people (Ps 147:19f.; Eph 2:11ff.), (4) gave Israel a Godly standard by which they might continue to inhabit Canaan (Dt 5:29ff.; Judg 2:19-21), (5) prepared Israel for the coming of the Promised Seed (Gal 3:24), and (6) illustrated in various forms and ceremonies the person and work of Christ (Heb 10:1).

In the third month after the Israelites left Egypt, they came to the Desert of Sinai. They encamped in front of the mountain to await word from God. The date is given in 19:1 because of the importance of what follows (19:1-2).

PREPARATIONS FOR THE LAW
Exodus 19:3-25

In Exodus 19 Moses made three trips into Mt. Sinai. In each case he came back with a message from the mount.

A. A Message of Challenge (Ex 19:3-8).

The first time Moses ascended Sinai, God spoke and Moses listened. The Lord directed Moses to first take a challenge back to his people. The basis of that challenge is set forth in 19:4: (1) God's power ("what I did to the Egyptians"), (2) God's protection ("bore you on eagle's wings"), and (3) God's patience ("brought you unto myself").

God set forth a twofold condition to the challenge, and a threefold promise. Israel must (1) obey God's voice and (2) keep God's covenant. If they met this challenge they would be (1) God's special possession, (2) a kingdom of priests, and (3) a holy nation. These words are considered by some to be the center and theme of the entire Pentateuch (19:5-6).

Moses went back and challenged the elders with the words of God. Speaking for the people, the elders expressed their commitment to do everything which the Lord had spoken (19:7-8).

B. A Message of Consecration (Ex 19:9-15).

Moses returned to the mount with the answer of the people. Again only divine monologue is recorded. The Lord indicated that when he spoke to Moses a thick cloud would come down upon the mount. The glory of God was thus concealed so that the people could come close enough to be able to hear his voice when he spoke with Moses on the mountain. God spoke to Moses within earshot of the people so that he might underscore the authority of his servant.

Moses returned immediately to the people and spent the next two days consecrating them for the descent of God on Sinai. Israel's response to God's first word at Sinai was verbal; their response to his second word was to be concrete action. They would symbolize their consecration by (1) washing their clothes, (2) abstaining from sexual relations for those three days, and (3) restricting their movements. The mount was to be off limits. Any who came near the mount, even animals, were to be stoned or shot through with arrows. Only when the ram's horn sounded was it safe for them to go up to the mountain.

C. A Message of Caution (Ex 19:16-25).

The people spent the better part of three days preparing to meet God. On the morning of the third day a theophany occurred. God descended on Mt. Sinai. The mount was not God's domicile, but only his temporary abode.

Five signs accompanied this manifestation: (1) thunder and lightning, (2) a thick cloud on the mount, (3) an exceedingly loud sound of a trumpet, (4) fire and smoke, and (5) earthquake. This is not the eruption of a volcano as some would like to believe, for no lava or ashes are mentioned.[1] Moses led the trembling people forward to the base of the mount. The prophet spoke to God, and God answered him (19:16-19).

Moses was called again into the mount. The Lord instructed him to once again warn the people about attempting to break through the barriers at the foot of the mount. Those who saw Yahweh on that mount would die. Even priests must consecrate themselves before they approached the Lord or he would break forth in wrath against them. Moses was confident that the barriers erected around the mountain were sufficient to keep the people away (19:20-23).

The Lord directed Moses to bring Aaron into the mount. Once again he warned Moses that no one, priest or people, should attempt to come up to the Lord. The tip of Sinai had become a holy of holies into which only Moses and Aaron, the future high priest, might enter. The "priests" here are either (1) the firstborn who were already consecrated to God or (2) the priests designates, the sons of Aaron. Moses returned to the camp and told the people what the Lord had said (19:24-25).

PRINCIPLES OF THE LAW
Exodus 20:1-26

Exodus 20 records how God spoke the Decalogue (Ten Commandments) and how the people responded to that heavenly voice.

A. The Decalogue (Ex 20:1-17).

God spoke directly to the people in this chapter. The God of Sinai first identified himself in three ways. I am (1) Yahweh, the Eternal One; (2) your God; (3) who brought you out of Egypt. He was their redeemer; they were his people. He had a right to govern their national and personal life (20:1-2). Having identified himself and established his right to set forth principles of conduct, God spoke the ten majestic words of the Decalogue.

1. No other gods (20:3). The first word protected the area of theology. This word is fundamental to all the others. The "who" of worship is emphasized here. The assumption is that (1) it is possible to worship surrogates for God, (2) such worship is at times attractive, and (3) man has a tendency in this direction.

2. No graven images (20:4-6). The second word spoke to the "how" of worship. The God of Sinai was invisible and no attempt was to be made to represent him in any way. They were not to bow down to (i.e., show respect for), let alone worship, such images. The worship of God must not be transferred from the realm of the spirit to that of the senses. Religious art was permitted, for it was abundant in the Tabernacle and the Temple. The intent here is to prohibit idolatry. The classic definition of idolatry was formulated by Augustine: Idolatry is worshiping anything that ought to be used, or using anything that is meant to be worshiped.[2]

A reason is attached to this prohibition. Yahweh is a jealous God and will brook no rival. He does not tolerate divided allegiance. Those who continue to hate him face his wrath even to the fourth generation. Those who love him and keep his commandments experience God's love throughout their generations.

3. No profanity. The Hebrew word translated *vain* comes from a root meaning "to be empty, or worthless." Invoking God's name in jest, in an unworthy cause, or in religious lip service are examples of

the violation of the third command. God's name was not to be misused in any way (20:7).

4. Observe the sabbath. The seventh day was to be a holy day. The Israelites were to rest from their labors. God himself set the pattern for this observance. After the six creative days he rested or ceased from his creative activity. Seven types of living beings are commanded to observe the seventh day (20:8-11).

5. Honor parents. This word protected the family. *Honor* includes but goes beyond obedience. Several times this verb is used with God as the object (e.g., 1 Sam 2:30). This underscored the seriousness of the injunction. A promise is attached to this word. Those who honor parents would live long in the land which God was giving them. The requirement to honor mother as well as father shows that the woman in Israel occupied a place of honor in her family (20:12).

6. No murder (20:13). The Law regarded life as sacred. Life could be taken from a man only on God's terms. Unnecessary taking of life out of anger or greed was prohibited. Jesus extended this commandment to include anger and verbal abuse of another (Matt 5:21-22).

7. No adultery (20:14). This word protected the sanctity of marriage. Jesus expanded this prohibition to include lust (Matt 5:27-30).

8. No stealing. Property rights were protected by this word. The attempt to get something for nothing is prohibited (20:15).

9. No lying. Truth was protected here. The whole spectrum of sins of the tongue was prohibited (20:16).

10. No coveting. The heart as well as actions were to be guarded from evil. This is the most comprehensive of all the commandments (20:17).

B. Observations Regarding the Decalogue.

1. The Decalogue as found in Exodus differs in several points from Moses' restatement of it in Deuteronomy 5. The main difference is the motivation for observance of the Sabbath.

2. The Decalogue was inscribed on front and back of two stone tablets the size of which cannot be precisely determined. Since the tablets were kept in the ark, the maximum dimensions would have been three by two feet.

3. No consensus exists as to the number of commands on each

tablet. Kline has suggested that the tablets were duplicate copies of the Decalogue.[3]

4. Major bodies within Christendom disagree on the enumeration of the commands. Roman Catholics and Lutherans regard 20:1-6 as one command; they split the command on coveting into two commands.

5. Eight of the ten words are really prohibitions rather than commandments. The Hebrew negative *lo'* points to categorical prohibition. Law is essentially restrictive.

6. The pronoun throughout the Decalogue is second masculine singular. God intended for the ten words to apply to every individual.

7. The first five words speak of "the Lord your God" which constitutes a repeated appeal to Israel's gratitude.

Chart No. 22

THE TEN COMMANDMENTS Exodus 20:3-17	
DUTY TO GOD	**DUTY TO MAN**
Protection of...	Protection of...
1. God's Sovereignty ("No other gods")	1. Man's Life ("Do not murder")
2. God's Service ("No graven images")	2. Man's Mate ("Do not commit adultery")
3. God's Sanctity ("No profanity")	3. Man's Property ("Do not steal")
4. God's Sabbath ("Remember the Sabbath")	4. Man's Reputation ("No false witnesses")
5. God's Servants ("Honor parents")	5. Man's Heart ("Do not covet")
SUMMARIZED "You shall love the Lord your God with all your heart" (Mt 22:37).	SUMMARIZED "You shall love your neighbor as yourself" (Mt 22:39).

C. Fear of the People (Ex 20:18-26).

The people were terrified at the sights and sounds of Sinai. They kept their distance from the mount. They requested that Moses be a mediator between them and God. Moses assured them that they had nothing to fear. God was testing them. A healthy fear of God would keep them from sinning. Moses then turned from the people and walked back up into the thick cloud which covered the mount, into the presence of God (20:18-21).

The first item of business on the mount was to set forth a means by which people who fear the Lord could nonetheless approach him in worship. Since the invisible God had spoken directly to them at Sinai, they were not to attempt in any way to make representations of him to aid them in worship. In the religious context of that day this would be a revolutionary requirement.

The proper place to meet God was at the altar. The regulations concerning the altar were these:

1. The altar was to be made of earth or stones.

2. If the altar was made of stone it was not to be built of dressed stones, i.e., cut stones. The purpose here was to avoid any temptation to carve images on the stones of the altar.

3. The altar could be located wherever God caused his name to be honored, i.e., appeared in vision, voice or action.

4. The altar was not to have steps. If a priest were to climb steps to an altar, the nakedness of his ankles would be seen. Sacrifice depicted a *covering* of sin; exposed nakedness destroyed that symbolism (20:24-26).[4]

PRECEPTS OF THE LAW
Exodus 21:1–23:19

Four collections of precepts are found in this section of Exodus. Many of the laws here are *casuistic*, i.e., they are framed in a conditional way. This section of Exodus is called the Book of the Covenant (24:7) or simply the Covenant Code.

A. Precepts Regarding Servants (Ex 21:1-11).

A Hebrew[5] might have to sell himself into servanthood if he could not meet his financial obligations. In such a case the debtor could not be made to serve more than six years. The basic principle regarding his release was that he should go free in exactly the same condition in which he came into servanthood. If he was married when he became a servant, his wife would go out with him. If he married a maidservant of his master during the six years, he did so realizing that when he went free his wife and children stayed with his master. In this case he might choose to remain a servant rather than surrender his wife and children. If so, he declared his intention before the judges (NIV). The pierced ear was the symbol of perpetual servanthood voluntarily chosen (21:2-6).

The law protected a female servant who might be sold into servanthood to pay family debts. Normally when this was done, marriage was contemplated, either to the master or to his son. If the master chose not to marry the servant girl, he had to allow her to be redeemed by relatives; he could not sell her to a third party. If he married another, he could not deprive the servant girl of food, clothing, or accessories.[6] If he was unwilling to give her these three things, he must release her (21:7-11).

B. Precepts Regarding Penalties (Ex 21:12–22:20).

The basic principle of Mosaic jurisprudence was the *lex talionis* stated in 21:24-25. The "eye for eye" principle was not intended to be a guideline for *personal* ethics, but a principle for *national* justice. Stated simply Exodus 21:24-25 argues that the punishment must always fit the crime. Jesus did not repudiate this principle in Matthew 5:38-42; he rejected the misuse of *lex talionis* in *personal* vengeance.

In the Covenant Code no provision is made for imprisonment or punishment by physical mutilation. The death penalty was stipulated for seven of twenty-one crimes which are enumerated.[7] This does not mean that the death penalty was inevitably administered in all these cases, but that it was the maximum sentence. Chart 23 summarizes the crimes and penalties which were set forth in the Book of the Covenant.

C. Precepts Regarding Abuse (Ex 22:21-31).

Six prohibitions next appear which have no stipulated penalties. God's people were not to mistreat the following:

Chart No. 23

PENALTIES OF THE LAW		
Basic Principle: Lex Talionis **Exodus 21:24-25**		
NO. REF.	**CRIME**	**MAXIMUM PENALTY**
1. 21:12-14	Murder	Death *
2. 21:15	Smiting Father or Mother	Death
3. 21:16	Kidnapping	Death
4. 21:17	Cursing Father or Mother	Death
5. 21:18-19	Battery	Compensation
6. 21:20-21	Mistreatment of a Slave	Punished *
7. 21:22-25	Injury to a Pregnant Woman	Fine/Death *
8. 21:26-27	Battery against a Servant	Release of Servant
9. 21:28-32	Cattle Kill a Person	Fine *
10. 21:33-34	Property Liability	Restitution
11. 21:35-36	Cattle Kill Cattle	Restitution
12. 22:1	Nonrecoverable Theft	Restitution + Penalty
13. 22:2-4	Recoverable Theft	Restitution + Penalty
14. 22:5	Mismanagement of Cattle	Restitution
15. 22:6	Property Negligence	Restitution
16. 22:7-13	Trust Violations	Restitution *
17. 22:14-15	Bailment Damage	Restitution *
18. 22:16-17	Premarital Sex	Compensation + Marriage
19. 22:18	Witchcraft	Death
20. 22:19	Bestiality	Death
21. 22:20	Sacrifice to False God	Utterly Destroyed
		*Exceptions or modifications

1. Strangers (22:21). They must remember that they once were strangers in Egypt.

2. Widows and orphans (22:22-24). If God should hear the cry of these destitute ones, his anger would be aroused. He would bring a sword against the nation making their wives widows and their children fatherless.

3. The poor (22:25-27). Money was to be lent without interest to a destitute brother. A cloak taken as security for a loan must be returned at sundown so that the poor brother would not suffer in the cold.

4. Those in positions of authority (22:28). They should not blaspheme their judges (lit., *'elohim*, gods), or curse the ruler of the people.

5. God (22:29-30). They should not withhold from him their offerings of grain, wine or cattle. Firstborn sons and cattle belonged to God. Yet here there was to be consideration for the animals, for the calf was to be left with its mother for seven days before being given to the Lord.

6. Themselves as holy men (22:31). They were to eat only the meat of animals properly slain. Animals torn by wild beasts were not fit for consumption by a holy people.

D. Precepts Regarding Justice (Ex 23:1-12).

The first twelve verses of Exodus 23 spell out obligations to treat all men justly and with compassion.

1. False testimony was forbidden. This could be testimony which slandered a righteous man or freed a guilty man. A witness was not to allow himself to be swayed by the majority view or to be influenced by the destitution of the party against whom he might testify (23:1-3).

2. Taking advantage of an enemy was forbidden. His straying livestock were to be returned to him. In an emergency, such as a donkey collapsing under its burden, the enemy was to be assisted (23:4-5).

3. Perversion of justice was forbidden. The poorest of men was entitled to a fair trial. False charges against the innocent were to be rejected. Those who lied in court and thus brought about the execution of an innocent man would not be accepted by the Lord. Bribes to judicial officers or witnesses were forbidden. Bribes blind the eyes to truth and twist the words of testimony (23:6-8).

4. Oppression of foreigners living in the land was forbidden. Israelites were never to forget their own experience as aliens in the land of Egypt (23:9).

5. The poor as well as wild animals were to be allowed free access to field, vineyard and olive grove in the sabbath years (23:10-11).

6. Dependents, man and beast, were to be given rest on the weekly sabbath (23:12).

E. Precepts Regarding Worship (Ex 23:13-19).

The reference to the sabbath in 23:12 suggested the transition to precepts relating to worship.

1. Israelites were never to invoke the names of other gods in worship, oaths, curses or prayers or any way which suggested that those gods really existed (23:13).

2. Annual feasts. Three times a year Israelite males were required to appear before the Lord to celebrate religious festivals. In the first month of the year the Feast of Unleavened Bread (including Passover) commemorated the Exodus from Egypt. As a general principle the Law stipulated that a worshiper at these festivals was not to appear empty handed (23:14f.).

The Feast of Harvest, later known as Pentecost, was observed fifty days after Passover. Firstfruits of the harvest were to be presented to the Lord on this occasion. At the end of the year, in the seventh month, the Feast of Ingathering or Tabernacles was celebrated. This was like a thanksgiving festival at the conclusion of the harvest (23:16f.).

The sacrifices offered at these festivals were strictly regulated by the Law. Nothing containing leaven (yeast) could be offered along with a blood offering. The fat portions of animals were to be offered on the altar on the day the animal was slaughtered. Only the best of firstfruits were to be offered. The pagan custom of cooking a young goat in its mother's milk was strictly forbidden (23:18f.).

PROMISES OF THE LAW
Exodus 23:20-33

Exodus 23 concludes with three promises designed to encourage obedience to the Law. First, God would send an angel to guard Israel along the way to the Promised Land. God warned his people to pay special heed to this angel for the divine Name (attributes) was in him. He would not overlook their rebellions. Obedience to this angel would make God their ally against all opposition (23:20-23).

Second, if they destroyed every vestige of paganism and worshiped only the Lord, he would give them prosperity in the land. He would bless their food and water, heal their diseases, and give them a full and fruitful life (23:24-26).

Third, God would gradually give them possession of the land. The fear of God, like the sting of a hornet,[8] would cause the inhabitants of Canaan to turn and flee. The borders of their inheritance would extend from the Red Sea in the southeast to the Mediterranean Sea in the west, from the southern desert to the Euphrates River in the north. All the native inhabitants of that area were to be driven out. No covenant was to be made with them lest they lure God's people into pagan worship (23:27-33).

POSSESSION OF THE LAW
Exodus 24:1-11

Before leaving the mount with this body of laws, Moses was directed to bring Aaron, his sons, and the seventy elders back to the mount. They were to worship the Lord at a distance, albeit much closer than the people. Moses alone would be permitted to approach the Lord (24:1f.).

Israel took possession of the Law in two stages. The law was received in the camp and celebrated in the mount.

A. Received in the Camp (Ex 24:3-8).

Moses reported to the people all that the Lord had said. They responded enthusiastically to all the words and laws of God. Moses then wrote down all that the Lord had said (24:3-4a).

The following day Moses led in a formal commitment service. An altar was constructed with twelve pillars representing the tribes surrounding it. Unnamed young men offered burnt and peace offerings to the Lord. Blood was sprinkled on the altar to sanctify it. Then the Book of the Covenant was read before the people. Again the people committed themselves to obey the word of the Lord. Moses sprinkled blood on the people (possibly as represented by the seventy elders). The blood symbolized the fact that God had now entered into a covenant with Israel (24:4b-8).

B. Celebrated in the Mount (Ex 24:1,2,9-11).

Aaron, Nadab, Abihu and the seventy elders accompanied Moses into the mount. They became the guests of God at a glorious banquet. The text states that these leaders saw the God of Israel as they looked up at a blue "pavement" clear as the sky itself. They feasted in the presence of deity, yet God never raised a hand against them. Fellowship with God at this table was possible because of the atonement made through the blood.

ENDNOTES

1. On the supposition that Exodus 19:16-18 describes a volcanic distur-
bance, several writers have attempted to locate Sinai in southern Arabia, the
nearest volcanic region in historic times. No lava or ash is mentioned, however, in Exodus 19:16-18.

2. Cited by Hamilton, *Handbook*, p. 203.

3. Meredith G. Kline, *Treaty of the Great King* (Grand Rapids: Eerdmans, 1963), pp. 13-26.

4. Rawlinson, *Pulpit Commentary*, II:164. Gispen (*Exodus*, p. 204),
however, sees the purpose here to prevent the first step on the road to immorality in worship.

5. The "Hebrew servant" of Ex 21:2 and the "brother" of Lv 25:39 are
probably equivalent. Noordtzij, however, thinks that an "Israelite" had a higher status than a "Hebrew." *Leviticus*, Bible Student's Commentary (Grand
Rapids: Zondervan, 1982), p. 259.

6. NASB, "conjugal rights." The Hebrew word *'onatah* is a *hapax
legomenon*. S.M. Paul suggests that the word should be translated "oint-
ments" on the basis of certain parallel Sumerian and Akkadian texts. Cited in
Walter C. Kaiser, *Toward Old Testament Ethics*, (Grand Rapids: Zondervan,
1983), p. 185.

7. Kaiser (*Ethics*, pp. 91ff) cites references for the sixteen capital offenses
of the Law.

8. Garstang suggested that the "hornets" were the Egyptians. Cited by
Gispen, *Exodus*, p. 235.

BIBLIOGRAPHY: THE LAW

Charles, R.H. *The Decalogue*. Clark, 1923.

Coffin, Henry Sloane. *The Ten Commandments with a Christian
Application*. Doubleday, 1915.

Daube, D. *Studies in Biblical Law*. Cambridge: Cambridge University
Press, 1947.

Falk, Z.W. *Hebrew Law in Biblical Times*. Jerusalem: Wahrmann
Books, 1964.

Galer, R.S. *Old Testament Law for Bible Students*. 1922.

Goldman, Solomon. *The Ten Commandments*. Chicago: University
Press, 1963.

Jukes, Andrew. *The Law of the Offerings*. Grand Rapids: Kregel,
1976.

McMillen, S.I. *None of These Diseases*. Westwood, NJ: Revell, 1963.

Morgan, G. Campbell. *The Ten Commandments*. Grand Rapids: Baker, 1974.

Paul, S.M. *Studies in the Book of the Covenant in the Light of Cuneiform and Biblical Law*. Leiden: Brill, 1970.

Rand, Howard B. *Digest of the Divine Law*. Merrimac, MS: Destiny, 1943.

Rushdoony, Rousas. *The Institutes of the Biblical Law*. Philadelphia: Presbyterian and Reformed, 1973.

Stamm, J.J., and M.E. Andrew. *The Ten Commandments in Recent Research*. London: SCM, 1967.

Wallace, R.S. *The Ten Commandments*. Grand Rapids: Eerdmans, 1965.

Weatherly, Owen M. *The Ten Commandments in Modern Perspective*. Richmond: John Knox, 1961.

CHAPTER TWENTY-SEVEN

The Golden Calf Tragedy
Exodus 24:12-34:35

AIM: To demonstrate the mercy and severity of God in response to apostasy.

THEME: The tragedy of apostasy.

The people had formally agreed to abide by the commandments of the Lord. God could now dwell in their midst in a special way. The Tabernacle was to be his abode among them as they traveled toward Canaan. For forty days Moses was instructed in detail about the construction of the Tabernacle. Before he could return to the camp with these plans, however, the people were led into a serious transgression by Aaron. Moses had to employ all of his skills as intercessor to save Israel from immediate destruction by the Lord and to secure divine agreement to continue the journey with the people. Thus in this unit of Exodus the Tabernacle was designed by God (chs. 25–31) and delayed by sin (chs. 32–34).

Exodus 24:12-18 introduces the present unit. Moses was directed to go higher into the mount to receive the tables of stone containing the Law written by God. He instructed the elders to "wait here," i.e., remain behind in the camp. Aaron and Hur were to serve as judges until Moses returned. Then Moses and his aide Joshua went higher into the mount.

The cloud of divine glory covered the mountain for six days. On the seventh day God spoke to Moses from the cloud. For forty days the prophet stayed in the mount. To the Israelites in the plain below, the glorious cloud looked like a consuming fire.

INSTRUCTIONS FROM THE LORD
Exodus 25:1–31:18

In Exodus 25-31 God speaks seven times (25:1; 30:11,17,22,34; 31:1,12). Scholars have called attention to similarities between this section and the creation narrative of Genesis 1. Certain parallels stand out. (1) Like Genesis 1, Exodus 25–31 narrates divine creation. (2) The phrase "thus the heavens and the earth were finished" (Gn 2:1) is parallel to Exodus 39:32, "Thus all the work of the Tabernacle . . . was finished." (3) The phrase "God finished his work which he had done" (Gn 2:2) is parallel to Exodus 40:33, "So Moses finished the work." (4) The phrase "So God blessed the seventh day" (Gn 2:3) is parallel to Exodus 39:43, "And Moses blessed them." (5) The Genesis account concludes with the thought, "And God saw everything that he had made and behold, it was very good (Gn 1:31). The Exodus account ends with the words, "And Moses saw all the work, and behold, they had done it; as the Lord had commanded, so had they done it (Ex 39:43). (6) In both the creation of the world and the creation of the Tabernacle the Spirit of God was active (Gn 1:2; Ex 31:3; 35:31).[1]

The instructions given to Moses in the mount pertained to (1) the Tabernacle, (2) the priesthood and (3) related matters.

A. Design of the Tabernacle (Ex 25:1–27:21).

The Israelites were to bring a freewill offering to the Lord consisting of precious metals, stones, cloth, spices, oil and incense as well as

314

wood and skins. Fourteen kinds of material would be needed (25:1-7). Two of these materials need special comment.

The acacia tree grew in the Sinai region. This is a heavy wood, indestructible by insects. The tree grows to a height of about twenty feet and produces yellow flowers. The *tachash* skin is not "badger skin" (KJV) but is the skin of a marine animal. Probably the dugong which grows to about eleven feet long is intended.[2]

The Israelites were to construct a tabernacle and all its furnishings exactly like the pattern revealed by God (25:8-9). See also Hebrews 8:5. Detailed instructions were given for the construction of the ark, table, lampstand, and altar of sacrifice. The veils, curtains, boards, bars and screen were fully described (25:10–27:21).

Chart No. 24

THE PLAN OF THE TABERNACLE

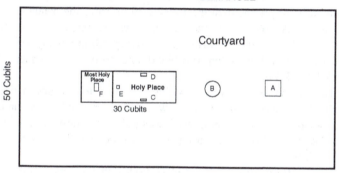

100 Cubits

A. Bronze Altar; B. Laver; C. Lampstand; D. Table;
E. Altar of Incense; F. Ark of the Covenant

Biblical critics have argued that the Tabernacle as described in Exodus never existed. They say that later priests invented this structure and wrote it back into the Mosaic history, so as to legitimize the Temple.[3] Prefabricated and portable worship structures, however, are attested in the ancient Near East. An Egyptian structure with frame construction dating to about 2600 BC was found at Gaza. In Ugarit the Canaanite god El had a portable shrine, according to Albright.[4] Also the Arabs had a tent shrine called a *qubbah* made of leather which they carried with them into battle. The existence of the Tabernacle in the wilderness then has support from archaeological discoveries.[5]

B. Ministers of the Tabernacle (Ex 28:1–30:38).

The sons of Aaron were to officiate as priests in the Tabernacle. Several matters related to their priesthood are discussed in this section of Exodus.

1. *Priestly garments (28:1-43).* Aaron and his four sons were designated as priests (28:1). Special garments were to be constructed for Aaron to wear when he officiated as high priest. These included (1) breastplate, (2) ephod, (3) robe, and (4) turban. Four other garments were worn by all the priests: (1) coat, (2) girdle, (3) cap, and (4) linen undergarments.

2. *Priestly consecration (29:1-34).* In 28:41 God alluded to the fact that Aaron and his sons were to be dressed appropriately and consecrated to their priestly ministry. Exodus 29 provides the details of that ordination. A special ordination sacrifice was required (29:1-3). The ritual was to include (1) washing, (2) robing, (3) anointing with oil, (4) sacrificing, (5) anointing with blood, and (6) eating of a sacrificial animal (29:4-34).

The ordination of Aaron and his sons was to last seven days. Each of the above-named rituals was to be repeated seven times. The blood of the sin offering which was put on the horns of the altar and then poured out at its base (29:12) consecrated the altar to God (29:35-37).

3. *Priestly duties (29:38–30:21).* Four duties of priests are next described. These may be summarized as follows:

First, priests were to present the regular burnt offering. Two lambs were to be offered each day, one in the morning, the other in the afternoon. A grain offering (fine flour mixed with oil) and a drink offering of wine were to accompany the offering of the lambs. Because of these daily offerings God promised to make the entrance of the tent a place of meeting with Moses and the Israelites (29:38-43). Only when the tent, the altar, and the priesthood were consecrated could God consent to dwell in the midst of his people (29:44-46).

Second, priests were to burn incense. The gold-covered altar of incense was positioned directly in front of the curtain which separated the Holy of Holies from the Holy Place in the Tabernacle. Morning and evening Aaron and his successors were to burn incense on that altar. Once a year that altar was to be reconsecrated to the Lord by the blood of a sin offering (30:1-10).

Third, priests were to administer the atonement money. Each Israelite counted in a census was required to pay a half shekel ransom for his life. These monies were to be used for the service of the Tent of Meeting (30:11-16).

Finally, priests were to wash before serving. At the bronze laver in the courtyard of the Tabernacle the priests were to wash hands and feet before entering the tent or offering sacrifice on the altar in the courtyard (30:17-21).

4. *Sacred substances (30:22-38).* Specific instructions were given regarding two substances which were to receive extensive and exclusive usage in the sacred services. (1) The anointing oil could be used only for anointing the priests, the Tent of Meeting, and the furniture of the tent. (2) A special incense was restricted to use on the Altar of Incense in front of the Testimony, i.e., the ark of the covenant (30:34-38).

C. Construction of the Tabernacle (Ex 31:1-18).

The Lord not only gave the blueprints for the Tabernacle and its furniture, he also appointed the craftsmen. Bezalel of Judah and Oholiab of Dan were to be commissioned to supervise the construction of all that was associated with the Tabernacle. The craftsmen were not to attempt to be innovative; they were simply to carry out the instructions of the Lord. Bezalel is the first individual in the Bible said to be filled with the Spirit (31:1-11).

The instructions in the mount concluded with a reminder that the sanctity of the Sabbath was to be maintained even during the time of Tabernacle construction. Sabbath observance was to be a sign between God and the Israelites (31:12-17).

After the lengthy set of instructions had been given, God gave to Moses the two tablets of the Testimony upon which the Ten Commandments had been written by the finger of God (31:18).

INSURGENCY AMONG THE PEOPLE
Exodus 32:1-30

The account of the great apostasy at Sinai is one of the saddest in the Old Testament. The narrative relates four developments.

A. Leading in the Apostasy (Ex 32:1-6).

The people in the camp began to despair of ever seeing Moses again. He had been in the flaming, cloud-covered mount for forty days without food or water. The people came to Aaron with the request that he make gods to lead them. With the disappearance of Moses they believed they had also lost the possibility of fellowship with Yahweh. They spoke contemptuously of their former leader (32:1).

Aaron did not argue with the people. He gave them instructions to bring their earrings to him. Some think that he was attempting to dissuade them by demanding the sacrifice of that which was very dear to easterners. Nonetheless, he melted down this gold and fashioned an idol cast in the form of a calf. Most likely this image had a solid core of wood which Aaron covered with gold leaf. Aaron presented the idol to Israel with the announcement, "These are your gods who brought you up out of Egypt." Aaron intended this image to be a visible representation of Yahweh, or at least of the sacred animal upon which Yahweh rode. Most gods in that period were associated with a sacred animal upon which they rode. He may have used the plural "gods" to suggest that more of these images could be constructed (32:2-4).

An altar was built before the new image and a festival was proclaimed in honor of Yahweh. Whole burnt offerings were presented and peace offerings in which the worshipers ate a portion of the animal. The people sat down to eat and drink and rose up to indulge in revelry (32:5-6).

B. Learning of the Apostasy (Ex 32:7-18).

In the mount Moses learned of what was taking place in the camp. God was prepared to wipe out that stiff-necked nation and build a new one from the descendants of Moses. This proposal was designed to test Moses with regard to any possible ambition on his part (32:7-10).

Moses passed the test. He immediately began to pray for the people. He urged the Lord to consider three things: (1) the power he had already displayed on behalf of Israel, (2) the possible blasphemous thoughts of the Egyptians if he should destroy the people, and (3) the promises he had made to the patriarchs. God responded to the logic of this model intercessory prayer. He relented concerning the destruction which he had threatened. Forgiveness of the people had not yet been secured, but the Lord's first burst of anger was averted by Moses' prayer (32:11-14).

Moses descended the mount carrying the two tablets of the Testimony which had been inscribed on both sides by God himself. At some point in the descent Joshua rejoined Moses. Joshua interpreted the noise coming from the camp as the sound of war. Moses pointed out that the noise was neither the sound of victory nor defeat, but the music of revelry (32:15-18).

C. Dealing with the Apostates (Ex 32:19-30).

When Moses saw the calf and the dancing of the people, his "anger waxed hot" (KJV). He cast down the precious tablets and smashed them at the foot of the mountain. He burned the wooden parts of the calf and pulverized the overlay. He scattered the remains on the water and made the guilty drink of it. Then he confronted his brother, and rebuked him for leading in the apostasy. Aaron blamed the people for pressuring him, and then blamed the fire. All he did was throw the gold earrings into the fire and out came the calf! Aaron's explanation was not even worthy of response from Moses (32:19-24).

Even at this point some of the people persisted in their orgy. Moses stood in the gate of the camp and cried, "Who is on the Lord's side?" The Levites, perhaps feeling guilty because of the leadership of their fellow Levite Aaron, rallied to Moses' side. They were told to strap on their swords and pass through the camp sparing no one who was still indulging in licentious conduct. Three thousand died that day. Moses commended the Levites for their zeal. They had put loyalty to their God above loyalty to their brethren. The next day Moses reminded the people of the enormity of their sin. He then promised to return to the mount to make atonement for them through prayer (32:25-30).

319

INTERCESSION BY MOSES
Exodus 32:31-34:9

Moses was a great man of prayer. His intercessory prayers skillfully wove together compassion and logic. He loved his people, and he did not fail to pour out his heart on their behalf. In the present unit, Moses' intercession passed through three stages.

A. Moses in the Mount (Ex 32:31-33:6).

In his prayer Moses acknowledged the great sin of the people. He begged God's forgiveness. If God would not forgive them, then he wished for his own name to be blotted from the Book of Life. This book apparently contained the names of those who found favor with the Lord. He wished to share the fate of his people (32:31f.).

The Lord assured Moses that only those who actually sinned in the apostasy would be blotted from the Book of Life. Moses needed to get back to the business of leading the people to the Promised Land. God had led the people to this point, now it was to be Moses and an angel. Shortly thereafter the Lord sent a plague among the people to punish them for participation in the calf episode (32:33-35).

In a further word to Moses, God indicated that he would send an angel (but not the angel of the Lord) before them to dispossess the inhabitants of Canaan; but he personally would no longer travel with them. Therefore no purpose would be served by constructing the Tabernacle, which symbolized God's presence, and by transporting it through the wilderness. This decision was actually in the best interest of the people, for God in his absolute holiness would not be able to tolerate their frequent lapses into sin. He would have to destroy them along the way (33:1-3).

The announcement that God would not accompany them on the way caused the people no little distress. God required them to take off the earrings which had figured so prominently in the calf apostasy. The penitent people immediately obeyed (33:4-6).

B. Moses in the Tent (Ex 33:7-23).

Moses pitched for himself a tent where he could fellowship with God at a distance from the camp. The tent was a visible prayer that the Lord would be reconciled to his people. When Moses entered the tent, the pillar of cloud came down. People stood reverently at the entrance of their tents to observe. In the tent God spoke to Moses "face to face, as a man might speak with his friend." When Moses returned to the camp, Joshua would remain behind at the tent, perhaps to summon Moses should the Lord call for him (33:7-11).

After Moses had communed with God in the tent for several days, he made yet another attempt to reconcile God to the penitent people. In 32:34 and 33:1-3 God had promised to send an angel before Israel even though he himself must withdraw from leading them. Accustomed as he was to God's presence, Moses was not too excited about following the lead of an angel. Yet he knew that he was not capable of leading Israel to the Promised Land by himself. Moses wanted more information about who would help him lead the people. God had indicated by word and deed that Moses was very special to him; but how could God so regard Moses and not the people of which he was a part? This was an oblique way of asking that God himself agree to lead the people (33:12-13).

Context seems to require that 33:14 be rendered as a question: "Shall my Presence go with you?" The Lord was helping Moses state his petition more explicitly. That was exactly what Moses wanted. The people would prefer to remain at Sinai where they could at least observe some evidence of God's presence, rather than go to the Promised Land without him. God's special favor for Moses and the people he represented could only be demonstrated if God accompanied them on their journey. The Lord agreed to this request. He would lead the people, not because they deserved his presence, but because of the high regard he had for Moses (33:14-17).

Emboldened by the divine response, Moses made another request: "Show me your glory." If God would grant this request, Moses' faith in the promise of God's guiding presence would be strengthened. A man, however, cannot bear the full vision of divine radiance. God promised to make his "goodness," i.e., a part of his glory, pass before Moses. He would be shielded in the cleft of the rock, where he would see the back parts of God, but not his face. Apparently the theophany would be in human form (33:18-23).

C. Moses in the Cleft of the Rock (Ex 34:1-9).

Moses was directed to hew out two tables of stone and return to the top of the mount alone. When Moses complied with these orders, Yahweh descended in the cloud and stood there with him. The emphasis here, however, is not on what Moses *saw,* but on what he *heard* (34:1-5).

As Yahweh passed before Moses he proclaimed his own "name," i.e., nature. Seven positive attributes of the God of Sinai are announced, all of which point to his compassion and forgiveness. Nonetheless, this wonderfully compassionate God does not leave the wicked unpunished. Sometimes children to the third and fourth generation suffer the consequences of the sins of their fathers (34:6-7).

Moses seized upon the emphasis on the compassion of God. He asked anew that God would (1) go with them, (2) forgive their wickedness, and (3) claim Israel as his inheritance (34:8-9).

COVENANT RENEWAL BY THE LORD
Exodus 34:10-35

Because God had a covenant with Israel, he would do wonders on their behalf. Israel, however, must obey the commands of God. This unit sets forth the mandate of God for his people and the mediator he provided for them.

A. Covenant Mandate (Ex 34:10-28).

In covenant renewal, restatement of the major stipulations of the original covenant is necessary. These were: (1) Maintain an attitude of absolute intolerance toward anything Canaanite. No treaty was to be made with Canaanites, and no intermarriage was permitted. Pagan shrines were to be demolished. (2) Make no molten image. (3) Appear three times annually before the Lord for the celebration of the major festivals. (4) Present firstborn males of man and beast as well as first-fruits of the harvest to the Lord (34:12-26).

Moses was directed to write down these principles of the covenant. This was the second time Moses explicitly was told to record a portion of the Law (cf. 24:4). The renewed covenant is first with Moses ("with *you* and with Israel"). Verse 28 is ambiguous as to whether

Moses or the Lord wrote the Decalogue on the newly cut stone tablets. According to 34:1, however, the Lord did the writing, thus underscoring the foundational authority of the Decalogue (34:27f.).

B. Covenant Mediator (Ex 34:29-35).

After forty days and nights in the mount, Moses returned to the camp with the two tablets of the Testimony. His face glowed with a radiance which struck fear in the hearts of the Israelites. Nonetheless Moses made them come near while he delivered to them the commands of God. When he had finished speaking to them, he put a veil over his face. From then on he only removed his veil when he entered into the Lord's presence.

ENDNOTES

1. Hamilton, *Handbook*, pp. 233-235.
2. A marine animal resembling the seal. John Davis, *Moses*, p. 252.
3. Rylaarsdam, "Exodus," I:845. Frank M. Cross states that the "priestly account is schematized and idealized" and contains "theological interpretations and historical developments of later ages." Yet Cross allows that an "important historical witness to the Mosaic age" is contained in this "priestly tradition." "The Priestly Tabernacle," *The Biblical Archaeologist Reader*, I:209.
4. Cited by Davis, *Moses*, p. 242.
5. Ibid.

CHAPTER TWENTY-EIGHT

God's Dwelling Place
Exodus 35-40

AIM: To demonstrate the spiritual significance of the Tabernacle.

THEME: All things according to the pattern.

The Mosaic records refer to the central place of worship in five different ways. It is called (1) the sanctuary (*miqdash*) which refers to the sanctity of the place (Ex 25:18); (2) tabernacle (*mishcan*) or residing place (Ex 25:9); (3) tent (*'ohel*), a collapsible dwelling (Ex 26:36); (4) tent of meeting (*'ohel mo'ed*) in Exodus 29:42; and tabernacle of the testimony *(mishcan ha'eduth)* because it housed the tablets of the Ten Commandments. The Tabernacle was the center of Israelite worship for five hundred years.

The importance of the Tabernacle is indicated in the manner in which it is presented. First God described in tedious detail this structure and its furnishings (Ex 24–31). Then the narrator emphasizes how all of these directions were carefully carried out by the Israelites (Ex 35–40).

THE PREPARATIONS
Exodus 35:1–36:7

The construction of the Tabernacle was a project which occupied the Israelites for several months. To prepare for this mammoth undertaking, materials were gathered and superintendents were appointed over the project.

A. Materials Gathered (Ex 35:1-29).

Moses assembled the people to convey to them the instructions which he had received in the mount. First he reminded them of the primacy of Sabbath observance. Even during the construction of the Tabernacle the sacred day was to be observed. The detail is added that not even a fire should be started on the Sabbath. Those who violated Sabbath law were to be executed (35:1-3).

Moses then challenged the people to bring a freewill offering to the Lord. The offering was to consist of (1) metals (gold, silver, bronze), (2) cloth materials (fine linen and various colored yarns), (3) animal skins (goat, ram, and dugong), (4) acacia wood, (5) olive oil, (6) spices, and (7) precious stones (35:4-9).

Skilled craftsmen among the people were encouraged to volunteer their services to construct the various components of the Tabernacle. Metal workers and seamstresses were in special demand for the project (35:10-19).

The people responded with enthusiasm to Moses' challenge. Everyone who was willing and whose heart moved him came and brought an offering to the Lord for the work. Men and women brought their gold jewelry of all kinds and presented it as a wave offering to the Lord. The same was done to offerings of silver, bronze, acacia wood, skins, yarns and fine linen. The skilled women spun yarn, linen and goats hair. The leaders brought onyx stones, gems, spices and olive oil. Everyone caught the spirit of the enterprise (35:20-29).

B. Supervisors Appointed (Ex 35:30–36:7).

After the materials began coming in, Moses announced the Lord's choice of Bezalel of Judah and Oholiab of Dan as superintendents of the project. These two men were filled with the Spirit of God. This filling manifested itself in their skill, ability and knowledge in all kinds of crafts. What is more, these two master craftsmen both possessed the ability to teach others these skills. God had blessed a whole troop of laborers with the skills necessary to construct the Tabernacle as he had commanded (35:30–36:1).

Moses summoned the labor crew and delivered over to them the offerings which the people had been giving to him. The offerings continued to pour in morning by morning. Finally the workmen left their work and sought out Moses to inform him that more than enough had been contributed toward the project. Moses then issued the order that the contributions should cease. This is probably the last time in all the history of the people of God when a leader told his flock to cease giving! (36:2-7).

THE CONSTRUCTION
Exodus 36:8-38

A number of questions confront the serious interpreter of the Tabernacle narratives. For one thing, the exact length of the cubit in this period is unknown. The biblical cubit ranged in length from the standard cubit of 17.5 up to the royal Egyptian of 20.65 inches. Did the structure have a sloping roof (Ferguson; Whitelaw) or a flat roof (Kennedy, Nichol)? The flat roof theory seems best. Details are omitted leaving open many questions about this structure. In six paragraphs Moses describes the construction of the Tabernacle proper.

1. The ten inner curtains (36:8-13) were made of linen and blue, purple and scarlet yarn. Cherubim or winged guardian angels were embroidered on them. Each curtain was twenty-eight by four cubits (forty-two by six feet). These curtains were joined in two sets of five curtains each. Each set was attached to the frame of the Tabernacle by fifty gold clasps.

2. The outer coverings (36:14-19) were three in number. The innermost covering was of goat's hair. Eleven curtains each thirty by four cubits (forty-five by six feet). These were sewn together in sets of five and six each. The two sets were then joined by fifty bronze clasps to make a single unit. Over the goat's hair covering was a covering of ram skins dyed red, and over that a covering of hides of dugongs.

3. The "boards" of acacia wood set in bases of silver formed the walls of the Tabernacle on three sides. The "boards" (KJV) are probably best understood as frames (NIV). Twenty frames formed the north and south walls of the structure, six frames formed the west walls. Double frames on the corners gave stability to the structure. Each frame was supported by two of the silver bases (36:20-30).

4. The bars (36:31-34) gave stability to the frames. Five were located on each of the three sides. The bars were overlaid with gold and attached to the frames with gold rings.

5. The veil which separated the Holy Place and the Holy of Holies was made of linen with embroidery of blue, purple and scarlet yarn. Figures of cherubim decorated this veil. It hung by gold hooks from four wooden pillars overlaid with gold. The pillars were supported by four silver bases (36:35-36).

6. The entrance hangings were made of the same substance as the inner veil. These curtains hung from five pillars with gold trim. The supporting bases here were of bronze (36:37-38).

THE FURNITURE
Exodus 37:1–38:20

Counting the mercy seat with its guardian cherubim as one distinct piece, seven articles of furniture adorned the Tabernacle and its court.

A. Furniture of the Tent (Ex 37:1-29).

Five pieces of furniture were constructed for placement within the Tabernacle. Each of these objects played an important role in the priestly ministries of the Mosaic era.

1. The ark (37:1-5) was made of acacia wood overlaid inside and out with pure gold. Long poles, also overlaid with gold, were inserted through rings on the side of the ark. By means of these rings the ark was to be transported. The ark was small, forty-five inches long and twenty-seven inches wide.

2. The mercy seat (KJV) or atonement (NIV) was constructed atop the ark. This sacred spot was overshadowed by the wings of two cherubim of hammered gold. The cherubim faced each other with faces turned downward toward the mercy seat (37:6-9).

Fig. 1 The Ark

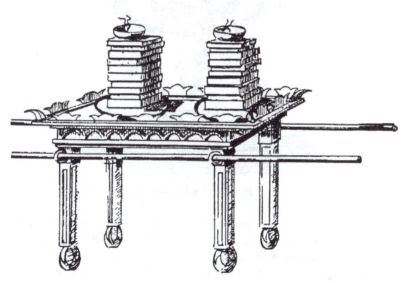

Fig. 2 The Table

3. The table (37:10-16) was positioned in the Holy Place. It was made of acacia wood overlaid with pure gold. A gold molding decorated the top. The table was thirty-six inches long, eighteen inches wide, and twenty-seven inches high. Like the ark, the table was also carried on staves inserted through golden rings attached to the four legs. All the vessels associated with the table—plates, bowls, ladles and pitchers—were also made of pure gold.

4. The lampstand (37:17-23) which adorned the Holy Place was one solid piece of hammered gold. It had six branches, each with three cups shaped like almond flowers. The lampstand itself had four similarly shaped cups. All the accessories of the lampstand — the wick trimmers and trays — were of pure gold.

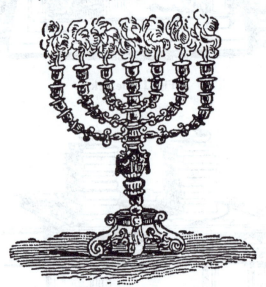

Fig. 3 The Lampstand

5. The altar of incense (37:25-29) was also a furnishing of the Holy Place. It was made of acacia wood overlaid with gold. It was a square of eighteen inches and stood thirty-six inches tall. Four horns and a decorative molding were part of the top. This altar was carried by poles overlaid with gold which were inserted into rings on its sides.

A footnote to the description of the altar describes how a perfumer made the anointing oil and the fragrant incense, the latter of which was used in conjunction with the altar of incense.

Fig. 4 Altar of Incense

B. Furniture of the Courtyard (Ex 38:1-20).

The most conspicuous furnishing of the courtyard was the altar of burnt offering. It was made of acacia wood overlaid with bronze. This altar was a square of ninety inches and it stood fifty-four inches high. Molded into the four corners were protrusions called horns. The altar was hollow. A bronze grating was placed half way up in the hollow square. Bronze covered poles inserted in rings on the sides were used to transport the altar. All of the utensils associated with the altar of burnt offering — pots, shovels, bowls, meat forks and firepans — were made of bronze.

Fig. 5 Altar of Burnt Offerings

The second piece of furniture in the courtyard was the bronze laver (35:8). It was made from the mirrors contributed by the women who served at the entrance of the Tent of Meeting. No further details are given about this group of women.

The courtyard itself was 150 feet long and seventy-five feet wide. A linen curtain supported by fifty-six bronze covered pillars marked off the courtyard. The entrance to the courtyard was to be on the east side. A beautiful embroidered linen curtain thirty feet in length hung at the entrance. This curtain was supported by four posts.

THE ACCOUNTING
Exodus 38:21-31

Moses had ordered a careful accounting of the materials used in the construction of the Tabernacle and its furnishings. The Levites under the direction of Ithamar did the audit. The amounts of the materials utilized were as follows:

Fig. 6 The Laver

1. Gold — twenty-nine talents and 730 shekels, or about 1,900 pounds.

2. Silver — a hundred talents and 1,775 shekels, or 6,437 pounds. This had been secured from the half-shekel sanctuary tax imposed on all the 603,550 men (age twenty and up) who had crossed the Red Sea. The silver was used to make bases, hooks, and decorative bands and caps for the pillars.

3. Bronze — seventy talents, 2,400 shekels, or about 4,522 pounds. Bronze was used to make the bases for the pillars of the courtyard as well as the bronze altar and the tent pegs.

Critics have questioned whether or not the Israelites had available in the wilderness sufficient quantities of the necessary metals and fabrics to build the Tabernacle as it is described in Exodus. The metal would be altogether just less than 13,000 pounds, or six and a half tons! The fabric involved was about 5,500 square yards! The Bible speaks several times of wealth which the Israelites took with them when they left Egypt (e.g., 12:35f.). No doubt much plunder was taken from the Amalekites (17:8-16). Perhaps some goods could have been secured through barter with trade caravans passing through the region.

THE PRIESTLY GARMENTS
Exodus 39:1-31

From the various colored yarns which had been contributed, the women wove "sacred garments" for Aaron and "garments for ministering" for his sons who served under him. The following were the sacred garments:

1. The ephod (39:2-7) was a sleeveless garment made of linen and various colored yarn. It is called the "ephod of gold" because it actually had thin strands of gold woven into the cloth. A beautiful waistband was of one piece with the ephod. Onyx stones mounted in gold settings were fastened to the shoulder pieces of the ephod. On these stones the names of the sons of Israel were inscribed, six names on each stone.

2. The breastplate (39:8-21) was made of the same cloth combination as the ephod. It was a square of nine inches. On this breastplate were four rows of precious stones mounted in gold settings. The exact identity of some of these stones is unknown, but each bore the name of one of the tribes of Israel. Every tribe was precious in God's sight. By means of gold rings and chains the breastplate was attached to the garments of the high priest.

3. The robe of the ephod (39:22-26) was made of blue cloth. The garment was pulled over the head. Balls of yarn resembling pomegranates interspersed with bells of gold adorned the hem of this robe. The bells told the worshipers when the high priest was busy in ministry within the unseen areas of the Tabernacle.

4. The turban worn by the high priest (28:36-38) had attached to it the sacred diadem (39:30f.). This plate of pure gold was engraved with the words *Holy to Yahweh*.

In addition to the four garments worn only by the high priest, four garments were worn by all the priests. These included (1) a coat, (2) sash, (3) headband and (4) linen undergarments (28:40-42). No mention is made of any footwear. Perhaps priests performed their duties barefoot since they were walking on holy ground (cf. Ex 3:5).

Fig. 7 High Priestly Garments
(1) Turban, (2) Ephod, (3) Robe of the Ephod,
(4) Coat, (5) Sash, (6) Breastplate

THE DEDICATION
Exodus 39:32–40:37

When the project was finished, the workers brought all the things which they had made to Moses for his final inspection. Three times the text emphasizes that they had made everything just as the Lord had commanded Moses. The Lawgiver then pronounced a blessing upon these dedicated workers for the efforts which they had put forth (39:32-43).

At the command of the Lord the Tabernacle was erected. The date was considered important enough to be recorded: the first day of the first month of the second year. Thus in just fifteen days short of a year, the Israelites had traveled to Sinai, received the Law and constructed a rather elaborate place of worship (40:1-2).

True to the literary pattern of Exodus, the Lord first gave precise orders regarding how the Tabernacle was to be erected, then Moses carried out those instructions. After the Tent was properly arranged, Moses was told to anoint the furniture with oil to consecrate it to the Lord. Then he was to conduct a consecration service for Aaron and his sons. They were to be washed. Aaron was to be dressed in the sacred garments and anointed with oil. Then Aaron's sons were to be dressed in their garb and anointed (40:3-16). Details of this consecration service are described in Leviticus.

Moses carefully narrates the details of the erection of the Tabernacle. First the bases were put in place and the frames, supported by the crossbars, inserted into them. After the interior posts were set up, the coverings were then put over this shell. The furniture of the Tabernacle was placed in position in the following order:

1. The Testimony (tablets of the Ten Commandments) was put into the ark. The poles were attached and the mercy seat was put over the ark. The ark was then placed in the far western end of the Tabernacle, the area known as the Holy of Holies.

2. The curtain was put in place to shield the ark and mark off the limits of the Holy of Holies.

3. The table and its accessories were placed in the outer area of the tent called the Holy Place on the north side. Twelve loaves of unleavened bread were placed on the table.

4. The lampstand was next set in its place within the Holy Place opposite the table on the south side.

5. The golden altar was placed directly in front of the ark of the Testimony within the Holy Place. Incense was burned on it.

6. The curtain was then put up at the entrance of the Tabernacle.

7. The bronze altar was placed at the entrance of the Tabernacle. Burnt offerings and grain offerings were offered on it.

8. The laver was placed between the tent of meeting and the altar of burnt offering. Water was then placed in it. Here the priests washed before entering the tent of meeting or approaching the altar in the courtyard.

9. The curtains which formed the courtyard were then set up (40:17-33).

When everything was in place according to the commandment of the Lord, the cloud which shielded the divine glory covered the Tabernacle. The glory was so bright that not even Moses could enter the sanctuary. From this day forward the glorious cloud directed the movements of the Israelites. When the cloud lifted above the Tabernacle, they broke camp. At night fire appeared in the cloud. Throughout their journeys the Israelites observed day and night this supernatural manifestation of the divine presence (40:34-38).

OBSERVATIONS REGARDING THE TABERNACLE

1. The Tabernacle is rooted in divine revelation. The Israelites merely implemented the directives of God. Eighteen times in the last two chapters the narrator emphasizes the precise compliance to the commandments of God. This emphasis appears two additional times in Exodus 36. God's commands are meant to be executed.

2. The dimensions of the Tabernacle were symmetrical. The length of the court was twice that of the width. The Holy Place was twice the size of the Holy of Holies. The latter was a fifteen foot cube.

3. The choice of metals is indicative of greater degrees of sanctity. "Pure gold" was used on of objects within the tent; courtyard furnishings were made of bronze. Ordinary gold was used for moldings, rings, and poles. Silver was used for the bases which held pillars near the veil.

4. Fabrics also reflected degrees of sacredness. The inner veil before the Holy of Holies was made of blue, purple and scarlet wools, along with fine linen. The Tabernacle curtains were primarily of linen embroidered with blue, purple, and scarlet yarns.

5. The Tabernacle perpetuated and intensified the Mt. Sinai experience. The glory of the Lord settled on Mt. Sinai (24:16) and later in the Tabernacle (40:34). In one sense the glory of God was more intense in the Tabernacle than it had been on the mount. Moses could enter the glory on the mount (24:18), but he could not enter the cloud when it filled the Tabernacle (40:35).

Fig. 8 The Tabernacle

6. The sanctity of the Tabernacle was derived, not from the precious metals it contained, or the godly men who labored therein, but from the fact that God chose to dwell there (29:43-46). Later the special presence of God in the Tabernacle came to be known as *Shekinah* glory. Here is where God and man could meet (29:42-43).

7. The Tabernacle in the words of Davies is "the principal bridgehead in the Old Testament to the doctrine of the Incarnation."[1] As God dwelt among his people in an earthly edifice, so he later "tabernacled" among his people in Jesus Christ (John 1:14; Col 1:19).

ENDNOTES

1. G. Hinton Davies, s.v. "Tabernacle," *The Interpreter's Dictionary of the Bible*, IV:506.

BIBLIOGRAPHY: THE TABERNACLE

Green, W.H. *The Hebrew Feasts* (1885).

Olford, Stephen F. *The Tabernacle: Camping with God.* Neptune, NJ: Loizeaux, 1978.

Ridout, Samuel. *Lectures on the Tabernacle.* Neptune, NJ: Loizeaux, 1976 reprint.

Slemming, C.W. *These Are the Garments.* Fort Washington, PA: Christian Literature Crusade, 1974.

Soltau, Henry W. *The Tabernacle, the Priesthood and the Offerings.* London, n.d.

THE BOOK OF
LEVITICUS

CHAPTER TWENTY-NINE

Getting Acquainted with Leviticus

AIM: To demonstrate the relevance of Leviticus for believers today.

THEME: Holiness is essential!

With twenty-seven chapters, 859 verses and 24,546 words Leviticus is the shortest book in the Mosaic collection. A somewhat cynical analyst observed: "Leviticus is a dust heap containing a single pearl — "You shall love your neighbor as yourself" (19:18). To the casual reader, this book represents the epitome of Old Testament irrelevance. Leviticus is full of minute descriptions of ancient rituals which have not been performed now for almost two thousand years. Christian theology argues that all these ceremonies have been rendered obsolete by the once-for-all-time sacrifice of Jesus Christ. As the name suggests, here is a handbook for a priesthood long since replaced in the plan of God by the priesthood of believers in Christ. So why study Leviticus?

The third book of the Bible is probably the least read of the sacred sixty-six. Three reasons can be suggested for this aversion to Leviticus: (1) Some think that it will be impossible for them to master all the ritual and symbol in the book so as to gain much spiritual benefit. (2) Others regard the material here obsolete, with no living application to the present day. (3) Others point to laws here so severe or trivial that they seem to be at variance with what is known of God from the rest of Scripture.

The prejudice against it notwithstanding, Leviticus is a Christian book. The Bible of Jesus contained this book. More than forty New Testament references to Leviticus have been identified. What appears on the surface to be a barren wasteland proves to be a gold mine to those with the patience to plumb its depths. William Hendriksen observed: "As ceremonial requirements, these laws are no longer valid. Their underlying principles are as valid today as during the old dispensation."[1]

DESCRIPTION OF LEVITICUS

What can a believer expect to find when he opens the book of Leviticus? What kind of book is this? Four introductory observations are appropriate.

1. Leviticus is a divine book. Modern critics argue that the material in Leviticus was written about a millennium after the time of Moses; that the book is the product of a priestly caste of the exilic period! A believer cannot possibly entertain such an idea. God directly speaks more here than in any other book in the Bible. Fifty-six times this book claims that God gave these laws to his people through Moses. Jesus himself underscored the authority of this book by commanding a cleansed leper to offer at the Temple the gift required by the law (Matt 8:4). Mary obeyed the law of Leviticus when she observed the days of purification and then presented an offering at the Temple (Luke 2:22).

The teaching of Leviticus is another indication of its divine origin. The lofty theology of this book towers like Everest over the pagan literature of the second millennium BC. Fundamental theological

344

themes are emphasized here. Some have referred to Leviticus as the "Book of Atonement" or "the Romans of the Old Testament."

2. Leviticus is a legal book. Only two historical incidents are narrated in Leviticus: (1) the consecration of the priests and the deaths of Nadab and Abihu (chs. 8–10); and (2) the punishment of a blasphemer (24:10-14). On the other hand, Leviticus is full of laws general and specific, severe and merciful. It contains (1) civil, (2) ceremonial, (3) moral, (4) religious, and (5) sanitary laws. For the sacred writer, however, law was law. To him distinctions between types of law were nonexistent.

In Leviticus God sought to govern either by broad principle or specific precept the whole of the life of his people. The divine expectation as revealed in this book may be summed up in the words of the Apostle Paul, "Whether therefore you eat, or drink, or whatsoever you do, do all to the glory of God" (1 Cor 10:31). According to Sell, "Everything is calculated to stimulate the spiritual life. Sanitary and dietary laws are not laid down as such but are made distinctive marks of a consecrated life of a chosen people; details of ritual are prescribed to express the sense of the holiness of God in whose service they are exercised. The effect of the law was to make Israel a Holy Nation."[2]

3. Leviticus is a priestly book. The name "Leviticus" suggests that this book has to do with Levites. Actually the priests are mentioned far more often than Levites — about 730 times versus 290 times. The principal figure in Leviticus is Aaron the high priest. Yet the book should not be regarded as a manual to guide Aaron and his sons through intricate ceremonies. While in eight passages Moses is directed to speak to the priests, in seventeen places he is told to speak to the children of Israel. Leviticus is a book of instructions for the priestly nation and their priestly representatives. The people were entitled and expected to know exactly what was required of them, and of their priests, in that service of the sanctuary which so deeply concerned every true Israelite.

4. Leviticus is a picture book. Here is set forth in ritual typology the redemptive program of God. Payne found here twenty-seven types involving 462 verses.[3]

SETTING OF LEVITICUS

Both the introduction (1:1) and the conclusion of Leviticus (27:34) clearly indicate that the setting in this book is the same as in the final chapters of Exodus. The book contains laws given to Moses at Mt. Sinai. Another strong tie to Exodus is found in the account of the ordination of Aaron and his sons which is the implementation of the instructions found in Exodus 29. Leviticus stresses the exact compliance with the stipulations of the previous book (8:9,13, etc.). The Levitical laws of impurities (chs. 11–16) and holiness (chs. 17–26) presuppose the establishment of the covenant which was narrated in Exodus.

The last event in Exodus, the erection of the Tabernacle, is dated to the first day of the first month of the second year of the Exodus (Ex 40:17). The first event in Numbers, the census at Sinai, is dated to the first day of the second month of the same year (Nm 1:1). Leviticus, therefore, covers only one month. This chronological framework is diagramed in Chart 25.

Chart No. 25

CHRONOLOGY OF LEVITICUS		
LAST EVENT IN EXODUS	L E V I T I C U S	FIRST EVENT IN NUMBERS
ERECTION OF THE TABERNACLE		CENSUS AT SINAI
2ND YEAR 1ST MONTH 1ST DAY		2ND YEAR 2ND MONTH 1ST DAY
ONE MONTH		

That Leviticus is an essential part of the Pentateuchal sequence is apparent. Genesis identified God's remedy for man's ruin — the Seed of woman. Exodus revealed God's answer to man's cry — the blood of the Lamb. Now Leviticus speaks of God's provision for man's need — sacrifice and priesthood. Leviticus is central in the Pentateuch

346

chronologically; it is also central theologically. With its doctrine of mediation through sacrifice and priesthood, and reconciliation at the altar, Leviticus is the very heart of the Mosaic books — and the gospel as well. The progression of thought in the first three books of the Pentateuch is illustrated in Chart 26.

Chart No. 26

THOUGHT PROGRESSION IN THE PENTATEUCH		
GENESIS	**EXODUS**	**LEVITICUS**
God's Remedy for Man's Ruin	God's Answer for Man's Cry	God's Provision for Man's Need
The Seed of Woman (Gn 3:15)	The Blood of a Lamb (Ex 13–14)	Priest/Altar/ Sacrifice
The Problem of Sin	The Possibility of Salvation	The Provision for Service

While continuity between Leviticus and the preceding books is obvious, a marked contrast between Exodus and Leviticus is also obvious. Exodus begins with enslaved sinners, Leviticus with redeemed saints. In the former book God got his people out of Egypt; in the latter, he got Egypt out of his people. Exodus is the book of deliverance emphasizing the fact of sacrifice; Leviticus is the book of dedication and sets forth the doctrine of sacrifice. In Exodus God speaks from the mount, and he approaches man. In Leviticus God speaks from the tent, and man learns to approach God. Exodus dwells at length on the erection of the Tabernacle while in Leviticus Tabernacle duties are set forth.[4]

STRUCTURE OF LEVITICUS

The Book of Leviticus can be summarized in the caption "Sacrifices and Sanctity." The first half of this book charts the way into the presence of God. Chapters 1–7 describe the five basic sacrifices through which an Israelite could approach God. The law of mediation (chs. 8–10) identified the Aaronic priesthood as the avenue of approach. The law of separation (chs. 11–15) emphasizes pure food, pure bodies, and pure houses. The law of expiation (ch. 16) provides for the nation as a whole to approach God through the annual sacrifices on the Day of Atonement. Chapter 17 serves as a kind of appendix to the first half of the book.[5]

Chart No. 27

STRUCTURE OF LEVITICUS			
("THE SANCTIFICATION OF THE NATION")			
THE WAY TO GOD Chs. 1–7	**THE WORK OF GOD** Chs. 8–15	**THE WALK WITH GOD** Chs. 16–22	**THE WORSHIP OF GOD** Chs. 23–27
Attaining Fellowship through Worship		**Maintaining Fellowship through Practice**	
SACRIFICE		**SANCTIFICATION**	
Ceremonial and Physical Defilement		**Moral and Spiritual Defilement**	
CLEANSING		**CLEAN LIVING**	

If the first part of Leviticus told an Israelite how he might approach a holy God, the second part told him how he might maintain his relationship to the Lord. Leviticus stresses *the sanctification of the nation*. Here God emphasized that his people must be set apart to his service. Holiness must govern every aspect of their life. The abiding lesson in the book is that *holiness is essential*.

Examining the second half of Leviticus more closely reveals the following breakdown: Chapters 18–22 speak of the law of dedication. Israel was not to follow the leading of Egypt or Canaan. They were especially to avoid unlawful marriages and Molech worship. Priests were to set the example in commitment. Directions are given concerning the holiness, the marriage, bodily perfection and purity of those who minister at God's altar. Chapters 23–25 reveal the law of the feasts. The Passover, Pentecost, Trumpets, the Day of Atonement, Tabernacles, the Sabbatical Year and Year of Jubilee are discussed. The law of obligations is set forth in the last two chapters of the book.

Thus Leviticus is a literary bifid illustrating the twofold emphasis of 1 John 1:7. The first half of Leviticus stresses that "The blood cleanses us," and the second half of the book focuses on "If we walk in the light." Chart 27 summarizes the structure of the third book of the Pentateuch.

TEACHING OF LEVITICUS

While Exodus spoke of redemption and instruction, Leviticus speaks of fellowship with God, holiness and worship. Griffith Thomas[6] has offered an excellent analysis of the teaching of Leviticus under seven heads:

1. The Great Problem: Sin. The fact of sin is recognized in the whole book. Sin is unlikeness to God, distance from God, and wrong done against God. By sin man is excluded from nearness to God and communion with him.

2. The Great Provision: Sacrifice. The words *offering* and *sacrifice* appear over ninety times. Two other words of high frequency are *blood* and *life*. The key phrase in the book, "before the Lord," appears some sixty times. The fact of redemption is the key to the whole book. The redemption is achieved through substitution, imputation, and death. The innocent animal pays the death penalty for the guilty sinner. Redemption from death is founded on righteousness and therefore is possible only through blood (life) poured out.

3. The Great Power: Priesthood. Man can and must approach God through divinely appointed mediators. Reading the Book of Leviticus, the Christian is reminded of his need for an intercessor, a priest superior to Aaron and his kin. That need is met in Jesus who offered up his own blood once for all time on behalf of sinful man.

4. The Great Plan: The Day of Atonement. Once each year the high priest was to enter the Holy of Holies with blood to atone for the

sins of the priesthood and the nation. A goat was driven into the wilderness to symbolize the removal of sin.

5. The Great Possibility: Access to God. Man can come into fellowship with God and can maintain that fellowship.

6. The Great Principle: Holiness. God's holiness demands holiness on the part of those who are his people. The word *holy* and its cognates appear some 131 times in the book. Closely related is the concept of cleanness. The word *clean* with its cognates and contrasts appears some 186 times. Leviticus stresses (1) clean food (ch. 11), (2) clean bodies (12:1–13:46), (3) clean clothes (13:47-59), (4) clean houses (14:33-57), (5) clean contacts (ch. 15), and (6) a clean nation (ch. 16). The verse which captures the essence of the book is Leviticus 19:2, "Ye shall be holy, for I the Lord your God am holy."

7. The Great Privilege: the Presence of God. When man approaches God in the prescribed manner, he enjoys the presence of God and consequent blessing.

TYPOLOGY OF LEVITICUS

No hint is found within the Book of Leviticus itself that this material should be interpreted in anything other than a straightforward and literal way. The statutes here are not regarded as temporary, but permanent obligations imposed by God upon all those who claim to be his children. For this reason some Jewish and Christian sects have insisted on implementation of the ordinances prescribed in this book. At the opposite extreme are those, like Philo, who have attempted to cut Leviticus free from its historical moorings. They have attempted to interpret the book in an abstract, symbolic way.

Two religions — Judaism and Christianity — claim Leviticus as divinely authoritative. Yet neither religion practices the rituals prescribed in this book. For Judaism the destruction of the Temple signaled a period of punishment. Modern Jews believe that study of Torah (the Law) supersedes sacrifice. Orthodox Jews, however, continue to look forward to a restoration of the sacrificial ritual and priesthood in a restored Temple. Christianity has approached the book in a different way. The apostles looked upon the book typologically as a foreshadowing of the sacrifice made by Christ. The apostles rejected the notion that the authority of Leviticus was bound to a literal observance of its laws. The Mosaic law in its entirety was part of a system which anticipated its own replacement with a better system, a new covenant (Jer 31:31).

Chart No. 28

TYPOLOGY OF THE OFFERINGS				
CONSECRATION OFFERINGS			CLEANSING OFFERINGS	
Focus: *The Value of Christ's Sacrifice*			Focus: *The Virtue of Christ's Sacrifice*	
BURNT OFFERING	MEAL OFFERING	PEACE OFFERING	SIN OFFERING	TRESPASS OFFERING
His Perfect Commitment	His Perfect Character	His Perfect Communion	His Perfect Atonement	His Perfect Payment

Allis wrote concerning Leviticus, "This is the New Testament gospel for sinners stated in Old Testament terms and enshrined in the ritual of sacrifice; and it finds its fullest expression in the ritual of the day of atonement."[7] The typology of Leviticus is evident in four different areas: (1) the sacrifices, (2) the appointed times, (3) the priesthood, and (4) the high priest.

A. Sacrifices.

Each of the five basic sacrifices of Leviticus points forward to a feature of Christ's one sacrifice: (1) The burnt offering, in which the animal was wholly burnt on the altar, portrays Christ's perfect commitment. His sacrifice was a sweet smelling savor (Eph 5:2). (2) No corrupting element (e.g., leaven) could be added to a meal offering. This sacrifice pointed to the perfect manhood of Christ which made his sacrifice acceptable. (3) The peace offering symbolized fellowship with God. According to Ephesians 2:14 "Christ is our peace." (4) The sin offering depicted sin covered by blood, removed and judged. Christ is called the Christian's sin offering (1 Cor 5:21; 1 Pet 2:24). (5) The trespass offering required payment of a penalty. Christ gave his life as a ransom (Mt 20:28).

B. Appointed Times.

Eleven appointed times are commanded in Leviticus. At least nine of these have more or less obvious typological significance: (1) The weekly Sabbath points to the eternal sabbath rest of God's people (Heb 4:9). (2) The lamb of the annual Passover depicts Christ, the Christian's Passover (1 Cor 5:7). (3) The feast of Unleavened Bread suggests the holy walk of believers (1 Cor 5:8). (4) The required presentation of firstfruits each year reminds the believer that Jesus was the firstfruits of those who sleep (1 Cor 15:33). (5) The Feast of Weeks (Pentecost) reminds the Christian of the coming of the Holy Spirit (Acts 2:4).

In the sacred seventh month three appointed times convey typological truth: (1) The blowing of trumpets at the beginning of the year points to the gathering of God's people (Matt 24:31). (2) The Day of Atonement sets forth the death, resurrection and ascension of Christ in beautiful symbolism. Kellogg has stated: "What the fifty-third of Isaiah is to Messianic prophecy, that...is the sixteenth of Leviticus to the whole system of Mosaic types, the most consummate flower of the Messianic symbolism."[8] (3) The Feast of Ingathering (Tabernacles) portrays the worship in the Messianic kingdom (Zech 14:16-18).

In the fiftieth year (Jubilee) a release was proclaimed throughout the land. The gospel age is depicted in the freedom and restoration which was part of this celebration (Isa 61:2; Luke 4:19).

C. Priestly Consecration Service.

Exodus 29 and Leviticus 8 list eight steps in the consecration of the Old Testament priesthood. Each of these steps finds a counterpart in the ordination of the New Testament priesthood of all believers.

1. The sons of Aaron were called to be priests (Ex 29:4). Believers are called to priesthood through the gospel (1 Pet 2:9).

2. The Old Testament candidates were washed with water (Lv 8:6). Candidates for Christian priesthood have been washed in baptism (Acts 22:16; Heb 10:22; Titus 3:5).

3. After washing came robing (Lv 8:7-9). In baptism the believer has "put on Christ" (Gal 3:27; Rev 3:18; Rom 13:14).

4. Anointing with oil came next (Lv 8:12). The believer has received of the Lord that which the oil of the Old Testament symbolized, namely, the gift of the Holy Spirit (1 John 2:20,27; 4:13; Acts 2:38).

5. Blood was applied to the garments of Aaron and his sons (Lv 8:30). So also the heart of the believer has been sprinkled with the blood of Christ (Heb 10:22).

6. Through this ceremony the sons of Aaron were consecrated or made holy (Ex 29:21). Christians are a holy people (Heb 10:10).

Chart No. 29

A BETTER HIGH PRIEST	
AARON AS HIGH PRIEST	CHRIST AS HIGH PRIEST
Called from among Men (Ex 28:1)	Called from among Men (Heb 5:4,10)
Compassion for the Wayward (Heb 5:2)	Prayed with Tears (Heb 5:7)
Spotless in Dress (Lv 16:4)	Spotless in Character (Heb 4:15)
Entered Earthly Tabernacle (Lv 16:3)	Entered Heavenly Temple (Heb 6:19)
Entered Once Each Year (Lv 16:2)	Entered Once for All (Heb 9:25)
Entered beyond the Veil (Lv 16:12)	Rent the Veil (Heb 10:20)
Offered for His Own Sins (Lv 16:11)	Offered Only for Our Sins (Heb 7:27)
Offered Blood of Animals (Lv 16:15)	Offered His Own Blood (Heb 9:12)

7. The sacrifices were then eaten by the candidates (Lv 8:31). Believers too partake of their sin offering which is Christ (Heb 13:10-12).

D. High Priesthood.

That Aaron was a type of Christ is made clear in the book of Hebrews. Some of the many points of analogy are set forth in Chart 29.

SIGNIFICANCE OF LEVITICUS

What is the abiding value of Leviticus? Baxter[9] has the following helpful suggestions: (1) Leviticus reveals to the Christian the character of God as much as it revealed that character to Israel of old. God has not changed. (2) Leviticus symbolically sets forth the basic principles which underlie all dealing between God and men. These principles have not changed. The Levitical priesthood and sacrifices have been fulfilled in Christ and hence abolished; but the spiritual realities which they pictorially presented abide for all time. (3) Leviticus suggests principles which should govern civil legislation today. The book sheds light on property rights, marriage and divorce, capital and labor, religion and the state and many similar issues. (4) Leviticus is a treasury of symbolic and typical teaching. Here the great facts of the New Covenant are illustrated in the great types of the Old.

ENDNOTES

1. William Hendriksen, *Bible Survey* (Grand Rapids: Baker, 1947), p. 228.

2. H.T. Sell, *Bible Study by Books* (London: Revell, 1896), p. 21.

3. J. Barton Payne, *Encyclopedia of Biblical Prophecy* (New York: Harper and Row, 1973), p. 674.

4. Adapted from John Phillips, *Exploring the Scriptures* (Chicago: Moody, 1965), p. 27.

5. Geisler recognizes the twofold character of Leviticus but divides it after chapter 10. He outlines this way: (1) the way to the Holy One (chs. 1-10), that being by sacrifice and priesthood; and (2) the way to holiness (chs. 11-27), that way involving both sanitation and sanctification. *A Popular Survey of the Old Testament* (Grand Rapids: Baker, 1977), pp. 67f.

6. Griffith Thomas, *Through the Pentateuch*, p. 110.

7. O.T. Allis, "Leviticus," in *New Bible Commentary*, ed. F. Davidson (Grand Rapids: Eerdmans, 1954), p. 135.

8. S.H. Kellogg cited by Allis, ibid.

9. J. Sidlow Baxter, *Explore the Book* (Grand Rapids: Zondervan, 1960), I:114-115.

BIBLIOGRAPHY: THE BOOK OF LEVITICUS

Bonar, A. *A Commentary on Leviticus*. Grand Rapids: Baker, 1978 reprint.

DeWelt, Don. *Leviticus*. Bible Study Textbook Series. Joplin, MO: College Press, 1975.

Knight, G.A.F. *Leviticus*. The Daily Study Bible Series. Philadelphia: Westminster, 1981.

Noordtzij, A. *Leviticus*. Bible Student's Commentary. Grand Rapids: Zondervan, 1982.

Wenham, G.J. *The Book of Leviticus*. The New International Commentary on the Old Testament. Grand Rapids: Eerdmans, 1979.

CHAPTER THIRTY

The Way to God
Leviticus 1-7

AIM: To demonstrate the principles undergirding the Mosaic sacrificial system.

THEME: Sacrifice provides a way to God.

The Tabernacle had now been constructed according to the detailed instructions given by the Lord. God himself had taken up residence in the tent (Ex 40). This tent, however, was also the place where the covenant people would offer their sacrifices to the Lord. Only if these offerings were presented in the proper manner could they accomplish their intended purpose, namely, procuring atonement and demonstrating self-surrender.

Leviticus opens with an emphasis upon the divine origin of what follows. For the third time the Lord *called* to Moses (cf. Ex 3:4; 19:3) and spoke to him from the tent of meeting. The sacrificial system of the Old Testament was ordained of God and revealed to Moses.

Mosaic sacrifices may be classified in various ways: (1) official and private, (2) bloody and nonbloody, and (3) "sweet savor" and non-"sweet savor." Overlaps between various sacrifices is evident, yet each of the five basic types had its own distinctive emphasis. Basic requirements for each sacrifice are set forth and yet adaptations were authorized for special circumstances. Frequently these sacrifices were offered in combination. The opening seven chapters of Leviticus speak of (1) the voluntary consecration offerings, (2) the mandatory cleansing offerings, and (3) the special regulations governing all the offerings.

CONSECRATION OFFERINGS
Leviticus 1:2–3:17

The first three of the five basic offerings of Israel—the burnt, meal and peace offerings—are distinguished from the other two in five ways: (1) They were "a pleasing odor to Yahweh."[1] (2) No particular violation or occasion prompted these sacrifices. (3) They are characterized by the expression "it (i.e., the sacrifice) shall be accepted for him." (4) They were voluntary.[2] (5) The blood associated with these offerings was thrown against the outer altar.[3] These consecration offerings were designed to help a believer maintain his fellowship with God.

A. Burnt Offering (Lv 1:3-17).

The burnt offering is first discussed because it set forth most clearly the foundational principle of the sacrificial ritual. For this reason Israel was commanded to present a lamb as a burnt offering every morning and evening at the entrance to the tent of meeting. The Hebrew term which designates this offering ('olah) signifies that which rises or ascends. The animal was completely consumed in the fire and ascended in the smoke to the Lord.

The burnt offering could be taken from the herd (1:3), from the flock, either sheep or goat (1:10), or from fowl, either dove or pigeon (1:14). The general principle which applied to the larger animals was "male without blemish." The same language is used in Hebrews 9:14 and 1 Peter 1:19 in reference to the offering by Christ.

The ritual of the burnt offering consisted of six steps, three by the worshiper, and three by the officiating priest. The worshiper was to do the following: (1) He was to present his offering at the entrance of the tent of meeting. (2) He then placed his hand(s) upon the head of the animal and leaned upon it. This action was called *semikah* and symbolized the sinner's identification with the animal and his dependence upon the sacrificial ritual. The animal was being substituted for the sinner. The offering could then "make atonement" for him (1:4). According to some, the word "atonement" (*kipper*) points to the covering of sin; others say the basic idea is that of cleansing. (3) He then slew the animal as the priest caught the blood in a pan. Thus the worshiper had vividly impressed upon his mind that the wages of sin is death (1:3-5a).

The three acts performed by the priests were to (1) sprinkle the blood of the animal on the four sides of the bronze altar; (2) skin the animal, cut it into pieces[4] and burn its head and fat; and (3) wash and burn the remaining pieces of the animal (1:5b-9).

This ritual was the same for sheep and goats as for bullocks (1:10-13). With birds the procedure differed slightly. The priest wrung off the head of the bird at the altar and burned it. The blood was poured out at the altar. The crop was removed and thrown into the ashes. The carcass of the bird was then torn open by the wings and burned on the altar (1:14-17).

The distinguishing feature of the burnt offering was that the entire animal was burned on the altar. The offering of these animals in faith and the obedience to the prescribed ritual rendered the burnt offering an aroma pleasing to the Lord (1:9).

B. Meal Offering (Lv 2:1-16).

Meal offerings were presented independently, or in conjunction with a bloody offering. The main ingredient here was "fine flour" or "raw meal" as some prefer. Oil, frankincense and salt (2:1,13) were to be added to the meal. Oil perhaps symbolizes the Holy Spirit, and salt the concept of preservation. Leaven and honey (2:11) were strictly forbidden. Both of these substances, while perfectly acceptable in ordinary food, were considered corrupting elements in sacrifices.

Cooked meal offerings — cakes or wafer — could be prepared

using oven, griddle, or pan (2:4-10). Another type of meal offering consisted of crushed heads of new grain roasted in the fire (2:14-16).

The ritual of the meal offering was very simple. The offering in whatever form was given to the priests. They burned a memorial portion on the altar. This, like the burnt offering, is described as an aroma pleasing to the Lord. The rest of the meal offering was deemed holy and was reserved for Aaron and his sons.

C. Peace Offering (Lv 3:1-17).

The peace or fellowship offering was actually a class of three offerings according to Leviticus 7:12-18. These offerings could come from the herd (3:1), the flock (3:6) or from goats (3:12). The animal could be male or female, but it had to be without blemish.

The ritual of the peace offering was similar to that of the burnt offering through the first five steps outlined above. The distinguishing feature of this offering was that part of the animal — the breast and thigh — was given to the priests; the rest of the animal was eaten by the worshiper and his family. Essentially what happened was this:

Chart No. 30

	BURNT OFFERING	MEAL OFFERING	PEACE OFFERING
VOLUNTARY CONSECRATION OFFERINGS			
MATERIAL OFFERED	Bullocks, Goats, Sheep, Rams, Lambs, Doves, Pigeons	Fine Flour, Green Ears, Incense, Oil, Salt	Male & Female of Flock & Herd, Bullocks, Lambs, Goats
GOD'S PART	All Burnt	A Handful	All the Fat
PRIESTS' PORTION	Skin	All the Remainder	Heave Shoulder, Wave Breast
MANIPULATION OF THE BLOOD	Sprinkled upon the Bronze Altar		Sprinkled upon the Bronze Altar
SYMBOLISM	Consecration of Life	Consecration of Possessions	Communion with God & His People
PURPOSE	TO MAINTAIN FELLOWSHIP WITH GOD		

After the memorial portion of the animal was offered up to God, the rest was cooked for a religious meal. The regulations stipulated that the worshipers must never eat any fat or blood. The fat covering connected with kidneys and liver belonged to God! The prohibition against eating fat applied only to the fat of sacrificial animals and in these only to those portions that were expressly mentioned.

CLEANSING OFFERINGS
Leviticus 4:1–6:7

Two offerings were required when sin entered the life of an Israelite: (1) the sin offering, and (2) the trespass offering. These offerings were introduced by Moses, and thus a more detailed description of the meaning and purpose of them is given. Nine times the text states that the one who offered these two offerings "shall be forgiven." The sin and trespass offerings were designed to restore a

Chart No. 31

COMPULSORY CLEANSING OFFERINGS		
	SIN OFFERING	**GUILT OFFERING**
MATERIAL OFFERED	Male or female of herd or flock; doves, pigeons, ⅒ ephah of fine flour.	
GOD'S PART	All the fat.	
PRIESTS' PART	Entire offering where the blood was not taken into the Tabernacle.	
MANIPULATION OF THE BLOOD	Poured out at the base of the bronze altar and in some cases smeared on the horns of the incense altar.	
PURPOSE	Restore broken fellowship with God	
DISTINCTIVES	Focus on Penalty. Results in Expiation. Covered the Principle of Sin. For public acts.	Focus on Payment. Results in Satisfaction. Covered the Practice of Sin. For private acts.

believer's fellowship with God once that fellowship had been broken by sin.

A. Sin Offering (Lv 4:1–5:13).

Emphasis is continually placed on the fact that sin offerings were valid only if the transgression was unintentional. The guilty party was "unaware of the matter" and was only "made aware of the sin" later. That his action constituted a sin had not occurred to him. The assurance is given throughout that the presentation of the sin offering would be followed by atonement and forgiveness (4:20,26 et al.)

The sin offering was graded according to the status of the person who committed the sin. In the case of a priest (4:1) or the entire congregation (4:13) a young bull was required; in the case of a ruler a male goat (4:22). A private citizen was required to bring a female goat (4:27) or lamb (4:32). In the case of a poor brother, a dove or pigeon might be offered (5:7) or even the tenth of an ephah of fine flour (5:11). In the case of the flour no oil or incense was to be put on it since it was a sin offering. Otherwise the offering of flour was to be treated like a meal offering (5:12-13).

The ritual of the sin offering as far as the worshiper was concerned was the same as with the burnt and peace offering: presentation, identification and slaughter of the animal. The priestly ritual, however, was more extensive, and involved six steps: (1) The priest was to sprinkle the blood seven times in front of the curtain of the sanctuary. (2) He was then to smear blood on the horns of the altar of incense inside the Holy Place. This constituted a plea for atonement since from this altar ascended a cloud of incense which was a symbol of supplication. (3) Next, blood was to be smeared on the horns of the bronze altar. (4) The remaining portion of the blood was poured out at the base of bronze altar. (5) The fat of the animal was then burned on the altar. (6) The rest of the animal was taken outside the camp and burned on an ash pile (4:6-30).

Leviticus 5 discusses some special applications of the sin offering. Three specific sins which might require a sin offering are first named. These are (1) withholding testimony, (2) accidental ceremonial defilement, and (3) idle swearing (5:1-4). In these cases a female sheep or goat was required as a sin offering. If he was unable to afford this, the sinner was to bring two doves or pigeons, the one for a sin offering and the other for a burnt offering.

B. Trespass Offering (Lv 5:14–6:7).

The trespass offering had the following in common with the sin offering: (1) both were required following an unintentional transgression; (2) both procured atonement. The trespass offering differed from the sin offering in that (1) it applied only to an individual, (2) the animal was slaughtered and eaten by the priest, (3) it could consist only of a ram, (4) it pertained to misappropriation of what belonged either to the Lord (5:15-19) or to a fellow Israelite (6:1-7), and (5) it required a restitution penalty of twenty per cent. The trespass offering was presented after an act of unfaithfulness *(ma'al)*, a term which refers to a violation of God's holiness. In the case of theft from a fellow Israelite, the sacrilege was committed when a false oath was taken which called upon God to confirm that which was not true.

SPECIAL INSTRUCTIONS
Leviticus 6:8–7:34

Certain special instructions regarding each of the five major offerings are directed to the priests.

A. For Burnt Offerings (Lv 6:8-13).

The burnt offerings described here are not those offered voluntarily by individuals in Leviticus 1, but rather the morning and evening offerings which were to be brought by the nation (Ex 29:38-46). The daily routine was as follows: (1) Wearing his ministerial garb, the priest first stirred up the fire by removing the ashes and temporarily depositing them at the foot of the altar. The priests were never to allow the altar fire to go out. (2) The priest was then to put on other clothing and remove the ashes to a ceremonially clean place outside the camp. (3) Wearing his ministerial garb again, the priest was to add wood to the altar fire and then burn the morning burnt offering.

B. For Meal Offerings (Lv 6:14-18).

The meal offering dealt with here is not that brought by the individual in Leviticus 2, but the required daily meal offering. Four stipulations are set forth: (1) A memorial portion of the flour mixed with oil and incense was burned on the altar. (2) The rest of the meal offering was to be eaten without leaven in the courtyard of the tent of meeting. (3) Any male descendant of Aaron could partake of this portion of the meal offering. (4) The portion eaten by the priests was considered holy and whatever it touched thereby became holy to God.

C. For Priestly Grain Offerings (Lv 6:19-23).

At the priestly consecration a special meal offering was to be offered. This was to consist of the tenth part of an ephah prepared with oil on a griddle. The candidate himself was required to prepare this offering. The large cake thus prepared was presented in two portions, one in the morning and one in the evening. The offering was burned completely on the altar.

D. For Sin Offerings (Lv 6:24-30).

Regarding the sin offering the following stipulations applied: (1) The portion of a sin offering which was eaten by the priests had to be consumed in the courtyard of the tent of meeting. (2) Any part of the sin offering, including the blood which was spattered during the slaughter, was considered holy. Whatever it touched was rendered holy. (3) If cooked in a clay pot, the pot had to be broken; if in a bronze pot it must be scoured and rinsed with water. (4) A sin offering in which blood was taken within the tent could not be eaten.

E. For Trespass Offerings (Lv 7:1-10).

Only the interior fat portions of the animal were burned on the altar. The rest was to be eaten by the males of a priest's family within a holy place, i.e., the tent of meeting (7:1-6).

A parenthetical statement regarding portions of offerings which belonged to the priests is appended to the brief discussion of the trespass offering (7:7-10). Whatever was left over from the sin and trespass offerings (e.g., the hide) belonged to the officiating priest. The hide of the burnt offering also belonged to the priest. Meal offerings prepared in ovens, pans or griddles belonged to the officiating priest. Uncooked meal offerings were to be divided equally with all the sons of Aaron.

F. For Peace Offerings (Lv 7:11-34).
Three offerings were categorized as peace or fellowship offerings: the (1) thanksgiving, (2) votive, and (3) freewill. As noted above, the distinguishing feature of the peace offering was the communal meal. Several stipulations on that aspect of the peace offering are set forth in this section of Leviticus.

1. A thanksgiving peace offering was to be accompanied by a meal offering consisting of cakes and wafers made without leaven as well as cakes made with leaven. One of each type of cake was given to the priest who officiated. The meat of the peace offering had to be eaten on the day it was offered (7:11-15).

2. A peace offering which was offered as a result of a vow or which was simply a freewill offering could be eaten on the second day, but absolutely not at all on the third day (7:16-18).

3. Meat which touched anything unclean was thereby rendered unclean and had to be burned up. Only those who were ceremonially clean could partake of the meat. Any other person would be cut off, i.e., excommunicated, from the people (7:19-21).

4. No fat of a sacrificial animal was to be eaten under penalty of excommunication. That portion belonged to God. Fat of animals found dead could be used for other purposes, but could not be eaten. No blood of any animal was to be eaten under penalty of excommunication (7:22-27).

5. The worshiper was to wave the breast of the peace offering before the Lord. That portion was then given to the priests. The right thigh also belonged to the priests (7:28-34).

This section closes with a reminder that the sacrificial system outlined above was commanded by Yahweh. The Law made clear that those who served at the altar were to live by the altar (1 Cor 9:13).

BASIC PRINCIPLES OF MOSAIC SACRIFICE

The seven sacrifices of Leviticus 1–7 (burnt, meal, sin, trespass and three types of peace offerings) have several common features. These are:

1. A worshiper could never come into the presence of God empty-handed.

2. The Hebrew word translated "offering" (qorban) means literally "a thing brought near." This word contains a clue as to the significance of the sacrificial system. The sacrifices provided the means by which a worshiper could come into the presence of God.

3. In most cases, the offering was a domesticated animal. That which was most costly and valuable was given to the Lord. Moreover, the Law required that the animal offered had to be one without blemish or spot.

4. The gift which was offered depended upon the financial resources of the worshiper. The very poor could substitute birds in the burnt offering and grain in the sin offering.

5. The worshiper was an active participant in the ritual. He laid his hands on the head of the sacrificial victim, thus identifying with that animal. The animal was a substitute for the worshiper. He slew the animal.

6. The priest had the responsibility to apply the blood. The blood would be scattered around or on either the outer or inner altar, depending on the sacrifice.

7. Either all or selected parts of the animal victim were placed on the outer altar and burned by the priests.

8. Depending on the sacrifice, those portions of the animal not burned on the altar were (1) given to the priest, or (2) given to the worshiper, or (3) taken outside the camp and burned.

Scholars frequently have asserted that the Mosaic sacrificial system made no provision for deliberate sin. The terms "unwittingly," "in ignorance," and "inadvertently" are repeatedly used in reference to the sin and trespass offering. Numbers 15:27-31 explicitly states that a person guilty of "high handed" sin must be cut off from among his people. Other scholars, however, point out that the particular situations covered in Leviticus 6:1-7 — sins against another person — could not possibly be sins done inadvertently. Numbers 5:6-8 seems to supply the key. Confession was essential in the case of deliberate sin. This confession would come after conviction and precede restitution (Nm 5:7). Apparently this confession had the effect of moving the sin into the category of inadvertent sins which could be expiated. If this analysis is correct, then under the Law the only sins which could not be expiated were those which were not acknowledged and renounced.

ENDNOTES

1. This expression, used ten times of the first three offerings, is employed but once in reference to the other three.

2. The voluntary nature of the first three sacrifices is indicated by the words "when any of you brings an offering" (1:2).

3. In the sin and trespass offerings the blood at times was carried within the Tabernacle.

4. According to Jewish tradition, the animal was cut into ten pieces.

CHAPTER THIRTY-ONE

The Work of God
Leviticus 8-15

AIM: To demonstrate that God requires consecration and separation of those who would approach him in worship.

THEME: The high calling of God.

In Leviticus 1–7 the focus was on the altar. The laws which were set forth concerned the various offerings. The word which summarizes those chapters is *oblation*. In chapters 8–15 the focus is on the work of the priesthood. The ordination of the priestly family is described in great detail (chs. 8–10). This section is followed by regulations governing purity and purification, matters about which the priesthood was to be especially concerned (chs. 11–15).

ORDINATION REGULATIONS
Leviticus 8:1–10:20

In Israel only members of the family of Aaron could serve as priests at the altar. In three chapters Moses sets forth (1) the ordination of these priests, (2) their entrance into the priesthood, and (3) the transgression of two of the original priests.

A. Consecration to Ministry (Lv 8:1-36).

Leviticus 8 records the implementation of the detailed instructions for the consecration of Aaron and his sons which were set forth in Exodus 29. In this chapter and the next two as well, Moses is supervisor and Aaron is subordinate. The Hebrew expression for "ordain" means literally, "fill the hands" (8:33). A priest's life was to be filled with nothing except holy things. The steps in the ordination ceremony were as follows:

1. Aaron and his sons were first washed at the entrance to the Tent. According to tradition this was done behind a linen sheet. Jewish tradition is divided as to whether only hands and feet were washed, or the body entirely immersed (8:6).

2. Aaron was robed with the special garb which he as high priest was entitled to wear. This consisted of the (1) coat, (2) robe, (3) ephod, (4) sash, (5) breastplate with the Urim and Thummim, (6) turban, and (7) the sacred diadem (8:7-9).

3. Moses anointed the Tabernacle and everything in it. He also anointed the bronze altar seven times and the laver as well. Then some of the anointing oil was poured on the head of Aaron to consecrate him (8:10-12).

4. The sons of Aaron were robed with their special garb (8:13).

5. Aaron and his sons placed their hands on the head of a bull to identify with it. The animal was then slaughtered. Moses applied some of the blood to the horns of the altar to purify it. The rest of the blood was poured out at the base of the altar. The fat portions of the animal were burned on the altar; the rest were burned outside the camp (8:14-17).

6. Moses offered a ram as a burnt offering on behalf of Aaron and his sons to symbolize their complete dedication to the Lord (8:18-21).

7. The special ordination ram was slain. Some of the blood of this animal was applied to the right ear, thumb and big toe. Blood was then sprinkled on the sides of the altar. Parts of the ram were ceremonially waved before the Lord and then burned on the altar together with various types of bread offerings. Moses also received a portion of this ordination ram (8:22-29).

8. Moses sprinkled the priestly candidates and their garments with a mixture of blood and oil (8:30).

9. The rest of the meat of the ordination ram was cooked and eaten along with bread from the basket of ordination offerings. What was not eaten on the day of sacrifice was destroyed. The meal served as a confirmation of the covenant that had been enacted between the Lord and the house of Aaron (8:31-32).

10. Aaron and his sons had to remain within the area of the sanctuary for seven days. Apparently the various ordination acts were repeated each of the seven days (8:33-36; cf. Ex 29:35ff.).

B. Commencement of Ministry (Lv 9:1-24).

On the day following the week of consecration, Aaron and his sons began their ministry. Under the direction of Moses, they were to present offerings in the presence of both the elders and the entire congregation. First, two offerings were to be made for Aaron and his house. Then a complete round of sacrifices was to be presented on behalf of the people. These sacrifices would prepare the way for the appearance of the glory of the Lord which would be a final confirmation of the Aaronic priesthood (9:1-7).

With the assistance of his sons, Aaron offered the sin offering of purification (9:8-11) and the burnt offering (9:12-14) as prescribed by the Lord. These offerings atoned for the sins of the priesthood. Once the priests were in a right relationship with the Lord, they could begin their ministry of atonement for the people. Aaron offered the sin, burnt, meal and peace offerings on behalf of the people in the prescribed manner (9:15-21). Then with arms upraised, Aaron pronounced a blessing upon the people. He then "stepped down," apparently from the raised platform of the altar (9:22).

Moses and Aaron then entered the tent of meeting. This was the first time Aaron was permitted to be in the tent. Entering the tent with his brother was the confirmation of the legitimacy of his priestly office. When the brothers emerged from the tent, they pronounced a second blessing upon the people. Then the glory of the Lord appeared to all the people. Fire came out from the presence of the Lord and consumed the burnt offering and the fat portions of the peace offering on the altar. This was not the initial kindling of the

371

altar fire, but rather this gave evidence that the Lord had accepted the offerings of the priests and the people. The congregation shouted for joy and fell in reverence to the ground (9:23-24).

C. Priestly Transgression (Lv 10:1-20).

Aaron's two sons, Nadab and Abihu, took their censers, put fire in them and added incense. They were offering "strange fire" before the Lord. Fire, which only moments before had betokened God's approval, came out from the presence of the Lord and consumed the two young priests (10:1-2).

Moses immediately made clear to Aaron why the Lord had manifested himself in this way. He reminded Aaron of a statement which the Lord had made earlier. God is absolutely holy. Those who by virtue of their office must constantly enter his presence are in peril. Such is the gist of the saying which Moses quoted to his brother. Aaron remained absolutely silent, and by so doing he was acknowledging the righteousness of the display of divine wrath which he had just witnessed (10:3).

What exactly was the sin of Nadab and Abihu? Their sin seems to have involved one or more of the following elements:

1. Disobedience: they were offering incense at the wrong time and place. According to Exodus 30:7-9 the high priest was to present on the altar of incense the daily offering.

2. Desecration: they may have used the wrong materials. Exodus 30:9 commands that no strange incense was to be offered.

3. Drunkenness: Is it merely coincidence that warnings against priestly drunkenness follow immediately the offering of the strange fire?

4. Disrespect: All were on their faces in reverent awe except Nadab and Abihu.

The swift reaction of the Lord to the "strange fire" was designed (1) to punish the sinners, (2) magnify the law, (3) teach obedience, and (4) warn future generations to approach God only in the manner prescribed.

Two cousins of the dead men were commissioned to bury Nadab and Abihu. The two priests were buried in their priestly garb outside the camp, away from the front of the sanctuary. Aaron and his sons were not present at the burial. They were not permitted to leave the sanctuary because shortly they were to participate in a sacrificial meal. Neither were they permitted to manifest external signs of mourning such as tearing their clothes or leaving their hair unkempt (10:4-7).

The Lord then spoke directly to Aaron. A strict law was enunciated which forbade any intoxicants from being consumed before priestly ministry in the tent of meeting. In every action Aaron and his sons must make a clear distinction between the profane and the holy. By example and by verbal directive the priests were to impress upon the Israelites strict compliance with all the commands which God gave through Moses (10:8-11).

Moses then gave directions to Aaron concerning the disposal of the offerings which had been presented to the Lord. That which remained from the grain offering was to be eaten by the priests in a holy place. The females of the priestly family could join the males in eating the breast and thigh which had been waved before the Lord. The only restriction was that this meat had to be eaten in a ceremonially clean place, i.e., it had to be eaten within the camp (10:12-15).

Moses was angry with the other two sons of Aaron, Eleazar and Ithamar, when he learned that they had not eaten the portion of the sin offering which had been assigned to them. They thus engendered the suspicion that they were superstitiously afraid to eat. Aaron excused their deed by (1) referring to the confusion that had arisen on that day, and (2) questioning the appropriateness of eating the sin offering on a day when the Lord had broken forth in wrath (10:14-20).

PURIFICATION REGULATIONS
Leviticus 11:1–15:33

Ceremonial defilement debarred an Israelite from worship assembly. Ceremonial defilement, however, is not be be equated with sin, for in many instances the defilement could not be helped. The priests were the guardians of the sanctuary. They were to make sure that no unclean person appeared there for worship. For this reason God speaks to both Moses and Aaron in this section three times (11:1; 13:1; 15:1). Both leaders were commissioned to pass on these regulations to the people. Four areas of ceremonial purity are discussed in Leviticus 11–15.

A. Food Prohibitions (Lv 11:1-47).

The Law regulated the diet of the Israelites. Apparently all fruits and vegetables were acceptable. The following principles governed the meat which was regarded as clean. (1) The quadrupeds which had cloven hoof and chewed the cud were considered clean. Camels, the coneys (NIV) or rock badgers (NASB), rabbits and pigs were specifically excluded. (2) Aquatic animals had to have both fins and scales to qualify. (3) Most birds were considered clean except birds of prey. (4) Flying insects with jointed legs for hopping on the ground were clean. These included locust, katydid, cricket or grasshopper (11:1-23).

An Israelite was rendered unclean by contact with the carcass of an animal whether clean or unclean. An object which had been rendered unclean by contact with a carcass of an animal had to be washed or, in the case of inexpensive pottery, destroyed (11:24-42).

God demanded holiness of his people. They must separate themselves from all which God said was defiling. The dietary law was thus grounded in the holiness of the God who had brought them up out of Egypt (11:41-47).

Five rationales have been advanced to justify the dietary laws: (1) The ethical. Abstaining from blood tamed a man's instinct for violence. So said Aristeas, a Jew who lived in the first century BC. (2) The aesthetic. Certain animals are naturally repulsive to man. (3) The cultic. Animals which were associated with pagan cults were regarded as "detestable." (4) The hygienic. The meats prohibited are damaging to the body. Maimonides (12th century AD) argued this position. (5) The pedagogic. God was teaching the Israelites self-discipline and submission to him even in the most routine affairs of life.

B. Purification after Childbirth (Lv 12:1-8).

After childbirth a mother was considered ceremonially unclean for seven or fourteen days depending on whether the child was male or female. The days for the purification of the mother extended thirty-three days following the birth of a male child, and sixty-six after the birth of a female (12:1-5). Birth per se did not render the woman unclean, but rather the postnatal flow of blood.

At the conclusion of the days of purification the new mother was to present a lamb for a burnt offering and a pigeon or dove for a sin offering. Her first trip out of the home was to go to the place of worship! Following these sacrifices the woman would be regarded as purified from her flow of blood. If the mother were very poor she could offer two pigeons or doves, one for a sin offering and the other for a burnt offering (12:6-8).

Why the more extended time of uncleanness after the birth of the female child? Given the obsession with seeking male offspring, the regulation may have been to protect the wife from an overzealous husband. He might be inclined to resume marital relations too soon after the birth of a female to the physical discomfort and possible jeopardy of the wife. Circumcision on the eighth day also may have cut short the days of uncleanness after the birth of a male child.

C. Purification after Leprosy (Lv 13:1–14:57).

The term "leprosy" in the English versions is used of a whole range of infectious skin diseases. Those suspected of having such an ailment were disqualified from the public assembly. The priests were the health officers of the community. For this reason the text sets forth rules for (1) the identification, (2) isolation and (3) cleansing of infectious skin diseases as well as (4) principles for dealing with the contaminated fabrics and objects.

1. Identification (13:1-44). Six guidelines were given to the priests regarding skin diseases: (1) The priests were to look for three initial symptoms: swelling, rash, or a bright spot. If there was any doubt about the nature of the ailment, the patient was to be put in isolation for a week and then checked again. (2) In more advanced stages the disease would develop open lesions. In other cases, the patient would be covered with the symptoms from head to foot. In either case, the patient was immediately declared unclean. (3) The priests were to be especially watchful for boils or burns which healed in an abnormal manner. (4) Itching sores on head or chin were to be inspected for signs of infectious disease. (5) A rash of white spots or loss of hair did not render a man unclean unless secondary symptoms were in evidence (13:1-44).

2. Isolation (13:45-46). The clothing and hair of one with an infectious skin disease were to indicate a state of mourning. That person had been cut off from the fellowship of the community. The person had to cover his mouth so as not to communicate to another his infectious disease. He was to warn those who approached him by crying "Unclean!" The victim had to live outside the camp alone.

3. Cleansing (14:1-32). The purification ritual for a cleansed leper was not a healing ceremony, but a testimony that healing had occurred. Three rituals were performed in an eight-day period: (1) On the first day, the priest went outside the camp to certify that the person was healed. A bird was killed over a pot of fresh water. The water and blood were thus mingled. A live bird was immersed in the bloody water along with hyssop and cedar wood. The bird was then set free. Just as the bird was restored to fullness of life, so the cleansed leper had been restored from his deadly disease (14:2-8).

(2) On the seventh day the former victim had to purify himself— shaving, washing himself and his clothing. (3) On the eighth day, a series of offerings was presented "before the Lord" in order to demonstrate the restored status. Some of the blood of the trespass offering was smeared on the former victim's right ear lobe, right thumb, and right big toe. The same was done with oil after some of it had first been sprinkled seven times "before the Lord" (14:10-20).

As in the case with a woman who had recovered from childbirth, special concessions were made for those who were unable to afford the standard offerings of cleansing (14:21-32).

4. Contamination (13:47-59; 14:33-53). Fabrics and leather might also be contaminated, but the precise nature of this contamination remains unclear. A priestly inspection was required. If after seven days the contamination had spread, the affected object was to be burned. If no spreading had occurred, the object was washed and examined again after seven more days. If the contaminated area had not faded, that part was to be torn away. If that did not stop the spread, the whole object was to be destroyed (13:47-59).

Once in Canaan, Israelite houses would have to be inspected by the priests for contamination. Mildew is probably the culprit here. Contaminated houses were to be ordered closed for seven days, then re-inspected. If the contamination had spread, the affected stones were to be replaced, and the rest of the interior walls scraped. If the mildew reappeared, the entire house was to be destroyed (14:33-45).

If replacement of the affected stones solved the problem, the priest was to pronounce the house clean. In the purification ceremony, a bird was killed over fresh water in a clay plot. Cedar wood, scarlet yarn and a branch of hyssop and a live bird were to be dipped into the mixture of blood and water. The house was to be sprinkled with the bloody water; the live bird was to be released outside the town. In this way atonement was made for the house (14:48-53).

D. Purification after Bodily Issues (Lv 15:1-33).

All bodily issues connected with the reproductive organs required ceremonial purification. Normal emissions required bathing only; abnormal emissions required sacrifices. When the issue had been stopped seven days, the affected person came to the priest to present sacrifices. The purpose here was to prevent defilement of the sanctuary (15:31). Sanitary considerations also entered into these regulations.

Three male discharges are discussed in 15:1-18: (1) A bodily discharge, i.e., of mucus, rendered a man unclean. Those who came in contact with him or any object he had touched were also unclean and had to wash their clothes and bathe. After seven days the victim himself had to wash and present two doves and two pigeons as sin and burnt offerings. (2) A nocturnal emission rendered a man unclean until evening. He was required to bathe and wash anything which had come in contact with the semen. (3) Emission of semen during normal marital intercourse rendered husband and wife unclean until evening. Both were required to bathe (15:1-18).

A woman was rendered unclean by her monthly period for seven days. Any one or any thing which came in contact with her was also rendered unclean for seven days. After her period of separation the woman was to offer two doves or young pigeons as sin and burnt offerings (15:19-30).

CHAPTER THIRTY-TWO

The Walk with God
Leviticus 16-22

AIM: To demonstrate that God's grace in providing cleansing at the altar demands a dedicated life on the part of the believer.

THEME: Without holiness no man shall see God!

The first seven chapters of Leviticus underscored the truth that the way to God is through sacrifice, the shedding of blood. Chapters 8-15 then took up the responsibilities of priestly ministers. The climax of that sacrificial system and of that priestly work came on the annual Day of Atonement (ch. 16). Through the rituals of that day God graciously condescended to cover the sins of the nation for another year. The only appropriate response to such marvelous grace was holiness on the part of both the people (chs. 17–20) and their priests (chs. 21–22).

HOLINESS THROUGH ATONEMENT
Leviticus 16:1-34

Under the Law the tenth day of the seventh month was the pinnacle of worship. Jewish tradition asserts that this was the day that Moses came down from Mount Sinai for the second time with new tablets of the Law and announced the Lord's gracious pardon for the sin of the golden calf. On this day atonement covered three areas: (1) the high priest himself, (2) the sanctuary, and (3) the people.

A. Aaron's Preparation (Lv 16:1-10).

The sudden stroke against Nadab and Abihu in chapter 10 had put the fear of the Lord in Aaron. The question uppermost in his mind must have been how he would be able to go about his priestly ministry within the tent without suffering a similar fate. He needed guidance in this respect.

Aaron was first warned that he was not to enter the Holy of Holies whenever he chose. He would be placing his life in jeopardy if he did, for the cloud of divine glory filled that part of the Tabernacle (16:1-2). At the prescribed time the high priest was required to take the following steps. First, he was to designate a bull for a sin offering and a ram for a burnt offering for the priesthood. Seven times the account uses the phrase "for himself." If one was to serve as a mediator, his own sins first had to be removed. Then the high priest was to bathe and don sacred vestments. He was not, however, to be clothed in the full attire of the high priest on this occasion. He wore only the normal priestly garments. Only his turban set him apart from his subordinates (16:3-4).

From the Israelite community the high priest was to secure two goats for a sin offering and a ram for a burnt offering. He then was to offer the bull as a sin offering to make atonement for himself and his household. Next, the high priest was to cast lots over the two goats at the entrance of the Tabernacle. One goat was thereby designated for the Lord and the other was designated "for Azazel." The first goat was then offered as a sin offering. The next step was to take a censer of burning coals from the altar and two handfuls of incense (16:5-12).

The expression "for Azazel" has provoked no little discussion.

380

Three major views have been advanced. (1) Some regard Azazel as the place to which the goat was taken. (2) Others think that Azazel was one of the desert demons, and one of the *shedim* (Dt 32:17) or *se'rim* (Lv 17:7). The ceremony would then be a strong expression of contempt for those who offered sacrifices to these demons. (3) Traditionally *'aza'zel* has been regarded as a compound word meaning "goat" and a verb meaning "to go." Hence Azazel was the goat which goes, or scapegoat. The sins of the nation were carried away by the goat symbolically.

B. Aaron's Presentation (Lv 16:11-17).

The high priest entered the Holy of Holies three times on the sacred day. First, he entered carrying the censer filled with burning incense. The clouds of incense were to conceal the mercy seat so that the high priest would not die. Aaron then returned to the altar and took some of the blood from the bull of the sin offering of the priestly household. An assistant had stirred continually the blood to prevent coagulation. Aaron then returned with this blood to the Holy of Holies. Some of this blood was sprinkled on the east (i.e., front) side of the mercy seat, and also seven times on the ground directly in front of the ark. Thus the entire Holy of Holies was brought in contact with the blood (16:13-14).

Aaron was then to slaughter the goat for the sin offering for the people. He re-entered the Holy of Holies to sprinkle the goat's blood on the mercy seat. This action made atonement for the Holy of Holies because of the uncleanness and transgression (*pesha'*) of the Israelites. This latter word, the gravest word in the Hebrew language for sin, occurs twice in Leviticus 16 and nowhere else in the book. Transgression is deliberate sin, willful rebellion. Because sin in its most gross manifestation was in view, on the Day of Atonement the blood had to be carried into the Holy of Holies itself.

The high priest then made atonement for the tent of meeting. No one was to be within the tent while Aaron went about his sacred business of making atonement for himself, his household and the whole community (16:15-17). All areas of the tent had now been restored to a state of holiness. The possibility of communion with God had thus been preserved for another year.

C. Other Activities of the Day (Lv 16:18-34).

Using the blood of both the bull and the goat, Aaron next made atonement for the bronze altar. The blood was applied to the horns of the altar and then sprinkled on it seven times. This action consecrated the altar from the uncleanness of the Israelites (16:18-19).

Aaron then laid both hands on the head of the live goat and confessed over it all the wickedness and rebellion of the Israelites. The goat was then sent into the desert in the care of a man appointed for the task. The goat was to be taken to a solitary place, i.e., a place from which it could not return. The release of the goat in the wilderness symbolized the removal of the sins of the nation.

Aaron then removed his linen garb, bathed, put on his regular high priestly garments, and offered up burnt offerings for himself and the people. The fat of the sin offering was burned at the same time (16:23-25).

The concluding portion of Leviticus 16 was addressed to the people. These verses seek to make clear the role which they would play in the annual Day. Their responsibilities were as follows: (1) They were to "humble" or "deny" themselves. The language used here (*'annah nephesh*) is used elsewhere in connection with fasting (Ps 35:13; Isa 58:3,5). The Day of Atonement was Israel's only legally prescribed day of fasting. (2) The people were also to make this day a "sabbath of rest," i.e., they were to abstain from all work.

Leviticus 16 concludes with three reminders that the Day of Atonement regulations were a lasting ordinance. The successors of Aaron were to conduct these rituals every year. Every part of the sanctuary which had come into close contact or proximity with sinful man was to be cleansed annually of the defilement which had become attached to it. Further information on the Day of Atonement appears in Leviticus 23:26-32.

HOLINESS IN DAILY LIFE
Leviticus 17:1–20:27

In four chapters the Lawgiver describes holiness in regard to (1) food, (2) marriage, and (3) social contact. He then sets forth the punishment for unholiness.

A. Holiness in Regard to Food (Lv 17:1-16).

To the prohibitions regarding certain kinds of meat (Lv 11), four additional principles are added in Leviticus 17. The penalty for one who violated these commands was to be "cut off from his people." This phrase has been interpreted to mean (1) judicial execution, (2) excommunication, and (3) premature death at the hand of God with the possibility of judgment in the life to come.

1. No domestic animals were to be killed outside the Tabernacle area. This regulation was designed to prevent sacrifices to demons (se'irim), lit., goats, which were believed to inhabit the wilderness (17:3-7). Such a law could be effective only when eating meat was a rare luxury and when everyone lived close to the sanctuary.

2. No sacrifices were to be made outside the Tabernacle (17:8-9). This law safeguarded the unity of the nation and assured the payment of the priestly dues. The "sojourner" (ger) or resident alien was required to observe this law as well as the main rules of Israelite society.

3. No blood was to be eaten (17:10-12). This law refers to drinking blood or eating meat from which the blood had not been drained. In southern Thailand to this day the marketing of the blood of poisonous serpents is a thriving business. The blood is believed to be a cure for a host of physical infirmities as well as an aphrodisiac. The blood is taken from live cobras and mixed with potent alcoholic beverages. Some of the brave suck the blood straight from the bodies of the snakes. Similar practices must have existed in the pagan world of Old Testament times. For the Israelites, however, blood was sacred because of sacrificial usage. Life was in the blood. To abstain from eating blood was thus to honor life and sacrifice. The prohibition, which here appears six times in five verses (vv. 10-14), was already in force in the days of Noah (Gn 9:4). Gentile Christians were instructed to abstain from blood (Acts 15:29). On the other hand, Jesus told his disciples that they must drink his blood to have eternal life, i.e., they must partake of his life (John 6:54).

4. The meat of animals found dead was to be avoided (17:13-16). To violate this command rendered one unclean. He was required to wash and change clothes to rid himself of the contamination. When game was killed, God required that its blood be covered with dirt. Again the purpose was to teach respect for blood.

B. Holiness in Marriage (Lv 18:1-30).

Leviticus 18 repeats seven times the warning that Israelites were not to imitate the Egyptian or Canaanite mores. Five times this chapter grounds sexual morality in the character of God. Those who observed these decrees were promised true life (18:1-5).

First, God strictly forbade sexual relations, and consequently marriage, between close blood relatives and those related by marriage (i.e., in-laws). Twelve specific cases mentioned in the text are summarized in Chart 32.

Chart No. 32

FORBIDDEN MARRIAGES			
Leviticus 18:6-17			
BLOOD RELATIVES First Degree	BLOOD RELATIVES Second Degree	STEP RELATIVES	MARRIAGE RELATIVES
1. Mother	4. Aunt (vv. 12-13)	6. Stepsister (v. 11)	10. Sister-in-law (v. 16)
2. Sister	5. Granddaughter (v. 10)	7. Stepdaughter (v. 17)	11. Daughter-in-law (v. 15)
3. Half-sister		8. Stepgranddaughter (v. 17)	12. Uncle's wife (v. 14)
		9. Stepmother (v. 8)	

Several basic principles stand out in this section of Leviticus. (1) Marital intercourse made the man and wife as closely related as parents and children. This is the "one flesh" concept of Genesis 2:24. (2) Marriage made a girl not just a daughter-in-law, but a daughter of her husband's parents and a sister to all his brothers. Even if her husband died, his brother could not marry her, for that would be equivalent to a brother-sister marriage. The custom of Levirate marriage (Dt 25:5ff.) was the exception to this principle. (3) A man could not marry any woman who was a close blood relative. (4) A man could not marry any woman who had become a close relative through a previous marriage to one of the man's close relatives. (5) The New Testament writers assume that the laws on incest still bind the Christian conscience (1 Cor 5:1ff.).

Leviticus 18:18 has been interpreted by some as a prohibition of the most odious form of polygamy, namely, taking to wife the sister of one's present wife. Others think that "sister" in this verse refers to any Israelite woman. Taken in this way Leviticus 18:18 prohibits polygamy altogether. Other sexual sins prohibited in this section are: (1) sexual relations with a menstruous woman, (2) adultery, (3) sodomy, and (4) bestiality. A prohibition against sacrificing children to the god Molech is included among the sins commonly practiced among the Canaanites (18:19-23).

The section on sexual sin ends as it began with a solemn warning. This kind of sin defiled the land of Canaan. Consequently God had decreed the expulsion of the inhabitants of that land. If Israel permitted these vile acts to be practiced among them, the land would vomit them out even as it had vomited out the Canaanites before them. Consequently, anyone who did these detestable things was to be cut off from his people (18:24-30).

C. Holiness in Social Affairs (Lv 19:1-37).

Leviticus 19 contains various laws most of which have to do with social relationships. The section begins with the basic principle: "Be holy because I, Yahweh your God, am holy."

1. The first four laws have to do with recognition of God. Honoring parents is a recognition of God's authority. Holiness begins in the home. Sabbath observance recognized God as sovereign over time. Avoiding idolatry recognized God's sole divinity. The peace offering recognized God's claim on material things (19:3-8).

2. In 19:9-18 the basic principle is: "You shall love your neighbor as yourself" (19:18). All duties toward one's fellow man are summed up in this command (Matt 22:39; Rom 13:9). During the harvest of the field or vineyard Israelites were to leave grain or fruit for the poor. The Law prohibited robbery and deceit, false swearing, and withholding wages from a hired man. A believer was not to take advantage of the handicapped. No favoritism was to be shown either toward the great or the poor in court. Spreading slander was forbidden. They must guard their heart from hatred or revenge. They were to frankly

rebuke a neighbor who sinned so that they would not be counted guilty of his transgression.

3. From the lofty heights of "love your neighbor" the section proceeds to three concise "decrees" regarding unnatural associations (19:19). The Law prohibited the crossbreeding of animals, the cultivation of two different crops in the same field, and the weaving of two different fabrics into a single article of clothing. Those who see a religious background to these prohibitions are in all likelihood correct. Man was to keep separate what God had created separate.

4. Another unnatural association is addressed in 19:20-22. A man who had sexual relations with a servant girl who had been promised to another had to be given "due punishment" (*biqqoret*). Jewish scholars interpreted this to mean (1) a monetary penalty or (2) corporal punishment. The death penalty was not assessed here because the woman was not free. Nonetheless, this adultery was a sin against God as well as man, for a sacrificial offering was required of the guilty man.

5. Fruit trees were to be regarded as "uncircumcised" for three years. The fruit of the fourth year was regarded as holy to the Lord, and consequently could only be given to the priests. Only in the fifth year was it permitted for an owner to eat the fruit of this trees (19:23-25).

6. Leviticus 19:25-31 contains a series of laws which prohibit pagan worship customs. These were: (1) eating blood, (2) attempting to unveil the future by divination or sorcery, (3) clipping the sides of the head or beard, (4) self-inflicted bodily lacerations for the dead, (5) tattoos, (6) cult prostitution, (7) profaning sacred times or places by pagan impurity, and (8) consulting spirit mediums. Item number 3 above may have something to do with the pagan custom of making hair offerings to various deities.

7. Three additional laws governing social relations are recorded in Leviticus 19:32-36. These are: (1) showing respect for the elderly, (2) treating foreigners fairly, and (3) employing honest standards in commercial transactions.

D. Punishment for Unholiness (Lv 20).

Leviticus 20 stipulates the punishments for several of the sins mentioned in the previous chapter. Anyone who engaged in Molech worship was to be stoned by the community. If an Israelite secretly sacrificed his children to Molech, the Lord himself would cut him off, probably by disease or accident. The same applied to those who knew of Molech worship by a neighbor but who failed to see to his execution (20:1-5).

Direct action by God was threatened against anyone who consulted a spirit medium. Such action would be necessary because of the difficulty of legally establishing the guilt for this sin in court. Anyone who cursed father or mother, i.e., treated them lightly or contemptuously, was to be executed. The phrase "his blood will be on his own head" which occurs six times in this section means that the guilty had forfeited his life, i.e., had caused his own death (20:6-9).

The penalty for the sexual sins forbidden in the previous chapter was death (20:10-21). Most likely stoning was the means of execution. The "burning" in one case (20:14) probably followed stoning. In two cases, God punished with childlessness the guilty parties (20:20-21). Spirit mediums were also to be stoned (20:27).

The remaining verses in Leviticus 20 contain an exhortation to (1) keep the laws of God so that they might be allowed to remain in the land, (2) distinguish between clean and unclean animals, and (3) be a holy people, set apart from all other nations (20:22-26).

HOLINESS IN MINISTERIAL DUTY
Leviticus 21:1–22:33

The basic principle underlying Leviticus 21–22 is this: Spiritual privileges and sacred duties involve larger responsibilities and greater perfection of character and conduct. Six areas of priestly requirements are treated in these chapters.

A. Priestly Ceremonial Purity (Lv 21:1-6).

A priest was to avoid contact with a corpse. Six blood relatives are named as exceptions. The bond between husband and wife was such that it was taken for granted that a priest might defile himself by contact with the dead body of his spouse. When a priest was in mourning, he was not to imitate pagan customs such as shaving his head or beard, or cutting his body.

387

B. Priestly Marital Purity (Lv 21:7-9).

A priest could not marry a woman defiled by prostitution or even a divorced woman. He was holy and set apart to the holy purpose of offering up the "food for God," i.e., presenting the sacrifices. A priest's daughter who defiled herself in prostitution was to be burned, probably after being stoned to death.

C. Standards for the High Priest (Lv 21:10-15).

A high priest was not even permitted to allow his hair to go loose or tear his clothes in times of mourning. The high priest could never come near a corpse even for father or mother. The high priest could marry only a virgin. Even marriage to a widow was forbidden. The purpose here was to maintain the purity of the high priestly family.

D. Physical Perfection for Priests (Lv 21:16-23).

Priests with physical blemishes enjoyed many privileges of priesthood, but they were disqualified from worship leadership. Twelve physical defects are specifically mentioned, but the precise meaning of some of the Hebrew words is uncertain. The one who served at the altar as well as the sacrificial animal upon that altar had to be completely sound in body. Under the principle that the physical requirements of the old law point to the spiritual requirements of the new, the following observation is appropriate: New Testament priests (believers) with defects of the spirit (e.g., hasty temper or jealousy) are disqualified from worship leadership.

E. Ministerial Privileges (Lv 22:1-16).

Because of the principle that familiarity breeds contempt, the priests were commanded to "treat with respect" the sacred offerings of Israel. A portion of these offerings formed the daily sustenance of the priests. By partaking of this food while in an unclean state or in an unclean place the priests would be guilty of profaning the name of the Lord. Holy gifts could be shared by any member of the priestly family in a clean place; most holy gifts could be eaten only by male descendants of Aaron in the courtyard of the sanctuary (22:1-3).

A priest or a member of his family was disqualified from eating sacred food by (1) an infectious skin disease, (2) a bodily discharge,

(3) contact with a corpse, or (4) contact with one who had an emission of semen. A priest who had thus become unclean remained in that condition until evening. After bathing he was allowed again to partake of the sacred food. A priest was never allowed to eat meat of animals that had died a natural death or that had been killed by wild animals (22:4-9).

No unauthorized person could eat the sacred offerings. A guest, hired worker or daughter who married outside the family were specifically excluded. A slave, however, and a daughter living at home were allowed to eat. If by accident someone partook of the holy food, he was required to restore the quantity eaten, plus a penalty of twenty per cent. The priests were to take every precaution to see that the sacred food was not inadvertently eaten by those unqualified to do so (22:10-16).

F. Ministerial Duties (Lv 22:17-33).

The law set forth the rules governing the selection of animals for freewill and votive offerings. The animals had to be (1) male, (2) without blemish, (3) of the cattle, sheep or goats. A number of defects which might disqualify an animal for sacrificial use are listed in the text, but the translation of the Hebrew words is not always certain. An animal with limbs too long or too short could be offered as a freewill sacrifice, but not in fulfillment of a vow (22:17-25).

A sacrificial animal must be older than seven days. To counter some pagan custom, the law forbade offering a mother animal and her young on the same day. A thanksgiving offering had to be eaten on the same day it was offered (22:26-33).

CHAPTER THIRTY-THREE

The Worship of God
Leviticus 23-27

AIM: To demonstrate that celebration and commemoration are essential ingredients of worship.

THEME: Sacred appointments.

Leviticus has pointed out the way to God (chs. 1–7), the priestly work of God (chs. 8–15), and the believer's walk with God (chs. 17–22). The last section of the book focuses especially on the worship of God. These chapters speak of holy times (chs. 23–25) and holy obligations (chs. 26–27).

HOLY TIMES
Leviticus 23:1–25:55

Leviticus 23–25 contains laws governing (1) sacred seasons, (2) the Tabernacle, and (3) the Jubilee. A brief narrative relating the disposition of a deliberate violation of the Sabbath law is also included.

A. Appointed Feasts (Lv 23:1-44).

Leviticus 23 presents in chronological order a list of "the Lord's appointed feasts." Nine times these feasts are said to be accompanied by *miqra' qodesh.* The NIV renders this expression "sacred assembly." The verb *qara'* means "to call out" or "proclaim." Israel's reckoning of time was based on the moon. When the new moon was attested by reliable witnesses the precise day of the appointed feast was made known by official proclamation, a *miqra' qodesh.* Little evidence exists to support the idea of a public assembly on these days. In any case, eight of these "appointed feasts" are discussed in Leviticus 23.

1. At the head of the list is the weekly Sabbath (23:2-3). The day was celebrated by suspension of all labor. The Sabbath commemorated the original creation rest and the deliverance of Israel from Egypt.

2. The Passover began at twilight on the fourteenth day of Nisan, the first month (23:4-5). Each family ate a roasted lamb which memorialized the lamb slain and eaten on the night Israel was delivered from Egypt.

3. The Feast of Unleavened Bread commenced on Passover and lasted seven days (23:6-8). The first and last days of the feast were sabbaths in which no regular work was permitted. Special offerings were presented each day of the feast.

4. On the first day of the new week following Passover the Feast of Firstfruits was scheduled (23:9-14). A barley sheaf was waved before the Lord to express gratitude for the spring harvest. Special burnt, meal and drink offerings were presented.

5. The Feast of Weeks — later called Pentecost — was observed fifty days after the presentation of the firstfruits (23:15-22). This was a sabbath day on which wheat loaves were waved before the Lord. A burnt offering consisting of seven male lambs, two rams and a bull were presented. Two lambs and a male goat were offered as a sin offering.

6. The sacred seventh month was ushered in with the Feast of Trumpets (23:23-25). The blowing of a ram's horn signaled that all regular work was to be suspended. Special offerings were presented. The trumpets may be a memorial to the giving of the Law at Sinai.

7. The Day of Atonement, the most sacred day on the Israelite calendar, was scheduled for the tenth day of the sacred seventh month

(23:26-32). This was a sabbath day, and the only required fast day of the year. The rituals of this day are discussed in detail in Leviticus 16.

8. The Feast of Tabernacles (also called Ingathering) began on the fifteenth day of the seventh month (23:33-43). The first day of the seven-day festival was a sabbath. So also was the day after the week of celebration. During the week the people lived in booths to remind them of the wilderness wandering. Numerous special sacrifices were made during the week.

The sabbath principle undergirds all the laws regarding festivals. Seven festivals were scheduled during the year. During these festivals seven days of rest were designated. The majority of the festivals fall in the seventh month. Every seventh year was a sabbatical year. The Year of Jubilee came after forty-nine (7×7) years.

B. Tabernacle Rules (Lv 24:1-9).

Laws about the holy place have been included here to remind the people that they were obligated to provide for the worship of God at all times and not just at the festivals detailed in the preceding chapter. Two matters are here discussed: (1) the lampstand and (2) the showbread.

The lamps on the lampstand were to be kept burning continuously. The finest oil was to be brought by the people and prepared by the priests. Under no condition could the lamp be allowed to go out during the night (24:1-4).

The "bread of the face" (presence) is elsewhere called "bread that is continually there" (Nm 4:7) and "consecrated bread" (1 Sam. 21:6). Twelve loaves of unleavened bread were arranged on the table in two rows of six each. Incense added to each row made them a "memorial portion" to the Lord. Tradition says the incense was placed next to the bread in two golden cups, but this is not certain. At the end of a week this bread was to be eaten by the priests within the sanctuary (24:5-9).

C. Shelomith's Son (Lv 24:10-23).

Chronological rather than topical considerations dictated the location of this account. A man of mixed blood, the son of Shelomith of Dan, in a fit of anger "cursed" the name of Yahweh. The Hebrew actually uses two verbs here. The first (*naqab*) means "to pierce;" the second (*qillel*) means to declare someone to be worthless and without any significance. That someone would have the nerve to pierce God's name and declare him to be worthless was such a heinous crime that the people brought him directly to Moses for judgment (24:10-11).

That the man would be worthy of death was a foregone conclusion in the light of Exodus 21:17. Moses, however, was uncertain about the manner of execution for such a high-handed crime, and whether or not some special treatment should be given to the corpse after execution. Shelomith's son was put in custody until the will of God was made known. God directed that the blasphemer should be taken outside the camp. Those who heard him blaspheme were to place their hands on his head as a testimony to his guilt. Then the entire assembly, beginning presumably with those who had been witnesses, were to stone the man to death (24:12-13).

Growing out of this incident a new principle was articulated. A person who cursed his god would bear whatever punishment his god might mete out. A person who "pierced" the name of Yahweh was to be executed forthwith. The implication here is that since pagan deities were nonentities, one incurred no guilt by cursing them. Yahweh, however, would defend the honor of his holy name. This incident induced the Jews eventually to forbid the utterance of the name Yahweh except by the high priest once each year on the Day of Atonement (24:15-16).

The Lord also made clear at this time a few other punishments which were to be administered. Whoever killed a neighbor's animal must make restitution, but whoever murdered a man must pay with his life. Injury to a neighbor, presumably deliberate and premeditated, was punishable by the *lex talionis*, comparable punishment principle (24:17-22).

This account closes with a note that the children of Israel obeyed the directive of the Lord and stoned the blasphemer (24:23).

D. Jubilee Laws (Lv 25:1-55).

As in the preceding chapters, the phrase "I am Yahweh your God" signals the close of units in Leviticus 25. Each of the units so marked ends with an exhortation which sets forth the spiritual reason for observing the Law. Moses records here the laws pertaining to (1) a sabbath for the land, (2) the redemption of property, and (3) the redemption of slaves.

1. The sabbath for the land (25:2-22). Every seventh year the land was to enjoy a sabbath. Crops were not to be planted, and that which grew of itself was not to be harvested. The notion of a sabbath rest for everyone and everything is a concept found only in Israel in the ancient world (25:1-7).

The fiftieth year was a special time in Israel. Scholars have taken three positions regarding the Year of Jubilee. Some regard this as a mini-year of about fifty days designed to bring the lunar calendar back into harmony with the seasons. Others think that the Year of Jubilee coincided with the seventh sabbatical year. Still others view the Year of Jubilee as an ordinary year which followed the seventh sabbatical year.

The general requirements of the Jubilee Year are set forth in 25:8-13. The Year of Jubilee was introduced by the blast of a ram's horn on the Day of Atonement. Land reverted to original owners. Persons sold as slaves were allowed to return to their families. The Year of Jubilee was also a sabbath year. No sowing and reaping were permitted, but food taken directly from the fields could be eaten.

Regarding the purchase and sale of land the following principles applied: Israelites were to be careful not to take advantage of one another in land transactions. The price of a field depended on the number of harvests which remained before the Jubilee (25:14-17).

Observance of Jubilee laws would involve a measure of faith. God would provide for all the material needs of his people if they would obey his statutes. This included their needs in the seventh year when no crops could be grown. God would give them such harvests in the sixth year that they would have sufficient to carry them through the seventh sabbatical year and the Jubilee which followed (25:18-22).

2. The redemption of property (25:23-38). Regarding the redemption of property the following principles applied: The land belonged to the Lord, and his people were merely tenants. The Lord of the land decreed that a seller always retained the right to cancel the sale by redemption of the property. The seller might acquire the wherewithal to redeem his property, or a close relative might do it for him. The redemption price was determined by the number of remaining har-

vests until Jubilee. The land reverted to the original owner in the Jubilee regardless (25:23-28).

A house within a walled city could be sold permanently, but the seller had a twelve-month period in which to cancel the sale. Houses in villages were considered to belong with the land. The seller retained the right of redemption. Houses of Levites could never be sold in perpetuity even if they were located in walled cities (25:29-34).

This unit of Leviticus 25 closes with an exhortation to help any brother who became impoverished. No attempt was to be made to profit from the misery of this brother. He was to be charged no interest on loans (25:35-38).

3. The redemption of slaves (25:39-55). Regarding debtor's servitude the Law stipulated the following: An Israelite was never to be treated as a slave if, because of debt, he was forced to sell himself to his creditor. He was to be treated as a hired worker or a temporary resident. In the Year of Jubilee he and his children were to be released from servitude. Every Israelite was the Lord's servant and therefore could not be the servant of a fellow Israelite. An Israelite, then, enjoyed a higher status than the "Hebrew" of Exodus 21:1-4 who could be made to serve as a servant for six years. The regulations did not apply to non-Israelite slaves. They could be made slaves for life and could be passed on to children as inheritance (25:35-46).

An Israelite retained the right of redemption if he was forced to sell himself to an alien in the land. He might redeem himself or a relative might pay the redemption price for him. The price to be paid was an amount equivalent to the annual wage of a hired man times the years remaining until the Jubilee. Fellow Israelites were carefully to monitor the way in which the alien treated the Israelite servant. Since the Israelites were God's servants they could not be permanently enslaved (25:47-55).

HOLY OBLIGATIONS
Leviticus 26:1-27:34

The final two chapters of Leviticus point to the holy obligations which Israel had before God, and the holy obligations which God assumed with regard to his people.

396

A. God's Assurances to Israel (Lv 26:1-45).

Leviticus 26 contains three divine assurances to Israel. God promises blessing for obedience, but he warns of judgment for unfaithfulness. He commits himself to remember his people when they turn to him.

1. Promises of blessing (26:1-13). The fundamental commandment to ancient Israel was that they should never waver in their commitment to Yahweh as sole deity. This commitment expressed itself negatively in refusal to utilize any object associated with pagan deities. Positively, the commitment to Yahweh expressed itself in the faithful observance of the Sabbath from week to week (26:1-2).

Israel would enjoy rich blessings if they lived a life of complete obedience to the Lord. The blessings included the following: (1) rain, (2) abundant harvest, (3) protection from plunderers, (4) removal of savage beasts, (5) victory over enemies, (6) population growth, (7) plentiful food supply, and (8) the presence of God in their midst (26:3-13).

2. Warnings of calamity (26:14-39). If Israel disobeyed, the Lord threatened the following: (1) sickness, (2) defeat by their enemies, (3) withholding of rain, (4) crop failure, (5) attacks by wild animals, (6) siege, (7) plague, (8) food rationing, (9) cannibalism, (10) desecration of sacred places, (11) devastation of cities and sanctuaries, and (12) deportation to foreign lands (26:14-33).

As a result of the calamities listed above, the land of Canaan would lie desolate. The land would enjoy the yearly sabbath rests which the disobedient people had neglected to give it (26:34-35).

The remnant which would be deported to foreign lands would become spineless cowards. They would stumble over one another in their flight from their enemies. Their numbers would steadily diminish. Gradually they would be "devoured" by the land of their enemy (26:36-39).

3. Assurances of remembrance (26:40-45). The experience of exile would cause some to confess their sins and humble their hearts. God then would remember the covenant which he had made with their fathers. They would have to pay the price for their sins. Yet God would not utterly reject them. He would be faithful to the covenant even though they had not been.

B. Israel's Commitment to God (Lv 27:1-34).

Vows were made out of the desire to lend weight to a prayer by promising a gift to God if he granted certain requests. Sometimes after an emergency had passed, a person might try to escape the consequences of his vow. No one was compelled to make a vow, but a vow once made was sacred and had to be kept. This unit deals with vows regarding people, animals and property. Miscellaneous regulations then follow.

1. *Vows regarding people (27:2-8).* A person might be dedicated to the Lord in sanctuary service. A person so dedicated could be redeemed by payment of an equivalent value in silver. The values assigned were related to the amount of manual labor that the respective persons could be expected to perform in the sanctuary. Children younger than one month were not given a value. The set amounts for the various age categories were as follows:

Age	Male	Female
over 60	15 shekels	10 shekels
20-60	50 shekels	30 shekels
5-20	20 shekels	10 shekels
up to 5	5 shekels	3 shekels

2. *Vows regarding animals (27:9-13).* A clean animal, if vowed to the Lord, was in all cases to be given to the sanctuary for use in the offerings. No substitutions could be made. An unclean animal which had been vowed to the Lord had to be sold for the price set by a priest. The money was then given to the sanctuary.

3. *Dedication of property (27:14-24).* A house might be vowed to the Lord. The house was to be sold at the price determined by the priest and the proceeds then given to the sanctuary. If the owner changed his mind, he could buy back his house by adding a twenty per cent penalty to the appraised value (27:14-15).

The value of land vowed to the Lord was to be determined by (1) the amount of seed it required, and (2) by the number of harvests remaining until the Year of Jubilee. If the owner did not redeem it or sell it to another, the land would not revert to him in the Jubilee. That land would then belong to the priests. To redeem land which had been vowed to the Lord, the owner would have to pay a twenty per cent penalty. If a man vowed a field he had purchased from another, he paid the evaluation price. In the Jubilee that field reverted to the original owner (27:16-25).

4. Exclusions regarding vows (27:26-33). Three exclusions on vows are stipulated: (1) Firstborn animals could not be given to the Lord since they already belonged to him. Unclean firstborn animals could, however, be redeemed by paying to the sanctuary the value of the animal and a twenty per cent penalty. (2) That which had been devoted to the Lord unconditionally could not be redeemed nor sold. That property remained an inalienable possession of the sanctuary. Persons devoted to the Lord, i.e., judicially condemned to death, could not be redeemed. (3) Tithes belonged to the Lord and therefore could not be dedicated to him in a vow. Every tenth animal which passed under the shepherd's rod was holy to the Lord. If it was redeemed, a twenty per cent penalty had to be paid.

The book of Leviticus closes with a final declaration of the divine origin of the previous laws, and the Mosaic mediation through which they were given. The so-called Sinai laws conclude with this verse (27:34).

THE BOOK OF
NUMBERS

CHAPTER THIRTY-FOUR

Getting Acquainted with Numbers

AIM: To demonstrate the relevance of Numbers for the believer today.

THEME: Perseverance is essential!

By word count Numbers with 32,902 words is the largest book of the Pentateuch. This book, the fifth largest in the Old Testament, is divided into thirty-six chapters and 1,288 verses. The name comes from the Latin (*Numeri*) which in turn is based on the name in the Greek version (*Arithmoi*). This name reflects the two censuses which are recorded here. While the names given to the other four books of the Pentateuch in the Greek version are reasonably appropriate descriptions of those books, "Numbers" only fits chapters 1 and 26 and possibly one or two other chapters in this book. The name has tended to discourage study of the book among Christians. The Jews, on the other hand, designated the book by the fifth key word in the text, *bemidhbar,* "in the wilderness." This title is an excellent description of the contents of the book for it is concerned with the wilderness period of Israel's history.

SETTING OF NUMBERS

Numbers makes a strong claim to Mosaic authorship. The itinerary of the journey in chapter 33 is directly attributed to him. The regulations and laws in the book were given through the agency of Moses (e.g., 1:1). Twelve times the events narrated here are linked to Sinai. Numbers was probably written toward the end of the wilderness period, about 1407 BC.

The trip from Egypt to Sinai took a month and a half (Ex 19:1). During the next ten months the Israelites received instructions from the Lord and constructed the Tabernacle. The priesthood was then consecrated to the service of God. The command to take the first census came twelve and a half months after they left Egypt, or after they had encamped at Sinai for eleven months.

PURPOSE OF NUMBERS

That Numbers derives its ultimate significance within the framework and context of the greater Pentateuch cannot be denied. That the book has no special significance peculiar to itself must be resisted.[1] The canonical process has maintained the integrity of Numbers as a distinct book. The legal content of the book clearly sets it apart from Leviticus. Numbers focuses on the laws of Israel while on the march. Only in this book are found the military order of the tribes, the census of the fighting force, and the travel duties of Levites. Leviticus emphasizes the believer's worship and purity; Numbers, the believer's walk and pilgrimage. Numbers begins with a date formula indicating a new section of material, and concludes with a summary which sets it apart from the following book.

The Book of Numbers can be summarized in the caption "Marching and Murmuring." The immediate purpose of the book is to relate the history of God's people from the time of the first census until the final encampment before they entered the Promised Land. For the most part during that period Israel was on the march from Mt. Sinai to the Plains of Moab just across Jordan from Jericho. Although they were being led by the Lord, all during that march God's people complained about their circumstances.

The key thought in Numbers is *discipline*. Part of the schooling and discipline of Israel took place in Egypt. Another, and very different part, took place during the years of wandering in the wilderness. Freedom needs discipline as well as law (Ex; Lv). In Genesis the theme was the formation of the nation of Israel; in Exodus, the salvation of the nation; in Leviticus, the sanctification of the nation. The theme of Numbers is *the education of the nation*. The key passage is 14:29-30 where God sentenced an entire generation to wander in the wilderness for forty years because of their lack of faith. Through various punishments God was training his people for their special role in the scheme of redemption.

The ultimate purpose and abiding lesson of Numbers is that *perseverance is essential*. Only two adults of those who left Egypt were permitted to enter the Promised Land. Those who make a good start are not crowned, but those who finish the course! Paul drew the lesson from this book that Christians must avoid presumption (1 Cor 10:1-12). The writer of Hebrews saw here a warning against unbelief (Heb 3:19).

STRUCTURE OF NUMBERS

Following geographical indicators, the Book of Numbers can be divided into three main divisions: (1) the preparation for march at Sinai, (2) the march from Sinai to the Plains of Moab, and (3) the completion of the march.

A. Preparation for March (Nm 1:1–10:10).

General agreement exists among scholars that the first major division of Numbers extends from 1:1 through 10:10. The setting of this material is Sinai, the same venue which has been the focus from Exodus 19 through Leviticus. So closely is this unit linked to the second book of the Pentateuch that one scholar has even suggested that these chapters should be appended to Exodus.[2]

Before leaving Sinai, Israel had to make preparation for the journey. This preparation is evident in (1) the mustering of the tribes and the care of the Tabernacle (chs. 1–4), (2) the enforced purity of the camp (chs. 5–6), (3) the offerings for proper worship (chs. 7–8), (4) the second observance of the Passover (ch. 9), and (5) the signals for service (10:1-10).

B. The March (Nm 10:11–22:1).

The long journey from Sinai to Moab is covered in these few chapters. Here is the record of all that is known of the thirty-eight years of wilderness wandering. At best it is only the record of a series of episodes.

1. The journey to the borders of Canaan (10:11–ch. 13) included the following episodes: the burning in the camp at Taberah, the sending of quail, the sedition of Miriam and Aaron, and the expedition of the spies with their report.

2. The curse of wandering was pronounced because the nation lost faith in God and refused to enter Canaan (chs. 14–20). The following episodes are narrated: the rebellion of Korah and Dathan; Moses' striking the rock; the plague of serpents; and various special enactments.

3. The defeat of Sihon, king of the Amorites and Og, king of Bashan (ch. 21) in Transjordan were the first events following emergence from the wandering.

Chart No. 33

STRUCTURE OF NUMBERS *("The Discipline of the Nation")*		
PREPARATION FOR THE MARCH	THE MARCH TO CANAAN	COMPLETION OF THE MARCH
Nm 1:1–10:10	Nm 10:11–21:35	Nm 22–26
Organization at Sinai	Disorganization on the way	Reorganization in the Plains of Moab
THE OLD GENERATION		THE NEW GENERATION Nm 21:10; Dt 2:14

The exact point of termination for the second main division of Numbers is not readily apparent. Gray set it at 21:9 and Noth at 21:13. A better suggestion is 22:1 as the concluding verse of this section. The arrival in the Plains of Moab which this verse narrates, and the subsequent threats to Israel's very survival mark a clear break with the period of desert wandering.[3]

C. Conclusion of the March (Nm 22:2–36:13).

At the conclusion of the march five episodes are recorded: (1) the efforts of Balaam to destroy Israel (chs. 22–25), (2) the second numbering of the people (ch. 26), (3) the naming of a successor for Moses (chs. 27–30), (4) the triumph over the Midianites and distribution of the Transjordan territory (chs. 31–33), and (5) the directions for settlement in Canaan (chs. 34–36).

HISTORY OF NUMBERS

Numbers features five main literary forms: (1) lists, (2) census tallies, (3) laws, (4) poetic oracles, and (5) historical narratives. The book also contains quotations from an ancient Hebrew poetic composition known as "The Book of the Wars of the Lord" (ch. 21).

Moses did more than merely record facts in Numbers. He also interpreted the history of his people. In every event he saw the hand of God shaping his people for their witness to the world. The Lord provided for their needs, guided their journeys, kept his covenant in spite of their unfaithfulness, and disciplined them. Through all these experiences God revealed his true nature to Israel.[4]

The main characters in Numbers are Moses, Aaron, and Miriam. Aaron's sons Eleazar and Phinehas figure prominently in the narratives, as do Caleb and Joshua. Numbers bridges the gap between the giving of the Law to Moses and the death of the great Lawgiver. The action revolves around seven crises:

1. A leadership crisis. Miriam and Aaron questioned the authority of Moses (ch. 12).

2. A faith crisis. At Kadesh the people believed the reports of the ten spies and refused to trust God for victory in Canaan (chs. 13–14).

3. A second leadership crisis. The leadership of Moses and Aaron was challenged by Dathan and Korah and their followers (ch. 16).

4. A personal crisis. Moses arrogantly and angrily smote a rock when he was but to speak to it. The people received water from the rock, but Moses lost the opportunity to lead his people into Canaan (ch. 20).

5. A program crisis. When they were not permitted to pass through the land of Edom, Israel was forced to take a detour through the desert. Poisonous snakes in the region caused havoc and death (ch. 21)

6. A military crisis. Israelite soldiers were forced to go to war against walled cities in Transjordan for the first time (ch. 21).

7. A religious crisis. Balak king of Moab used beautiful temptresses to lure the men of Israel into Baal worship at Peor (ch. 25).

CHRONOLOGY OF NUMBERS

Chronological indicators appear in Numbers 1:1, 9:1, 10:11 and 33:38. The interest of the author, however, was not primarily chronological for in 20:1 the year is missing in a date formula. Furthermore, the temporal sequence in the book is disrupted by 9:1. Practically no events during the forty years of wandering have been recorded. All of this suggests that, while chronology was of concern to the writer, it was not the overriding concern.

Chronologically, the first event in Numbers was the observance of the second Passover in the first month of the second year after leaving Egypt (9:1). This event, however, seems to have been narrated only to establish the background for the celebration of the supplemental Passover in the second month. That second month was the chronological departure point for this book.

On the first day of the second month of the second year of the Exodus a census was taken at Sinai (Nm 1:1). Two other events are assigned by the calendar to the same month. The supplemental Passover was observed on the fourteenth day (9:11). On the twentieth day the Israelites departed from Sinai (Nm 10:11). Normally the trip from Sinai to Kadesh took eleven days (Dt 1:2). Since Israel, however, moved only at the direction of God, their journey to Kadesh took about eleven months (Nm 20:1).

Chart No. 34

CHRONOLOGY OF NUMBERS					
CENSUS AT SINAI	LEAVE SINAI	ARRIVE KADESH	AARON'S DEATH	ARRIVE ZERED	MOSES' ADDRESS
2nd Year 2nd Month 1st Day	2nd Year 2nd Month 20th Day	3rd Year 1st Month 1st Day	40th Year 5th Month 1st Day	?	40th Year 11th Month 1st Day
Nm 1:1	Nm 10:1	Nm 20:1	Nm 33:38	Dt 2:14	Dt 1:3,5
19 Days	11 Months	37+ Years	4+ Months	6 Months	
38 Years Dt 2:14					

The main historical-chronological problem facing the interpreter of Numbers is whether the Israelites made two trips to Kadesh, or just one. Israel arrived at Kadesh in the first month, but unfortunately the text does not name the year (Nm 20:1). For this reason some have proposed a *second* trip to Kadesh in the first month of the fortieth year when Aaron died. No second trip to Kadesh, however, is mentioned in the journey summary (Nm 33) or in the historical review in Deuteronomy 1–2.

About thirty-eight years elapsed between the arrival at Kadesh and the conclusion of Numbers. Almost nothing is known of that period. Most of the time was probably spent at Kadesh. Scripture indicates that circumcision and Passover were suspended during the thirty-eight years of wandering (Josh 5).

The dating of Aaron's death at Mt. Hor in the fortieth year, the fifth month, the first day (Nm 33:38) is the final time note in the book. Israel mourned for Aaron thirty days (Nm 20:29). The Israelites therefore departed from Mt. Hor on the first day of the sixth month. The *terminus ad quem* of events in Numbers was the first address of Moses on the first day of the eleventh month (Dt 1:3,5). Fitting all the events of Numbers 21–36 into a period of five months creates problems for all interpreters.

The chronological data relating to Numbers is displayed in Chart 34.

GEOGRAPHY OF NUMBERS

A geographical analysis of Numbers indicates six stages in the movement of God's people.

1. At Sinai. Israel's departure from Mt. Sinai is narrated in 10:10. All events recorded from Exodus 19 to Numbers 10 took place at the holy mount. As noted above, in Numbers this involves only nineteen days, during which time a census was taken and the people prepared for the journey to Canaan.

2. From Sinai to Kadesh (10:11–12:16). According to Numbers 33:16-36 Israel encamped at twenty spots between Sinai and Kadesh. The three most important of these were Taberah, where the fire from God burned in the outer edges of the camp; Kibroth Hattaavah, where many died of food poisoning; and Hazeroth, where Aaron and Miriam rebelled against Moses. Identifying the camping spots between Sinai and Kadesh is next to impossible. The text indicates that Taberah was a three-day journey from the mount. Since Taberah is not mentioned in the itinerary of Numbers 33 it is possible that this spot and Kibroth Hattaavah were one and the same.

3. At Kadesh. Almost seven chapters (13:1–20:21) speak of events at Kadesh. The Tabernacle was located here for some thirty-eight years. Actually very little is known of this "wandering" period. Perhaps the individual tribes ranged far and wide through the Wilderness of Zin, with Kadesh being the hub which held them together as a nation.

4. From Kadesh to the Valley of Moab near Pisgah (20:22–21:20). Eight camping spots are enumerated in the itinerary of Numbers 33:36-48. Eight additional camping spots in this phase of the journey are mentioned in Numbers 21, but undoubtedly some of these are the same as those in Numbers 33. The general location of some of these spots is made possible by the notation of more familiar landmarks (e.g., Red Sea, Zered Valley, Arnon River). Nevertheless, precise location of these spots is impossible.

5. From the valley of Moab to the Plains of Moab opposite Jericho (21:21-35). Israel engaged Sihon, an Amorite king, in warfare and captured his capital of Heshbon. Jazer was also captured from the Amorites. Israel then marched north into Bashan where king Og was defeated at Edrei.

MAP 11
JOURNEY TO CANAAN
NUMBERS 10-20

6. In the Plains of Moab opposite Jericho (22:1–36:13). The Moabite king Balak sent to Pethor near the Euphrates to secure the services of a soothsayer named Balaam. During this encampment Israel launched a holy war against the Midianites. The boundaries of the Promised Land were spelled out (34:1-12).

THEOLOGY OF NUMBERS

The theology of Numbers emphasizes how God interacts with his people. The book illustrates Romans 11:22, "Behold the kindness and severity of God." The theology here can be summarized in five statements which are as relevant today as they were in ancient Israel.

1. God is present with his people. The guiding presence of the Lord was visibly made known in the cloud which hovered over the Tabernacle day and night. The Israelite camp moved at the direction of the cloud (9:15-23). When the leadership of Moses came under attack, God explained to the rebels his unique presence with his servant. Moses was permitted to view the form of God, and the Lord spoke with him "mouth to mouth" (12:6-8).

2. God provides for his people. God gave ample provision for his people en route to Canaan (physically and spiritually). The daily supply of manna was a constant reminder of the provision for Israel. When they complained of having only the manna, God brought them the quails (Nm 11). Their thirst led God to provide water from a rock (20:8).

3. God is patient with his people. The Israelites constantly grumbled against the provision of God. At times the divine patience wore thin and the people experienced disciplinary judgments. God's forbearance, however, is indicated in the fact that he did not abandon his people.

4. God listens to the prayers of his people. Numbers contains several examples of dramatic intercession especially by Moses. He prayed for the healing of his sister who had rebelled against his leadership (12:9-15). When the people rebelled at the report of the ten spies, Moses prayed for pardon on the grounds of God's reputation and merciful character (14:13-16).

5. God protects his people. The would-be curses of a pagan diviner were turned into blessings. Magical incantation and ritual, so feared

in the ancient world, could not harm the people of the Lord. Sihon and Og, with mighty armies, were not able to prevail against Israel.

TYPOLOGY OF NUMBERS

The book of Numbers is important to the Christian student for four reasons. The book (1) narrates the history of God's dealings with Israel at this vital stage of national development, (2) supplies background for understanding the many allusions to its history and laws which occur in later sections of the Bible, (3) illustrates rich spiritual lessons, and (4) contains Messianic prophecy and numerous types.

In his fourth oracle, Balaam uttered a wonderful prophecy which reaches down to the Messianic age. He beheld in the distant ages a ruler called poetically the "star" and the "scepter." This future ruler would crush the enemies of his people. He would arise after Amalek had passed from the scene, after the Assyrian captivity, after the Greek conquest of Mesopotamia, and after the subsequent fall of the Greek empire. That is to say, according to Balaam the future ruler would arise during the days of the Roman empire (Nm 24:15-24).

The typological teaching of Numbers can be summarized as follows: (1) The Nazirite of Numbers 6 may be a type of the Christian. A Nazirite took a voluntary vow to live a life especially consecrated to God. (2) Aaron's rod that budded (ch. 17) points to the resurrection of Jesus which established his right to serve as the high priest of the new Israel of God. (3) The ashes of the red heifer (ch. 19) together with those of cedar wood, hyssop and scarlet wool were used to produce the waters of purification. So the benefits of the death of Jesus can be appropriated by obedience in the watery grave of baptism. (4) The brazen serpent (ch. 21) erected in the wilderness brought healing to snake-bitten souls. So the son of man lifted up on a tree brings spiritual healing to sin-smitten souls (John 3:14).

ENDNOTES

1. Cf. the dictum by Martin Noth: "We can scarcely speak of a special significance peculiar to the book of Numbers." *Numbers, a Commentary,* Old Testament Library (Philadelphia: Westminster, 1968), p. 11.

2. G.B. Gray, *A Critical and Exegetical Commentary on Numbers,* The International Critical Commentary (Edinburgh: T. & T. Clark, 1903), p. xxiv.
3. B.S. Childs, *Introduction to the Old Testament as Scripture* (Philadelphia: Fortress, 1979), p. 197.
4. J. Lawrence Eason, *The New Bible Survey* (Grand Rapids: Zondervan, 1963), p. 98.

BIBLIOGRAPHY: THE BOOK OF NUMBERS

Budd, Philip J. *Numbers.* Word Biblical Commentary. Waco, TX: Word Books, 1984.

Gaebelein, A.C. *The Book of Numbers.* New York: Dodd, Mead, 1913.

Greenstone, J.H. *Numbers with Commentary.* Philadelphia: The Jewish Publication Society of America, 1939.

Huey, F.B. *Numbers.* Bible Study Commentary. Grand Rapids: Zondervan, 1981.

Jensen, Irving L. *Numbers: Journey to God's Rest-land.* Chicago: Moody, 1964.

Noordtzij, A. *Numbers.* Bible Student's Commentary. Grand Rapids: Zondervan, 1983.

Riggans, Walter. *Numbers.* Daily Study Bible Series. Philadelphia: Westminster, 1983.

Wenham, Gordan J. *Numbers: An Introduction and Commentary.* Tyndale Old Testament Commentaries. Downers Grove, IL: InterVarsity, 1981.

CHAPTER THIRTY-FIVE

Preparing to March
Numbers 1-10

AIM: To demonstrate that God's people must prepare for their heavenly march.

THEME: To Canaan's land!

The Tabernacle was erected on the first day of the second year of the Exodus. One month later God ordered Moses to take a census of the people (cf. Ex 40:1; Nm 1:1). Nineteen days later the Israelites broke camp and started north toward Canaan. During those final days at Sinai several important matters were addressed.

NUMBERING THE TRIBES
Numbers 1:1–2:34

The first steps in organizing Israel for the march to Canaan were the numbering of the potential fighting force and the arrangement of the camp.

A. The Census (Nm 1:1-51).

The Lord ordered Moses to take a census of the whole Israelite community. Every male from twenty years old and upward was to be counted and his name listed in the official records. The purpose of this census was both military and religious (see Ex 30:14). Moses and Aaron were to supervise the census assisted by the leaders of each of the tribes (1:1-16).

One by one the ancestry of every male by tribe, clan and family was recorded (1:17-19). Since this was a military census, the tribe of Levi was exempt. Three duties are assigned to the Levites here: transporting the Tabernacle, dismantling it, and reassembling it (1:47-51).

The census indicated a total of 603,550 who were available for military service. The tribe of Judah (74,600) was the largest and the tribe of Manasseh (32,200) was the smallest (1:20-46).

B. The Camp (Nm 1:52–2:34).

The Levites were to set up their tents around the Tabernacle of the Testimony. Thus they provided a shield so that other Israelites would not inadvertently wander too close to the sacred structure (1:53-54). The other tribes formed an outer square around the Levites. Each tribe had its own standard. Tradition says that these standards matched the color of the twelve precious stones which represented each tribe on the breastplate of the high priest. Judah, Ephraim, Reuben, and Dan were the four leading tribes on the four sides of the Tabernacle. Chart 35 illustrates the arrangement of the camp.

ORGANIZING THE LEVITES
Numbers 3:1–4:49

Numbers 3 begins with an expression which was observed ten times in Genesis: "These are the generations of." Four sons of Aaron had been ordained along with their father to the priesthood. Two of those sons, Nadab and Abihu, had been smitten dead. Therefore, only three priests served Israel during the wilderness period (3:1-4).

Twice in Numbers 3 the following ominous threat appears: "If any one else comes near, he shall be put to death" (vv. 10,38). To "come

Chart No. 35

ARRANGEMENT OF THE CAMP
Numbers 2,3

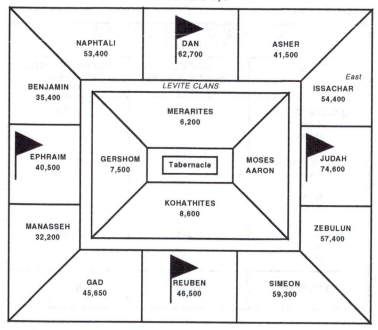

near" means to pass beyond the prescribed limits of one's position. Levites could not usurp the privileges of priesthood, and laymen could not lay claim to the prerogatives of the Levites.

The tribe of Levi was given to Aaron. The Levites were to serve under the direction of Aaron as assistants to the priests. The Lord had a claim upon the firstborn of Israel ever since he spared them when he passed through the land of Egypt. Now the Lord announced that he would accept the tribe of Levi in lieu of the firstborn (3:5-13).

A. First Levitical Census (Nm 3:14-51).

In the first census every male Levite of a month or older was to be counted. No upper limit was set. The Levites included in this census are being appointed to a lifelong service. The tribe of Levi had three main divisions which were subdivided into eight clans. Chart 36 summarizes the results of this special numbering.

Chart No. 36

CENSUS OF THE LEVITES Numbers 3,4		
LEVITE CLANS	**1ST RECKONING** (From Age 1 Month) Nm 3	**2ND RECKONING** (Age 30-50) Nm 4
GERSHONITE CLANS Libni Shimei	7,500	2,750
KOHATHITE CLANS Amram Izhar Hebron Uzziel	8,600	2,630
MERARITE CLANS Mahli Mushi	6,200	3,200
TOTALS	22,300	8,580

Firstborn Israelites of a month old numbered 22,273. Levites of one month old and upward numbered only 22,000. This meant that 273 Israelite firstborn could not be redeemed from the Lord's service by the substitution of Levites. For these 273 a redemption price of five shekels apiece was established. Probably Moses determined by lot which 273 Israelites had to be redeemed. The firstborn of Israel's livestock were also redeemed by the firstborn of the livestock of the Levites (3:40-51).

B. Second Levitical Census (Nm 4:1-49).

In the second Levitical census Moses was to count all males "from thirty years old up to fifty years old" (4:3). This census pertains to those qualified to engage in the strenuous physical labor of assembling, dismantling and transporting the Tabernacle. Moses found 8,580 Levites in this age bracket.

Detailed instructions regarding the work of the Levites are given in Numbers 4. Each clan had its own specific ministry, supervised by one of the sons of Aaron. The Kohathites (4:4-20) had the responsibility of transporting "the holy things." The actual work of preparing those items for transport was the responsibility of the priests. The ark and the table required three coverings, the lampstand and altars two. The laver for some reason is not here mentioned. Wrapping these objects necessitated temporary removal of the carrying poles (cf. Ex 25:15). The Kohathites were warned three times (4:15,18,20) not to infringe on priestly prerogatives. This clan had the greatest responsibility and consequently was in the greatest jeopardy. Kohathites numbered 2,750.

The Kohathites were under the supervision of Eleazar, Aaron's eldest son. He also was directly responsible for the oil of the lamp, the incense, the anointing oil, and the regular burnt offering (4:16).

The second division of Levites was the Gershonites (4:21-28). Gershonites numbered 2,630. Their work consisted of transporting the Tabernacle curtains or at least standing guard over the wagons which carried these curtains.

The Merarites (4:29-33) were the third division of the tribe of Levi. Merarites numbered 3,200. They were guardians of the wooden frames and pillars as they were carried in wagons.

PROTECTING THE CAMP
Numbers 5:1–6:27

The first four chapters of Numbers emphasized the sanctity of the Tabernacle by the placement of the tribes around the structure, and by the role assigned to the Levitical clans. Each of the chapters ends with a note underscoring the obedience of the people or Moses to the divine commandment. In the next two chapters various ordinances which will maintain the sanctity of the camp are enunciated. The negative and then the positive aspects of keeping the camp holy are discussed.

419

A. Things to Be Avoided (Nm 5:1-31).

In contrast to the positive directives of the first four chapters, Numbers 5 is largely negative. It deals with the avoidance of three types of defilement.

1. Physical defilement. Those with infectious skin diseases, bodily issues, or any other defilement were to be expelled from the camp. The purity of the camp must be maintained (5:1-4).

2. Willful transgression. Those who had wronged a brother were required to make oral confession and make restitution. The transgressor was to add twenty per cent to what was stolen. These monies were to be paid to the victim or a close relative. In the event there was no close relative, the restitution belonged to the priests. All of this preceded the atonement ritual performed by the priest (5:5-10).

3. Potential unfaithfulness. In the sanctified camp of Israel, not only was it necessary to deal with inadvertent impurity and deliberate transgression, even possible sin had to be investigated. The law of jealousies (5:11-31) was designed to reduce domestic strife. A man who suspected his wife of unfaithfulness but had no proof might make life miserable for his spouse. The man was required to take his wife to the priest along with a special offering. The offering served to bring the legal case between the spouses before the Lord for a decision. This was a "put up or shut up" option which a husband could employ, and presumably a wife could demand, to establish once and for all her innocence.

The ritual proceeded as follows: The priest prepared a brew consisting of holy water and dust from the floor of the Tabernacle. Curses against unfaithfulness were written on a scroll and then washed off into the water. The woman stood before the Lord in front of the sanctuary and took an oath that she had been faithful to her husband. If the woman had been unfaithful, the bitter water made her thigh rot and her abdomen swell. Perhaps some disease of the ovaries is intended that would cause her to look continually pregnant. She would thus be accursed among the people. If, however, she drank the water with no ill effect she was vindicated. The note "she will be able to have children" suggests that this test was designed for a childless woman who might be suspected of being under the curse of barrenness because of unfaithfulness.

B. Things to Be Encouraged (Nm 6:1-27).

The sanctity of the camp was encouraged through the ministry of the Nazirites and through the priestly blessing.

1. The Nazirite ministry (6:1-21) was designed to challenge all Israelites to a life of deeper dedication to the Lord. God is said to have raised up the Nazirites (Amos 2:11). No one was barred from the Nazirite ministry on the basis of sex or tribe as was the case in the priestly ministry.

A Nazirite was to be "holy to Yahweh" (6:8). Three requirements were placed on those who took this vow: (1) They were to abstain from all fruit of the vine or any fermented drink. (2) They were not allowed to cut their hair or (3) go near a dead body. The hair was the symbol of the consecration. If the Nazirite was accidentally defiled by a sudden death, he was required to shave his hair, present a special offering to the Lord, and start the period of his vow all over again (6:1-12).

When the term of the vow was over, the Nazirite was to bring to the Tabernacle a burnt offering, sin offering, and peace offering, together with the appropriate grain and drink offerings. In addition he was to present a basket of cakes and wafers made of flour mixed with oil. The Nazirite was to shave off his hair and burn it under the peace offering which he offered. After the priest took his portion of the sacrifices, the Nazirite was once again permitted to drink wine (6:13-21).

2. The priestly blessing (6:22-27) also served to sanctify the camp. Actually, it is Yahweh—his name is used thrice in the blessing—who did the blessing, not Aaron. Omitting from count the name Yahweh, the blessing consists of twelve words in accordance with the twelve tribes. The blessing is directed to the whole people, rather than the individual. It consists of three parts: (1) *bless* (material wealth) and *keep* (protection from all that could oppose fullness of life), (2) *make his face to shine* (indicative of pleasure) *and be gracious* (unmerited favor), (3) *lift up his face* (give love) *and give you peace.*

The priestly blessing would serve to put God's name upon the Israelites, i.e., make them especially conscious that their blessing was derived from Yahweh. The Lord indicated that he would honor that priestly blessing.

OFFERINGS FOR THE LORD
Numbers 7:1-89

Numbers 7 is the longest chapter in the Pentateuch. It records an incident which antedates the material in chapters 1–6 by one month. Here is narrated a twelve-day ritual of contribution by the tribal leaders to the work of the newly dedicated Tabernacle. The chapter begins with another reminder of God's holiness. God's shrine and all its contents were anointed and consecrated (7:1-2).

To assist in the sacred service the princes presented six carts and twelve oxen to Moses at the Tabernacle. The Lord instructed Moses to accept these gifts and distribute them as he saw fit among the Levites for use in their work. Moses gave two wagons to the Gershonites and four to the Merarites along with two oxen for each of the carts. The carts would be essential in transporting the Tabernacle. The Kohathites did not receive carts because they were to carry on their shoulders the holy vessels of the Tabernacle (7:3-9).

At the dedication of the altar each tribe presented a special offering. The contributions were made over a period of twelve days (7:10-83). Each tribal leader is identified and his offering described. The list starts with Judah and ends with Naphtali. In each instance the chieftain brought not only precious objects, but various animals to be used in burnt, sin and peace offerings. The total gifts for the twelve days were as follows:

12 Silver Bowls	72 Rams
12 Silver Plates	72 Lambs
12 Golden Spoons	12 Kids
36 Bullocks	60 Goats

Numbers 7 closes with the note that God *spoke* with Moses from the Holy of Holies. Moses did not *see* the Lord within the Tent. The promise of Exodus 25:22 was fulfilled immediately after the Tabernacle and the altar had been dedicated.

CONSECRATING THE LEVITES
Numbers 8:1-26

In its description of the consecration of the Levites, Numbers 8 parallels chapter 8 of Leviticus which narrates the ordination of the priests. The description of the Levitical ordination service is preceded by a note (8:1-4) prescribing the duty of the priests in lighting the lamp within the Holy Place. The seven lamps were to be positioned so that they gave light to the area immediately in front of the lampstand. The note reiterates that the lampstand was made of hammered gold exactly like the pattern the Lord had shown Moses in the mount. This is the second time Numbers has placed a directive to priests immediately before a passage containing information concerning Levites (cf. 4:5-15 and 4:16-49). Apparently the author's purpose in so arranging the material was to continually remind his readers of the priority of the Aaronic priesthood in the Mosaic worship system.

Three steps were involved in the setting apart of the Levites:

1. Purification. Three times Moses was told or said to cleanse the Levites. Three times the Levites are said to purify themselves. Aaron was to sprinkle the water of cleansing upon them. The Levites were then to shave their whole bodies and wash their clothes. Even in ordination a gap separated priests and Levites as Chart 37 indicates.

2. Presentation. The Levites were substitutes for the firstborn of the nation, and as such had to receive the laying on of the hands of the people (doubtless through their tribal representatives). Aaron was then to present them as a wave offering to the Lord. The high priest made the prescribed motions in front of the Levites.

Chart No. 37

ORDINATION TO MINISTRY	
THE PRIESTS **Leviticus 8**	**THE LEVITES** **Numbers 8**
Made Holy	Made Clean
Washed with Water	Sprinkled with Water
Put on New Garments	Washed Garments
Blood Applied to Person	Blood "Waved" before God

3. Sacrifice. The Levites laid their hands upon the heads of two bulls and these were offered up as a sin offering and a burnt offering on their behalf (8:5-14).

Thus consecrated the Levites began their ministry in the Tabernacle. They were regarded as a gift to Aaron, i.e., they were assistants to the priests. They began to assist their brethren at age twenty-five; regular service began at age thirty (4:3,23,30). They were required to retire from regular service at age fifty (8:15-26).

OBSERVING THE PASSOVER
Numbers 9:1-14

Prior to the census (Nm 1:1), God had commanded Israel to observe the Passover. This second observance of the sacred feast was done on the evening of the fourteenth of Nisan, the first month. Some, however, were unable to participate in the observance because they had become defiled by a dead body. The Lord made a special concession to the sincerity of these Israelites, and granted them permission to celebrate the Passover one month later. A person on a long journey might also postpone Passover observance for one month. Any person, however, who merely neglected to observe Passover was to be cut off from his people.

ORDERING THE MARCH
Numbers 9:15–10:36

The paragraphs in this unit are designed to prepare the reader for Israel's departure from Sinai.

A. The Heavenly Cloud (Nm 9:15-23).

On the day the Tabernacle was erected, the heavenly cloud covered it. At night the cloud looked like fire. When the cloud lifted above the Tent, the Israelites broke camp. They camped for a long time at some spots; on other occasions the cloud remained only overnight. The paragraph emphasizes no less than ten times how Israel followed divine direction faithfully (9:15-23).

Chart No. 38

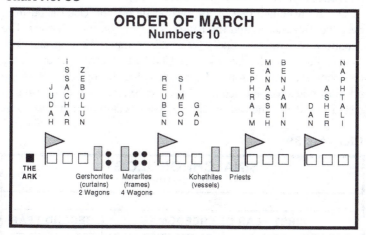

B. The Silver Trumpets (Nm 10:1-10).

Two silver trumpets were used by the priests (1) to assemble the camp at the door of the Tabernacle, (2) to call the heads of the tribes together, (3) to signal camp movement, (4) to sound the alarm when the nation was under attack, and (5) to serve as a memorial at feasts and festivals (10:1-10).

C. The Request to Hobab (Nm 10:29-32).

Moses asked Hobab his brother-in-law (Reuel the Midianite is another name for Jethro) to accompany Israel on the journey. God had promised good things to Israel, and Hobab would share in that blessing if he chose to join the trek toward Canaan. Hobab was reluctant to leave his desert home and his people. Moses then suggested that Hobab, because of his intimate knowledge of the desert, would be invaluable to the group in their journey. Hobab could be the eyes of Israel. Some regard this statement of Moses as an indication that he did not fully trust in the leading of the Lord during the journey. Others have suggested that Moses was merely trying to make Hobab feel needed so that he would choose to cast his lot with the people of the Lord. In any case, there is in this passage an evangelistic thrust, a concern that this Gentile share the blessings which God had in store for his people.

D. Departure from Sinai (Nm 10:11-36).

On the twentieth day of the second month the cloud lifted from over the Tabernacle, and the Israelites set out on their journey. The departure was majestic and joyous with trumpets blowing and flags waving. Each tribe fell into place as God had directed. The ark of the covenant was out in front. Moses celebrated the movements of the ark with poetic verse whenever the sacred symbol set out or came to rest. The order of the rest of the procession is illustrated in Chart 38.

Chart No. 39

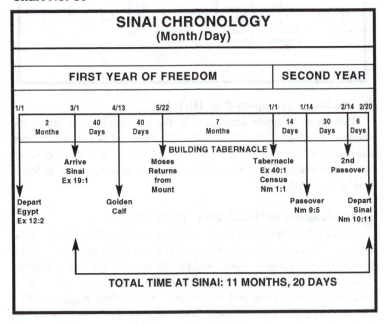

CHAPTER THIRTY-SIX

Calamity at Kadesh
Numbers 11-16

AIM: To demonstrate the necessity of faith, obedience and respect for God-given authority.

THEME: A failure of faith!

A frequent phrase in the wilderness account is "and they journeyed from . . . ." Seven times the narrator uses this departure formula in Exodus and five times in Numbers. Moses delighted in noting every movement which would bring his people closer to Canaan. Of all the departures, however, that from Sinai was the most significant and spectacular. The orderliness and confidence of their march soon and unexpectedly gave way to disarray and fear. This unpleasant chapter in Israel's journey unfolds in three movements: (1) en route to Kadesh, (2) encampment at Kadesh, and (3) enactments at Kadesh.

427

EN ROUTE TO KADESH
Numbers 11:1–12:16

According to Numbers 33, Israel camped at twenty spots en route to Kadesh. This journey took several months. Only three episodes along the way are narrated, and one of those only briefly.

A. Complaint about the Way (Nm 11:1-3).

Apparently Israel had traveled for only three days when the complaints started. The people grumbled about their hardships in the hearing of the Lord, i.e., publicly, and he was moved to anger against them. Fire from the Lord began to consume them on the fringes of the camp. In other words, God unleashed a tremendous lightning storm over Israel. Yet God's mercy is manifest even in judgment, for only the outskirts of the camp were destroyed. Nonetheless, Moses went to God in prayer on behalf of the people and the punishment ceased. The spot was given the name Taberah ("burning").

B. Complaint about Food (Nm 11:4-35).

The second crisis after leaving Sinai was triggered by the mixed multitude who had joined Israel in the Exodus. They had become dissatisfied with the diet of manna. They craved meat and the fresh vegetables which they had enjoyed in Egypt. Why the Israelites did not slaughter some of the flocks and herds which accompanied them out of Egypt is not stated. In any case, their contempt for the manna ("this manna") is quite clear (11:4-9).

Murmuring is contagious! The complaint of the rabble soon became the lament of the whole camp. Every family was wailing at the entrance to its tent. Two reactions to this development are noted: the Lord became angry, and Moses became discouraged. He took the complaint of the people as an indictment of his leadership. Moses became as guilty as the people by complaining to God that he had thrust upon him this leadership role. His prayer is full of self-pity. It is permeated by personal pronouns. Moses seems to have become more concerned about his personal status than with God's glory. He wanted out of his ministry. Death would be preferable. "The burden of this people is too great," he complained (11:10-15).

428

God exercised great patience with both Moses and the people. The leadership problem would be solved by endowing some of the elders with the same Spirit which was on Moses. They would then be able to help him carry the burden of the people. The food problem would be solved quickly. God would bring meat to their camp the very next day. They would eat meat until it "comes out of your nostrils and you loathe it!" The miracle of provision would at the same time become an occasion of punishment (11:16-20).

In his discouragement Moses displayed a lack of faith. If all the flocks and herds were to be slaughtered and all the fish in the sea were caught, that would not be enough meat for this throng! Moses took into consideration only what he saw *now*, not what he *had seen* of God's power. God asked doubting Moses a question which he would likewise address to any other skeptic among his people: "Is Yahweh's arm too short?" Is God incapable of reaching down to assist his people? (11:21-23).

Moses gathered seventy elders and stationed them around the tent. True to his word, God came down and talked with Moses there. The Spirit which rested on Moses was then given to the seventy and "they prophesied." The exact nature of this prophesying is not clear. Perhaps a vigorous, ecstatic praising of God is intended. In any case, the prophesying was designed to be evidence that the Spirit indeed had come upon these men (11:24-25).

Two of the seventy, Eldad and Medad, remained in the camp. No reason is given for their absence. They too began to manifest the gift of prophesying. Joshua, jealous for his mentor, urged Moses to make these men cease. Magnanimous Moses did not covet exclusive rights to God's Spirit. He wished that all of the people were prophets and shared the Spirit which had filled him since his call (11:26-30).

By means of wind currents, God disrupted the migratory pattern of quails. The wind forced the birds down all around the camp to within three feet of the ground where they were easily captured with nets. No family gathered less than ten homers (about sixty bushels). Following Egyptian custom they spread the catch out around the camp to dry in the sun. Some apparently could not wait until the meat was ready. While the meat was still between their teeth God smote them with a plague. The spot was named Kibroth Hattaavah, "graves of greed" (11:31-34).

C. Complaint against Moses (Nm 12:1-16).

From Kibroth Hattaavah the people moved to Hazeroth were a leadership crisis of a different sort developed. Miriam and Aaron began to criticize Moses because of his Cushite wife. Had Zipporah died? Or had Moses taken a second wife? Or was "the Cushite" a designation for Zipporah? Since Cushan is mentioned in connection with Midian (Hab 3:7), and since Zipporah was from the land of Midian, it is possible that Zipporah is intended. The influence of Miriam the sister had waned after the arrival of Zipporah at Sinai. In any case, the marriage issue was merely a pretext. Miriam and Aaron wanted more power for themselves. God had spoken through them just as much as through Moses, they claimed (12:1-2).

Moses was not inclined to deal with the dissidents because "he was more humble than anyone else on the face of the earth." Modern critics have argued that these words are incongruous with Mosaic authorship of the Pentateuch. Interpreted as braggadocio this verse would be difficult to square with Mosaic authorship. Perhaps Moses, however, intended the words to be understood as a confession of weakness in leadership. Because of his very low self-esteem he did not exercise boldness in dealing with the rebels (12:3).

God intervened in the crisis by calling the three leaders to the door of the tent. This is the only instance where the Lord spoke "at once" or immediately. He was quick to defend his servant Moses. In the pillar of cloud the Lord came down and stood there. He directed Aaron and Miriam to take one step forward (12:4-5).

The Lord then indicated in no uncertain terms the unique role of Moses. To ordinary prophets God revealed himself in dreams and visions. Moses, however, spoke "face to face" with the Lord. He had the privilege of viewing the form of the Lord. That which the elders had seen only once (Ex 24:10), Moses saw every time he spoke with God. Just as Joseph had been faithful over all things in the house of Potiphar, so Moses was the dependable majordomo of God's house. He was God's servant par excellence! Because of this standing with the Lord, others should be afraid to speak out against Moses (12:6-8).

The anger of Yahweh burned against Aaron and Miriam. When the cloud lifted from above the tent, Miriam was leprous, as white as snow. This indicates that Miriam was the instigator of this act of rebellion.

430

Aaron got off with a fright as is indicated by the structure of the Hebrew sentence. He turned to Moses and begged him not to "hold against us the sin we have so foolishly committed." Perhaps to evoke Moses' sympathy, Aaron compared his sister to a child who suffered from a fatal disease when it is born (12:9-12).

Moses said nothing in defense of himself, nothing by way of rebuke to his detractors. He earnestly prayed for the healing of Miriam. God healed the woman; but her disease was a divine rebuke of no small consequence, comparable to the act of a father spitting in his child's face after the child misbehaved. A child who had been the victim of such indignity would not dare show his face for a week. So Miriam was to be confined outside the camp for seven days. So that everyone might know what had happened to her, the nation was delayed for a week at Hazeroth ("villages") until Miriam was restored to the camp (12:9-15).

ENCAMPED AT KADESH
Numbers 13:1-16:50

In the first month of the third year of the Exodus, eleven months after leaving Sinai, the Israelites reached Kadesh in the Wilderness of Paran (20:1). Kadesh appears to have remained the base camp for Israel during the next thirty-eight years.

A. Paralyzing Doubt (Nm 13:1-14:38).

Kadesh was to be the staging area for the invasion of Canaan. The people wished to reconnoiter the land before the attack (Dt 1:20-23), and the Lord gave permission for this to be done. One leader from each tribe was dispatched on this mission. These are not the same tribal leaders mentioned in Numbers 1. Perhaps younger men were selected by the tribes. The only representatives who are significant are those of Ephraim (Hoshea who was given the name Joshua by Moses), and of Judah (Caleb). The twelve were under commission to investigate the defensive capabilities of the Canaanites and the potential of that land for agricultural prosperity (13:1-20).

The spies explored the entire length of Canaan as far north as Rehob and the entrance of Hamath. Debate over the geography of

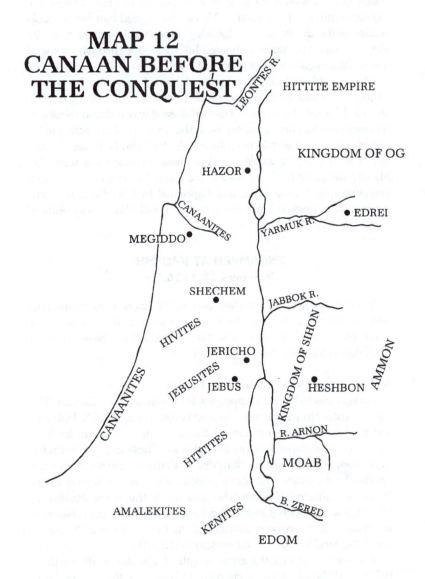

MAP 12
CANAAN BEFORE
THE CONQUEST

LEONTES R.

HITTITE EMPIRE

KINGDOM OF OG

HAZOR

CANAANITES

YARMUK R.

EDREI

MEGIDDO

SHECHEM

JABBOK R.

HIVITES

JERICHO

JEBUSITES

JEBUS

KINGDOM OF SIHON

HESHBON

AMMON

CANAANITES

HITTITES

R. ARNON

MOAB

AMALEKITES

KENITES

B. ZERED

EDOM

the exploration of Canaan continues. About all that can be said is that Rehob and the entrance of Hamath were very near what would later be the northern border of Israel's territory. The spies returned after forty days, carrying a cluster of grapes from the Valley of Eshcol and other fruits of the land as well (13:21-24).

The spies reported to Moses that indeed Canaan was a land flowing with milk and honey and they presented the fruit as evidence. They also noted that (1) the inhabitants were powerful, and (2) the cities were large and fortified (13:25-29).

Caleb confidently urged an immediate attack for "we can certainly do it!" The other spies, however, convinced the people that the Canaanites were invincible. The land devoured its inhabitants, i.e., it was the battleground of the nations. This "evil report" suddenly made all the inhabitants of the land giants. The descendants of Anak were a giant race which made the Israelites regard themselves as grasshoppers (13:30-33).

The majority report of the spies sent a shock wave through the camp. The people wept aloud all night. They murmured against Moses and Aaron. Better to die in the wilderness than to face those giants! In the agony of their soul they cried out "Why?" They accused the Lord of all kinds of sinister plans to kill them. They were ready to return to Egypt! Since they knew Moses would never agree to that, they were fully prepared to select another leader and depart (14:1-4).

To demonstrate their agony over the attitude of the people, Moses and Aaron fell down upon their faces before the assembly. Caleb and Joshua tore their clothes as a sign of mourning for the godlessness of their people. They reminded the assembly of the positive words which had been reported concerning the land. "If the Lord is pleased with us, he will lead us into that land," they argued. Israel, however, must not (1) rebel against the Lord, nor (2) be afraid. They were confident that with God's help Israel could "swallow up" the inhabitants of the land. The "protection" (lit., shadow) of the Canaanites had been removed. They would now be subjected to the scorching rays of God's judgment. The Canaanites were no match for Israel, for their gods were no match for Israel's God (14:5-9).

The assembly, unswayed by the emotional appeals, was ready to stone Joshua, Caleb, Moses and Aaron. At that moment, however, the glory of the Lord appeared at the tent. God expressed to Moses his disappointment with the lack of faith in Israel even after all of the miraculous signs which he had performed in their midst. The Lord expressed his intent to strike down Israel and build a new and even greater nation of Moses. The Lord was conducting an attitude check on the leader of his people (14:10-12).

Moses passed the test. Again he pled for mercy and forgiveness as he had done at Sinai. He pressed two arguments in his intercessory prayer. (1) He pled that God's reputation among the heathen depended upon his involvement with Israel. If Yahweh destroyed his people all at one time, the heathen would conclude that he was unable to fulfill the land promise which he had made to them. (2) Furthermore, Moses reminded the Lord of how he had described himself earlier (Ex 34:6,7) as a God of patience, love and forgiveness, who did not punish indiscriminately. He called upon his God to once again pardon his people as he had done time and again since they had left Egypt (14:13-19).

In response to the prayer of Moses the Lord made four points: (1) The nation would be spared, but the unbelieving generation would be deprived of seeing the Promised Land. They had seen God's glory and his miraculous signs and yet they had tested God "ten times," i.e., numerous times. (2) The nation was to turn away from Canaan. Their new destination was to be the Red Sea. (3) The Israelites had pronounced sentence against themselves. Everyone twenty and older would fall in the wilderness. Their children would be shepherds in the desert for forty years, a year for each day the spies were in Canaan. (4) Because Caleb was of a different spirit, wholeheartedly committed to God, he and Joshua would be permitted to enter the land (14:20-35).

God's wrath immediately was poured out on the ten spies who spread the bad report through the camp. They were struck down by a plague before the Lord (14:36-38).

B. Reckless Repentance (Nm 14:39-45).

When Moses reported these things to the people, they mourned bitterly. Early the next morning they prepared to march toward the hill country to conquer Canaan. The people assumed the appearance of obedient faith and of unconditional trust in God's promise. They

434

believed that an admission of guilt would undo their recent failure of faith (14:39-40).

Moses warned them that they were proceeding without the presence of the Lord; they surely would be defeated. Even though Moses and the ark remained in the camp, the people marched "presumptuously" (lit., they were "swollen, puffed up") into the high country. The Amalekites and Canaanites living in that region engaged and defeated Israel in battle and beat them down all the way to Hormah (14:41-45).

C. Encouraging Instruction (Nm 15:1-41).

Following the disastrous defeat in south Canaan, Israel was plunged into despair. The gracious Lord refrained from adding to their misery by verbally chastising them. He elected rather to continue their spiritual education. Israel had failed to penetrate Canaan from the south. The instruction contained in Numbers 15 begins with these words: "When you come into the land you are to inhabit." In their hour of defeat, God gave his people a ray of hope. They would one day enter the Promised Land, but that would occur according to God's timetable.

Six regulations were set forth. (1) The quantities of grain, wine and oil which were to accompany the voluntary burnt offerings and "sacrifices" (i.e., peace offerings) were specified. (2) Israelite and non-Israelite alike would be expected to abide by the demands of the Law in Canaan "for the generations to come." (3) The law regarding first fruits was sharpened.[1] (4) Provision was made for the forgiveness of sins due to ignorance and oversight.[2] (5) The penalty for commission of a "high handed" sin was being cut off from the people. (6) Tassels were to be worn on the four corners of their outer garments to remind them of their duty to obey all the commands of the Lord (15:1-31,37-41).

An incident in the desert tested Israel's resolve to execute those guilty of high-handed sin. A man was found gathering sticks on the Sabbath. Moses' problem here was twofold: was gathering wood in the same category as lighting a fire (Ex 35:3)? And did the man deliberately set out to violate the Sabbath? The man was kept in custody until the Lord himself rendered a verdict. The decision was that the man was to be stoned. This indicates that (1) gathering wood did fall under the category of "work" and was thus forbidden on the Sabbath, and (2) the man could know this and therefore did sin presumptuously. The people willingly carried out the execution (15:32-36).

D. Troublesome Dissidents (Nm 16:1-50).

At some point during the Kadesh encampment Moses and Aaron faced a serious challenge to their leadership. The dissidents were Korah, a Levite, and Dathan and Abiram of the tribe of Reuben. These rebels were joined by 250 princes. Korah wished to abolish the distinction between priests (family of Aaron) and the rest of the tribe of Levi. The Reubenites apparently felt that they had a claim to the priesthood over the tribe of Levi because they were descendants of the firstborn of Jacob (16:1-2).

The three leaders and their followers came to Moses and Aaron as a group. They accused the brothers of taking more authority than was rightfully theirs. The slogan of the dissidents was this: "The whole congregation is holy." Every Israelite was thus holy, and the Lord was with them just as much as he was with Moses and Aaron. The brothers therefore had no right to set themselves over the assembly (15:3).

In the face of this attack, Moses fell face down in an attitude of prayer. How long he remained in that position is not stated. After the prayer experience Moses announced a test which would prove who had the right to approach God as worship leaders. In the morning Korah and his company must do what had heretofore been the exclusive prerogative of Aaron's family: they must burn incense before the Lord. Whoever could burn incense before the Lord without being destroyed by the fire of God's holiness would prove that he had been divinely chosen for priestly ministry. Moses concluded this challenge by using the very words of the rebels: You Levites have gone too far! Moses hoped thereby to (1) reveal who were the real instigators of the rebellion, and (2) drive a wedge between the conspirators (16:4-7).

Moses then met with the Levites separately. He was attempting to sever their association with Korah and his Reubenite allies. He reminded the Levites of the noble ministry to which God had called them. God had separated them from the rest of the congregation, and had brought them near to himself to do the work at the Lord's Tabernacle and to minister before the people. He warned them that by seeking the priesthood they were attacking the Lord, not Aaron (16:8-11).

Moses next summoned the Reubenites to a confrontation, but they refused to meet with him. They repudiated Moses' leadership by accusing him of (1) leading them out of a land flowing with milk and honey into a barren desert, (2) lording it over them, (3) failing to deliver on his promise to lead them to a land of abundance, and (4) attempting to blind others to the true circumstances so that he could retain his leadership (16:12-14).

For the first time the text declares that Moses was very angry. He prayed in bitterness prior to the contest at the Tabernacle. He had never harmed the dissidents in any way. He asked the Lord not to accept the offering of incense which they were about to make (16:15).

Moses' efforts to head off the rebellion had failed. Korah and his followers assembled with their fire censers and incense and stood opposite Moses and Aaron at the entrance of the Tent. The glory of the Lord appeared to the entire assembly. He instructed Moses and Aaron to separate themselves from the assembly so he could put an end to all of them at once. Moses and Aaron cried out to the Lord that he punish only those guilty of rebellion (16:16-22).

The Lord then gave direction for the assembly to remove themselves from the area occupied by the tents of the dissidents. Moses and the elders went to the tents of Dathan and Abiram. Moses warned the assembly to move away from the tents of those wicked men. The dissidents and their families came out and stood defiantly before their tents. The test here in the camp was this: if the earth opened and swallowed these men the assembly would know that they had treated the Lord with contempt (16:23-30).

The judgment of the Lord was decisive. In the camp the earth opened up and consumed the rebels. At the Tabernacle fire came out from the Lord and consumed the 250 men who were offering incense. Eleazar, at the direction of the Lord, gathered the censers of the dead Levites and had them hammered out to overlay the altar. That overlay was to be a perpetual reminder that no one except a descendant of Aaron might approach that altar without the risk that the Lord would consume him just as he had consumed Korah and company (16:31-40).

The spirit of rebellion was not suppressed by the divine judgment upon the Reubenite and Levite dissidents. The next day the whole assembly turned against Moses and Aaron, accusing them of having "killed the Lord's people." The cloud of divine glory again covered the Tent. The Lord directed Moses and Aaron to separate themselves from the assembly so that God could put an end to them at once. Moses directed Aaron to hasten into the assembly with his censer to make atonement for the plague of God's wrath. Aaron raced to take his stand between the living and the dead. This was Aaron's finest hour. He risked his own life to stay the plague. Even so, 14,700 people died in that judgment (16:41-50).

ENDNOTES

1. The law of first fruits was first articulated in Ex 22:29 and 23:19.

2. A similar provision is made in Lv 4, but the earlier passage contemplated sins of commission while this passage envisioned sins of omission.

CHAPTER THIRTY-SEVEN

Developments in the Desert
Numbers 17-21

AIM: To illustrate that no obstacle is too great to be overcome by those who march toward Canaan.

THEME: More than conquerors!

Not much is known about the punishment phase of the wilderness period. Besides the Korah rebellion (ch. 16) nothing happened during those long years of wandering that was of importance in the further development of God's program. Kadesh seems to have been the hub of activity for most of that period. Circumcision was suspended, and possibly also parts of the sacrificial system (Josh 5; Amos 5:25). Numbers 17-21 stresses the success with which Israel was able to cope with problems which arose while they were still camped at Kadesh or en route to Canaan.

PROBLEMS AT KADESH
Numbers 17:1–20:21

While still at Kadesh Israel faced five problems. These were the problems of (1) authority, (2) worship phobia, (3) defilement, (4) death, and (5) lack of water.

A. Problem of Authority (Nm 17:1-11).

Immediately following the Korah rebellion the Lord moved to give a dramatic and permanent evidence of the selection of Aaron as the priestly head. Each tribe was required to present a staff to Moses. The name of the tribal leader was inscribed on each staff. Aaron's name was written on the staff of the tribe of Levi. The thirteen staves were placed in the tent in front of the Testimony (i.e., the ark). God was to cause the staff of the man he had chosen to sprout. Thus the constant grumbling of the tribes against the priestly leadership of Aaron would be silenced.

When Moses entered the tent the next morning he discovered that the staff of Levi with Aaron's name upon it had not only sprouted, it had actually produced almonds. After showing the staves to the leaders, Moses put Aaron's staff back in front of the ark where it remained a perpetual reminder of the choice of Aaron.

B. Problem of Worship Phobia (Nm 17:12-18:32).

The Israelites were filled with fear as a result of what they had witnessed in the past few days. They had seen (1) Korah and company consumed by fire from heaven, (2) Dathan and Abiram swallowed up by the earth, (3) a plague which killed thousands stayed by the incense Aaron offered, and (4) the divine attestation of Aaron in the miraculous budding of the rod. The conventional wisdom was that it was far safer to stay away from the Tabernacle. God needed to deal with this worship phobia.

Numbers 18 begins by declaring that the priests "shall bear the responsibility for offenses against the sanctuary, and you and your sons alone are to bear the responsibility for offenses against the priesthood." According to 18:23 "the Levites shall do the service of the tent of meeting and they shall bear their iniquity." Thus sins inadvertently committed within the sanctuary impacted upon the clergy, not the congregation. The priests and the Levites were given this awesome responsibility so "that there be wrath no more upon the people of Israel" (18:5).

Some of the other points of emphasis in Numbers 18 are these: (1) The Levites were responsible to the priests when they performed their duties (vv. 2,3,6). (2) The priesthood was a gift of God to the sons of Aaron. Only they could serve at the altar in the courtyard and within the tent proper. Anyone else who came near was to be executed (v. 7). (3) Some of the income of the priests included "the most holy offerings" which could be eaten only by the priests themselves in the Tabernacle; offerings which were merely "holy" which could be eaten in a clean place by the household of the priests; firstfruits; everything "devoted to the Lord"; and the firstborn of every womb, both man and animal (vv. 8-19). (4) Neither Levites nor priests would have an inheritance in the Promised Land. The tithes of the people, however, belonged to the Levites (vv. 20-24). (5) The Levites were to give a tithe of their income to the Priests (vv. 25-29).

C. Problem of Defilement (Nm 19:1-22).

Numbers 19 is concerned with defilement caused by contact with a corpse. In the immediately preceding chapters the theme of death has been prominent. Thus (1) Korah and his company were smitten dead by fire from heaven (16:35), (2) 14,700 died in a plague (16:49), (3) Aaron stayed the plague of death with an incense offering (16:48), (4) fear of death seized the people (17:12-13), and (5) ritual encroachment would result in death (18:3,7,22).

The regulations here differ somewhat from Numbers 5:2-3 which required one who was unclean by virtue of contact with a corpse to be put out of the camp. Numbers 5 was a temporary enactment designed for the wilderness period. Numbers 19 looked forward to the settlement in the Promised Land: "and it shall be a perpetual statute for them" (19:21).

Directions were given for the preparation of the "waters of purification." A red heifer without blemish which had never been used in profane work was to be presented. The animal was to be slaughtered outside the camp under the supervision of Eleazar. The priest then sprinkled the blood of the heifer with his finger seven times (the number of completeness) toward the front of the sanctuary. Then the remains of the animal were incinerated outside the camp along with cedar wood, hyssop and scarlet. This is reminiscent of the procedure used in the cleansing of a leper (Lv 14:4-6). The supervising priest and the man who took care of the burning became ceremonially unclean by these actions. Both were required to wash their clothes and bathe. They could enter the camp, but they remained unclean until evening (19:1-8).

The ashes of the red heifer were collected and stored in a clean place outside the camp. The man who performed this chore was considered unclean until evening. When the need arose, these ashes were used to make the "water of cleansing" (lit., the water of impurity). This water was ordained by God to remove impurity (*niddah*) which was viewed as being attached to the body. This was a lasting ordinance for the Israelites and for the resident aliens living among them. No record of the use of this water is found, however, in the historical books of the Old Testament (19:9-10).

Primarily the water of cleansing was used to purify the defilement of death. Outdoors one became impure by touching a corpse, bone, or grave. Indoors merely being in the same room where someone had died rendered a person unclean. The uncleanness lasted seven days (19:11-16).

The waters of cleansing were made by pouring living (i.e., fresh) water over the ashes of the heifer. Any person ceremonially clean could administer the cleansing. The water was sprinkled by means of a bunch of hyssop upon the tent and its furnishings where death had occurred. Unclean persons had to be sprinkled twice, on the third and seventh days of the week of uncleanness. Then the person being cleansed had to wash his clothes and bathe. He was declared clean on the evening of the seventh day. Any person who refused to purify himself was to be "cut off from the congregation" because he was guilty of defiling the sanctuary of the Lord (19:17-20).

Any person who had any connection with the water of cleansing became impure. Even the one who administered the water was considered unclean until evening. Anything touched by an unclean person became unclean, and anyone who touched that unclean object became unclean till evening (19:21-22).

The writer of Hebrews (9:11-13) refers to the ashes of the heifer and draws a parallel between the water of cleansing and the blood of Jesus. Some have seen in the red heifer outside the camp a type of Christ's death on the cross, and in the water of cleansing a type of baptism.

D. Problem of Death (Nm 20:1).

Miriam died and was buried at Kadesh. Thus ended the life of one of the truly great women of Israelite history. That no mention is made of mourning following Miriam's death is strange. Her death is dated to the first month, but of what year is not stated.

E. Problem of Water (Nm 20:2-13).

At one point in the encampment at Kadesh a shortage of water developed. The people gathered in opposition to Moses and Aaron. They wished they had died with those who had been smitten dead before the Lord rather than die by degrees in that desert (20:2-5).

Moses and Aaron went to the door of the tent and fell face down in intercessory prayer. The glory of the Lord appeared to them. Moses was told to take his rod and Aaron, gather the assembly, and *speak* to the rock. Water in abundance would come forth for the people and their livestock. *The rock* must refer to the only rock in that area (20:6-8).

When Moses addressed the congregation in front of the rock, he seemed to take credit for himself and Aaron for the miracle which was about to take place. Moses spoke when he should have been silent. Then in anger he *smote* the rock twice, when he should have spoken once. Water came forth. That ended the opposition against Moses and Aaron. Because of his arrogant indiscretion, however, God informed Moses that he would not lead the people into Canaan. This area was called Meribah ("quarreling"). This Meribah is named after the spot in the Wilderness of Sin (Ex 17:1-7) where Israel earlier had quarreled with God.

F. Problem with Neighbors (Nm 20:14-21).

Having failed to enter Canaan from the south, Israel next tried to enter from the east. From Kadesh Moses sent messengers to the king of Edom requesting permission to pass through his territory. Moses sketched the history which brought Israel to the borders of Edom. He impressed upon the Edomite king the power of Yahweh who had sent his "angel" to deliver Israel from Egypt, the most powerful people on the face of the earth. Edom should think twice before opposing this people. Moses promised that the Israelites would not stray from the "king's highway" to trample the fields or vineyards of Edom. The king responded, however, with a categorical "no." If Israel attempted to enter the narrow mountain passes, Edom would attack.

Moses dispatched other messengers who reiterated the request, but added the promise of paying for any water the livestock might drink in Edom. Again the Edomites responded negatively. They marched a powerful army to the border in a show of force designed to discourage Moses from attempting to march through that land.

PROBLEMS EN ROUTE TO CANAAN
Numbers 20:22–21:35

As the years of wilderness punishment drew to an end, Israel set out from Kadesh. They faced four problems along the way: (1) death, (2) attack, (3) detour, and (4) battle.

A. Problem of Death (Nm 20:22-29)

At Mount Hor near the border of Edom the Lord announced that Aaron would be "gathered to his people." He would not live to enter Canaan because he had rebelled against the Lord along with Moses at Meribah. In the sight of the nation Moses took Aaron and his son Eleazar to the top of the mount. He removed Aaron's high priestly garments and put them on his son. Aaron died there, and presumably was buried by Moses and Eleazar. Israel mourned for thirty days over the death of their first high priest. According to Numbers 33:38 Aaron died in the fortieth year of the Exodus, in the fifth month on the first day of the month.

B. Problem of Attack (Nm 21:1-3).

The Canaanite king of Arad attacked Israel while they were traveling along the road to Atharim (location unknown). Some Israelites were taken captive. Israel vowed to destroy the Canaanite cities of that area if God would deliver this army into their hand. The Lord listened to Israel's plea and delivered the Canaanites over to them. Israel completely destroyed their cities and named the area Hormah ("destruction"). Hormah was the place where Israel was first defeated by the Canaanites (14:45). Now that place of defeat had become a place of victory.

The chronological placement of the attack by the king of Arad and the retaliation by Israel is difficult. Some think that this attack may have come while Israel was camped at Kadesh. Numbers 33:40, however, seems to place this event between Aaron's death and Israel's departure from Mount Hor. That is also the position taken in the present text. Therefore, the Israelite attack against the Canaanite cities of the Negev must have occurred while Israel was camped at Mount Hor.

C. Problem of a Detour (Nm 21:4-20).

From Mount Hor Israel journeyed toward the Red Sea to bypass the land of Edom. This detour made for unpleasant travel through hostile desert. The people became impatient because of the way and began to speak out against God and Moses. Ignoring the miraculous daily provision of manna, they complained of no food and water. They wished they had never left Egypt (21:4-5).

To punish the murmurers, God sent poisonous snakes among the people. Many died of the painful and deadly bite of these serpents. That region even today is infested with several varieties of venomous snakes. In desperation the people turned to Moses. They acknowledged the sin of rebellion, and requested their leader to pray that the snakes might be removed from the camp. The great intercessor was only too glad to comply with their request (21:6-7).

God's plan was not to remove the cause of their suffering, but to provide a remedy for it. The solution would require both faith and obedience on the part of the stricken people. A bronze serpent was to be constructed and put on a pole where it could be seen from a distance. Someone who was bitten had only to look toward the elevated serpent to find an antidote for the deadly poison in his body (21:8-9).

The bronze snake gradually became an object of worship in Israel until it was finally destroyed in the days of Hezekiah (2 Kings 18:4). Jesus found in this episode a picture of his work on the cross. When

Christ was uplifted on the cross he provided the remedy to a far more deadly poison (John 3:14-15).

The rest of the detour was apparently uneventful. Finally Israel crossed the Zered Valley and camped alongside the Arnon River, the border between Moab and the more recently established Amorite kingdom of Sihon. To underscore the strategic importance of the Arnon, Moses quotes from "the Book of the Wars of the Lord." All that is known of this book is that it was contemporary with the author of Numbers and that it was in poetic verse. This book is not mentioned elsewhere in the Bible. That not all ancient Israelite documents were accepted as inspired of God and preserved as part of the sacred literature of the nation is clear (21:10-15).

Pressing northward from the Arnon, Israel came to Beer ("well") where God promised to give them much-needed water. The people composed a song to commemorate the digging of the well, and Moses incorporated that poetic composition into Numbers. In the valley of Moab beneath Mount Pisgah the nation camped and waited permission to pass through Amorite territory (21:16-20).

D. Problem of Battle (Nm 21:21-35).

The request made of Sihon, the Amorite king, is essentially the same request made earlier of the king of Edom. Israel wished to pass through Moab on the main north-south corridor known as the King's Highway. Sihon, however, was no more willing than the Edomites to allow such a vast throng to pass through the midst of his land. He mustered his entire army and marched out to engage Israel at Jahaz. In the ensuing battle Israel defeated Sihon and overran his land from the Arnon to the Jabbok. All the Amorite settlements were captured including the capital of Heshbon (21:21-26).

The victory over Sihon is mentioned over a dozen times by Old Testament preachers and poets. The victory was important as a confidence builder for Israel. This was Israel's first victory over an organized state. As such it was a token of the mighty conquests to come.

The territory which Israel took from Sihon had formerly belonged to the Moabites. The Amorites regarded the dislodging of Moab as a tremendous accomplishment. Amorite poets had composed a song to celebrate the victory. That ancient Amorite poem was incorporated

MAP 13
TRANSJORDAN
CAMPAIGNS
NUMBERS 21

ASHTAROTH

KINGDOM OF OG

R. YARMUK

EDREI

SECOND CAMPAIGN

R. JABBOK

JAZER

FIRST CAMPAIGN

JERICHO SHITTIM
GILGAL

KINGDOM OF SIHON

HESHBON
NEBO

BAMOTH

DIBON

AROAR

R. ARNON

AMMON

MOAB

into the sacred text (21:27-30). But why? Probably to put the Israelite victory over Sihon in proper perspective. The mighty king who had defeated Moab had been destroyed by Israel with one mighty blow.

After spying out Jazer, Moses was able to capture that city from another group of Amorites. As Israel marched on toward Bashan they encountered the armies of King Og at Edrei. The Lord gave comforting assurance that Israel would be able to defeat Og as they had defeated Sihon. And so it happened. Israel wiped out the entire army of Og and took possession of the region of Bashan.

CHAPTER THIRTY-EIGHT

The Two-Faced Prophet
Numbers 22-25

AIM: To demonstrate the sovereignty of God over the spoken word.

THEME: Speak only God's Word!

Balaam is a perplexing character! He was a non-Israelite, yet he knew the Lord. He was a soothsayer, yet he uttered some of the most magnificent prophecies in the Bible. He faithfully proclaimed God's word, yet was responsible for leading Israel into immorality.

Balaam was brought into the action by Balak the king of Moab. Having seen how Israel had crushed Sihon and Og, Balak feared that Moab would be next. The Israelites were at this time camped in the plains of Moab across from Jericho. Balak and his allies the Midianites decided to resort to magic in their effort to thwart the advance of God's people (21:1-4).

BALAAM'S DILEMMA
Numbers 22:1-20

Balak knew of a soothsayer living at Pethor near the Euphrates River. This man had the reputation of being able to bring either blessing or cursing on people by his spoken word. Twice in Numbers 22 Balak sent messengers to Balaam in an effort to persuade him to come and curse Israel.

A. First Visit of the Messengers (Nm 22:5-14).

The appeal to Balaam was carried by elders of Moab and Midian. They took with them a substantial fee for the services of this diviner. The substance of their message was this: "A people has come out of Egypt. They are very numerous. Curse them for me so that perhaps I will be able to drive them from my land." Balak hoped to immobilize Israel through the curse and thus render them powerless to resist his own army (22:5-7).

Balaam invited the dignitaries to lodge with him overnight. Apparently he was accustomed to receiving communications from Yahweh during the night. He would determine God's will with regard to the curse on Israel and give his guests answer in the morning (22:8).

God did appear to Balaam that night. He asked a question designed to make the diviner analyze the proposition of his guests: "Who are these men with you?" This question involves an element of rebuke. Balaam should have dismissed these guests and sent them on their way. He should not have encouraged them with his hospitality to think that he might yield to their offer. Ignoring the implied rebuke, Balaam repeated to God the request of Balak. Since Balaam was so obtuse that he could not see the inconsistency of the request, God spelled it out for him. He must not go with these men. He must not put a curse on a people so obviously blessed of God (22:9-12).

The next morning Balaam reported to Balak's messengers what had transpired. He blamed his negative reply on God for "Yahweh has refused to let me go with you." These words suggest that Balaam really wanted to go and earn the reward which had been offered to him. He had no personal scruples about cursing Israel, but reluctantly he must submit to the will of God. The messengers then returned to Balak to report Balaam's refusal (22:13-14).

B. Second Visit of the Messengers (Nm 22:15-21).

Balak decided in his desperation to try once again to persuade Balaam to come to him. He sent another delegation more numerous and more distinguished than the first. He promised to reward Balaam handsomely, virtually give him *carte blanche* if he would ignore whatever restraints he felt God had put on him and come to curse Israel. In the face of this greater temptation Balaam at first seemed adamant: "Even if Balak gave me his palace filled with silver and gold, I could not do anything great or small to go beyond the command of Yahweh my God."

Having made what appears to be a noble declaration, Balaam wavered. He asked these dignitaries to spend the night. He would see if perhaps God had changed his mind in the matter. This invitation suggests that Balaam did not have a high view of God's immutable will, nor did he have a personal commitment to that will. Nothing really had changed since the first offer except that his personal reward had been increased significantly. God already had expressed his will in the matter. Balaam was playing the role of a hypocrite when he indicated that he would again see what the Lord might say about the invitation (22:15-19).

God appeared again that night to Balaam. Since Balaam truly desired to go with the messengers and earn his reward, God gave him permission to do so. This is not to be interpreted as a change in the will of God. Rather God is here permitting Balaam to do what he really wanted to do so as to teach him, as well as Balak and the modern reader, a lesson (22:20).

BALAAM'S DENUNCIATION
Numbers 22:21-41

The episode of Balaam's talking donkey is humorous to everyone except Balaam. The account unfolds in three units.

A. Balaam and His Donkey (Nm 22:21-30).

Balaam was quite eager to depart with the princes of Moab. God was very angry with him, however, for Balaam intended to carry through on a curse of God's people. The angel of the Lord stood in the road to oppose him. This is reminiscent of the time when the Lord blocked the path of Moses and sought to slay him (Ex 4:24).

Three times Balaam's donkey sensed the danger in the path of disobedience and spared her master's life. Seeing the angel in the road with drawn sword, the donkey darted off into a field. Balaam had to beat the donkey to get her back on the road. In a narrow spot between two vineyard walls again the donkey saw the angel. To avoid the danger she pressed against one of the walls crushing the foot of Balaam. The irate master beat his animal again. In another narrow spot the donkey could go neither to the left or right to escape the danger, so she just laid down in the road. Balaam again beat the animal (22:21-27).

At this point the Lord opened the mouth of the donkey and the dumb beast began to speak. The animal first asked why she had been beaten. Balaam was so angry he was not shocked that the animal had spoken. If he had brought a sword with him, he would have slain the animal for making a fool of him three times. The donkey simply reminded Balaam of her years of faithful service. From her actions he should have concluded that there was danger in the path (22:28-30).

Interpreters have responded in four ways to this narrative of a talking donkey. Most regard the narrative as legendary. Others laud the narrative as containing a profound truth encapsuled in a form which could be grasped by the peoples of antiquity: he who follows his own will in opposition to that of God has less spiritual discernment than a donkey. Others have seen here an internal, subjective experience on Balaam's part. He heard the donkey talk while in a vision or dream. Finally, some emphasize the words "the Lord opened the donkey's mouth" and simply accept the event as a miracle. Peter accepted the historicity of the narrative when he wrote: "He was rebuked for his wrongdoing by a donkey — a beast without speech — who spoke with a man's voice and restrained the prophet's madness" (2 Pet 2:16).

B. Balaam and the Angel (Nm 22:31-35).

The Lord now opened Balaam's eyes just as he had earlier opened the donkey's mouth. Balaam saw the angel of the Lord standing in the road with drawn sword. In fear he bowed low and fell face down. The angel explained that Balaam's way was contrary (or reckless)

452

before him. If the donkey had not turned away, the angel would have slain Balaam in the way (22:31-33).

Balaam confessed his sin in mistreatment of his donkey. He offered to turn back since the Lord was obviously displeased with his mission. The angel told Balaam to go on with the Moabite princes. For the second time Balaam was warned to speak only what God told him to speak (22:34-35).

C. Balaam and Balak (Nm 22:36-41).

Balak received advanced word of Balaam's arrival. He went out to the border of his land at the Arnon River to meet his guest. Rather than thank Balaam for coming, Balak rebuked him for not coming sooner. Balaam warned Balak that he could speak only what God put into his mouth. The two men then went to Kiriath Huzoth where Balak offered sacrifices. To his shame, Balaam participated in the meal which followed the pagan sacrificial ritual. The next morning Balak took his diviner to Bamoth Baal (the high place of the god Baal) where he could view a part of the encampment of Israel.

BALAAM'S DECLARATIONS
Numbers 23:1-24:25

Balaam delivered four oracles while in the land of Moab. On the first three occasions he made elaborate preparation before attempting to speak a word concerning Israel. He requested that seven altars be built on the high place. The king and the diviner then offered a bull and a ram on each altar. Perhaps the intent here is to induce the Lord to give a word which would be favorable to Balak (23:1-3).

A. Balaam's First Oracle (Nm 23:1-12).

Balaam left Balak at the altars and went off alone to await a word from the Lord. God met with Balaam there, and the diviner called attention to the sacrifices he had just offered. God then put a message in Balaam's mouth, and the diviner returned to Balak and his princes to deliver the message (23:4-6).

In the oracle Balaam first set forth the proposition that he could not curse what God had not cursed. True curses are statements of

453

judgment originating in heaven; they are not conjured up in the minds of men. Balaam then went on to describe what he saw as he surveyed the encampment of Israel. He saw Israel as a special people separate from all other nations. He forecasted the increase of Israel as the dust of the earth. He concluded the oracle with a prayer that he might die as a righteous Israelite might die, obviously an allusion to a hope of life beyond the grave (23:7-10).

Balak was upset by what he heard from Balaam. He protested that he had brought the diviner to Moab to curse his enemies, and what Balaam had said amounted to a blessing. Balaam responded that the oracle was out of his control. He could only speak what the Lord put in his mouth (23:11-12).

B. Balaam's Second Oracle (Nm 23:13-26).

Balak then took Balaam to the field of Zophim on the top of Mount Pisgah. From this spot Balaam could again see only part of the Israelite encampment. The sacrificial ritual with seven altars was repeated. Again the Lord put a word in Balaam's mouth. When he returned to Balak waiting beside the altars, the king asked, "What did Yahweh say?" Not everyone who asks that question really wants to know the answer! (23:13-17).

This second oracle begins with the proposition that God is absolutely true to his word. He never lies, nor changes his mind. Balaam had received a command to bless because God had blessed Israel. Nothing Balaam said could change this blessing. Balaam could see no misfortune or misery in Israel because Yahweh their King was in their midst. The supreme proof of the divine acceptance of Israel was the fact that he had delivered them from Egyptian bondage. With God in their midst Israel had the strength of a wild ox. Sorcery and divination had no power against Israel because God was working in their midst. Israel, like a powerful young lion, would consume all enemies! (23:18-24).

Balak's patience began to wear thin. If Balaam could not curse Israel, at least let him not bless them! Balaam again reminded the king that he could communicate only what the Lord commanded (23:25-26).

C. Balaam's Third Oracle (Nm 23:27–24:14).

Balak still thought that God might allow Balaam to curse Israel. He took the diviner to the top of Peor. Balaam did not hesitate to comply with Balak's third request, proof that he wanted to accommodate his host as much as possible. On the mount the sacrificial ritual with seven altars was repeated. Missing this time was any request for Balak to stay beside the altars. Balaam did not "go out to meet the Lord" as in the first two occasions, i.e., Balaam did not resort to sorcery. As he looked out over the encampment of Israel, the Spirit of God came upon him. Thereafter Balaam's statements began with solemn *ne'um*, "oracle." This word was used by prophets to make a declaration of divine inspiration (23:27–24:2).

The oracle began with a description of Balaam's condition when he received the revelation from God. Balaam knew himself to be a different person, filled with God's Spirit. He was prostrate, but his eyes were open. He saw a vision from God and heard his words. Balaam described the impression which the sight of Israel's camp had made on him. He compared the rows of Israel's tents to valleys with streams and abundant plant life. These words were addressed to Israel (24:3-6).

In 24:7 Balaam ceased to speak to Israel, but rather about them. He pictured Israel's prosperity under the image of a man returning from a well with buckets overflowing. He foresaw a powerful king in Israel, one more powerful than Agag. He saw Israel exalted over other nations. With the strength of a wild ox Israel would devour all hostile nations. Enemies would hesitate to rouse this crouching lion. The oracle concludes with a thought taken from the promise made to Abraham: "May those who bless you be blessed, and those who curse you be cursed" (24:7-9).

Balak's anger came to a boil. He struck his hands together, not in amazement, but as a sign of contempt! He ordered Balaam to leave his land. No reward would be given this diviner who could not deliver a curse. "Yahweh has kept you from being rewarded," the king said sarcastically. Balaam reminded Balak of what he had repeatedly said, namely, that he could say only what Yahweh had revealed. Before leaving for home, however, Balaam wanted to present to Balak what Israel would do to his people "in the end of days." This phrase usually signals that some part of the succeeding prophecy embraces the age of Messiah (24:10-14).[1]

455

D. Balaam's Fourth Oracle (Nm 24:15-25).

Again Balaam began by making a strong declaration of the divine origin of what he was about to speak. Though prostrate, his eyes could see clearly the vision from the Almighty. Balaam shared in his fourth oracle the words which God had revealed to him. He went on to describe a glorious future king, one which he figuratively designated as "the star" and "the scepter." The future king would crush all the enemies of Israel. These enemies were represented in Balaam's day by Moab and Edom. Some think that the king which Balaam foresaw was David; Jewish tradition sees here a reference to the Messiah (24:15-19).[2]

The remaining portion of Balaam's final oracle seems to have the purpose of setting forth four events which must transpire before the glorious king would rise in Israel: (1) The nation of Amalek, so powerful in that day, would come to ruin. (2) The Kenites, who dwelled in safety, would be destroyed when the Assyrians took them into captivity. (3) A people would come from the west (Kittim) to subdue the Mesopotamian powers represented in the prophecy by Asshur and Eber. The reference is to the invasion of the Greek armies by Alexander the Great. (4) These Greek conquerors would themselves come to ruin. The Romans succeeded the Greeks as masters of the world. Thus the stage was set for the coming of the glorious King in Israel (24:20-24).

BALAAM'S DEGRADATION
Numbers 25:1-18

Balaam could not curse Israel. God would not let him. Nonetheless he wanted the honor and money which had been promised. So before leaving Balak he whispered a suggestion that he knew would defeat the people of God (Nm 31:16). Numbers 25 describes the outworking of Balaam's plan.

A. Israel's Filthy Behavior (Nm 25:1-5).

While Israel camped at Shittim, beautiful Midianite and Moabite women lured the men of Israel into the debasing rites of the god Baal. According to the NIV, "the men began to indulge in sexual immorality with Moabite women who invited them to the sacrifices to their gods." At their first exposure to the fertility cult of Baal, the

456

Israelites yielded. They bowed down and worshiped the Baal of Peor (25:1-3).

The Lord's anger burned against Israel. He instructed Moses to execute the leaders of the apostate people and impale them (i.e., hang their corpses over pointed poles) throughout the day before the Lord. Their exposed bodies would be a warning to others. Only by this action could the fierce wrath of God be turned away from Israel. Moses carried out these orders by instructing the judges to execute the guilty. The text does not directly indicate that these orders were carried out. Some commentators think this sentence is implicit in the text; others think that Moses was negligent in carrying out this order from God (25:4-5).

B. Phinehas's Faithful Action (Num 25:6-18).

Up to this point the men of Israel had at least respected the purity of Israel's camp. Now, however, a prince of Israel, a Simeonite named Zimri, took a Midianite princess named Cozbi into his tent "in the sight of Moses and the congregation" while they were weeping in repentance at the door of the Tabernacle. This brazen act of defiance provoked Phinehas, the grandson of Aaron. He seized a spear and followed Zimri into the tent. With one mighty blow he drove the weapon through the Israelite and into the woman's body as they were engaged in sexual immorality. This dramatic action stopped a plague which had broken out against the Israelites. Nonetheless, some 24,000 died in the plague (25:6-9), 23,000 of them in one day (1 Cor 10:8).

The Lord spoke a word of commendation to Phinehas. He was as zealous for the honor of God as was God himself. His decisive action had turned away God's anger from Israel. As a reward he and his descendants would have a covenant of lasting priesthood. This means that the high priesthood would be reckoned through Phinehas and his sons (25:10-13).

Moses then received a divine directive to regard the Midianites as enemies of Israel. This is reminiscent of the experience at Rephidim where an oath was taken that peace between Israel and Amalek would never again be possible (Ex 17:16). Cozbi and the Midianite women had deceived Israel at Peor, and for this Midian must pay the price (25:16-18).

ENDNOTES

1. See comments on Gn 49:1.
2. See James E. Smith, *What the Bible Says about the Promised Messiah* (Joplin, MO: College Press, 1984), pp. 59-64.

CHAPTER THIRTY-NINE

Unfinished Business
Numbers 26-36

AIM: To encourage faithfulness until death.

THEME: Set your house in order for you shall die!

Moses was approaching the end of his life. This fact is mentioned twice in Numbers 26-36 (27:13; 31:2). With respect to Israel's future the section is optimistic. The actions taken here were in anticipation of the conquest; the enactments were binding on future generations. In those final days Moses needed to take care of six items of unfinished business.

A CENSUS TO TAKE
Numbers 26:1-65

After the plague at Peor, the Lord gave directions to Moses and Eleazar to take another census. As in the census some thirty-eight years earlier, those twenty years old or older who were able to serve in the army were to be counted. The results of this census which was conducted in the plains of Moab are depicted in Chart 40.

Chart No. 40

CENSUS FIGURES Numbers 1, 2, 26				
TRIBE	BEFORE THE WANDERINGS	AFTER THE WANDERINGS	DIFFERENCE	%
REUBEN	46,500	43,730	-2,770	-6%
SIMEON	59,300	22,200	-37,100	-63%
GAD	45,650	40,500	-5,150	-11%
JUDAH	74,600	76,500	+1,900	+2.5%
ISSACHAR	54,400	64,300	+9,900	+18%
ZEBULUN	57,400	60,500	+3,100	+5.5%
EPHRAIM	40,500	32,500	-8,000	-20%
MANASSEH	32,200	52,700	+20,500	+63%
BENJAMIN	35,400	45,600	+10,200	+29%
DAN	62,700	64,400	+1,700	+2.5%
ASHER	41,500	53,400	+11,900	+28%
NAPHTALI	53,400	45,400	-8,000	-15%
TOTALS	603,550	601,730	-1,820	-0.3%

In comparing the two censuses the following facts become apparent: (1) The tribe of Simeon experienced a sizable decline, perhaps because the Simeonites had been leaders in the apostasy at Peor. (2) The tribe of Manasseh experienced a disproportionate increase. The reason for this is not clear. (3) The tribes here are listed in the same order as in Numbers 1, except for Manasseh and Ephraim which have exchanged places. (4) The second census differs from the first in that the various clans in each tribe are here listed. (5) Comparing the list of the heads of families who went into Egypt in 1877 BC (Gn 46:9-25) with the clans enumerated here indicates that some fluctuation in the structure of the tribes had taken place. (6) The totals in both censuses were approximately the same (a decrease of 1,820, or about .3 percent), but population of individual tribes fluctuated markedly.

The purpose of the census in Numbers 26 was to provide statistical data for the allocation of land to the various tribes in Canaan. Two principles were to guide this distribution: (1) it must be by lot and (2) it must be based on the numerical strength of each tribe. The mechanics of how these two principles were to be implemented are not detailed here, nor in 33:54 where the subject is again discussed (26:52-56).

Chart No. 41

ORGANIZATION OF THE TRIBE OF LEVI			
TRIBAL DIVISIONS	**Exodus 6 Numbers 3, 4** c. 1446 BC	**Numbers 26** c. 1406 BC	**1 Chronicles 23** c. 1000 BC
GERSHONITES	Libni Shimei 7,500	Libni	Ladan Shimei
KOHATHITES	Amram Izhar Hebron Uzziel 8,600	Hebron Korah	Amram Izhar Hebron Uzziel
MERARITES	Mahli Mushi 6,200	Mahli Mushi	Mahli Mushi
TOTALS>>>	22,000 From 1 month	23,000 From 1 month	38,000 From Age 30

As in the first census, Levites were counted separately. Again as in 3:17-33 the clans of Levi with their subdivisions are enumerated. In the earlier listing the subdivisions numbered eight; here they number five. Since in David's day the original eight subdivisions were intact (1 Chr 23), it is difficult to determine why they are not listed here. Perhaps the missing clans had supported the cause of Korah and consequently here are all lumped together under the designation Korahite clan. In any case, Moses found the number of Levites one month old and older to be 23,000, a thousand more than was found in the Sinai numbering (26:57-62).

The narrative concludes with a note identifying the location of the census as the plains of Moab. Of those counted in the earlier census only Caleb and Joshua had survived to be counted in the second. God's judgment word against the previous generation had been fulfilled (26:63-65).

AN ISSUE TO DECIDE
Numbers 27:1-11; 36:1-12

The five daughters of Zelophehad of the tribe of Manasseh came to the entrance of the tent of meeting to present a case to the leaders of the nation. Women in ancient Israel had the right to bring legal matters before the court. The issue was this: Should daughters be given inheritance rights if there was no male heir? The father of these women had died in the wilderness leaving no sons to inherit his portion in the Promised Land. The women emphasized that their father had in no way supported Korah in his rebellion. Rather he died in the wilderness "for his own sin," i.e., he had fallen under the general judgment on the nation. Why should his name disappear from the clan records merely because he had no sons? (27:1-4).

Moses sought a ruling from the Lord in this case. The Lord instructed Moses to rule in favor of the five women. They were to be given an inheritance among the relatives of their father. A general legal principle grew out of this specific case. Property passed on to nearest of kin in the following order: sons, daughters, brothers and uncles (27:5-11).

The case ruling raised some legal complications which were brought to the attention of Moses by some of the clan leaders of the tribe of Manasseh. What if women who inherited property married outside their tribe? Would not their property then pass over to another tribe? Would this not then deplete the tribal allotment of a tribe? These questions led to a further amplification of the law regarding the inheritance of daughters. Daughters who inherited property could marry anyone they pleased within the clan of their father. If the daughters chose to marry outside their tribe, they forfeited their inheritance rights. No inheritance was to pass from one tribe to another. The daughters of Zelophehad complied with this condition. They married within the clans of the descendants of Manasseh (36:1-12).

A SUCCESSOR TO APPOINT
Numbers 27:12-23

Moses received instructions to ascend Mount Pisgah (Nebo) in the Abarim range. There he was to view the Promised Land before being gathered to his people in death. To see but not enter Canaan was a punishment imposed on Moses in the Desert of Zin when he failed to honor the Lord at Meribah (27:12-14).

In the face of this death announcement, Moses' only concern was the welfare of the people. He did not want them to be like sheep without a shepherd. He prayed that the Lord would appoint a man "to go out and come in before them." This language points to the need for a military leader. To the end, and even under judgment, Moses had the heart of a pastor (27:15-17).

The census officially enrolled the second generation; the daughters of Zelophehad were the successors to their father. Moses also needed a successor, and the new generation needed a new leader. The Lord chose Joshua for this task, and in so doing again underscored the certainty of Israel's agenda. Joshua's natural qualifications were not what commended him for this position of leadership. He was supernaturally prepared, for the Spirit of the Lord was in him (28:18).

Joshua was to stand before Eleazar the high priest and the entire assembly. Moses was to lay his hand upon him in a ceremony of ordination. Thus would some of Moses' authority be put on Joshua, and the community would thereafter obey his directives. Joshua, however, would not have access to the presence of the Lord as had Moses. He would have to obtain divine decisions through the Urim and Thummim stones carried by Eleazar in or on his breastplate. The exact means by which these stones revealed the will of God is not known (27:19-21).

Moses carried out the instructions regarding Joshua. His enthusiasm for his successor is indicated in that he did not just lay one hand upon him as directed in verse 18, but both hands (27:22-23).

463

INSTRUCTIONS TO PASS ON
Numbers 28:1–30:16

Before he went to meet his Maker, Moses felt the need to communicate with the people some regulations. These regulations pertained
to the areas of sacrifice and women's vows.

A. Instructions Regarding Sacrifices (Nm 28:1–29:40).

The divine origin of the sacrificial system is again underscored in
the opening verses of Numbers 28. Sacrifices are figuratively called
"food." The burning of this food upon the altar by God-fearing worshipers created an aroma pleasing to the Lord (28:1-2). The sacrifices
prescribed periodically in Israel can be summarized as follows:

1. Daily two lambs were to be offered, one in the morning and the
other in the evening. The offering of each lamb was to be accompanied with a grain offering (flour mixed with olive oil) and a drink offering of wine which was poured out before the Lord. This was known
as the regular burnt offering (28:3-8).

2. Weekly on the Sabbath day an additional two lambs with appropriate grain and drink offerings were offered (28:9-10).

3. On the first day of the month a burnt offering of two bulls, one
ram and seven lambs was made. Grain and drink offerings varying in
size accompanied these offerings. In addition, a male goat was offered
on the new moon for a sin offering. Some scholars believe that the
new moon was celebrated quarterly rather than monthly (28:11-15).

The special sacrifices required at the annual festivals are next delin-
eated. Essentially, certain days during the annual festivals were treated
as Sabbath days and the prescribed offerings were made: a burnt
offering of two bulls, a ram and seven lambs with proportionate grain
and drink offerings. This was true for each of the seven days of the
Feast of Unleavened Bread (28:16-25), and the Feast of Weeks
(28:26-31). On the Feast of Trumpets (29:1-6) and Day of Atonement (29:7-11) only one bull was required.

During each of the seven days of the Feast of Tabernacles fourteen
lambs, two rams, and a male goat for a sin offering were required,
along with a descending number of bulls. Thirteen bulls were offered
on the first day, seven on the seventh day. The day after the week-

long celebration of Tabernacles was also regarded as a Sabbath. A bull, a ram, and seven lambs were presented as a burnt offering and a male goat as a sin offering (29:12-38). This one feast accounted for a large percentage of the total annual sacrificial requirement of bulls (59%), rams (40%) and goats (36%).

Chart 42 depicts the regular communal sacrifices required under the Law. These figures do not include freewill and votive offerings.

Chart No. 42

REQUIRED COMMUNAL OFFERINGS				
	BURNT OFFERINGS			**SIN OFFERING**
Occasion	**Bulls**	**Rams**	**Lambs**	
Daily (x 364)*			728	
Sabbath (x 52)			104	
New Moon (x 4)*	8	4	28	4
Unleavened Bread (x 7)	14	7	49	7
Pentecost	2	1	7	1
Trumpets	1	1	7	1
Atonement	1	1	7	1
Tabernacles	71	15	105	8
Annual Totals >>>	**97**	**29**	**1035**	**22**

*Based on the so-called Jubilee Calendar which postulates a year consisting of thirteen months of twenty-eight days each, yielding a total of 364 days in a year. The chart assumes that New Moon was a quarterly rather than a monthly celebration.

B. Instructions Regarding Vows (Nm 30:1-16).

Three principles govern this section of Numbers: (1) vows are binding, (2) a vow or pledge must be reported to one's immediate superior, and (3) persons in authority can cancel commitments made by subordinates. Thus, a father could overrule the vow of an unmarried daughter, and the Lord would release her from that vow. A husband could nullify the vow of his wife. If, however, the father or the husband said nothing immediately after hearing of the vow, then the terms of the vow stood. The woman was obligated to fulfill the terms of her vow. Any vow taken by a woman living alone (e.g., a widowed or divorced woman) was binding.

A BATTLE TO FIGHT
Numbers 31:1-54

Just before his death, Moses received a divine directive to take vengeance on the Midianites for the trouble caused at Peor. After this matter of unfinished business was concluded Moses would be gathered to his people. "Vengeance" here does not mean revenge; it is the legitimate expression of divine authority when that authority is challenged. Israel here was to be the tool of God's justice (31:1-2).

In response to this command, Moses mobilized an army of twelve thousand, one thousand from each tribe. To underscore that this was a holy war, Phinehas the priest accompanied the army. He took with him some of the holy vessels from the Tabernacle and the silver trumpets to use in signaling the host (31:3-6).

The Israelites won a decisive victory over the Midianites. The five kings of Midian were killed in the battle. Balaam, who apparently had not returned to his home in Pethor, also was slain. The towns of Midian were plundered and then burned. The Midianite women and children and livestock were taken as plunder back to the camp (31:7-12).

Numbers 31 does not go into detail about the actual battle. The chapter primarily has a legal function. Moses set forth the necessary cleansing of an army returning from battle and the laws that governed the division of spoils. These matters had to be settled at this point, for Israel soon would be engaged in extended warfare in Canaan.

The leaders of Israel met the returning army outside the camp. Moses was furious when he saw that the Midianite women had been spared. These women had followed Balaam's advice and turned the men of Israel away from the Lord with their wiles. Their enticement had resulted in a plague against Israel at Peor. If anyone deserved to die, they did. On the theory that any Midianite woman who had experienced sexual relations had participated in the immoral rites of Baal, Moses ordered them executed. The young males were also to be executed lest when they reached maturity they would be especially vengeful toward Israel. Only the virgin maidens were spared to become house servants in Israel (31:13-18).

The soldiers had been rendered unclean by contact with corpses during the battle. Moses required them, and the captives as well, to remain outside the camp for seven days. On the third and seventh days they had to purify themselves by washing. Eleazar stipulated that spoils should be cleansed by fire where possible as well as washed with the water of cleansing. Only after seven days of purification could the soldiers return to the camp (31:19-24).

The Lord himself gave the directions as to how the spoils of victory were to be divided. First, all the captive women and animals were to be counted. Half of these were to be given to the soldiers. From their share the soldiers were to give tribute to the Lord of one out of every five hundred in each category of captives. Eleazar would receive this tribute on behalf of the Lord and use it for the upkeep of the priesthood. From the half of spoil which belonged to the people, one in fifty was given as tribute to the Lord. This portion was given to the Levites for their upkeep (31:25-47). The specifics regarding this booty are set forth in Chart 43.

Chart No. 43

DIVISION OF MIDIANITE SPOILS				
CATEGORY	WARRIORS' PORTION	LORD'S PORTION	PEOPLE'S PORTION	LORD'S PORTION
Sheep	337,500	675	337,500	6,750
Cattle	36,000	72	36,000	720
Donkeys	30,500	61	30,500	610
Virgins	16,000	32	16,000	320
Totals	420,000	840	420,000	8,400

The commanders of thousands and hundreds counted their men and found that none were missing in battle. They were moved by this miracle to bring a special offering to the Lord of the spoils of the battle. The gold brought to Moses weighed 16,750 shekels or about 420 pounds. The golden items (bracelets, earrings and the like) were kept in the tent of meeting as a memorial for the Israelites before the Lord (31:48-54).

THE LAND TO APPORTION
Numbers 32:1–35:34

The material in this unit of Numbers is concerned with apportioning the land which Israel would shortly claim as its own. Six matters are treated here.

A. A Special Tribal Request (Nm 32:1-42).

The Reubenites and Gadites had large herds and flocks. They noted that the region of Gilead which had already fallen to Israel was ideal for raising cattle. They came to Moses and the other leaders of the nation requesting that they might be permitted to claim this region for their tribal inheritance. They had no desire to cross the Jordan into Canaan (32:1-5).

Moses was obviously angry with this request. In his reply to the Gadites and Reubenites he made the following points: (1) For their countrymen to go to war in Canaan while they sat idle in Transjordan would be unfair. (2) By choosing to remain in Transjordan they were discouraging the others from claiming the Promised Land beyond Jordan. (3) The wandering in the wilderness was punishment for the discouragement which the negative report of the spies had produced at Kadesh. (4) They were a "brood of sinners" like their fathers and their proposal would make God even more angry with Israel. (5) They would be at fault if Israel refused to follow God into Canaan and consequently meet with destruction in the wilderness (32:6-15).

The petitioners put the whole matter in a different light when they explained their plan. They would build pens for the livestock and leave their women and children in Transjordan. They would be glad to cross over to help their brethren conquer Canaan. When the war was over they would return to their homes east of Jordan (32:16-19).

On condition that they would fight with their brethren until the land was conquered, Moses granted the request of the two tribes. If they failed to stand by their brethren until the land was divided, they would be sinning. They could be sure that their sin would find them out! Once again the two tribes committed themselves to fight with their brothers. Moses then gave orders to Eleazar and Joshua to give Gilead to the Gadites and Reubenites if they fought for Israel (32:23-32).

Apparently half of the tribe of Manasseh decided to join Gad and Reuben in this land request. The clan of Makir within the tribe of Manasseh had been instrumental in conquering a part of Gilead. Two of their commanders, Jair and Nobah, had conquered various settlements there and renamed them after themselves. Thus did the former kingdoms of Sihon and Og come to be the possession of the two and half tribes. A number of cities were built or rebuilt to protect the women and children while most of the men crossed the Jordan (32:33-42).

B. Israel's Camping Itinerary (Nm 33:1-49).

Numbers 33 contains a parenthetical list of the stages in the journey from Egypt to the plains of Moab. Not all the camping spots are here listed. Most of those which are named cannot be located with certainty. Not counting the starting place (Rameses) and the endpoint (the plains of Moab), forty names are listed, possibly one name for each of the forty years of wandering. Sixteen of the places mentioned here are not found elsewhere in the Pentateuch.

The list divides Israel's wilderness journey into three phases: (1) from Rameses to Sinai — eleven stages (33:5-15); (2) from Sinai to Kadesh — twenty-one stages (33:16-36); and (3) from Kadesh to the plains of Moab — nine stages (33:37-49). Phase one covered three months, phase two several months, and phase three the last year of the wandering.

Why the list appears in this location in the book is not clear. Numbers 33 is the only chapter in this section which is oriented toward the past. Perhaps the list is intended to reinforce the thought that God had guided them thus far in their travels, and would continue to do so as they moved across Jordan.

C. Apportionment of the Land (Nm 33:50–34:29).

In the plains of Moab the Lord gave to Moses some general instructions regarding the apportionment of the land. The Israelites first had the task of driving out the inhabitants of Canaan and removing all their pagan objects and shrines. They should not hesitate to take Canaan, for God had given it to them. Once they controlled the land they were to distribute it by lot to the tribes.

Moses warned Israel that if they failed to drive out the Canaanites they would make life miserable for God's people. Furthermore, should Israel fail to do as God directed to the inhabitants of the land, then God would do to Israel as he had intended to do to their enemies.

Numbers 34 describes the borders of the Promised Land. Not all the geography here is clear, but this much can be said: The western boundary was the Mediterranean Sea. Lebo Hamath was the northernmost point and Kadesh the southernmost. The Jordan River formed the eastern boundary. This was the area which was to be apportioned to the nine and a half tribes.

The Lord revealed to Moses the names of the men who were to serve on the apportionment committee. Eleazar and Joshua were to be co-chairmen. One representative from each of the ten tribes affected by the apportionment also served on the committee.

D. Designated Cities (Nm 35:1-34).

The Levites were to be given towns within the tribal areas. A thousand cubits (1500 feet) surrounding each of these towns was designated as part of the town. An additional two thousand cubits (3000 feet) on all sides of the town served as pasturage (35:1-5).

Six towns of the forty-eight given to Levites were to be designated cities of refuge. A person guilty of manslaughter could flee to one of these cities and find refuge until he stood trial. Three of these towns were on the east of Jordan, and three on the west. Those guilty of deliberate murder could not be spared in the city of refuge. The avenger of blood, a near kinsman of the dead man, would put him to death (35:6-21).

One who was judged to have taken a life accidentally was required to remain for his own protection in the city of refuge until the death of the high priest. If he ventured outside the walls of the city, the avenger of blood could execute him without being culpable (35:22-28).

Attached to this provision for cities of refuge are other laws bearing on murder. More than one witness was required before a man could be executed for murder. No ransom could be accepted for the life of a murderer. This implies that a ransom might be accepted when other capital crimes had been committed. In other words, the judges had some discretion in certain capital cases (e.g., kidnapping), but not when the offense was murder. The general principle here is that bloodshed polluted the land. Only by the shed blood of the murderer could there be an atonement for the land. Otherwise the land became defiled and God could not dwell there. Once again the ultimate concern here is the purity of the land. Failing to execute murderers polluted and defiled the land! (35:29-34).

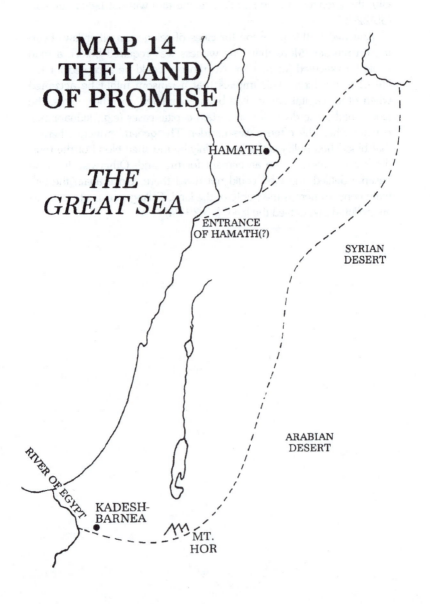

MAP 14
THE LAND
OF PROMISE

THE
GREAT SEA

HAMATH

ENTRANCE
OF HAMATH(?)

SYRIAN
DESERT

ARABIAN
DESERT

RIVER OF EGYPT

KADESH-
BARNEA

MT.
HOR

THE BOOK OF
DEUTERONOMY

CHAPTER FORTY

Getting Acquainted with Deuteronomy

AIM: To demonstrate that Deuteronomy forms a fitting conclusion to the ministry of Moses.

THEME: Obedience is essential!

The fifth of the "five scrolls" was named in the Greek Old Testament, *Deuteronomion*, "second law." This name is derived from the fact that Moses repeated and at times adjusted the Law just before his death. Some Rabbis called Deuteronomy "The Book of Exhortations," but most referred to it by the first key word *debharim*, "words."

The importance of Deuteronomy can be seen in the frequency with which it was quoted in the Dead Sea Scrolls and in the New Testament. When he was tempted, Jesus responded to the Devil in each instance with a quotation from Deuteronomy (Matt 4:4,7,10). When he was asked which was the first and greatest commandment (Matt 22:37f.), he cited Deuteronomy (6:5). He referred to specific points of the Law as formulated in Deuteronomy on several occasions (e.g., Matt 18:16; 19:8; 22:24).

AUTHORSHIP OF DEUTERONOMY

Deuteronomy has always been a battleground between those who accept the Bible's own view of itself, and those who have a contrary view. Two radically different opinions regarding the origin of Deuteronomy are current.

A. Claims of the Book.

According to Ridderbos, "Deuteronomy presents a clearer self-witness concerning its authorship than any of the other books of the Pentateuch."[1] The book presents itself as being the record of discourses spoken by Moses just before his death (1:5; 5:1; 29:2). In addition the actual writing of this material is attributed to Moses: "So Moses wrote this law, and delivered it unto the priests . . . and unto all the elders of Israel" (31:9). "This law" certainly includes Deuteronomy, and perhaps, as Keil thinks, the entire Pentateuch.[2]

B. Claims of the Critics.

Deuteronomy plays a key role in the critical reconstruction of Old Testament history. The basic contention of this theory is that Deuteronomy was a forgery created just prior to the great reformation of King Josiah over seven hundred years after the death of Moses. The priests pretended to discover this book in the Temple in 621 BC and it was then palmed off on the king and the gullible public as an ancient work of Moses (2 Kings 22). While more recent critics have acknowledged the antiquity of many of the laws in this book, few have dated this material to the age of Moses. To interact with these critical views is beyond the scope of this survey. Suffice it to say that conservative scholars have called attention to a host of details in Deuteronomy which undergird its claims to emanate from Moses.[3]

SETTING OF DEUTERONOMY

The first address in Deuteronomy is dated to the fortieth year of the Exodus, the eleventh month and the first day of the month.

According to Joshua 4:19 Israel crossed the Jordan river into Canaan in the forty-first year after leaving Egypt, the first month and the tenth day. This would be about seventy days after Moses' first address. Subtracting the thirty days of mourning following Moses' death (34:8), leaves roughly forty days for the addresses of Deuteronomy. This chronological scheme is set forth in Chart 44.

Chart No. 44

CHRONOLOGY OF DEUTERONOMY		
Deuteronomy 1:3	Deuteronomy 34:8	Joshua 4:19
Moses' First Address	Mourning for Moses	Israel Crossed Jordan
40/11/1		41/1/10

About Forty Days
Seventy Days

No new characters are introduced in this book. In his addresses, however, Moses does refer to a number of characters who were encountered earlier. Besides Moses himself, fifteen others are mentioned here. The listing below is included for review purposes.

1. Sihon	6. Caleb	11. Aaron
2. Og	7. Joshua	12. Eleazar
3. Abraham	8. Esau	13. Dathan
4. Isaac	9. Lot	14. Abiram
5. Jacob	10. Pharaoh	15. Balaam

The geographical setting for the entire Book of Deuteronomy is the plains of Moab opposite Jericho east of Jordan. Israel was camped in the valley near Beth Peor (3:29; 4:46) in a region known as the Arabah (1:1). Through the course of his addresses, however, Moses reviewed the entire history of the journey from Egypt. The maps included in the comments on Exodus and Numbers will be helpful in reviewing this material.

In the Book of Numbers the people finally arrived at the border of the Promised Land after forty years in the wilderness. In Deuteronomy Moses prepared them to enter that land. Seven factors made Deuteronomy necessary. (1) A new generation had arisen. (2) A new land filled with gross religious corruption was before them. (3) New dangers confronted them. (4) The new prospects, however, were for settlement at last in a homeland. (5) Militarily, economically and spiritually, new challenges faced God's people. (6) The transition from seminomadic to agricultural life necessitated the promulgation of new duties. (7) A new leader was about to emerge.

PURPOSE OF DEUTERONOMY

Some disagreement exists regarding the main purpose of Deuteronomy. To call it a law-book is a bit simplistic, although law is found in the book. Deuteronomy is not a commentary on the Law, nor is it an apologetic for that Law. The historic reality of the Sinai experience is assumed throughout. What then is the relation of Deuteronomy to the Law?

To a limited extent, Deuteronomy is a reshaping of the Law. On the eve of entering Canaan, adjustments in certain obligations were necessary. Deuteronomy indicates that some aspects of the Law were intended only for the wilderness period.

Deuteronomy aims at an internalization of God's Law. Moses was seeking to implant within his people the will to live by God's Law. The summarization of the Law in terms of loving God with heart, soul and mind (10:12f.) is a major contribution of this book. By this emphasis Deuteronomy was opposing all forms of legalism which might grow up around the Law of God.

The book serves to underscore the necessity of obedience to God's Law. The abiding lesson of Deuteronomy is that *obedience is essential* — essential to health, happiness and heaven itself.

DESCRIPTION OF DEUTERONOMY

The Book of Deuteronomy can be summarized in the caption "Preaching and Pleading." Here Moses poured out his heart in urging

Israel to be faithful to the Lord. The book contains thirty-four chapters, 958 verses, and 28,461 words. Almost every verse in the book is filled with exhortation, instruction, warning or promise. Deuteronomy speaks of the past but not with the purpose of presenting a chronicle. Rather Moses reminded his auditors of selected events which then become the basis for exhortation and warning in the present.

While Deuteronomy speaks of the past, it focuses on the future. The book possesses a Janus-like quality. Deuteronomy looks back to Sinai; it looks forward to the entrance to the Promised Land, and beyond that, to the ultimate salvation of God's people. The laws set forth here are clearly intended for the settlement period; the warnings point to the dangers which will be faced in the new land. The ultimate goal of the speaker/writer is to ensure that Israel will enjoy a long and prosperous possession of the Promised Land. The book emphasizes that God's covenant is offered anew to each generation. Commitment is the key to appropriating the benefits of that covenant.

According to 1:5 Moses began to expound (be'er) the Law to Israel. Like a master teacher, Moses was seeking to clarify and interpret the Law received at Sinai in order to ensure its proper understanding by the people. The theme of Deuteronomy is *the instruction of the nation.* Moses sets forth here in no uncertain terms the consequences of both obedience and disobedience. This material then is popular rather than technical. For this reason Deuteronomy is the version of the Law which has been most widely quoted over the centuries. This book must be regarded as one of the most influential ever written.[4]

Several verses have been nominated as the key verse in Deuteronomy. Since Jesus found in the fourfold obligation of the following passage the first and greatest commandment, it surely must top the list of outstanding verses: *"And now, Israel, what does the Lord your God require of you, but to fear the Lord your God, to walk in all his ways, and to love him, and to serve the Lord your God with all your heart and with all your soul, to keep the commandments of the Lord, and his statutes, which I command you this day for your good?"* (10:12f.).

The primary literary form in Deuteronomy is the address. In Exodus, Leviticus, and Numbers the Lord spoke to Moses or through

Moses to the people. Here Moses himself addressed Israel. The viewpoint of the book is that of a sermon, "a farewell message, by a wise and devoted leader."[5] Deuteronomy is written in a flowing oratorical style which makes constant appeal to motives and emotions. It is meant to move its readers and its hearers.[6] Moses' second discourse (chs. 5–26) has been ranked alongside the discourses of Demosthenes and Cicero!

In addition to the addresses the book contains a song (ch. 32), a blessing (ch. 33) and bits of historical narrative (4:41-49; 1:1-5; 34:1-12). While repetition is evident in Deuteronomy, the book is far from a verbatim copy of the preceding books. Deuteronomy has its own character both in form and in content. The book is more prophetic and religious than juridical. It is also more personal. Here Moses speaks like a father who earnestly and lovingly admonishes his children.

STRUCTURE OF DEUTERONOMY

Scholars have noted a similarity in the structure of Deuteronomy and the pattern which is observable in vassal treaties from the ancient Near East.[7] These treaties consisted of six component parts: (1) preamble (cf. 1:1-5), (2) historical prologue (cf. 1:6–4:43), (3) general stipulations (cf. 5:1–11:32), (4) specific stipulations (cf. 12:1–26:14), (5) divine witnesses invoked (cf. 26:15-19), (6) blessings and curses (cf. chs. 27–28).

Scholars differ as to how many addresses of Moses are recorded in Deuteronomy. Popular suggestions range from one to ten. The variety among the superscriptions makes it difficult to lay much emphasis on the scope of each speech. A fourfold breakdown of the speech section is perhaps best.

A. First Address (Dt 1–4).

Following an introduction to the book, Moses' first speech begins in 1:6. This speech brought to remembrance the history of Israel since they had left Egypt. The narrative material has been carefully selected to describe the historical situation and to lay the foundation for the theological argument which is developed in the rest of the book. The emphasis is upon God's providential care (chs. 1–3).

The purpose of the opening historical review is made clear in chapter 4. Israel had experienced both God's wrath and mercy. Moses was earnest and eloquent in his appeal to Israel to learn from their past, to enter into the Promised Land so that they might enjoy God's blessings (4:1-40). A new generation, a new leadership, and the prospect of a new land demanded a new application of the Sinai covenant. In conclusion Moses appointed three cities of refuge on the east side of Jordan (4:41-49).

B. Second Address (Dt 5-26).

Chapter 5 begins with a new introduction, but in fact the chapter is set in the same context as chapter 1. Moses addressed all Israel in order to explain the "statutes and ordinances" just before the entrance into Canaan. He repeated the Decalogue because it provides the basis of all the Mosaic legislation. Moses also set forth in detail his own role as mediator of God's revelation.

In chapters 6-11 Moses preached to the people. He chose as his text events in Israel's history, events which, with the exception of Sinai, were not mentioned in chapters 1-4. The appeal to obey the covenant is here as in the earlier chapters, but with even greater intensity. He then stressed (1) the duty of avoiding idolatry, and (2) the need of humility before God that they might not fall into the sin of self-righteousness and be destroyed as their fathers had been (chs. 7-11).

Chapters 12-26 contain legal material. Several laws are re-formulated to reflect the new situation in Canaan. Moses first set forth laws regarding religion. Only one sanctuary was to be tolerated. All idolaters were to be cut off. Regulations respecting clean and unclean animals were to be enforced. Three great feasts were to be observed: Passover, Weeks, and Tabernacles (12:1-16:17).

The laws pertaining to political life were next expounded. The authority of judges and priests was set forth. Methods of procedure in courts of justice were defined. The law of witnesses, cities of refuge and war were made known (16:18-20:20).

Laws respecting social and domestic relations came next. Moses discussed crimes against society, relations of husband and wife, humanity towards brethren, treatment of servants, vows, trespasses, divorce, charity, and matters of individual character (chs. 21-26).

481

C. Third and Fourth Addresses (Dt 27–30).

In his third address Moses provided for a covenant renewal in the Promised Land (chs. 27–28). The Law was to be preserved, a perpetual memorial and reminder to be placed upon great stones when the nation had passed over Jordan (ch. 27). Moses then stipulated the blessings of obedience, and the cursing upon disobedience (ch. 28).

In his fourth address Moses called for renewal of commitment (chs. 29–30). Here Moses gave his last exhortations to obey the Lord.

D. Appendix (Dt 31–34).

Chapters 31–34 constitute a kind of appendix to Deuteronomy. In chapter 31 Moses ceased preaching and entered into a series of actions. He fixed his addresses in written form (v. 9), commissioned Joshua as his successor, and deposited the Law beside the ark. A routine is established for the reading of the Law in future generations (v. 12). The chapter concludes with an introduction to the Song of Moses which the Lawgiver taught the people as a testimony against their future disobedience.

The Song of Moses (ch. 32) contrasts the faithfulness of God with the faithlessness of Israel. In this poem Moses offered a prophetic interpretation of history which encompassed past, present and future. The Song is not addressed to Moses' contemporaries, but to that future disobedient generation which would provoke God's wrath in the Promised Land.

The blessing of Moses (ch. 33) contains no exhortation or warnings. The Lawgiver simply invokes God's blessing upon his people for the future. Again the perspective is prophetic as Moses surveyed the future of his people. The poem begins with the fact that the kingdom of God has been founded. It concludes with a reference to Yahweh himself as the ultimate and eternal refuge of his people. A redeemed people have a blessed future! God's purposes will prevail in spite of the behavior of one or the other generation of his people.

The final chapter of Deuteronomy narrates the death of Moses and the assumption of leadership by Joshua. Before his death Moses was allowed to view the Promised Land. His work is evaluated. Moses was not to be remembered with grave-side tributes on the anniversary of his death. He was to be revered through the reading of the Law which he had recorded.

Chart No. 45[8]

STRUCTURE OF DEUTERONOMY				
("The Instruction of the Nation")				
First Discourse	Second Discourse	Third Discourse	Fourth Discourse	Last Words
Review of the Journey	Restatement of the Law	Reemphasis of Responsibility	Renewal of Commitment	Reminder of Duty
Chs. 1–4	Chs. 5–26	Chs. 27–28	Chs. 29–30	Chs. 31–34

TEACHING OF DEUTERONOMY

Three fundamental truths are taught in Deuteronomy. The first is that Yahweh is unique. "Hear, O Israel: The Lord our God is one Lord" (6:4). Besides him there is no other (4:35). Yahweh is God of gods, and Lord of lords, the great God, mighty and awesome (10:17). Therefore, he detests images (7:25).

The second fundamental truth is that Israel is a unique people. "For you are a holy people unto the Lord your God: the Lord your God has chosen you to be a special people unto himself, above all people that are upon the face of the earth" (7:6). God would not abandon nor destroy this people for he had made a commitment to their forefathers by an oath (4:31). "He brought us out from thence, that he might bring us in, to give us the land which he swore unto our fathers" (6:23).

A third fundamental truth is that a unique relationship existed between God and Israel. Israel had entered into a covenant with Yahweh (29:13). Yahweh was their father (32:6). Israel must therefore love and not merely fear him (6:5) "And now, Israel, what does the Lord your God require of you, but to fear the Lord you God, to walk in all his ways, and to love him, and to serve the Lord your God with all your heart and with all your soul, to keep the commandments

483

of the Lord, and his statutes, which I command you this day for your good" (10:12f.).[9]

Analyzing the emphasis on obedience in Deuteronomy, Griffith Thomas[10] offers the following:

1. The necessity of obedience: the Law of God.
2. The motive for obedience: the goodness of God.
3. The standard of obedience: the word of God.
4. The incentive to obedience: the faithfulness of God.
5. The alternative to obedience: the justice of God.

Christologically, Deuteronomy presents one outstanding personal Messianic prediction. God indicated to Moses that he would raise up a prophet like unto Moses (Dt 18:14-20). Peter and Stephen both saw in this prophecy a reference to Jesus (Acts 3:22,23; 7:37). The cities of refuge (19:1-13) and the kinsman redeemer (25:1-10) are regarded by some as types of Christ.

ENDNOTES

1. J. Ridderbos, *Deuteronomy*, Bible Student's Commentary (Grand Rapids: Zondervan, 1984), p. 19.

2. C.F. Keil, *The Pentateuch*, Biblical Commentary on the Old Testament, trans. James Martin (Grand Rapids: Eerdmans, 1959), III:518.

3. See, e.g., Gleason Archer, *A Survey of Old Testament Introduction* (Chicago: Moody, 1964), pp. 241-250; G.T. Manley, *The Book of the Law* (Grand Rapids: Eerdmans, 1957); and J.W. McGarvey, *The Authorship of Deuteronomy* (Cincinnati: Standard, 1902).

4. Eason, *New Bible Survey*, p. 106.

5. Ibid., p. 107.

6. Dwight E. Stevenson, *Preaching on the Books of the Old Testament* (New York: Harper, 1961), p. 43.

7. Meredith Kline, *Treaty of the Great King* (Grand Rapids: Eerdmans, 1963).

8. Adapted from Phillips, *Exploring*, pp. 44-48.

9. Hendriksen, *Survey*, p. 230; Gerald H. Twombly, *An Analytical Survey of the Bible* (Winona Lake, IN: BMH Books, 1975), pp. 30f.

10. Griffith Thomas, *Pentateuch,* pp. 166f.

BIBLIOGRAPHY: THE BOOK OF DEUTERONOMY

Clements, R.E. *God's Chosen People: A Theological Interpretation of the Book of Deuteronomy.* London: SCM, 1968.

Craigie, P.C. *The Book of Deuteronomy.* The New International Commentary on the Old Testament. Grand Rapids: Eerdmans, 1976.

Kline, Meredith. *The Treaty of the Great King.* Grand Rapids: Eerdmans, 1963.

McGarvey, J.W. *The Authorship of Deuteronomy.* Cincinnati: Standard, 1902.

Manley, G.T. *The Book of the Law.* Grand Rapids: Eerdmans, 1957.

Mays, A.D.H. "Deuteronomy." In *The New Century Bible.* Grand Rapids: Eerdmans, 1981.

Nicholson, E.W. *Deuteronomy and Tradition.* Philadelphia: Fortress, 1967.

Oberst, Bruce. *Deuteronomy.* Bible Study Textbook Series. Joplin: College Press, 1968.

Ridderbos, J. *Deuteronomy.* Bible Student's Commentary. Grand Rapids: Zondervan, 1984.

Rider, J. *Deuteronomy with Commentary.* Philadelphia: The Jewish Publishing Society, 1937.

Smith, George Adam. "The Book of Deuteronomy." In *The Cambridge Bible for Schools and Colleges.* Cambridge University Press, 1918.

Thompson, J.A. *Deuteronomy, An Introduction and Commentary.* Tyndale Old Testament Commentaries. Downers Grove, IL: Inter-Varsity, 1974.

von Rad, G. *Deuteronomy, A Commentary.* Old Testament Library. Philadelphia: Westminster, 1966.

CHAPTER FORTY-ONE

A Time to Remember
Deuteronomy 1:1-4:43

AIM: To demonstrate the value of remembering what God has done for his people.

THEME: Looking backward!

The first five verses of Deuteronomy constitute an introduction to the entire book. The contents of this book are described as the "words of Moses" (1:1) in which he "proclaimed" (1:3) all that the Lord had commanded him concerning Israel. Moses was a man under orders. By passing on these instructions he was exemplifying the obedience which he exhorted in his people. Moses "expounded" or "taught" (1:5) the law, i.e., he made it absolutely clear to them.

The recipients of the message are identified as "all Israel" (1:1). This phrase, which appears elsewhere in the Pentateuch only twice, is used fourteen times in Deuteronomy. It underscores the unity of the nation.

The chronology of Moses' words is specified in terms of the Exodus. The speech is dated to the fortieth year, eleventh month, the first day (1:3). This is the only exact date given in the book. Eventwise, the speech comes after the defeat of Sihon and Og, the Amorite kings who ruled east of Jordan (1:4). Some victories had already been experienced, and Moses anticipated further victories in the near future.

The location of the events in Deuteronomy is given in some detail. Israel was at this time camped in the territory of Moab, in an area known as the Arabah (1:1). The exact location of all the sixteen geographical proper names mentioned in this brief introduction is not certain.

The introduction contains one parenthetical note of importance. The travel time from Horeb to Kadesh by the Mt. Seir road normally was eleven days (1:2). Theoretically, Israel could have been in Canaan shortly after leaving Sinai. Now some thirty-eight years later they still had not claimed their inheritance.

Moses' first address consists of two unequal parts. He began with a review of Israel's journey, and concluded with a comparatively short exhortation to obedience. At the conclusion of the address he announced the appointment of three cities of refuge.

BASIC REVIEW
Deuteronomy 1:6–3:29

Moses' first address consisted mainly of a review of some of the major events of the past forty years. The Lawgiver presented the history of Israel from Horeb to Moab. Moses was looking backward. The material here, however, is interpretive and not merely repetitive. New bits of information and explanation are offered. These are indicated in the paragraphs below by an *asterisk* (*). Experiences associated with seven different areas are reported in this section.

The purpose of this section is to underscore that what God had done in the past he could continue to do in the future. Three times the divine charge had come to enter and possess Canaan — at Sinai (1:6), at Kadesh (1:19), and in Moab (3:18). With God's help they could do it!

God had been faithful, and he demanded faithfulness on the part of his people. This speech emphasizes, however, that the Israelites tended constantly toward unfaithfulness. The successes of the past were a cause for hope in the future; the failures provided a warning.

A. At Horeb (Dt 1:6-18).

After a long stay at Horeb/Sinai God ordered Israel to break camp and march toward Canaan. Concerning that land the Lord made the following points: (1) The land was vast, stretching from the Negev in southern Palestine to the upper reaches of the Euphrates. (2) Canaan was occupied by hostile peoples. (3) The land had already been given to Israel. (4) Nonetheless, the land would have to be conquered by Israel. (5) The land was part of the promise of God to their forefathers (1:6-8).

Prior to leaving Horeb it was necessary to organize the people. The reference here is to what is recorded in Exodus 18, not Numbers 11. God had blessed Israel with numerical growth, and *Moses prayed for even greater growth. At the same time, *Moses realized that he could not by himself bear all the responsibilities of leadership over such a large group. *He freely admitted this and suggested *that the people select wise, discerning, and experienced men who could be appointed to leadership positions. *They saw the wisdom in this. *Moses then appointed (1) commanders, (2) administrative officers (*shoterim*) who served as judges. *He instructed the latter in their responsibilities, and agreed to hear any cases which might prove too difficult for them. No mention is made of Jethro's role in this organization (1:9-18).

B. At Kadesh (Dt 1:19-46).

After traversing a hundred miles of great and terrible wilderness, Israel arrived at Kadesh. The words which follow echo the narrative of Numbers 13–14. Moses urged the people to go up and take the land. *The people, however, suggested that spies first be sent to explore Canaan. Moses approved the plan and appointed twelve men, one from each tribe, to undertake the mission. Returning with fruit from Eshcol, the spies reported on what a good land God had given them (1:19-25).

Fear paralyzed the people and perverted their understanding of God. They thought God hated them, that he wanted to exterminate them. The obstacles to conquering the land seemed insurmountable. Moses urged them not to fear, for God would lead the way into the land. He would fight for them as he had done in Egypt and in the desert when Israel had been attacked by Amalek. To underscore the love of God for them, Moses introduced father/son imagery. To this place God had carried them as a father carries his son. Even though they had seen the leading of the Lord in the fiery cloud, still they did not trust him (1:26-33).

The Lord was angry with their unbelief and pronounced the death sentence on that generation. Missing here is any reference to Moses' great prayer of intercession (Nm 14:13-19). *The unbelief of the people triggered in Moses an outburst which brought down divine wrath against him also. He would not be allowed to lead Israel into the land. That would be the privilege of Joshua. Meanwhile, God directed Moses to lead the people south toward the Red Sea, away from Canaan (1:37-40).

Too late the people determined that they would attempt a southern invasion of Canaan. They were warned that God would not go with them nor fight for them. In their arrogance Israel had marched up into the hill country. The Amorites swarmed against them like bees and chased them back to Kadesh. There the people wept before the Lord, but he "turned a deaf ear" to them. For quite some time the people remained at Kadesh in this miserable state of alienation from God (1:41-46).

C. At Mount Seir (Dt 2:1-8).

When they eventually left Kadesh Barnea, Israel spent many days traveling in the vicinity of Mount Seir. *This region had been given by Yahweh to the sons of Esau. *No hostile move was to be made against Edom. Israel was to pay for any food and water they consumed. Since they had been so blessed of God, they could afford to be magnanimous with the inhabitants of Mount Seir. Moses here made no mention of the advance party sent to Edom, the denial of permission, or the hostile show of force by the king of Edom.

490

D. In Moab and Ammon (Dt 2:9-23)

Nearing the region of Moab and Ammon, *again Israel received a directive not to go to war with these descendants of Lot. *Their land too was a divine allotment. *Parenthetically Moses pointed out that the Moabites, Edomites and Ammonites, with Yahweh's help, had dispossessed strong peoples in order to occupy their lands (2:9-12,19-23).

Crossing the Zered Valley into the the region of Moab was a milestone for Israel. Thirty-eight years had passed since Israel had departed Kadesh to attack the Canaanites. An entire generation of fighting men had died in the wilderness. Their demise was not due merely to natural causes for the hand of the Lord had been against them (2:13-15).

E. In the Kingdom of Sihon (Dt 2:24-37).

Crossing the Arnon Gorge, Israel came into the Amorite kingdom of Sihon. *Now God gave them permission to fight! The Arnon marks the beginning of the conquest. *Reports of their victory here would strike terror into the hearts of subsequent opposition (2:24-25).

First Moses attempted to negotiate passage through the area. He assured the king that (1) Israel had already passed through Seir and Moab peacefully; and (2) that the Amorite territory was not Israel's main objective. Sihon refused passage. Yahweh had made his spirit stubborn, i.e., permitted nothing to happen which might have softened his heart (2:26-30).

With God's assurance of victory, Israel engaged Sihon in battle at Jahaz. The entire Amorite army was wiped out. All the towns of the area were captured. *No survivors were spared. *The spoils were appropriated by Israel. Yet Israel was careful not to touch any Ammonite villages in the region just as *God had commanded (2:31-37).

F. In Bashan (Dt 3:1-11).

In the region of Bashan the Amorite king Og came out against Israel. Again The Lord gave Moses assurance of victory. Og was totally crushed *and sixty walled cities were taken. *Og was a descendant of the Rephaim. *His huge iron "couch" or sarcophagus (13×6 feet), was kept as a trophy in the city of Rabbah.

491

G. In the Plains of Moab (Dt 3:12-29).

In the Plains of Moab, Moses assigned the recently conquered Transjordan territory to the tribes of Reuben, Gad and half the tribe of Manasseh. The condition of this assignment was that the men of war from these tribes would assist their brothers in the conquest of Canaan (3:12-20).

*Moses gave Joshua encouragement. He should not fear. Just as God had destroyed the two kings of Transjordan, so would he do to all the kingdoms beyond Jordan (3:21-22).

*Moses prayed concerning a personal matter. He requested that he might go over Jordan and at least see the good land. God, however, would not listen to him. Moses could view the Promised Land from the top of Pisgah; but Joshua would lead the people across Jordan (3:23-29).

BASIC EXHORTATIONS
Deuteronomy 4:1-40

In Deuteronomy 4 Moses' first address moves from recollection to exhortation. In chapters 1–3 he employed frequent direct discourse; in chapter four he quotes God only once. He exhorts his auditors to obey the Law, and he grounds his exhortation in three different appeals.

A. Appeal of Experience (Dt 4:1-24).

Israel had now lived in possession of God's Law for forty years. They had experience with it. Moses therefore reminded his audience of five attributes of God's Law.

1. The Law points the way to life, i.e., life more abundant within the Promised Land. The judgment at Baal Peor made clear that only those who held fast to the Lord survived. Therefore Israel was to observe without alteration the commands they had been given through Moses (4:1-4).

2. The Law reflects divine wisdom. Observing these righteous laws would make them a great nation and give them a reputation for prudence. God would be near them and answer their prayers (4:5-8).

3. The Law originated with God. They must never forget the experience at Horeb/Sinai when God spoke to them out of the fire the ten

words and then wrote them on two tablets. The laws which they were to follow in Canaan had been given to Moses at the Mount (4:9-14).

4. The Law reflects reality. At Sinai they had not seen any form when God spoke to them. Therefore, they should not ever attempt to represent God by any object. The God of Sinai was sovereign over all celestial bodies and over history. Three times in this chapter Moses admonished Israel to guard against the temptation of idolatry. The various forms of graven images are listed in the opposite sequence which is found in the creation narrative of Genesis 1 — man, beast, bird, creeping thing, fish, and heavenly bodies.[1] Perhaps the thought is that idolatry is a complete reversal of the intention and direction of creation (4:15-20).

5. The Law plays no favorites. Even Moses was denied entrance to Canaan because he had sinned. God is a consuming fire, a jealous God who will tolerate no rivals. Anyone who engaged in idolatry would come under his wrath just as did Moses. Thus the sermon emphasized that Israel could learn from creation, from history and from the personal experience of Moses. Three times (1:37; 3:26; 4:21) in this first sermon he reminded them that he had been denied entrance into Canaan (4:21-24).

B. Appeal of Warning (Dt 4:25-31).

The Law is severe for lawbreakers. Those who disregarded it would be scattered among the nations. There they would worship pagan gods until they realized the futility of such worship. Then they would look again for the Lord, hear his voice and experience his compassion. Though Israel may forget her covenant obligations, God would forever remember the covenant which he swore to their fathers.

C. Appeal of Relationship (Dt 4:32-43).

Threat was never the ultimate word which God had for Israel. He constantly reminded this people that he loved them dearly. Reception of the Law was a privilege unparalleled in history. Israel had actually heard the voice of God at Sinai and had survived. They had seen the mighty power of God unleashed against Egypt. Yet this awesome God loved them and brought them out of Egypt. He would help them dispossess great nations (4:32-38).

The Law is solitary, the only expression of the sovereign will of the only God in heaven and earth. Only by observing this Law could Israel experience real life (4:39-40).

BASIC ANNOUNCEMENT
Deteronomy 4:41-43

Between the first and second addresses, Moses designated three cities east of Jordan as cities of refuge. This paragraph highlights the theme of life, a theme underscored in the preceding and succeeding chapters of Deuteronomy. A city of refuge meant life for one who had taken another life unintentionally. The three cities were Bezer in Reuben, Ramoth in Gad, and Golan in the territory assigned to Manasseh. The legislation concerning these cities is presented in 19:1-13.

ENDNOTES

1. Hamilton, *Handbook,* p. 397.

CHAPTER FORTY-TWO

Loving the God of Love
Deuteronomy 4:44-11:32

AIM: To prove that obedience is the greatest demonstration of love for God.

THEME: If you love me!

The first address of Moses emphasized the history of Israel. The second focuses on the holiness of Israel. In chapters 1–4 Moses employed the backward look; in chapters 5–11 the inward look. Chapters 1–4 contain a review of Israel's journey; chapters 5–11 a rehearsal of Sinai's laws. Remembrances of the past are followed by commandments for the present.

Moses' second address has two distinct parts. Chapters 5–11 are foundational and hortatory. Here are found the most basic principles of the Law. The second part of the discourse (chs. 12–26) sets forth specific legislation which would be in force once Israel entered the Promised Land. The first part of the discourse is surveyed in this chapter.

The introduction to the second address (4:44-49) stresses that the Law about to be presented in Transjordan was the same Law which had been proclaimed at Horeb/Sinai. Four focal points in the address are clear: (1) the Law, (2) the Lord, (3) the leader, and (4) the land.

FOCUS ON THE LAW
Deuteronomy 5:1–6:25

Deuteronomy 5-6 stresses the idea of oneness. There is one law, one mediator, and one Lord. Moses began by reminding Israel of the situation at Sinai when they received the Law. He then emphasized the fundamental components of that Law.

A. Sinai Covenant Recalled (Dt 5:1-33).

Moses called upon "all Israel" to obey the Law which God had communicated to them "face to face," i.e., personally through Moses the mediator. That covenant was not just with their fathers (4:31), but with each successive generation (5:1-5).

In some details the Decalogue as recounted here differs from the version in Exodus 20:1-17. The repetition serves the purpose of underscoring the eternality of God's Law. God's will regarding idolatry, murder, theft and coveting cannot be revised. The new generation must make this divine will the standard for its own lifestyle (5:6-21).

The Decalogue was proclaimed to the whole assembly on Sinai out of "the fire, the cloud and the deep darkness." God then recorded these ten words on two stone tablets and gave them to Moses. The Israelites were terrified by the awesome display of divine power on the mount. They feared for their lives if they should continue to hear God's voice. The elders of the tribes therefore requested that Moses approach the Lord on their behalf and then bring them the divine word. They pledged that they would obey whatever God commanded through Moses (5:22-27).

God endorsed the proposal of the people. They were told to return to their tents. Moses, however, stayed behind to receive from the Lord the ordinances which were to be observed in the Promised Land. The people were required to "walk in all the way" that the Lord had commanded if they were to prosper in the land they were about to possess (5:28-33).

These verses establish the credentials of Moses to be Israel's authoritative teacher. He had (1) congregational appointment and (2) divine approval. The one Law required but one mediator. In the first four chapters Moses spoke as a fellow Israelite using some ten times the phrase "our God." In the next twenty-four chapters Moses speaks mostly from the perspective of Israel's teacher. He uses in these chapters the expression "your God" almost exclusively.

B. Principal Commandments Reiterated (Dt 6:1-25).

Deuteronomy 6 begins with a reminder that the commands which Moses was about to give them (1) came from the Lord, (2) were intended for observance in the Promised Land, (3) were to be conveyed to future generations, (4) would test their fear of the Lord, and (5) would lead to a more abundant life and the fulfillment of all God's promises (6:1-3). Three principal commands are contained in Deuteronomy 6.

The Israelites were to love the Lord. Deuteronomy 6:4 is known to Jews as the *shema'*, the Hebrew word for "Hear." The verse is a foundational text for the doctrine of monotheism and the self-consistency of Yahweh. Because God is one, Moses could call upon Israel to render unto him undivided love and loyalty. Israel's love for God would be demonstrated by (1) embracing those commandments in their heart and (2) instructing their children in God's ways. They were to (figuratively?) bind those commands upon their hands, foreheads and doorposts (6:4-9). These verses are the basis for the Jewish practice of wearing phylacteries, small leather containers enclosing parchment with a number of biblical verses upon them. Orthodox Jewish homes have a *mezuzah,* a small box attached to the doorposts which contains various Scripture quotations.

The Israelites were to fear the Lord. The biggest danger facing Israel in the wonderful new land would be forgetting their divine benefactor. They must serve only the Lord, and use his name alone in their oaths. If they followed other gods they would provoke the Lord to anger. They would thus be testing the Lord as their fathers had done at Massah (cf. Ex 17:1-7). If they disobeyed God, they would lose the land; if they obeyed him, all their enemies would be thrust out before them (6:13-19).

The Israelites were to teach the grace of God. Israel was delivered from Egypt by grace. They were preserved in the wilderness by grace.

497

They would receive the Promised Land by grace. The only appropriate response to such grace was obedience to the commandments of this wonderful God (6:20-25).

FOCUS ON THE LORD
Deuteronomy 7:1–8:20

Moses next attempts to get his audience to look upward, to reflect on their great God. They needed to know that the Lord was leading them and testing them as they prepared for entrance into Canaan.

A. Leading of the Lord (Dt 7:1-26).

The key to successful effort on the part of God's people is the assurance that the Lord is leading. That assurance is possible through reflection on the word and works of God. Moses points out seven key facts which Israel needed to remember.

1. Israel needed to remember who the enemy was. The seven mighty nations of Canaan were to be totally destroyed. No treaty was to be made with them. No intermarriage was to take place with them. Fraternization with these pagans would lead to religious apostasy, which in turn would arouse the wrath of God. All pagan paraphernalia was to be destroyed (7:1-5).

2. Israel needed to remember her own identity. This nation was (1) holy to Yahweh, (2) chosen out of all people, (3) God's treasured possession, (4) the object of God's love, (5) the beneficiary of the divine oath, (6) the object of God's deliverance, and (7) the servant of the only true God (7:6-8).

3. Israel needed to remember her God. He is faithful to his covenant of love to a thousand generations of those who love him. On the other hand, he utterly destroys all those who hate him (7:9-11).

4. Israel needed to remember the key to blessing. Faithful execution of God's commands against the Canaanites would result in blessing: (1) population growth, (2) agricultural abundance, and (3) health (7:12-16).

5. Israel needed to remember the power of God. They would not be afraid to face the Canaanites if (1) they recalled what God had done to Pharaoh and all Egypt; (2) they understood that God would

send before them the "hornet," a metaphor for the fear of Israel; and (3) they realized that their awesome and great God was actually in their midst (7:17-21).

6. Israel needed to remember the plan of God. He would drive out the seven nations of Canaan "little by little" lest the land be uninhabited and overrun by wild beasts. Nonetheless, the Lord would throw their enemies into utter confusion until they were destroyed. No king of Canaan would be able to stand before them (7:22-24).

7. Israel needed to remember the command of God. No pagan image was to be spared. These detestable objects would bring destruction upon any house where they might be found (7:25-26).

B. Testing of the Lord (Dt 8:1-20).

Deuteronomy 8 is introduced in familiar words (see 4:1). The theme of the chapter is testing, past and future, of Israel's loyalty to God. Three tests are addressed.

1. Israel was tested in the wilderness. They were humbled through hardship. In their extremity, however, God provided for their needs whether food or clothing or physical strength. The manna was designed to teach them that the basic source of life was God himself and his words. Jesus quoted 8:3 ("Man shall not live by bread alone, but by every word that proceeds from the mouth of God") in his confrontation with the Devil (Matt 4:1-4). The point here is that God had given to Israel in the wilderness the loving discipline which a father might give his son (8:2-5).

2. Israel would face a very different kind of test upon entering the Promised Land. The test would be, not that of privation, but of plenty. They might be tempted to think that since they were living in a land of plenty, they would not need to depend upon the Lord for material blessing (8:6-9).

3. Israel would face the test of time. The longer they enjoyed the prosperity of Canaan, the greater the danger of forgetting the Lord and all he had done for them. They would tend to become proud and boast that through their own power and strength they had accumulated this wealth. Should that ever happen, Moses solemnly testifies that God would destroy them just as he had destroyed the pagan nations before them (8:10-20).

FOCUS ON THE LEADER
Deuteronomy 9:1–10:11

In this unit Moses sets the record straight regarding God's past dealings with Israel, and his personal role in those dealings. The contrast here is between the unfaithfulness of the people and the faithfulness of their leader.

A. Unfaithfulness of the People (Dt 9:1-17,22-24).

Moses started out by reassuring them that they quickly would destroy the feared Anakim—the giant race which occupied parts of Canaan. They might tend to think that their righteousness had enabled them to dispossess these people. Moses sets the record straight. Israel was undeserving, they were a "stiff-necked people." God, however, would give them possession of the land because (1) of the wickedness of the Canaanites and (2) of the solemn promise he had made to the Patriarchs (9:1-6).

Moses charged that for forty years Israel had provoked the Lord to anger by their rebellious spirit. He described at length the unfaithfulness of the nation while he was in the mount receiving the tablets of stone. The Israelites had constructed an idol for themselves at the very time Moses was receiving the commandments of the Lord. God was about to destroy them there at Sinai and make a new nation from the seed of Moses. He was ready to destroy Aaron as well. Moses also alluded to the Israelite rebellion at Taberah, Massah, Kibroth Hattaavah, and Kadesh where the supreme act of doubt and disobedience occurred (9:7-17,22-24).

B. Faithfulness of Moses (Dt 9:18-21;9:25–10:11).

Moses was faithful both to the Lord and to his people. At Horeb Moses prayed forty days and nights for his people. God responded to his intercession. Only by God's gracious response to earnest prayer had Israel survived their encampment at the mount. The ground of Moses' appeal was not the righteousness of Israel, but (1) the promise to the Patriarchs, (2) the reputation of God among the heathen, and (3) the effort which God had already invested in Israel's redemption from Egypt (9:18-21,25-29).

That the prayer of Moses was successful is indicated in four facts. First, a second set of tablets of stone was taken to the mount and engraved by the finger of God. Moses returned forty days later with the tablets and put them in a temporary ark which he had made for them (10:1-5). Second, Moses documented the success of his prayer by quoting from an ancient travel journal. His prayer for the preservation of Aaron was answered. He had died at Moserah, not at Mt. Sinai. Moserah must have been in the vicinity of Mt. Hor (Nm 33:38). The fact that Eleazar his son followed Aaron in office proved that Aaron again had found favor with the Lord (10:6-7).

For his third proof of the successful intercession, Moses mentioned the appointment of the Levites "at that time," i.e., at the time of his intercession. The ministry which God assigned to Levi proved that forgiveness had been extended to the entire nation. Levi was to (1) carry the ark, (2) stand before the Lord, and (3) pronounce blessings in his name. No distinction is made here between ordinary Levites and the priests who were of the family of Aaron (10:8-9). The final proof that Moses' intercession on the mount had been accepted on behalf of Israel was the fact that God had commissioned Moses to lead the people forth from Sinai (10:10-11).

FOCUS ON THE LAND
Deuteronomy 10:12–11:32

Moses next turned to God's expectations for his people as they prepared to enter the Promised Land. Five expectations are summarized in 10:12-13 and then developed in the rest of the unit.

1. "Fear the Lord your God" (10:12,20).
2. "Walk in all his ways" (10:12; 11:22).
3. "Love him" (11:1,13,22).
4. "Serve the Lord your God" (10:20; 11:13).
5. "Keep the commandments of the Lord" (11:1,8,13,22).

The God who spoke from Sinai was worthy of Israel's allegiance because of who he was and what he had done. Their God (1) was sovereign over heaven and earth, (2) loved the fathers, (3) chose Israel above all other nations, (4) was mighty and awesome, (5) was absolutely impartial, (6) defended the helpless, and (7) loved foreigners. For the past forty years he had performed great and awesome works in the sight of Israel. He had taken seventy souls who migrated to Egypt and made them as numerous as the stars in the sky. For all of this he was worthy of their highest praise, reverence, and service. They should "circumcise" their hearts, i.e., take an attitude toward God which was the opposite of stubborn and rebellious. They must hold fast to him. His name only was to be employed in their solemn oaths (10:14-22).

The expectation of loving God and keeping his requirements is reinforced by three lessons from history: (1) the Exodus, (2) God's presence in the wilderness, and (3) the rebellion of Dathan and Abiram. These events are called "the discipline of Yahweh," i.e., the education, positive and negative, provided by God (11:1-7).

The expectation of keeping God's commandments is reinforced also by anticipation of the future. The land they would inherit would not be like Egypt. In Canaan they would be dependent upon "the rain of heaven," not on human ingenuity reflected in the Egyptian irrigation system. Total dependence upon the providence of God would mandate compliance to his will (11:8-12).

The expectation is reinforced a third time by depiction of the consequences of not rendering obedience, love and service to the Lord in the new land. Turning to Canaanite weather gods (e.g., Baal) would result in (1) arousing the anger of the Lord, (2) shutting off the rain from heaven, (3) withering of the crops, and (4) banishment from the land (11:13-17).

As the hortatory part of his discourse draws to a close, Moses summarizes what he has been saying. The emphasis is on obligations and promises. The obligations are (1) to bind, as it were, the commandments of God on their hearts, hands, heads, and homes; and (2) to use every opportunity to pass on these commandments to children. The promises are (1) success in the conquest of Canaan, and (2) long years in the new land (11:18-25).

The first part of the address comes to a conclusion with an appeal for a decision. The alternatives before Israel are summed up in the words "blessing" and "curse." Obedience leads to the former, disobedience to the latter. When they entered the land, Moses called upon them to proceed to Mt. Ebal and Mt. Gerizim and there face again the alternatives of blessing and curse (11:26-32). The specifics of this future covenant renewal ceremony are found in Deuteronomy 27.

CHAPTER FORTY-THREE

Preparing for the Promised Land
Deuteronomy 12-18

AIM: To demonstrate how God provided guidance for his people for their life in a new land.

THEME: A guide for life!

The second half of Moses' second address — the next fifteen chapters of Deuteronomy — sets forth legislation designed to govern the life of Israel in the Promised Land. Some of the laws here are duplicates from earlier sections of the Pentateuch, some are adaptations of those laws, and some are introduced here for the first time. This word of Law is spoken only after God's word of grace (chs. 1–11). Israel was not to obey these laws in order to become the people of God; rather, they were to obey because they were, by God's grace, his people.

Most commentators regard this as a disparate collection of laws with no visible structure, unity or order. These laws, however, can be grouped under one of the commands of the Decalogue which was restated in Deuteronomy 5. The laws related to the first five of the Ten Commandments are discussed in this chapter.

WORSHIP LAWS
Deuteronomy 12:1-32

The first two words of the Decalogue prescribe the worship of Yahweh and proscribe the use of any image to represent him. More has been written about Deuteronomy 12 than any other chapter in the book. Four points are emphasized here:

1. All pagan sanctuaries and cultic paraphernalia in Canaan were to be destroyed. The latter included (1) altars, (2) sacred stones, (3) Asherah poles, and (4) idols. The very names of those deities were to be expunged. Never should Yahweh be worshiped as those gods were worshiped (12:1-4).

2. Legitimate worship could only take place at that spot designated by the Lord. The phrase "the place which the Lord will choose" is used six times in Deuteronomy 12 (plus eleven additional times in the book). At that sanctuary all tithes, gifts, and sacrifices were to be presented. Once the land had been subdued God would choose the place for "a dwelling for his name." The phrase "to put his name there" appears in the book three times, and the similar "to make his name dwell there" is used six times. In the secular literature of that period equivalent expressions were used (1) as an affirmation of ownership, (2) in the erection of victory monuments, and (3) on foundation stones of sanctuaries (12:5-14).[1]

3. Slaughtering and eating meat for ordinary meals could take place anywhere. The only limitation was that the blood had to be drained from the dead animal because "the blood is the life." This blood was to be poured out on the ground. Religious meals, however, were restricted to the central sanctuary. The blood of sacrificial animals could only be poured out at the altar of the Lord (12:15-28).

4. Israelites must not emulate the detestable worship practices of the Canaanites. These pagans went so far as to offer up their children as burnt offerings to their gods! (12:29-32).

The thrust of Deuteronomy 12 is not one sanctuary versus many sanctuaries, but rather pure worship versus false worship; between "their gods" (v. 2) and "your God" (v. 4); between "their name" (v. 3) and "his name" (v. 5); between all the "places" of false worship (vv. 2-3) and "the place" which the Lord will choose.

SANCTITY PRINCIPLE
Deuteronomy 13:1–14:27

The third commandment concerns proper use of the Lord's name. Two areas of profaning God's name are treated here.

A. Advocating Rebellion (Dt 13:1-18).

If the emphasis of Deuteronomy 12 is on idolatry, in Deuteronomy 13 the emphasis shifts to the idolater. In the previous chapter all outward, physical objects associated with idolatry were to be destroyed. This chapter deals with a more difficult form of temptation. Those who advocated following other gods were profaning God's name. Three cases are cited.

1. A false prophet. Such a one might accurately forecast a sign or wonder. Nonetheless, if he advocated following other gods, he should be rejected. That prophet was to be executed for preaching rebellion. The Lord would use these deceivers to test the loyalty of his people (13:1-5).

2. A relative or friend. Here is yet a more powerful temptation. Deuteronomy 12 portrayed the home as a place of worship, rejoicing, and festivity. The home, however, might also become a stumblingblock. No pity was to be shown such a one who secretly advocated conspiracy against the Lord in the home. He must be executed, and the person he tried to entice must cast the first stone. The death penalty would be a deterrent to others who might advocate similar evil (13:6-11).

3. Whole towns. Temptation is most difficult to resist when "everyone is doing it." Mass sinning, however, must be dealt with as surely as an individual sinner. An investigation was to be made of any town rumored to be advocating worship of other gods. If the rumors were true, the entire town was to be put to the sword and the plunder burned "as a whole burnt offering" to the Lord. The place was to be left in ruins forever (13:12-18).

B. Practicing Abomination (Dt 14:1-21).

Those who were part of the covenant family were expected to maintain the honor of the Father's name by totally separating themselves from the abominable practices of the surrounding peoples. This separation was to be reflected in mourning practices. Lacerating the body was a practice of the cult of the dead, and possibly also part of the seasonal rites of the fertility cult (14:1-2).

The separation from the heathen was also to be reflected in dietary practice. "Clean" (i.e., permissible) land animals had to (1) divide the hoof and (2) chew the cud. Water creatures had to have fins and scales. Most fowl could be eaten except scavengers. Swarming insects were forbidden. An animal found dead could not be eaten for it would not have been slaughtered in the proper manner. A kid was never to be boiled in its mother's milk. This practice apparently had some significance in the fertility cult (14:3-21).

Deuteronomy (14:3) uses the word *to'ebhah,* "abomination," in reference to the forbidden meats. This word is used primarily in reference to acts of perversion by the Canaanites. The parallel passage in Leviticus used a different word —*sheqets* — for "abomination." Here in Deuteronomy Moses is apparently suggesting a link between Canaanite cult practices and the list of unclean animals.

C. Dedicating the Produce (Dt 14:22-27).

On the more positive side, God's name was honored when tithes were paid on that which the land provided. These tithes were to be eaten in the religious festivals at the central sanctuary. Those coming from a distance could bring equivalent silver to invest in the festival for themselves, their families, and guest Levites. Festivals were not to be selfishly enjoyed by a man and his family. Those less fortunate were to be invited to the table.

SABBATH PRINCIPLE
Deuteronomy 14:28–16:17

The fourth word of the Decalogue requires observance of the Sabbath. This section of Deuteronomy amplifies the Sabbath principles of rest, release and rejoicing. Deuteronomy 14:22 speaks of what Israel was to do with her possessions every year. The emphasis on time continues in this section with directions about what was to transpire every third and seventh year.

A. Seven-year Cycle (Dt 14:28-15:18).

The Law organizes time into sabbatical cycles of seven years. Twice during each heptad — in the third and sixth years — the tithe was stored in the community rather than taken to the sanctuary. From these resources the community would care for the needy. Some scholars think that this tithe of the third year was in addition to the regular tithe (14:28-29).

Exodus 23:10-11 emphasized that the land was to lie fallow during the seventh year for the benefit of the poor. Leviticus 25:1-7 stressed rest for the land itself. Here in Deuteronomy, however, a new emphasis is seen. Debts of Israelite brothers were to be canceled at the end of the sabbatical cycle. Some scholars think this means totally canceled; others think that a one-year reprieve was granted. Ideally, faithfulness to the Law would bring such a blessing that borrowing among brothers would be unnecessary (15:1-6).

Being realistic, however, Moses recognized that there would always be poor folk in the land. He required an openhanded policy toward them, especially as the seventh year approached when a lender might tend to be tightfisted. A destitute brother might "appeal to the Lord" against such a selfish one in which case he would be found by the heavenly Judge to be guilty of sin. Selfishness is sin! (15:7-11).

Indentured Hebrew servants were to be released after six years of service. Whether these are the six years of the sabbatical cycle, or six years from the date of the sale is not clear. Slavery laws were discussed earlier in Exodus 21:2-11 and Leviticus 25:39-45. Some differences in these passages are apparent. Harmonizing all the details is not easy. Deuteronomy 15 is concerned with an Israelite who had been forced to sell himself into debtor's slavery in which he was required to work out his financial obligation.

When released from his obligation, the servant was to be endowed with ample provision so that he would not begin his new state of freedom in destitution. Servants were to be freed willingly because their six years of service were worth twice (*mishneh*) that of a hired hand for an equivalent period. Servants who because of love preferred servanthood to freedom were to be marked by a pierced ear (15:12-18).

B. Firstborn Animals (Dt 15:19-23).

The firstborn male animals, like the Sabbath, belonged to the Lord. These animals were not to be worked or used for the benefit of man. The firstborn were to be eaten at festivals in the sanctuary. Of course if the animal was flawed it could not be presented to the Lord. A substitution had to be made, and the flawed animal could then be eaten at home.

C. Annual Feasts (Dt 16:1-17).

Hamilton has pointed out that clusters of threes are frequent in this section of Deuteronomy.[2] In chapters 14–15 three references to years appeared. There were three categories of unclean animals (ch. 14), three temptations to idolatry (ch. 13), three prohibitions against eating blood (12:16,23; 15:23), three uses of the phrase "the place which the Lord your God will choose" in chapter 14 and six uses in both chapters 12 and 16. So now three times each year all the males are to appear before the Lord at the sanctuary. None was to appear empty handed. Each was to bring an offering in proportion to the way he had been blessed (16:16-17).

1. Passover and Unleavened Bread came in Abib (March/April). Passover was a celebration of deliverance from bondage. The unleavened bread was a reminder of the hasty departure from Egypt. Although the Passover lamb could only be sacrificed at the sanctuary, the seven days of unleavened bread applied throughout the land. The seventh day of the festival was a sabbath (16:1-8).

2. Seven weeks after the beginning of harvest the Feast of Weeks was celebrated. The more precise date for this festival is given in Leviticus 23:15-16. This one-day feast was a time for freewill offerings to the Lord and for celebration by the entire family. Generosity toward the needy was stimulated by recollections of their time of servitude in Egypt (16:9-12).

3. At the conclusion of the fall harvest the joyous Feast of Tabernacles was celebrated for seven days. Again, this was a time of family fellowship and sharing with the less fortunate. The entire feast was in

essence a sabbath celebrating work well done and blessing of God (16:13-15).

AUTHORITY PRINCIPLE
Deuteronomy 16:18–18:22

The fifth commandment, "Honor your father and mother," in essence deals with the issue of authority. That is the subject Moses next addresses in his discourse.

A. The Judge (Dt 16:18–17:13).

Judges were to be appointed by the people in every town. These men were not above the law. They were not permitted to show partiality, pervert justice or accept bribes. Most of this paragraph, however, is about the people themselves; "you" not "they." All of God's people are to measure up to the high standards set for judges (16:18-20).

The judges would have the special responsibility of investigating alleged religious corruption. This might include such things as (1) erecting an Asherah pole near an altar of the Lord, (2) erecting a sacred stone, (3) sacrificing defective animals, or (4) worshiping other gods. The Asherah and sacred stones served as divine emblems for the Canaanites and may have played a role in the judicial procedures in that society (16:21–17:1).

Israelites convicted of pagan worship by the testimony of at least two witnesses were to be executed by stoning. The witnesses had to cast the first stones (17:2-7).

Difficult cases were to be taken to the sanctuary to be adjudicated by the priests and "the judge who is in office at that time," (i.e., the high priest). Whether this constituted one or two levels of appellate judiciary is not clear. In any case, the decision of the priestly court was final. Anyone who rebelled against its decision was lawless and hence was to be executed (17:8-13).

B. The King (Dt 17:14-20).

Moses predicted that sometime after the land was settled the people would request a king. This would not necessarily be an evil request, since kings were part of the promises made to the Patriarchs.

They must be certain, however, to only appoint the king chosen by the Lord. He must not (1) multiply horses, (2) engage in trade relations with Egypt, (3) multiply wives or (4) accumulate large amounts of gold and silver. On the positive side, he was to be an Israelite, not a foreigner. He was to make a personal copy of the Book of the Law and read it throughout his reign. King and commoner alike were equal under the Law, and the king must recognize that fact if he wished to have an enduring dynasty.

C. The Priest (Dt 18:1-8).

The whole tribe of Levi, including the priests who were descendants of Aaron, were to have no inheritance in the Promised Land. The Lord was their inheritance. They would live from the gifts which the people brought to the Lord. These included portions of certain sacrificial animals and the firstfruits of crops and wool. Levites who became full time ministers at the sanctuary were entitled to their maintenance even though they might have acquired some wealth from the sale of family possessions elsewhere.

D. The Prophet (Dt 18:9-22).

People have a natural curiosity about the future. For the covenant people, however, certain means of attempting to ascertain and/or influence the future were forbidden. The list includes (1) pedosacrifice, (2) divination, (3) sorcery, (4) interpretation of omens, (5) witchcraft, (6) spell casting, (7) mediums, (8) spiritists, and (9) necromancers. All of these occult practices are detestable to the Lord and constitute one of the reasons he chose to dispossess the Canaanites (18:9-13).

The Lord had something better in store for his people. He would raise up from among them a prophet like Moses. At the request of the people Moses had been placed in the role of intermediary. He now revealed for the first time, that at Sinai the Lord had announced his intention to raise up a future prophet who would be an intermediary, a deliverer, and a lawgiver. This future prophet would speak flawlessly the word of God. Anyone who would fail to listen to what he said in the name of the Lord would have to give account directly to the Lord. Some commentators see in this passage the establishment of the prophetic office in Israel. Others interpret the words Messianically.[3]

Peter (Acts 3:22-23) and Stephen (Acts 7:37) saw in Jesus the fulfill-ment of this prediction (18:14-19).

Two kinds of future prophets were to be condemned to death: (1) one who only pretended to speak by God's authority, and (2) one who spoke in the name of other gods. False prophets could be identi-fied when their predictions failed to come to pass (18:20-22).

ENDNOTES

1. G.J. Wenham cited by Hamilton, *Handbook*, p. 420.
2. Ibid., p. 428.
3. Smith, *Messiah*, pp. 67-70.

CHAPTER FORTY-FOUR

More Laws for a New Land
Deuteronomy 19-26

AIM: To demonstrate the inner logic of God's Law.

THEME: God's expectations!

In this chapter the Deuteronomic legislation which relates to the last five words of the Decalogue is discussed. To this legal material are appended directions for two ceremonies to be performed shortly after entering the land.

SANCTITY OF LIFE
Deuteronomy 19:1–22:8

The sixth commandment establishes the sanctity of life. Several applications of this principle are grouped in this section of Deuteronomy.

A. Cities of Refuge (Dt 19:1-14).

Taking a life, even accidentally, was a serious matter under the Law. One guilty of manslaughter had to flee for safety to one of six cities of refuge. These cities were situated three in Transjordan and three in Canaan. The cities of refuge offered sanctuary from the "avenger of blood." Some think the "avenger of blood" was a kinsman of the dead person who in rage might kill the guilty party. Others have suggested that the avenger might be a government appointed functionary. No sanctuary was offered anyone guilty of premeditated murder. The elders of the hometown of the murderer would order him returned. He would then be handed over to the avenger of blood, presumably after a trial had been conducted. Only by execution of the murderer could the stain of innocent blood be removed from the land (19:1-13).

Another serious matter was the removal of a boundary stone. According to 27:17 one guilty of this crime came under the curse of God. Why this brief law is inserted here is unclear. Perhaps it has something to do with jurisdictional disputes in the prosecution of murderers (19:14).

B. Witnesses (Dt 19:15-20).

Israelite courts required at least two witnesses to secure conviction of any crime. A false witness was given the same punishment which the victim of his falsehood might have received had he been convicted. No pity was to be shown the perjurer even if the death penalty was involved (19:15-21).

C. Military Regulations (Deut 20:1-20).

Israel was not to fear in warfare even when facing overwhelming superiority for the Lord would be with them. Before every battle the priests were to remind the soldiers of this fact (20:1-4).

Military exemptions were granted to (1) one who had built a house and never lived in it, (2) one betrothed to a woman but who had not married, (3) and one who was faint-hearted. Commanders were appointed immediately prior to each battle (20:5-9).

An offer of peace was to be extended to a distant city before an attack was launched. Inhabitants of cities which surrendered were put to forced labor. The males of cities which did not surrender were slain; women, children and livestock were taken as plunder. Cities in Canaan, however, were to be utterly destroyed, every living thing put to the sword. If this were not done, these pagan peoples would eventually teach Israel their pagan ways (20:10-18).

During extended sieges the army of Israel was not to harm the fruit trees. Other trees, however, could be used to build siege works (20:19-20).

D. Unsolved Murders (Dt 21:1-9).

Murder brought guilt upon the whole land. An unsolved murder could not merely be ignored. The elders of the nearest town were responsible for conducting a ceremony of purification. An unworked heifer was to be taken to a flowing stream. Its neck was to be broken. The elders were to wash their hands over the heifer and declare before a priest that they had not killed the victim, nor did they know who had done so. They were to call upon the Lord to accept the death of the heifer as atonement for the land so that the people would not be held guilty of shedding innocent blood. The principle here is that only death could atone for the life of an innocent murder victim.

E. Personal Relations (Dt 21:10–22:12).

Respect for life as applied to personal relationships dominates the next section of the Deuteronomic legislation.

1. A female captured in war could be taken for a wife after certain conditions were met. She must have her head shaved, nails trimmed, and clothing she was wearing when captured removed. She must be allowed to have a month to mourn the separation from (and possible death of) her parents. These regulations would also help to insure that the attraction to the woman was not shortlived and purely physical. The Israelite could divorce his foreign wife if he pleased, but he could not after marriage or divorce treat her as a slave (21:10-14).

2. A man could not transfer the inheritance of the firstborn of one wife to the firstborn of a wife more beloved. Whether this law envisions polygamous marriage or the taking of a second wife after the divorce or death of the first wife is not clear (21:15-17).

517

3. Parents were required to side with law and order even against their own offspring. A rebellious son who could not be disciplined at home was to be brought to the elders of the city. The parents had to bear testimony against the son, identifying him as incorrigibly stubborn, rebellious, profligate and a drunkard. The son was to be executed by the men of the city. The parents were spared the ordeal of casting the first stones (21:18-21).

4. The bodies of those executed for capital crimes were to be impaled on a tree for the duration of the day. To leave the body there longer would bring God's curse on the land (21:22-23).

5. An Israelite was to be concerned for the property of a brother. Straying livestock was to be returned immediately to the owner or housed until it could be returned. Concern here is twofold: the potential loss to the neighbor, and the danger to the animal (22:1-3).

6. A neighbor's distressed animal was to be helped immediately (22:4).

7. Transvestism did not respect the God-ordained distinction between the sexes and consequently was an abomination to the Lord (22:5).

8. A nesting mother bird was not to be taken along with her young or eggs. This law has to do with the conservation of food supplies and respect for the parental relationship even in the animal world (22:6-7).

9. A parapet was to be constructed around the flat roof of a new home to prevent anyone from falling therefrom (22:8).

UNLAWFUL UNIONS
Deuteronomy 22:9–23:18

The seventh commandment is, "You shall not commit adultery." Unnatural and immoral unions of all kinds were prohibited by this command.

A. Mixing Kinds (Dt 22:9-12).

Three laws forbid the mixing of kinds: (1) two kinds of seeds were not to be planted in a vineyard; (2) an ox and an ass were not to be yoked together; and (3) clothes in which two types of cloth had been woven together were to be avoided. Similar laws are found in Leviticus 19:19. The purpose may have been to maintain distinctions within the created order. Some think these mixings grew out of some magical background and hence are here forbidden. Tassels (lit., twisted threads) were to be attached to the four corners of a cloak. Numbers 15:37-41 indicates that the tassels served to remind the people of the commandments of the Lord (22:9-12).

B. Sexual Violations (Dt 22:13-30).

Four categories of sexual misconduct are addressed in this section.

1. Premarital promiscuity was a serious crime in ancient Israel. If a husband alleged that his new bride was not a virgin at the time of the marriage, an investigation was conducted by the elders of the city. The girl's father had to prove her innocent of the charge by presenting the "tokens of her virginity," i.e., the bloodstained cloth from the wedding night. If the court found the husband guilty of slander he had to pay a fine of a hundred silver shekels (about 2.5 lbs.) to his father-in-law. He also lost the right to divorce his wife. If, however, the accusation was proved in court the men of the city were to stone the wife at the door of her father's house (22:13-21).

2. A couple caught in the act of adultery were both to be executed. The same penalty applied when a betrothed virgin slept with a man in a town. The law assumed that if the woman did not scream for help that she must have been a willing participant (22:22-24).

3. Rape of a betrothed virgin was punishable by death. He who raped a virgin who was not betrothed had a threefold penalty: (1) pay the girl's father fifty shekels of silver (1.25 lbs.), (2) marry the girl, and (3) never divorce her (22:25-29).

4. Sexual relations between a man and his stepmother were forbidden. Such activity came under the curse of God (22:30; cf. 27:20).

C. Admission to the Assembly (Dt 23:1-8).

Four categories of people were to be excluded from the assembly (*qahal*) of the Lord, i.e., the registry of citizens of the nation:

1. A man who had been emasculated. Such men had no stake in the future of the nation through posterity (23:1).

2. A person of illegitimate birth (*mamzer*). The exact meaning of

the term is unknown. It has been taken to mean (1) a bastard, (2) a child of a cult prostitute, (3) a child born of an incestuous relationship (23:2).

3. An Ammonite or Moabite was excluded until the tenth generation, i.e., permanently. This exclusion was based on the inhospitality of these peoples to Israel at the time of the Exodus. These peoples also had hired Balaam to come and curse Israel. A state of perpetual hostility was to be maintained with Moab and Ammon (23:3-6).

4. Edomites and Egyptians after the third generation could enter the assembly (23:7-8).

D. Uncleanness in the Camp (Dt 23:9-14).

Cleanliness in the camp was to be maintained during military campaigns. A man became unclean because of "what happens at night." The language here is not the same as in Leviticus 15:16. The reference may be to urinating at night either involuntarily or else because the man was too lazy to get up and go outside the camp. Such a one had to wash himself and stay outside the camp until sunset (23:9-11).

Soldiers were to relieve themselves outside the camp. They were required to cover their excrement with dirt. The reason for this is both hygienic and religious. The Lord moved about in the camp and therefore it must be kept holy and clean (23:12-14).

E. Miscellaneous Laws (Dt 23:15-18).

The section concludes with laws relating to escaped slaves and prostitution. (1) A foreign escaped slave was to be offered sanctuary on Israelite territory. He was not to be oppressed. (2) No Israelite man or woman was to become a temple prostitute. (3) No money earned through prostitution was to be used to pay religious obligations at the house of the Lord (23:15-18).

UNLAWFUL DEPRIVATION
Deuteronomy 23:19–24:7

The eighth commandment prohibits theft. In this short unit some ramifications of that commandment are explored. The first three paragraphs deal with theft of property; the last four with the theft of "life."

1. A fellow Israelite could not be charged interest on a loan. This did not apply to loans made to foreigners (23:19-20).

2. Vows to the Lord were to be promptly paid. Better not to make a vow than to make one and not fulfill it. Failure to pay a vow promptly constituted sin (23:21-23).

3. One passing through a vineyard or grainfield could partake of his neighbor's grapes or grain. This did not constitute theft. He could not, however, attempt to harvest or carry off any of these goods (23:24-25).

4. A woman once divorced by her husband and married to another could never under any circumstances return to the first husband. That would be an abomination in the sight of the Lord (24:1-4).

5. A new wife was entitled to the companionship of her husband for at least one year. The husband could not be drafted for military duty (24:5).

6. A millstone could not be taken as security for debt. That with which a man earned his livelihood could not be used for this purpose (24:6).

7. Kidnapping resulting in involuntary servitude was punishable by death (24:7).

FAIRNESS PRINCIPLE
Deuteronomy 24:8–25:4

Fairness is the essence of the ninth commandment, "You shall not bear false witness." Nine cases requiring fairness are considered.

1. A person with a leprous skin disease should not be allowed to jeopardize the well-being of the community. The sanitation laws were to be strictly followed as they had been in the case of Miriam (24:8-9).

2. A lender was not to enter the home of a borrower to secure the collateral. This law protected the privacy of the borrower's home and left up to him the choice of collateral. The creditor was also protected from covetousness (24:10-11).

3. The collateral of a poor man — most likely his cloak — was to be returned at sunset so that he would have something to protect him from the chill of night. This was regarded as a righteous act in the sight of God (24:12-13).

4. A hired man was to be paid daily. Should wages be withheld from such a one, the employer would be guilty of sin (24:14-15).

5. They must guard against overzealousness in punishing crime. Only the guilty was to be punished, not any other member of his family (24:16).

6. Foreigners were to be accorded justice. No collateral should be extracted from a widow which would cause her duress (24:17-18).

7. When harvesting crops — grain, olives, grapes — a farmer was not to be greedy and go through the process a second time. What was left in the field, the tree or the vine was to be for the poor who had the right to the "second" harvest (24:19-22).

8. Disputes between individuals were decided in court. The judges were to determine (1) who was guilty and (2) the extent to which he was to be flogged. The flogging was to be done in the presence of the judge to insure that no excess was administered. In no case was the number of lashes to exceed forty (25:1-3).

9. An ox used to thresh grain was not to be muzzled. The animal had a right to partake of the grain as he worked (25:4).

UNLAWFUL DESIRE
Deuteronomy 25:5-16

"You shall not covet." That is the tenth commandment. Five ramifications of that principle are addressed here. These laws deal with pairs.

1. Two brothers. A widow who had no sons was not to marry outside the family of her husband. Her brother-in-law was to take her to wife. The first son born to this union would carry on the name of the dead brother so that the family name would not be blotted out of the family registry. The principle here is family above personal wishes (25:5-6).

2. Two in-laws. Because of greed over greater inheritance a man might refuse to participate in a Levirate marriage. The refusal, however, involved great public shame. The widow would take her brother-in-law before the elders of the town. She would remove one of his sandals, symbolizing that he had relinquished his rights. Then she would spit in his face. That man's line would forever be known as the family of the unsandaled (25:7-10).

3. Two men. A woman might not grab the private parts of a man even in the defense of her husband. She might injure the man and thus deprive him of the right of procreation. Such a woman was to have her hand cut off. This is the only case of punishment by mutilation in the Law. It underscores the tremendous reverence the ancients had for the organs of procreation. The abiding lesson here is that the end does not justify the means (25:11-12).

4. Two weights. Israelite merchants were not to have two sets of weights, one for buying and one for selling. Heavier weights would acquire more than one paid for when buying; a lighter weight would provide less to the customer at the time of sale. Such practices were abominable to the Lord (25:13-16).

5. Two enemies. Israel was never to forget what Amalek did to them during the Exodus. They attacked the stragglers, showing no fear of the God of Israel. Once settled in the land, Israel was to erase the memory of Amalek from under heaven (25:17-19).

CEREMONIAL OBLIGATIONS
Deuteronomy 26:1-19

Two ceremonies were to be held as soon as Israel had taken possession of the land and had made the transition to the agricultural life. These were the offering of (1) the firstfruits and (2) the triennial tithe.

A. Offering of Firstfruits (Dt 26:1-11)
The firstfruits of Canaan were to be placed in a basket and taken to the sanctuary, and presented to the priest. The worshiper was then to recite what amounts to a creed. In this he declared that (1) he had arrived in the land which the Lord had sworn to the Fathers, (2) his ancestors had become a mighty nation in Egypt, (3) God had heard the cries of his oppressed people in Egypt, (4) the Lord had brought them out of Egypt with mighty hand and outstretched arm and had performed tremendous miracles in the process, (5) the Lord had brought them to the land flowing with milk and honey, and (6) the Lord had given them the firstfruits of the soil. After reciting this litany of praise, the worshiper, his household and invited guests (foreigners, Levites) were to join in celebration.

B. Offering of the Triennial Tithe (Dt 26:12-15).

The tithe of the third year was kept in the towns and shared with the needy: (1) the foreigners who mostly would be of the servant class, (2) the fatherless, (3) widows, and (4) Levites. On the first celebration of the triennial tithe a ritual prayer was to be uttered. In the prayer the worshiper declared that (1) he had laid aside the sacred portion and distributed it to the needy as required in the Law; (2) he had not desecrated the sacred portion by eating it during a time of mourning, touching it while unclean, or offering any portion of it to the dead; and (3) he had carried out the letter of the Law. He then was to call upon the Lord to look down from heaven and bless Israel in their newly acquired land.

C. Closing Remarks (Dt 26:16-19).

Moses brought his long second address to a close with brief remarks designed to remind Israel of several important facts. He reminded them of (1) the imperative of submitting to God's law enthusiastically ("with all your soul") and cheerfully ("with all your heart"); (2) the declaration they had made in the covenant renewal that Yahweh was their God; (3) the commitment which they had made to obey the Lord and walk in his ways; (4) the fact that the Lord had declared them to be his people, a treasured possession; (5) the promise that God would elevate them high above other nations in praise, fame and honor because of their holiness.

CHAPTER FORTY-FIVE

The Last Words of Moses
Deuteronomy 27-34

AIM: To demonstrate the importance of the last words of Moses.

THEME: Listen to the Word of God!

Moses' third (chs. 27–28) and fourth (chs. 29–30) sermons were not nearly as long as his second. In both addresses the focus was on what would befall Israel in the Promised Land into which they were about to enter. The last four chapters of the book focus on the hero of Israel, Moses himself.

MOSES' SERMONS
Deuteronomy 27:1–30:20

The theme in both the third and fourth sermons is the future of Israel. Far more space is devoted here to curse than to blessing, a pattern which has been observed in other law codes from the ancient Near East.[1]

A. Third Sermon (Dt 27:1–28:68).

The third sermon contains three major units: (1) covenant renewal, (2) blessing and curses, and (3) the threat of captivity.

1. Covenant renewal (27:1-26). Immediately upon entering Canaan, Israel was to prepare for a covenant renewal ceremony. They were to make a public copy of the Law. Large stones were to be erected at Mt. Ebal and coated with plaster. While the plaster was still drying, they were to inscribe on those stones "all the words of this law." Also at Mt. Ebal an altar was to be built. Only fieldstones untouched by iron tools were to be used. Burnt offerings and peace offerings were to be presented amidst joyous feasting while the stones were inscribed with the Law (27:1-8).

Moses was joined by the priests at this point in urging Israel to live up to her calling as God's people. By grace God had chosen them and redeemed them. The only appropriate response to that grace was obedience (27:9-10).

The tribes were given their instructions for the covenant renewal ceremony in Canaan. Six tribes were to stand on Mount Gerizim "to bless the people," and six on Mount Ebal "to pronounce curses." The Levites were to stand in the valley between the two mounts and loudly recite twelve terse curses. The people — apparently those standing on Ebal — were to respond with a hearty "Amen" (27:11-26).

2. Blessing and curses (28:1-48). Moses next enumerated fourteen blessings which would follow upon faithful obedience to the Law. The litany of blessings is followed by a list of thirty-two curses which would punish disobedience.

3. The threat of captivity (28:49-68). In the closing verses of Deuteronomy 28 Moses looked into the distant future and described the culminating chastisement of Israel. His description of the captivity moves through two phases.

Moses first described the devastation which a future enemy would bring to the land. The swiftness and fierceness of the nation is emphasized. The crops and livestock would be spoiled. Cities throughout the land would come under attack. Citizens would be in such dire straits that cultured men and women would resort to cannibalism, eating even their own children. Terrible plagues, prolonged disasters and severe illnesses would radically diminish the size of the nation (28:49-63).

Israelites would be scattered among the nations. There they would worship other gods. They would be filled with perpetual anxiety and despair. Some would return to Egypt and offer themselves for sale as slaves (28:64-68).

B. Fourth Sermon (Dt 29:1–30:20).

Moses' last sermon was delivered in the plains of Moab. There the Sinai covenant was renewed. This sermon consists of six parts.

1. He reminded his audience of four important things: (1) He reminded them of the powerful works which God had performed in Egypt. (2) Parenthetically he remarked that even to that day Israel did not fully comprehend what had transpired in Egypt. (3) Moses stressed God's providential care during the forty years in the wilderness. God had provided both food and clothing for them. (4) Finally Moses reminded them of the conquest of Sihon and Og. Their lands were now the possession of Reuben, Gad and half the tribe of Manasseh (29:1-8).

2. He dramatically described the solemn occasion which was unfolding there in the plains of Moab (29:9-15). They were standing in the presence of God in order to enter into a covenant with him. God would take upon himself an oath to recognize Israel as his people. This covenant would involve generations yet unborn.

3. He warned them about the wrath of God (29:18-29). Any person who might be inclined toward idolatry was sadly mistaken if he thought he could escape judgment because of the blessings associated with the covenant. Every curse written in Deuteronomy would fall upon that man, and his name would be blotted out from under heaven (29:18-21).

The land would suffer the wrath of God as well as the individual idolater. Future generations and foreigners would be amazed at the desolation of that once abundant land which would be as desolate as Sodom. How could such a thing be? Israel betrayed the Lord and worshiped other gods. Therefore they brought upon themselves all the curses of God's Law including deportation to a foreign land (29:22-28).

This passage of prediction closes with an important note. "The secret things belong to the Lord." He alone knows the future, and it is not for his people to probe those mysteries. "The revealed things," (namely, the Law) belong to his people. Their future is determined by their present walk. Obedient faith leads to blessing, but disobedience to disaster (29:29).

4. Moses promised that repentance and obedience would bring about a restoration of Israel. God would gather them from distant lands. He would circumcise their hearts, i.e., create circumstances such that they would willingly and lovingly follow the Law. God's curses would be turned against their enemies. Again they would be fruitful in their land (30:1-10).

5. Moses stressed the easy access to the key to life. This Law which would lead to life was not something far beyond them. They knew it in their heart and spoke it with their lips. All they needed to do was to obey it (30:11-14).

6. Moses concluded by setting before his audience the alternatives of life and death, prosperity and destruction. Obedience would lead to the former, disobedience to the latter. He urged his listeners to choose the path of life—to love, listen and hold fast to the Lord. The message reached its climax with the insightful declaration that "The Lord is your life" (30:15-20).

MOSES' SUCCESSOR
Deuteronomy 31:1-29

In Deuteronomy 31 Moses appears as the aging statesman. The focus here is on those who will lead after he has departed. The chapter contains seven speeches, four by Moses and three by the Lord.

1. Moses' speech to Israel. For the fourth time Moses reminded the people that he would not be leading them across Jordan. That, however, did not matter. The Lord would still lead them! He would be working through Joshua to give them victory over their enemies. When that happened, they must remember to do to those enemies as Moses had commanded. "Be strong and courageous," he urged, in view of the promise that the Lord would never leave nor forsake them (31:1-6).

2. Moses' speech to Joshua. Before the entire nation Moses delivered

a charge to Joshua. He too was urged to be "strong and courageous." These words became virtually a battle cry in Israel (Josh 1:6,7,9,18). The Lord would go before Joshua, but not so far as to separate himself from his servant. Assurance of the divine presence would banish fear and discouragement (31:7-8).

3. Moses' speech to the priests and elders. The Law which had been written down by Moses himself was delivered to the priests for safekeeping. He commissioned the priests to publicly read the law during the assemblies which were held in the sabbatical year. The concern here was that children would hear that Law and learn therefrom to fear the Lord (31:9-13).

4. The Lord's speech to Moses. The Lord directed Moses and Joshua to appear at the tent of meeting where the successor to the Lawgiver was to be divinely commissioned. The Lord appeared to the men at the entrance to the tent in the pillar of cloud (31:14-15).

5. The Lord's second speech to Moses. The Lord informed Moses of his impending death. He also informed him that his long hours of preaching would not prevent the people from straying into idolatry. When they broke the covenant, God would hide his face from them. All kinds of disasters and difficulties would then fall upon them. The Lord commissioned Moses to write a song and teach it to Israel. The song would be remembered long after the sermons had been forgotten. The song would testify for the Lord against the people in that day when they apostatized. Moses complied with the Lord's instruction. The song is included as chapter 32 of Deuteronomy (31:16-22).

6. The Lord's speech to Joshua. At the tent the Lord spoke a word of encouragement to Joshua. Again he was told to "be strong and courageous." He would succeed in his mission because the Lord would be with him (31:23).

7. Moses' speech to the Levites. The book in which Moses had recorded the Law was handed over to the Levitical priests. They were told to place the book beside the ark. The book would be a witness against the nation in the future when they fell away from the Lord. The elders were assembled once again, and Moses spoke to them words of warning about the future of Israel once they had entered the Promised Land (31:24-29).

MOSES' SONG
Deuteronomy 32:1-47

Deuteronomy 32–33 are replete with translation problems due to the presence of unusual vocabulary and Hebrew grammar. Radical differences can be observed in the standard English translations of these chapters. The song which Moses taught Israel had nine thought units.

1. In the introduction (32:1-2) Moses likened the words of his song to refreshing rain. He therefore called upon the heavens and earth to hear what he has to say.

2. Moses praised God for his greatness, his perfect works, and his just ways. God is the Rock, the stable and unchanging one (32:3-4). This same figure appears in verses 18,30,31.

3. Moses rebuked the people for their unfaithfulness to God. They were his children, but no longer. They had become a warped and crooked generation. They were foolish and unwise (32:5-6).

4. Moses reminded the people of God's grace. God had found Israel in a barren wilderness. He had cared for Israel like an eagle that "stirs its nest." The allusion is to the habit of the mother eagle to make the nest uncomfortable with sharp objects so that the baby will be forced to the edge. The mother pushes baby over the side. As the eaglet falls earthward, the mother swoops beneath at the last possible moment to rescue her young. Thus do eaglets learn to fly (32:7-12).

From the wilderness experience God would bring Israel into the heights of Canaan. There he would nourish his people with the choicest foods (32:13-14).

5. Moses predicted the future apostasy of Jeshurun,[2] "the upright one." In the midst of the prosperity with which God would bless them, they would abandon him. They would embrace idols and new gods which were in reality only demons (32:15-18).

6. Moses described the Lord's reaction to this apostasy. He would reject his sons and daughters and withdraw his face from them. He would punish them by means of a foreign nation. The fire of his wrath would be ignited. Various disasters would be hurled against them culminating in a scattering of the nation in exile (32:19-27).

7. Moses lamented the stupidity of his people. They would not

530

discern the signs of God's wrath against them. When Israelite armies were put to flight by foreigners, God's people should have realized that their Rock had abandoned them. What shame to fall to enemies who were as corrupt as Sodom (32:28-33).

8. Moses held out the hope of divine compassion even after judgment. Those enemies would receive their due. Eventually the Lord would vindicate his people and have compassion on them. The gods would not be able to save their own people. Seeing this, Israel would realize that these gods were totally unreliable (32:34-38).

9. Moses emphasized the greatness of God. He had the power to put to death and raise from the dead. This great God swore by himself that he would take vengeance on his adversaries. The theme of vengeance appears in verses 35, 41, and 43. This ultimate victory over all enemies calls for rejoicing (32:39-43).

After receiving the song from the Lord, Moses and Joshua spoke these words in the hearing of the people. He admonished the people to take his words to heart. These were not idle words; they were the life of Israel. If they followed these words, they would live long in the land (32:44-47).

MOSES' SUMMONS
Deuteronomy 32:48–34:12

The closing events of Moses' life are narrated in three units: (1) the directive, (2) the blessing, and (3) the death.

A. Divine Directive (Dt 32:48-52).

On the same day he sang his song, the Lord directed Moses to ascend Mt. Nebo to view the Promised Land. The Lord informed Moses that he would die on the mount. Again Moses was reminded of the sin he had committed at Meribah Kadesh, the sin which prevented him from entering the Promised Land.

B. Blessing of the Tribes (Dt 33:1-29).

In Deuteronomy 31 Moses was the statesman, and in chapter 32 the singer; now in chapter 33 he is the seer. Like Jacob in Genesis 49, Moses looked into the future of the tribes. He assumed the role of

531

a father to the tribes in these verses. While the tribal oracles in Genesis 49 contain judgmental elements, here the thrust is almost entirely positive.

The blessing begins with a poetic description of the great manifestation of Yahweh at Mt. Sinai. The verses are difficult to translate and interpret. Moses mentioned a brilliant light emanating from God which illuminated Mt. Sinai. With God were "holy ones," i.e., angels. The New Testament emphasizes that the Law was given through the mediation of angels.[3] This awesome God is at the same time a God of love (33:1-3a).

The people responded to Moses' words in 33:3b-5. Even holy ones, they said, bow before the Lord to receive his instruction. They declared Yahweh to be king in Jeshurun, i.e., Israel. Then followed the blessing on each of the tribes.

1. The tribe of Reuben would continue, but it would never be numerically strong (33:6).

2. Moses prayed that Judah, which normally led the tribes into battle, would (1) have prayers answered, (2) come back safely from battle, and (3) experience the help of God against foes (33:7).

3. The leaders of Levi, Moses and Aaron, were tested at Massah (Ex 17:1-7) and Meribah (Nm 20:1-13). Moses also recalled the judgment executed after the episode of the Golden Calf (Ex 32:26-29) in which the Levites acted as guardians of God's covenant. God had blessed the tribe with three main responsibilities: (1) the Thummim and Urim through which God revealed his will to Israel, (2) the ministry of teaching, and (3) the worship rituals. Moses called upon the Lord to bless Levi in his ministry and protect him from all his foes (33:8-12).

4. Joseph's sons Ephraim and Manasseh became two tribes in Israel, but Moses blessed them as one. The blessing relates to two areas: (1) material prosperity and (2) military might (33:13-17).

5. Zebulun and Issachar are called upon to rejoice in every aspect of their daily lives. The feasts of these tribes would come from the abundance of the Mediterranean Sea and from the treasures of the seashore. The latter reference is to shellfish, dye made from those shellfish, and glass made from sand (33:18-19).

6. Gad already had received its inheritance east of Jordan. Gad,

however, would also play a key role in the upcoming war of conquest in Canaan. This tribe would receive a lion's portion of the spoils of victory (33:20-21).

7. Dan is described as a lion's cub, young and timid but with potential for great strength in the future (33:22).

8. Naphtali would experience great blessing because of its location in the land (33:23).

9. Asher would be the most blessed among the tribes. "Dip his foot in oil" probably refers to the abundance of olive trees in his territory. The tribe would have strong fortifications which would enable Asher to enjoy blessing to the fullest (33:24-25).

The blessing concluded with a litany of praise for the Lord. He is praised for coming on the clouds of heaven to the aid of his people. This eternal God was the refuge of Israel. Israelites found security in the fact that they were enveloped in his everlasting arms. He would fight with, for and through his people in the coming conquest. Following the struggle would come peaceful security in the land of abundance. Israel was so blessed to have God as shield, helper and sword. Victory was assured! (33:26-29).

C. Death of Moses (Dt 34:1-12).

In obedience to the command of the Lord, Moses climbed Nebo to the very top of the peak called Pisgah. There he viewed the Promised Land which God had sworn to his forefathers. God reminded him once again that he could not enter that land. Then Moses died. The details of his burial are not given. The verb could be rendered either as an active or a passive. If the former, then God buried him. If the latter, then the text is simply stating that Moses was buried. The exact location of the burial site is not known, but it was in Moab in the valley opposite Beth Peor (34:1-6).

At the time of his death Moses physically was in remarkable shape. At 120 years this "servant of the Lord" still had his sight and vigor. The Israelites accorded him the honor of thirty days of mourning. The people immediately recognized Joshua as leader (34:7-9).

Joshua was equipped for leadership when he received the spirit of wisdom through the laying on of Moses' hands. Deuteronomy, however, closes with a section which emphasizes the uniqueness of

Moses. No prophet had arisen in Israel like Moses in two respects: (1) the Lord knew Moses "face to face," and (2) Moses was able to perform tremendous miracles in Egypt in the sight of all Israel (34:10-12).

ENDNOTES

1. K.A. Kitchen cited by P.C. Craigie, *The Book of Deuteronomy*, The New International Commentary on the Old Testament (Grand Rapids: Eerdmans, 1976), p. 340, n. 15.

2. This poetic name for Israel is found in four passages: Dt 32:15; 33:5,26; and Isa 44:2.

3. Acts 7:53; Gal 3:19; Heb 2:2.